Bronze Age Connections

Cultural Contact in
Prehistoric Europe

Bronze Age Connections
Cultural Contact in Prehistoric Europe

Edited by Peter Clark

Oxbow Books
Oxford and Oakville

Published by
Oxbow Books, Oxford, UK

© Oxbow Books and the individual authors, 2009

ISBN 978-1-84217-348-0

This book is available direct from:

Oxbow Books, Oxford, UK
(Phone: 01865-241249; Fax: 01865-794449)

and

The David Brown Book Company
PO Box 511, Oakville, CT 06779, USA
(Phone: 860-945-9329; Fax: 860-945-9468)

or from our website

www.oxbowbooks.com

A CIP record for this book is available from the British Library

Library of Congress Cataloging-in-Publication Data

Bronze Age connections : cultural contact in prehistoric Europe/edited by Peter Clark.
   p. cm.
Presentations from a conference held Sept. 2006 in Dover, England.
Includes bibliographical references.
ISBN 978-1-84217-348-0
  1. Bronze age--Europe--Congresses. 2. Acculturation--Europe--History--To 1500--Congresses. 3. Intercultural communication--Europe--History--To 1500--Congresses. 4. Europe--Antiquities--Congresses. 5. Excavations (Archaeology) Europe--Congresses. 6. Europe--History, Naval--Congresses. 7. Naval history, Ancient--Congresses. 8. Seafaring life--Europe--History--To 1500--Congresses. 9. Boats and boating--Europe--History--To 1500--Congresses. 10. Europe--Commerce--History--Congresses. I. Clark, Peter.
  GN778.2.A1B755 2009
  930.1'5094--dc22

          2009024737

Cover design by Mark Duncan,
photography by Andrew Savage and cover concept by Peter Clark

Printed and bound in Great Britain by
Hobbs the Printer Ltd
Totton, Hampshire

Contents

List of contributors vii

1. Introduction: Building New Connections *Peter Clark* 1

2. Encompassing the Sea: 'Maritories' and Bronze Age maritime interactions *Stuart Needham* 12

3. From Picardy to Flanders: Transmanche connections in the Bronze Age
   Jean Bourgeois and Marc Talon 38

4. British immigrants killed abroad in the seventies: The rise and fall of a Dutch culture
   Liesbeth Theunissen 60

5. The Canche Estuary (Pas-de-Calais, France) from the early Bronze Age to the *emporium*
   of Quentovic: A traditional trading place between south east England and the continent
   Michel Philippe 68

6. Looking forward: Maritime contacts in the first millennium BC *Barry Cunliffe* 80

7. Copper mining and production at the beginning of the British Bronze Age *Simon Timberlake* 94

8. The demise of the flint tool industry *Chris Butler* 122

9. Land at the other end of the sea? Metalwork circulation, geographical knowledge and the
   significance of British/Irish imports in the Bronze Age of the Low Countries *David Fontijn* 129

10. The master(y) of hard materials: Thoughts on technology, materiality and ideology occasioned
    by the Dover boat *Mary W Helms* 149

11. Exploring the ritual of travel in prehistoric Europe: The Bronze Age sewn-plank boats in context
    Robert Van de Noort 159

12. In his hands and in his head: The Amesbury Archer as a metalworker *Andrew Fitzpatrick* 176

List of Contributors

PROFESSOR JEAN BOURGEOIS
Department of Archaeology and Ancient
    History of Europe
Research Unit Prehistory and Protohistory
Blandijnberg 2
3rd Floor
Belgium-9000 Gent
Belgium

Jean.Bourgeois@UGent.be

MR CHRIS BUTLER
Rosedale
Berwick
Polegate
East Sussex BN26 6TB
UK

chris@reltub.fsbusiness.co.uk

MR PETER CLARK
Canterbury Archaeological Trust
92a Broad Street
Canterbury
Kent CT1 2LU
UK

pete.clark@canterburytrust.co.uk

PROFESSOR BARRY CUNLIFFE
Institute of Archaeology
36 Beaumont Street
Oxford OX1 2PG
UK

barry.cunliffe@archaeology.oxford.ac.uk

DR ANDREW FITZPATRICK
Wessex Archaeology Ltd
Portway House
Old Sarum Park
Salisbury,
Wiltshire SP4 6EB
UK

a.fitzpatrick@wessexarch.co.uk

DR DAVID FONTIJN
Faculteit der Archeologie
Postbus 9515
2300 RA Leiden
The Netherlands

d.r.fontijn@arch.leidenuniv.nl

MR MICHEL PHILIPPE
Musée Quentovic
8, place du General De Gaulle,
62630 Étaples-Sur-Mer
France

michel.philippe@etaples-sur-mer.com

PROFESSOR MARY W HELMS
407 N. Holden Road
Greensboro
North Carolina 27410
USA

DR STUART NEEDHAM
Langton Fold
North Lane
South Harting
West Sussex GU31 5NW
UK

DR ROBERT VAN DE NOORT
Department of Archaeology
University of Exeter
Laver Building
Exeter EX4 4QR
UK

R.Van-De-Noort@exeter.ac.uk

DR MARC TALON
Directeur interrégional Nord Picardie
Institut National de Recherches Archéologiques
    Préventives
518 rue St Fuscien
80 000 Amiens
France

marc.talon@inrap.fr

DR LIESBETH THEUNISSEN
National Service for Archaeology
Cultural Landscape and Built Heritage
P.O. Box 1600
3800 BP Amersfoort
The Netherlands

E.M.Theunissen@Racm.nl

DR SIMON TIMBERLAKE
19 High Street
Fen Ditton
Cambridge CB5 8ST
UK

simon.timberlake@ntlworld.com

1. Introduction: Building New Connections

Peter Clark

Standing beside the great Roman *pharos* on the towering heights east of Dover at the south-eastern tip of Britain, the distant coast of Europe can be clearly seen, a thin strip of greenish brown evocatively set between sea and sky. Below, the port rattles and booms as a seemingly endless succession of ferries load and unload, huge steel behemoths towering over the cars and lorries they carry, forever plying backwards and forwards across the waves. Dover is Britain's busiest port, with over fourteen million people passing through it each year, making the short sea crossing between England and France. This intimate connection has often been ambivalent, however; the great hills flanking the town are studded with the remains of gargantuan defences dating over many centuries, witness to times when the sea was a welcome barrier against continental threat rather than the populous highway it is today. Fittingly, it was deep below the streets of this bustling modern port that Europe's oldest sea going boat was discovered in 1992; the Dover Bronze Age boat – built some three and a half millennia ago – now has pride of place in the local museum, and is a focus of intense international interest and study. In particular, it has stimulated a desire to better understand what connections might have existed between peoples on either side of the Channel in this distant time. Archaeologists have long been aware of similarities in Bronze Age material culture in the modern countries of England, northern France, the Netherlands and Belgium; what can these tell us about the nature of relations between these transmanche com-

munities in the second millennium BC? The growing pace of research and new discoveries on both sides of the Channel together with the general public's appetite for information suggested the need for a colloquium where new data could be presented and new ideas discussed in open forum. There could be no better place for a debate about ancient seafaring and maritime connections than the modern port of Dover.

Thus, in September 2006, over 180 people gathered at Dover's Western Docks to attend some fifteen presentations by various scholars from Belgium, England, France, the Netherlands and the USA on the theme 'Bronze Age Connections: Cultural Contact in Prehistoric Europe'. This volume brings together twelve of those presentations for a wider audience and for the benefit of those conference delegates who found difficulty in hearing the original presentations as huge waves crashed on the walls and roof of the conference venue (Fig 1.1).

The conference was the second such event organised by the Dover Bronze Age Boat Trust (DBABT), a registered charity set up in 1993, whose aims are 'to protect, preserve and conserve for the public benefit the Dover Bronze Age Boat' and 'to advance the education of the public about all aspects relating to the boat, its design, construction, history, use and all other relevant matters…'. The first of these aims was achieved in November 1999 when an award-winning gallery of Bronze Age life was opened at Dover museum (Clark *et al* 2004), with the fully conserved Dover boat as

its centrepiece. The Trust continues to monitor the condition of the boat and the gallery as part of its remit; similarly the 'education of the public' is a continuing responsibility, realised in many ways, such as the production of a documentary video, appearances on television and radio, public lectures, the organisation of school visits, guided tours of the gallery and so forth. In the same vein, and in recognition of the international significance of the find, the DBABT organised a major conference focussing on the Dover boat in 2002 to celebrate the tenth anniversary of its discovery. With speakers from Denmark, England, the Netherlands, Northern Ireland, Norway, Sweden, Switzerland and Wales, some 130 delegates attended the conference, whose proceedings were published in 2004 as '*The Dover Bronze Age boat in context: Society and water transport in prehistoric Europe*'.

In the same year, a detailed technical monograph appeared on the Dover boat itself (Clark 2004a), the result of ten years of study by a large interdisciplinary team of specialists. The boat itself was found at the bottom of a 6 metre deep shaft during road construction in 1992, and has been dated to 1575–1520 cal BC (Bayliss *et al* 2004, 254). The surviving hull is around 2.2 m broad, and over 9.5m of the boat's length was salvaged. The northern end of the vessel, for various reasons, could not be recovered at the time of excavation. The state of preservation of the boat was remarkable, with the toolmarks of its fabrication clearly visible, in addition to the survival of organic materials used to make the boat watertight.

In essence, the boat remains consist of four planks, hewn from logs of huge, straight-grained oak trees (*Quercus* sp.) without side branches (Fig 1.2). It has been estimated that such trees must have originated in close set oak forests, with at least 11m between the basal buttresses and the first appearance of branches. Such trees are very rare in Western Europe today.

Two flat planks form the bottom, each carved out of a half log, leaving upstanding cleats and rails allowing its jointing with other boat timbers (Fig 1.3). These bottom planks were joined together along a central butt joint, with transverse timbers and wedges hammered through the cleats and central rails. Curved

Figure 1.2 The Dover boat in situ

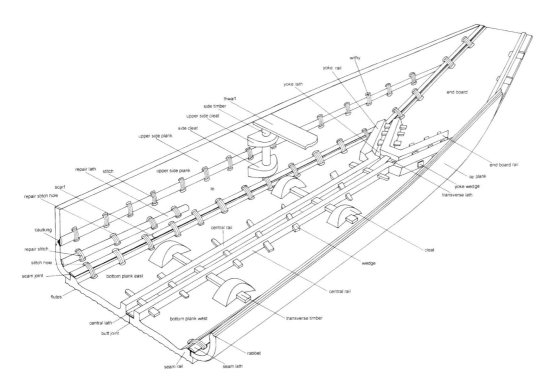

Figure 1.3 Schematic drawing showing main elements of the Dover boat's construction

side planks were stitched to the bottom of the boat with twisted withies of yew (*Taxus baccata*). These side planks also possess side cleats carved out of the solid wood. The timbers forming the end of the boat splay into a Y-shape, intricately carved from the main planks. This originally would have held a carved wooden board, reminiscent of a modern "punt". There was clear evidence for the presence and some dimensions of this missing end board; there was also evidence for at least two other main structural timbers. On the top of the curved side planks was another row of stitches, cut through in antiquity. There were clearly two further side planks, and the boat had been deliberately dismantled (albeit partially) when it was abandoned. She had been made waterproof by pressing in a mixture of beeswax and animal fat into the stitch-holes and along the seams, where the stopping was overlain by pads of moss wadding, compressed and held in place by long thin laths of oak under the yew stitches. The boat had clearly been used extensively. Tool marks on its bottom (outboard) surface were differentially worn away, suggesting it had been beached regularly on a sand or gravel shore (though see Sanders 2007, 188–190 for an alternative view). The main timbers had split and were repaired by stitching wooden laths over the damage.

The rarity of the discovery, the complexity and precision of its manufacture, the quality of its preservation and the circumstances of its abandonment make the Dover boat a pivotal resource for the study of prehistoric maritime archaeology. Indeed, the implications of the find have had ramifications for the understanding of Bronze Age archaeology in general, something that was central to the study of the boat from the beginning; 'The boat was made and used by people living three and a half millennia ago, and it was to better understand these people, their society and the world they lived in that was as much a focus of the analysis team's work as the study of the vessel itself' (Clark 2004b, 1).

It was apparent even at the time of publication of *The Dover Bronze Age Boat* that the primary results of analysis were not the final word; 'this volume does not attempt to be a final, definitive statement…; rather, it is a springboard for further study and a resource for the imagination' (Clark 2004b, 2). That sentiment has indeed been borne out; the Dover boat has stimulated an extensive debate amongst scholars around the world that continues to this day (*eg* Boon and Rietbergen forthcoming; Coates 2005a; 2005b; Crumlin-Pedersen 2003; 2006; Fenwick 2006; 2007; McGrail 2006a; 2006b; 2007; Roberts 2006a; 2006b; Sanders 2007; Von der Porten 2006; Ward 2005).

The first Dover conference focussed largely on prehistoric maritime transport, the cultural perception of the boat and the concept of voyage, along with the environmental context of the find (Clark 2004c). At the same time, attention was drawn to the geographical location of the discovery, in England's busiest port close to the shortest sea crossing to the continent. The nature of transmanche contacts in prehistory (a long-standing topic of interest; *see* Butler 1963, Briard 1965; Burgess 1968; Blanchet 1987) was reviewed in the light of recent discoveries, particularly from northern France (Clark 2004d), a study that was to provide the genesis of the theme for the 2006 conference. The boat has given physical form to the abstract notion of maritime voyaging and overseas social contact, contributing to a renewed appreciation of the nature and importance of sea travel to prehistoric communities.

Of course, whether the Dover boat itself ever crossed the sea to the continent will no doubt remain forever moot, though recent proposals have suggested avenues to further explore the technical possibility. At the time of writing, a re-assessment of the boat timbers is being undertaken, using alternative methodologies of analysis to those used previously in order to perhaps enhance our understanding of the vessel's original form and potential capabilities (*eg* McGrail 2007; Crumlin-Pedersen and McGrail 2006). At the same time, an international partnership of archaeologists and heritage institutions is exploring the possibility of building a full scale reconstruction of the Dover boat (Clark 2008), which will allow the experimental assessment of various hypotheses in a series of sea trials, an approach that has proved fruitful for a number of prehistoric boats of different types and building traditions (*eg* Gifford and Gifford 2004; Gifford *et al* 2006; Vosmer 2003; Rouzo and Poissonnier 2007; Crumlin-Pedersen and Trakadas 2003). Notwithstanding these continuing studies, the vessel remains symbolic of the voyages that are known to have taken place in the Bronze Age from material culture recovered on either side of the channel and indeed from the sea floor itself. Examples include pottery (*eg* Desfossés 2000a, 191–195; Marcigny and Ghesquière 2003; note also the distribution of Treviskar ware from modern-day Cornwall and Devon right along the southern coast of England and across the sea to Basse-Normandie and

Pas-de-Calais (Mariette 1961; Marcigny and Ghesquière 2003; ApSimon 2000; ApSimon and Greenfield 1972; Gibson forthcoming; Gibson *et al* 1997)), metalwork (Blanchet and Mordant 1987; Muckelroy 1981; Needham and Dean 1987), styles of architecture (*eg* Desfossés 2000b, 63, figs 15 and 16; Desfossés and Philippe 2002; Lepaumier *et al* 2005; Mare 2005; Sys and Leroy-Langevin 2004) and jewellery such as the British-style gold torcs recovered from the sea floor off the coast of Sotteville-sur-Mer (Seine-Maritime; Billard *et al* 2005). In this respect the discovery of the boat has in part inspired a renaissance of study and research in the transmanche area. Terrestrial archaeologists have become more willing to incorporate the maritime dimension in their studies, whilst nautical archaeologists have become more sensitive to the cultural context of the vessels they study, a coming together of the 'wet' and 'dry' archaeological communities (Adams 2007, 219).

The increasing recognition of maritime archaeology as an integral part of 'mainstream' archaeological thinking seems to have been reflected in an improvement of the legislative and governmental protection of the maritime heritage in recent years, under the aegis of the respective national heritage agencies in the region. In Belgium, the Vlaams Instituut voor het Onroerend Erfgoed (VIOE) was formally recognised as the 'preferred partner' of the Belgian federal government with regard to maritime heritage research in 2003 (Pieters *et al* 2006, 8), whilst in France maritime cultural assets were formally ratified as part of the 'Code du Patrimoine' (French Heritage Code) in 2004 with responsibility for scientific research entrusted to the Département des Recherches archéologiques subaquatiques et sous-marines (DRASSM; Massy 2006). In England, English Heritage were given responsibility for maritime archaeology out to the 12 mile Territorial Limit off the English coast in 2002 (Oxley 2006, 46), and in the Netherlands the Rijksdienst voor Archeologie, Cultuurlandschap en Monumenten (RACM) likewise had their responsibility for the maritime heritage extended to the Territorial Limit (24 miles in this case) as part of an amendment to the 1988 Monuments Act in 2007 (Andrea Otte, *pers comm*).

This increasing awareness has also meant a more satisfying and nuanced appreciation of new archaeological discoveries on either side of the channel, reflected in an increasing number of publications that recognise the inter-regional implications of their subject matter. Examples include the Bronze Age settlements at Highstead and Île Tatihou, the barrow cemeteries at Oedelen-Wulfsberg, Aartijke, Monkton-Mount Pleasant and Aire-sur-la-Lys in addition to the gold cup and associated finds from Ringlemere (Bennett *et al* 2007; Marcigny and Ghesquière 2003; Bourgeois *et al* 2001; Bourgeois and Cherretté 2005; Cherretté and Bourgeois 2002; Clark forthcoming a; Lorin *et al* 2005; Needham *et al* 2006). The study of the Ringlemere cup is particularly germane here, as in his discussion of the find Stuart Needham postulated a 'set of cultural relations which tied together communities in southern Britain, Northern France and the Low Countries' from the latter half of the Early Bronze Age onwards (Needham 2006, 75). How these relations manifested themselves in cultural and social terms remains debatable, though it has been suggested that a high level social grouping straddled the channel, a single 'people' or 'tribe' bound together by close social (perhaps familial) and economic relationships; 'the people of La Manche' (Clark 2004d, 7). Whatever the nature of this maritime community, it could only be maintained through the existence of boats, perhaps similar to that found in Dover in 1992. It was in the context of this international discussion of prehistoric maritime contact that the theme of the second DBABT conference was proposed in May 2005; *Bronze Age Connections: Cultural Contact in prehistoric Europe*. The conference was scheduled to coincide with the occasion of the temporary loan of the spectacular Ringlemere gold cup from the British Museum to Dover Museum, home of the Dover boat, the first time that these two icons of Bronze Age life had been seen together.

Sixteen speakers were invited to contribute a presentation on various aspects of the theme 'Bronze Age Connections'. Unfortunately, as the conference drew near, some speakers found that they were unable to attend; though this freed up some time to allow some very valuable alternative contributions, it meant that some critical topics were not addressed, notably the ceramic and metalwork evidence in the transmanche region.

The papers are presented here in a slightly

different order to that of the conference itself, a reflection of the changing emphases of the written texts in response to discussion both at the conference and in subsequent correspondence. Thus the volume begins with Stuart Needham's broad overview of the nature of maritime cultural contacts in the transmanche region (Chapter 2), where he debates the extent to which they might imply a unified cultural entity in the manner of the *Manche-Mer du Nord/People of La Manche* groups (Marcigny and Ghesquiere 2003; Clark 2004d). Jean Bourgeois and Marc Talon then set out the new evidence from northern France and Belgium (Chapter 3), whilst Liesbeth Theunissen presents us with a cautionary tale of how modern-day connections between archaeologists can affect our perception of prehistoric connections (Chapter 4). With our minds focussed on Dover and the connections between peoples in the Channel-Rhine-Friesian zone, where the great navigable rivers of the Rhine and Thames face each other across the seaways running along the western European coast ('The Great Crossroads'; Clark forthcoming b), we should not forget that there were other important routes of communication and connection across the seas, and that these changed over time. Richard Bradley (2007) has emphasised the strong links between Ireland and Scotland across the Irish Sea during prehistory, whilst others have focussed on the seaways along the southern coast of Britain (Wilkes 2004; 2007) and the connections between the British Isles, Ireland and Iberia (*eg* Almagro-Gorbea 1995; Cunliffe 2001). In Chapter 5, Michel Philippe traces the dominance of the Canche Estuary as a nodal point for connections between the continent and the British Isles from the 6th century AD *emporium* of Quentovic back into the Bronze Age at least (*see* Desfossés 1998, fig 1, for the palaeogeography of the estuary), and shows that even here the routes across the sea were fluid in more than one sense. The theme of complex and dynamic networks of interaction through time is pursued by Barry Cunliffe (Chapter 6) for connections in the first millennium BC; the subtler picture of complexity drawn from a richer set of data may give us a glimpse of the intricacy of maritime links in earlier periods.

The transmanche area (*ie* south-eastern England, northern France and the Low Countries) is devoid of the raw materials needed to make bronze; in the Bronze Age every scrap had to be imported, sometimes over great distances. It seems reasonable to assume that the vast majority of this bronze was imported on boats of some kind, along river systems and (certainly in the case of England), across the sea, a view perhaps supported by the assemblages of metal objects recovered from the seabed at Langdon Bay, Moor Sand and Salcombe (Needham and Dean 1987; Muckelroy 1981; Needham and Giardino 2008; Samson 2006). But where did the bronze come from? Initial analysis of the Dover boat suggested that the boat was capable of carrying a cargo of several tonnes (Roberts 2004), potentially representing a supply of several thousand bronze tools in a single voyage (Clark 2005). If such boats were employed for the importation of bronze, how many voyages would be required to satisfy the demands for bronze tools in the region? If the apparent demise of the stone tool industry is real, does this imply the ubiquity of metal tools within Bronze Age society? Simon Timberlake looks at the evidence for metal production in the early British Bronze Age in Chapter 7, with some important speculation on the scale of metal production and consumption during the period, whilst in Chapter 8, Chris Butler provides a more nuanced view of the decline of the stone tool industry during the Bronze Age.

Maritime archaeology has traditionally been avowedly determinist in its outlook, but we should remain sensitive to the contextual and perceptual frameworks that influenced past social behaviour and thereby the archaeological record we observe. David Fontijn gives us a critical assessment of the contemporary perception of the objects that travelled long distances to their final resting place in the soil of the Low Countries (Chapter 9), which stimulates introspection regarding the nature of the geographical world view and the understanding of long-distance connections in Bronze Age communities. Of course, the vessels that allowed these maritime connections were no doubt themselves imbued with cosmological significance; Mary Helms explores the magical elements involved in the creation of the Dover boat (Chapter 10), whilst in Chapter 11 Robert van de Noort sets out the chronological changes in the ritual perception of sewn plank boats during the second millennium BC.

Lastly, and most fittingly, we focus our attention on an individual who witnessed these ancient connections and travelled across the breadth of western Europe to his final resting place in the south of England. Andrew Fitzpatrick describes the Odyssey of the Amesbury Archer in Chapter 12, weaving together the themes of magic, metal, travel and power that form the warp and weft of our Bronze Age Connections.

We hope that this collection of papers will inform, entertain and stimulate further discussion about the Dover boat and its implications for Bronze Age society. There is still much to talk about, and new discoveries and new research will no doubt enrich the subject and help cast new perspectives on our current understanding of the issues. This is particularly pertinent in appreciating the social context of the boat, whether it be understood as a product of an Early or Middle Bronze Age society (Clark 2004d; van de Noort this volume). David Yates has recently drawn attention to the increasing evidence for land organisation in the Middle Bronze Age with 'considerable agricultural activity from at least the middle of the second millennium BC' (Yates 2007, 26), suggesting a period of social and economic flux in which we must contextualise the construction and use of the Dover boat. All who have seen the vessel have been impressed by the investment of time and effort involved in its creation; understanding the social need for such a vessel and the organisation required for its manufacture remains an important avenue of enquiry. In this sense, it is not clear what advantages the complex, heavy sewn-plank wooden hull would have over hide boats, which are widely assumed to have been the most likely form of maritime transport in early times (though there is no evidence for such vessels in western Europe until the Iron Age; Clark 2005; McGrail 1987, 185–187). Historically, hide boats are known to have cargo capacities easily within the postulated range of the Dover boat, and their seaworthiness in rough weather is well known (Petersen 1986; Stefansson 1942, 37–39; Clark 2004e, 306). What benefits were to be gained in the apparently significantly greater effort in constructing a sewn-plank boat as opposed to a hide boat? The reasons for this may no doubt

be manifold, but Stuart Needham has made an intriguing observation in his discussion of the Ringlemere gold cup (Needham 2006). Noting the apparent emergence of such vessels in the first few centuries of the 2nd millennium BC, he speculates that they might be perceived as a 'specialised artefact', like the contemporary 'special cups ', developed 'for the conduct of certain inter-regional relations which were becoming desirable for the acquisition of exotic materials and knowledge' (*ibid*, 79). Perhaps part of the rationale of constructing such splendid and complex vessels was not just the technicalities of seafaring, but issues of conspicuous display and the visible articulation of social connections and 'membership' of a specialised maritime community.

It is, however, easy to overlook how little data we actually have and to forget the complexities of social relationships in the Bronze Age. Much attention has been focussed on the Atlantic Zone and the maritime connections along the western European seaboard, but we should not forget that there were also connections with the interior, a point recently highlighted by the discovery of a Bronze Age hoard of central European bronze ingots found at the mouth of the River Somme in Saint-Valery-sur-Somme (Blanchet and Mille forthcoming), and that the Amesbury Archer spent some time in central Europe before making the long journey westwards to the British Isles (Evans *et al* 2006; Fitzpatrick this volume). As for our understanding of Bronze Age seafaring, the list of finds presented by Robert van de Noort (Table 11.1) at first sight looks impressive, but in truth it is a poor haul for over a millennium of known maritime contact, with several finds representing badly eroded and damaged fragments. The range of vessels depicted on Scandinavian rock carvings and northern European bronzes (Kaul 1998; 2004; Coles 1993; 2000), even allowing for artistic expression, is a tantalising suggestion of the range of boat types that may have existed in the period. We still have much to learn, and every new boat find will be of critical importance for the foreseeable future.

Notwithstanding this, several avenues of research have suggested the existence of a cultural unity between peoples living on either side of the Channel and southern North Sea; further fieldwork and new research can only clarify our understanding how this community operated, and how it related to other social groups along the coasts and inland. It perhaps came into existence in the early part of the 2nd millennium BC and continued for much of the Bronze Age, and perhaps even later; note the apparent continuity of *'relations transmanche'* into the Iron Age in Basse-Normandie at sites such as Mondeville and Île Tatihou (Marcigny *et al* 2005; Marcigny and Talon forthcoming). However during the second half of the millennium the geographical extent of this community diminished as other socio-political cultural entities gained ascendancy; in France and Belgium, for example, continental (RSFO) cultural influences become more dominant in the later Bronze Age (Bourgeois and Cherretté 2005; Blanchet and Talon 2005; Buchez and Talon 2005).

Our study of Bronze Age Connections in the transmanche area, which originated almost eighty years ago (*eg* van Giffen 1930; 1938), has made tremendous advances in recent years, and remains a fertile and exciting area of study. It is now sixteen years since the discovery of the Dover Bronze Age boat, at once a supreme example of the boatbuilder's art and a symbol of the human connections across the hazardous and unpredictable waters of the sea – the *mysterium tremendum et fascinus*. The find is a hugely important and influential contribution that continues to inspire debate amongst students of the Bronze Age around the world. In this sense it was very gratifying that so many of the delegates attending the 2006 conference were from countries other than England; apart from the speakers themselves, we welcomed people from France, Belgium, the Netherlands, Denmark and the USA, many of them students who joined an audience of British scholars and members of the local community for the two-day conference. The subject clearly has a widespread and international fascination, and as this introduction is being written, plans are already afoot for another conference focussing on the Dover boat and its implications in Boulogne-sur-Mer in 2012, organised by l'Association pour la Promotion des Recherches sur l'Âge du Bronze (APRAB). The study of ancient connections has encouraged a spirit of co-operation and communication between many people in the respective countries of the transmanche region, a network of new connections that resonates with those of the distant past.

Lastly, a reflection on the interconnectedness of all things; we have noted above how the Dover boat may act as a symbol of the maritime network of connections between Bronze Age peoples and communities. In Chapter 12, Andrew Fitzpatrick describes the family connection between the Amesbury Archer and his 'companion'; they could have been brothers, cousins, or father and son. The evidence for this intimate Bronze Age Connection is in their very bones; their feet share an unusual non-metric trait that demonstrates their genetic relationship. The bones involved (they both have pseudo-facets for articulation) are called the *calcaneus* and the *navicular*. The name *navicular*, of course, derives from the bone's physical resemblance to a small boat.

Acknowledgements

First and foremost, thanks must go to the Trustees of the Dover Bronze Age Boat Trust whose vision and commitment made the conference such a success; Paul Bennett, Steve Bispham, Bill Fawcus, John Moir, Frank Panton, Andrew Richardson, David Ryeland, Anthony Ward and Robin Westbrook. The practical co-ordination and organisation of the conference was undertaken by Denise Ryeland, who discharged her responsibilities with exemplary efficiency and good humour, and invaluable support and assistance was provided by Jon Iveson and the staff of Dover museum. Grateful thanks must also be extended to all those organisations that kindly provided financial assistance to make the conference possible; the Kent Archaeological Society, the British Academy, the Swire Charitable Trust, the University of Kent, the Tory Foundation, Tours of the Realm and the Dover Society.

List of references

Adams, J 2007 'Joined-up boats: maturing maritime archaeology', *Antiquity*, **81 (311)**, 217–220

Almagro-Gorbea, M 1995 'Ireland and Spain in the Bronze Age', in J Waddell and S Shee-Twohig (eds), *Ireland in the Bronze Age*, Dublin: Office of Public Works, 136–148

ApSimon, A 2000 'Two middle Bronze Age lug-handled jars and their wider implications', in M Allen and J Gardiner, *Our Changing Coast: A survey of intertidal archaeology of Langstone Harbour, Hampshire*, Council for British Archaeology Research Report, **124**, 146–151

ApSimon, A and Greenfield, E 1972 'The excavation of

a Bronze Age and Iron Age settlement at Trevisker Round, St Eval, Cornwall', *Proceedings of the Prehistoric Society*, **38**, 302–381

Bayliss, A, Groves, C, McCormac, C, Bronk Ramsey, C, Baillie, M, Brown, D, Cook, G and Switsur, R 2004 'Dating', in P Clark (ed), *The Dover Bronze Age Boat*, with illustrations by Caroline Caldwell, Swindon: English Heritage, 250–255

Bennett, P, Couldrey, P and Macpherson-Grant, N 2007 *Excavations at Highstead, near Chislet, Kent 1975–77*, Canterbury: The Archaeology of Canterbury (New Series), **4**

Billard, C, Eluere, C and Jezegou, M-P 2005 'Découverte de torques en or de l'Âge du Bronze en mer de Manche', in J Bourgeois and M Talon (eds), *L'Âge du Bronze du Nord de la France dans son contexte européen*, Paris: Editions du Comité des Travaux Historiques et scientifiques avec l'Association pour la Promotion des Recherches sur l'âge du Bronze, 287–301

Blanchet, J-C (ed) 1987 *Les relations entre le continent et les îles britanniques a l'âge du Bronze: Actes du colloque de Lille dans le cadre du 22ème congrès préhistorique de France*, Amiens: Supplément à la Revue Archéologique de Picardie

Blanchet, J-C and Mille, B forthcoming 'Découverte exceptionnelle d'un depôt de lingots du Bronze ancien à Saint-Valery-sur-Somme', in *L'isthme européen Rhin-Saône-Rhône dans la Protohistoire, actes du colloque de Besançon 2006*, Presses Universitaires de Franche-Comté

Blanchet, J-C and Mordant, C 1987 'Les premières haches à rebords et à butée dans le Bassin parisien et le Nord de la France', in J-C Blanchet (ed), *Les relations entre le continent et les îles britanniques a l'âge du Bronze: Actes du colloque de Lille dans le cadre du 22ème congrès préhistorique de France*, Amiens: Supplément à la Revue Archéologique de Picardie, 89–118

Blanchet, J-C and Talon, M 2005 'L'âge du Bronze dans la moyenne vallée de l'Oise: apports récents', in J Bourgeois and M Talon, M (eds), *L'âge du Bronze du nord de la France dans son contexte européen*, Paris: Editions du Comité des Travaux Historiques et scientifiques avec l'Association pour la Promotion des Recherches sur l'âge du Bronze, 227–268

Boon, B and van Rietbergen, E forthcoming 'Aspects of the analysis of structure and strength of prehistoric ships', in *Between the Seas – Transfer and Exchange in Nautical Technology*, Proceedings of the 11th International Symposium on Boat and Ship Archaeology, Mainz, Germany

Bourgeois, J and Cherretté, B 2005 L'Âge du Bronze et le Premier Âge du Fer dans les Flandres occidentale et orientale (Belgique): un état de la question', in J Bourgeois and M Talon (eds), *L'âge du Bronze du nord de la France dans son contexte européen*, Paris: Editions du Comité des Travaux Historiques et scientifiques avec l'Association pour la Promotion des Recherches sur l'âge du Bronze, 43–81

Bourgeois, J, Cherretté, B and Meganck, M 2001 'Kringen voor de doden: Bronstijdgrafheuvels te Oedelem-Wulfsbere (W–VI)', *Lunula: Archaeologia Protohistorica*, **9**, 23–27

Bradley, R 2007 *The Prehistory of Britain and Ireland*, Cambridge: Cambridge University Press

Briard, J 1965 *Les Dépôts Bretons et l'Age du Bronze Atlantique*, Rennes: Université de Rennes

Buchez, N and Talon, M 2005 L'âge du Bronze dans le bassin de la Somme, bilan et périodisation du mobilier céramique', in J Bourgeois and M Talon, M (eds), *L'âge du Bronze du nord de la France dans son contexte européen*, Paris: Editions du Comité des Travaux Historiques et scientifiques avec l'Association pour la Promotion des Recherches sur l'âge du Bronze, 159–188

Burgess, C 1968 'The later Bronze Age in the British Isles and northwestern France', *Archaeological Journal*, **125**, 1–45

Butler, J 1963 'Bronze Age connections across the North Sea: a study in prehistoric trade and industrial relations between the British Isles, the Netherlands, north Germany and Scandinavia, *c* 1700–700 BC', *Palaeohistoria*, **9**, Groningen: J B Wolters, 1–286

Cherretté, B and Bourgeois, J 2002 'Palenkrans uit de midden-bronstijd en nederzettingssporen uit de late ijzertijd te Oedelem-Wulfsberge, W–V1 (2001)', *Lunula: Archaeologica Protohistorica*, **10**, 13–15

Clark, P (ed) 2004a *The Dover Bronze Age boat*, with illustrations by Caroline Caldwell, Swindon: English Heritage

Clark, P 2004b 'Introduction', in P Clark (ed), *The Dover Bronze Age Boat*, with illustrations by Caroline Caldwell, Swindon: English Heritage, 1–3

Clark, P (ed) 2004c *The Dover Bronze Age boat in context: Society and water transport in prehistoric Europe*, Oxford: Oxbow books

Clark, P 2004d 'The Dover boat ten years after its discovery', in P Clark (ed), *The Dover Bronze Age boat in context: Society and water transport in prehistoric Europe*, Oxford: Oxbow books, 1–12

Clark, P 2004e 'Discussion', in P Clark (ed), *The Dover Bronze Age Boat*, with illustrations by Caroline Caldwell, Swindon: English Heritage, 305–322

Clark, P 2005 'Shipwrights, sailors and society in the Middle Bronze Age of NW Europe', *Journal of Wetland Archaeology*, **5**, 87–96

Clark, P 2008 'One step at a time: The Dover Bronze Age boat experimental research programme', in M-J Springmann and H Wernicke (eds), *Historical Boat and Ship Replicas: Conference-Proceedings on the Scientific Perspectives and the Limits of Boat and Ship Replicas, Torgelow 2007*, Maritime Kulturgeschichte von Bodden- und Haffwewässern des Ostseeraumes, Friedland: Steffen Verlag, 29–38

Clark, P forthcoming a 'Transformations of meanings: some implications of the prehistoric discoveries', in P Bennett, P Clark, A Hicks, J Rady and I Riddler, *At the Great Crossroads: Prehistoric, Roman and medieval discoveries on the Isle of Thanet 1994–95*, Canterbury Archaeological Trust Occasional Paper, **4**, Canterbury: Canterbury Archaeological Trust, 88–100

Clark, P forthcoming b 'Preface: The Great Crossroads', in P Bennett, P Clark, A Hicks and I Riddler, *At the Great Crossroads: Prehistoric, Roman and medieval discoveries on the Isle of Thanet 1994–1995*, Canterbury: Canterbury Archaeological Trust, xv–xvi

Clark, P, Corke, B and Waterman, C 2004 'Reassembly and display', in P Clark (ed), *The Dover Bronze Age boat*, with illustrations by Caroline Caldwell, Swindon: English Heritage, 290–304

Coates, J 2005a 'Early seafaring in northwest Europe: Could planked vessels have played a significant part?', *The Mariner's Mirror*, **91 (4)**, 517–530

Coates, J 2005b 'The Bronze Age Ferriby Boats: Seagoing Ships or Estuary Ferry Boats?', *International Journal of Nautical Archaeology*, **34 (1)**, 38–42

Coles, J 1993 'Boats on the rocks', in J Coles, V Fenwick and G Hutchinson (eds), *A Spirit of Enquiry; Essays for Ted Wright*, Exeter: WARP, The Nautical Archaeology Society and the National Maritime Museum, 23–31

Coles, J 2000 *Patterns in a Rocky Land: Rock Carvings in South-West Uppland, Sweden*, Uppsala: Department of Archaeology and Ancient History

Crumlin-Pedersen, O 2003 'British Bronze-Age Finds', in O Crumlin-Pedersen and A Trakadas (eds), *Hjortspring: A pre-Roman Iron-Age Warship in Context*, Ships and Boats of the North, **5**, Roskilde: Viking Ship Museum, 211–218

Crumlin-Pedersen, O 2006 'The Dover Boat – a Reconstruction Case-Study', *International Journal of Nautical Archaeology*, **35 (1)**, 58–71

Crumlin-Pedersen, O and McGrail, S 2006 'Some Principles for the Reconstruction of Ancient Boat Structures', *International Journal of Nautical Archaeology*, **35 (1)**, 53–57

Crumlin-Pedersen, O and Trakadas, A (eds), *Hjortspring: A pre-Roman Iron-Age Warship in Context*, Ships and Boats of the North, **5**, Roskilde: Viking Ship Museum

Cunliffe, B 2001 *Facing the Ocean: the Atlantic and its Peoples 8000 BC–AD 1500*, Oxford: Oxford University Press

Desfossés, Y 1998 'Les ateliers de saunerie laténiens de Sorrus (Autoroute A16, Pas-de-Calais)', in S Curveiller and C Seillier (eds), *Archéologie du littoral Manche – Mer du Nord, 1: Des origines à l'époque gallo-romaine, actes du premier colloque archéologique de Calais, 1997*, *Bulletin des Amis du Vieux Calais*, **160–161–162**, 469–478

Desfossés, Y 2000a 'Conclusion', in J-C Blanchet (ed), *Habitats et nécropoles de l'Age du Bronze sur le Transmanche et le TGV Nord*, Bulletin de la société préhistorique Française (Etudes et Travaux), **89 (10–12)**, 189–202

Desfossés, Y (ed) 2000b *Archéologie Préventive en Vallée de Canche: Les sites protohistoriques fouilles dans le cadre de la réalisation de l'autoroute A16*, Nord-Ouest Archéologie, **11**, Berck-sur-Mer: Centre de Recherches Archéologiques et de Diffusion Culturelle

Desfossés, Y and Philippe, M 2002 'Angleterre et France à l'Age du Bronze – Les Contacts Transmanche', *Archéologia*, **391**, 46–57

Evans, J, Chenery, C and Fitzpatrick, A 2006 'Bronze Age Childhood Migration of Individuals near Stonehenge, revealed by Strontium and Oxygen Isotope Tooth Enamel Analysis', *Archaeometry*, **48 (2)**, 309–321

Fenwick, V 2006 'Introduction', in *Keeping up with the Dover Boat: IJNA's Track Record*, Oxford: Blackwell, 1–9

Fenwick, V 2007 'The Dover Boat: the Reality of Deep-Mud Rescue', *International Journal of Nautical Archaeology*, **36 (1)**, 177–184

Gibson, A forthcoming 'The imported Cornish vessel', in P Bennett, P Clark, A Hicks, J Rady and I Riddler, *At the Great Crossroads: Prehistoric, Roman and medieval discoveries on the Isle of Thanet 1994–95*, Canterbury: Canterbury Archaeological Trust, 54–58

Gibson, A, Macpherson-Grant, N, and Stewart, I 1997 'A Cornish vessel from farthest Kent', *Antiquity*, **71 (272)**, 438–41

Gifford, E and Gifford, J 2004 'The use of half-scale model ships in archaeological research with particular reference to the Graveney, Sutton Hoo and Ferriby ships', in P Clark (ed), *The Dover boat in Context: Society and water transport in prehistoric Europe*, Oxford: Oxbow Books, 67–81

Gifford, E, Gifford, J and Coates, J 2006 'The construction and trials of a half-scale model of the Early Bronze Age ship, Ferriby 1, to assess the capability of the full-size ship', in L Blue, F Hocker and A Englert (eds), *Connected by the Sea: Proceedings of the Tenth International Symposium on Boat and Ship Archaeology, Denmark 2003*, Oxford: Oxbow Books, 57–62

Kaul, F 1998 *Ships on Bronzes: A Study in Bronze Age Religion and Iconography*, Publications from the National Museum, Studies in Archaeology and History, **3.1**, Copenhagen

Kaul, F 2004 'Social and religious perceptions of the ship in Bronze Age Europe', in P Clark (ed), *The Dover Bronze Age Boat in Context: Society and water Transport in Prehistoric Europe*, Oxford: Oxbow Books, 122–137

Lepaumier, H, Marcigny, C and Ghesquière, E 2005 'L'architecture des habitats protohistoriques de Normandie: quelques exemples de la fin du IIIème millénaire au début du second âge du Fer', in O Buchsenschutz and C Mordant (eds), *Architectures protohistoriques en Europe occidentale du néolithique final à l'âge du Fer*, Actes du 127ème congrès des Comité des Travaux Historique et Scientifiques, Nancy, 15–20 avril 2002, Paris: Éditions du Comité des Travaux Historique et Scientifiques, 231–264

Lorin, Y, Pinard, E, Trawka, H and Hannois, P 2005 'Aire-sur-la-Lys, Le Hameau Saint-Martin', in G Fosse (ed), *Bilan Scientifique de la région Nord-Pas-de-Calais 2004*, Lille: Ministère de la Culture et de la Communication, 128–131

Marcigny, C and Ghesquiere, E 2003 *L'Île Tatihou (Manche) à l'Âge du Bronze: Habitats et Occupation du Sol*, Documents d'Archéologie Française, **96**, Paris: Èditions de la Maison des Sciences de l'Homme

Marcigny, C, Ghesquière, E, Clement-Sauleau, S and Verney, A 2005 'L'âge du Bronze en Basse Normandie: définition par le mobilier céramique, une première tentative', in J Bourgeois and M Talon, M (eds), *L'âge du Bronze du nord de la France dans son contexte européen*, Paris: Editions du Comité des Travaux Historiques et scientifiques avec l'Association pour la Promotion des Recherches sur l'âge du Bronze, 303–332

Marcigny, C, and Talon, M forthcoming 'Sur les rives de la Manche. Qu'en est il du passage de l'âge du Bronze à l'âge du Fer?', in *De l'âge du Bronze à l'âge du Fer (X–VIIème siècle av. J-C)*, Actes du colloque international APRAB-AFEAF de St Romain-en Gal 2005, Revue Archéologique de l'Est

Mare, E 2005 'Le village de Malleville-sur-le-Bec (Eure)', in C Marcigny, C Colonna, E Ghesquière and G Verron (eds), *La Normandie à l'aube de l'histoire: les découvertes archéologiques de l'âge du Bronze 2300–800 av J-C*, Paris: Somogy Éditions d'art, 52–53

Mariette, H 1961 'Une Urne de L'Âge du Bronze à Hardelot (Pas-de-Calais)', *Helinium*, **1**, 229–232

Massy, J-L 2006 'French legislation on maritime cultural assets', in M Pieters, G Gevaert, J Mees and J Seys (eds), *Colloquium: To sea or not to sea – 2nd international colloquium on maritime and fluvial archaeology in the southern North Sea area, Brugge, 21–23 September 2006*, VLIZ

Special Publication, **32**, Oostende, Belgium, 53–54

McGrail, S 1987 *Ancient Boats in NW Europe: the archaeology of water transport to AD 1500*, London: Longman

McGrail, S 2006a 'The Dover Bronze Age Boat', *Antiquaries Journal*, **86**, 417–419

McGrail, S 2006b 'Experimental boat archaeology: has it a future?', in L Blue, F Hocker and A Englert (eds), *Connected by the Sea: Proceedings of the Tenth International Symposium on Boat and Ship Archaeology, Denmark 2003*, Oxford: Oxbow Books, 8–15

McGrail, S 2007 'The Re-assessment and Reconstruction of Excavated Boats', *The International Journal of Nautical Archaeology*, **36 (2)**, 254–264

Melton, N and Nicholson, R 2004 'The Mesolithic in the Northern Isles: the preliminary evaluation of an oyster midden at West Voe, Sumburgh, Shetland, UK', *Antiquity*, **78 (299)**, http://antiquity.ac.uk/ProjGall/nicholson/index.html

Muckelroy, K 1981 'Middle Bronze Age trade between Britain and Europe; a maritime perspective', *Proceedings of the Prehistoric Society*, **47**, 275–97

Needham, S and Giardino, C 2008 'From Sicily to Salcombe: a Mediterranean Bronze Age object from British coastal waters', *Antiquity*, **82 (315)**, 60–72

Needham, S 2000a 'Power pulses across a cultural divide: cosmologically driven exchange between Armorica and Wessex', *Proceedings of the Prehistoric Society*, **66**, 151–207

Needham, S 2006 'Networks of Contact, Exchange and Meaning: the Beginning of the Channel Bronze Age', in S Needham, K Parfitt and G Varndell (eds), *The Ringlemere Cup: Precious Cups and the Beginning of the Channel Bronze Age*, British Museum Research Publication, **163**, London: British Museum Press, 75–81

Needham, S and Dean, M 1987 'La cargaison de Langdon Bay à Douvres; la signification pour les échanges à travers la manche', in J-C Blanchet (ed), *Les relations entre le continent et les îles britanniques a l'âge du Bronze: Actes du colloque de Lille dans le cadre du 22ème congrès préhistorique de France*, Amiens: Supplément à la Revue Archéologique de Picardie, 119–24

Needham, S, Parfitt, K and Varndell, G (eds) 2006 *The Ringlemere Cup: Precious Cups and the Beginning of the Channel Bronze Age*, British Museum Research Publication, **163**, London: British Museum Press

Oxley, I 2006 'Legislation related to maritime archaeological heritage: England', in M Pieters, G Gevaert, J Mees and J Seys (eds), *Colloquium: To sea or not to sea – 2nd international colloquium on maritime and fluvial archaeology in the southern North Sea area, Brugge, 21–23 September 2006*, VLIZ Special Publication, **32**, Oostende, Belgium, 46–47

Petersen, H 1986 *Skinboats of Greenland*, Ships and Boats of the North, **1**, Roskilde: Viking Ship Museum

Pieters, M, Demerre, I, Lenaerts, T and Zeebroek, I 2006 'Maritime Archaeology and Heritage Afloat Unit of the VIOE: state of affairs', in M Pieters, G Gevaert, J Mees and J Seys (eds), *Colloquium: To sea or not to sea – 2nd international colloquium on maritime and fluvial archaeology in the southern North Sea area, Brugge, 21–23 September 2006*, VLIZ Special Publication, **32**, Oostende, Belgium, 8–9

Roberts, O 2004 'Reconstruction and performance', in P Clark (ed), *The Dover Bronze Age Boat*, London: English Heritage, 189–210

Roberts, O 2006a 'Interpretations of Prehistoric Boat Remains', *International Journal of Nautical Archaeology*, **35 (1)**, 72–78

Roberts, O 2006b 'The Dover Boat: Steady as She Goes!', *International Journal of Nautical Archaeology*, **35 (2)**, 334

Rouzo, P and Poissonnier, B 2007 'Fabrication expérimentale d'une pirogue monoxyle en chêne', *Archéopages*, **18**, 58–63

Samson, A 2006 'Offshore finds from the Bronze Age in North-Western Europe: The Shipwreck Scenario revisited', *Oxford Journal of Archaeology*, **25 (4)**, 371–388

Sanders, D 2007 'The Dover Boat; some responses to Ole Crumlin-Pedersen and Seán McGrail, concerning its propulsion, hull form, and assembly and some observations on the reappraisal process', *International Journal of Nautical Archaeology*, **36 (1)**, 184–192

Stefansson, V 1942 *Ultima Thule*, London: George Harrap

Sys, D and Leroy-Langevin, E 2004 *Escaudain-Erre (Nord). Fouilles préventives: Document Final de Synthèse*, Service archéologique du Douaisis

van Giffen, A 1930 *Die Bauart der Einzelgräber: Beitrag zur Kenntnis der ällteren individuellen Grabhügelstrukturen in den Niederlanden*, Leipzig: Mannus Bibliothek

van Giffen, A 1938 'Continental bell or disc-barrows in Holland with special reference to tumulus I at Rielsche Hoefke', *Proceedings of the Prehistoric Society*, **4**, 258–271.

Von der Porten, E 2006 'Minimal, Intermediate, and Maximum Reconstructions of the Dover Boat', *International Journal of Nautical Archaeology*, **35 (2)**, 332–333

Vosmer, T 2003 'The Naval Architecture of Early Bronze Age Reed-built Boats of the Arabian Sea' in D Potts, H Naboodah and P Hellyer (eds), *Archaeology of the United Arab Emirates: Proceedings of the First International Conference on the Archaeology of the U.A.E.*, London: Trident Press, 152–157

Ward, C 2005 'Dover Bronze Age Boat', *The International Journal of Nautical Archaeology*, **34 (2)**, 347–348

Wilkes, E 2004 *Iron Age maritime nodes on the English Channel coast: an investigation into the location, nature and context of early ports and harbours*, unpublished PhD thesis, University of Bournemouth

Wilkes, E 2007 'Prehistoric sea journeys and port approaches: the south coast and Poole Harbour', in C Cummings and R Johnston (eds), *Prehistoric Journeys*, Oxford: Oxbow Books, 121–130

Yates, D 2007 *Land, Power and Prestige: Bronze Age Field Systems in Southern England*, Oxford: Oxbow Books

2. Encompassing the Sea: 'Maritories' and Bronze Age maritime interactions

Stuart Needham

Our appreciation of the cultural place of the sea and sea-faring has developed radically in recent years. Earlier interpretation of coastal communities had always taken into consideration the exploitation of marine food resources and the use of the sea to reach other lands to engage in commerce, war or other interactions. But the sea was generally seen as simply a medium through which to achieve the objectives of harvesting, communicating and transporting, a rather inconvenient and at times perilous intervening tract. It was interpreted as a backdrop to land-based activities, a peripheral element that had to be confronted and engaged with, but which remained 'outside' of society in a way that the occupied territory did not. The latter is easier to recognise as being 'culturally constructed' because of abundant evidence for its utilization and modification in chosen ways not determined simply by ecological constraints. For the sea we are deprived of such evidence; 'occupation' can only be transient by its nature and most evidence for its use is either circumstantial, coming from the flanking lands, or the result of accidents rather than the positive actions that characterize the terrestrial record (Broodbank 2000, 70; Parker 2001).

Thinking on how early communities conceptualised the sea has however been shifting. Barry Cunliffe's book *Facing the Ocean* has been one influential source (Cunliffe 2001), as have been many papers in journals, for example, in the *World Archaeology* volume on *Seascapes*. In his introduction, Gabriel Cooney helps us to find ways of 'seeing land from the sea', a nice reversal of viewpoint (Cooney 2003;

also Parker 2001; Crumlin Pedersen 1996; Robinson 2007). The term *seascape* 'provides a context within which to move beyond a preoccupation with subsistence and its associated technology...'; the sea is instead 'contoured, alive, rich in ecological diversity and in cosmological and religious significance and ambiguity' (Cooney 2003, 323). The papers in this World Archaeology volume, among others, give us conceptual tools to understand how the sea can be embodied in the mental and practical constitution of coastal or island cultures. The sea may be an 'axis of movement' (Phillips 2003), a unifying medium because of common preoccupations (Ballard *et al* 2003) and a habitat richly inhabited by spiritual powers, frequently those linked to the Underworld (Bradley 2000, 12; Parker 2001, 38). Moreover, the sea can be central to the 'people who inhabit its dry edges but actually live across its fluid surface' (Cooney 2003, 323; Raban 1999). Compared to an entirely land-based existence, active engagement with the sea shapes human perception and experience very differently (O'Sullivan 2003; Parker 2001, 22).

But however central it is to a given culture, the sea is never simply an extension of the land, a point emphasized by the frequency with which the land/sea interface is regarded by early communities as liminal or transformative (*eg* Cunliffe 2001, 9; Scarre 2002; Van de Noort 2003, 404, 412). The sea tends to be associated with death and the Otherworld in opposition to the land of Thisworld. Among the traditional communities of northern Scandinavia the coast is seen as a meeting point between land, sea and sky and therefore a liminal place where communication could most readily take place between humans and spirit worlds (Helskog 1999). The margins of the world of the living are sometimes deliberately chosen as appropriate places for the disposal of the dead (Parker Pearson 1999, 124–125; Scarre 2002, 26; Lindendauf 2003). Such cosmological attitudes explain, in part at least, why the ships that cross the sea can become potent metaphors for states of transition (Broodbank 1993, 327; Ballard *et al* 2003; Van de Noort 2006, 283). But this cosmological schism between land and sea makes it all the more difficult to create integrated interpretations of cultural land-cum-seascapes.

Cosmological differentiation of the sea can have a marked effect on perceptual relations between communities separated by it, but does not necessarily do so. For example, in considering the Neolithic of the islands of Malta and Gozo, Robb has argued that there was a key change during the period. He interprets the marked cultural differentiation apparent in the Temple period in terms of a new social geography (Robb 2001, 191); 'travel forges and fixes relative identities… crossing the seas would have meant consciously crossing an ideological frontier to strange lands where people lived differently'. Robb's analysis helps comprehension of given cultures maintaining difference at the same time as participating within a unitary interaction system, which is relevant to my later discussion

There has also been discussion in the literature about whether it is possible to define specifically *maritime cultures*. Proposed initially by Keith Muckelroy, subsequent writers have doubted or at least qualified its utility (Hunter 1994; Westerdahl 1994; Parker 2001, 25). Hunter makes the point that 'many populations possess a maritime element within their social framework, but whether there are circumstances in which this element can be extended into a full-blooded 'maritime culture' requires questioning' (Hunter 1994, 261). He goes on to say that 'Maritime components are no more than extensions or reflections of the broader culture to which they belong and are integral rather than isolated economic or social elements' (*ibid*, 262). This is a valid perspective in that we should always be seeking holistic views of a given culture or cosmological

view: the sea and all it entails will be defined in relation to land, and the land in relation to sea. Nevertheless, schisms of perception still need to be sought in any given cosmology since the abundant ethnographic and folklore evidence shows that they are commonplace, presumably because of the special properties and difficulties that the maritime environment presents to humans. Westerdahl has addressed this point in suggesting (in an unpublished conference paper – Parker 2001, 38) that we should add the domain of *mare* to Hodder's *domus* and *agrios* in reconstructing ancient world views.

Mare thus gives us, at a general level, a psychological component which rationalises the maritime environment and maritime affairs within the broader cosmological construct. *Mare* will have been conceived differently by different cultures, at times even those linked by a special axis or network of maritime interaction. To talk of a 'maritime interaction network' gives emphasis to the mechanical and physical aspects of interaction without explaining what other factors – beliefs and particular practices – were important to the constitution of the said network. To embrace all of these constituent factors I will apply the term 'maritory' – adapted from 'territory' but not intended to be analogous in social construction.

The case study of this paper is the constitution of maritime interactions during part of the Early Bronze Age (*c* 2000–1500 BC). Some years ago research on this topic had little evidence at its disposal beyond that of exchanged objects and influences (as seen in artifacts, architecture and depositional practices). Early classic studies established that the Early Bronze Age was a time of growing inter-regional interactions that included regular contact across the seaways of northwest Europe, linking Ireland, Britain and neighbouring parts of continental Europe (*eg* Megaw and Hardy 1938; Piggott 1938; Butler 1963). The background to exchanges was traditionally seen to lie in 'trade' involving specialist 'middlemen' with the objective of commercial profit, or alternatively in the migration of people. In more recent decades migration on anything more than a small scale has been downplayed in interpretations and, meanwhile, the mode and purpose of exchange in prehistoric Europe has been much debated (*eg* Scarre and Healy (eds) 1993). Bradley and Edmonds' thorough critique of exchange models in archaeology emphasizes the non-commercial basis of exchange in pre-state/pre-monetary economies – *ie* in 'traditional' societies; a long line of anthropological research going back to Mauss (1970) and Malinowski (1922) has shown that there was an inextricable link between exchange and inter-personal or inter-group relations (Bradley and Edmonds 1993; Godelier 1999; see also Needham 2008).

The wide ranging surveys of long-distance travel and exchange in ethnographic societies by Mary Helms (1988; 1993; 1998) have inspired new approaches to the interpretation of archaeological evidence for pre-state societies (Beck and Shennan 1991; Broodbank 1993; Needham 2000a; Robb 2001; Van de Noort 2003; 2006; Kristiansen and Larsson 2005). Helms showed that the long-distance acquisition of goods in such cultural contexts usually involved valuables rather than 'bulk commodities'; those valuables could include foreign 'esoteric' knowledge as well as rare materials or objects. Exchange was not driven by commercial objectives, but instead there were two other dominant processes. On the one hand, there is an intrinsic yearning by people to reach out into the world beyond their immediate experience, to 'touch' the more distant and mythical realms which often have associations with the gods and ancestors. On the other hand, it was a way for aspiring high-ranking members of a community to prove themselves worthy of their would-be station by embarking on a difficult mission (also Kristiansen and Larsson 2005, 39–41; Van de Noort 2006, 279–282). The consequent acquisition of goods, materials or knowledge that was quite alien to the home territory and which could be identified with the outer cosmos would be a way of both forging a more lasting connection between the individual and the powers (including spiritual powers) that reside there *and* validating the accomplishment of the journeyer and the mission. Acquisition of this kind was not driven by a mutual desire to exchange 'commodities' and it must have operated within some kind of understood system of gift exchange between travelling group and host community or its leader. Robert Van de Noort draws the further inference that the journeyers of the Early Bronze Age

normally went the full distance themselves rather than relying on a chain of exchanges; in this respect it is analogous to 'directional trade' (Van de Noort 2006).

Stephen Shennan persuasively applied the framework offered by Helms to the case of the Early Bronze Age 'trade' in amber (Beck and Shennan 1991, 137–140) and a broader application of the same ideas to this period and region has been referred to by the present writer as *cosmologically-driven exchange* (Needham 2000a). It is now possible to interpret much of the exotica of the Early Bronze Age – trinkets of amber, jet, faience, tin, gold, shale, amongst other types of object – as specialized gear of the elite and ritual specialists, *ie* shamans (Woodward 2000; 2002; Sheridan and Shortland 2004), and their acquisition can be described as cosmologically-driven. The dominance of this *raison d'être* for long-distance acquisition may have waned after the mid second millennium BC (Van de Noort 2003).

As for the mechanics and practicalities of maritime exchange, significant advances have of course come in recent years from the full publication of Bronze Age boat finds, most notably the superb remains from North Ferriby and Dover (Wright 1990; Clark (ed) 2004a). Craft of this type were clearly available to service the Early Bronze Age maritime networks and Van de Noort (2006) has made the case that they were an innovation explicitly connected to the rise of cosmological acquisition in the Early Bronze Age. I will return to the significance of these in the conclusions. Van de Noort takes us beyond the underlying rationale of long-distance maritime travel by suggesting which members of society would have been involved and how they were linked together by the venture. However, relatively little attention has been paid to other social and organizational aspects of these maritime interactions: what kind of infrastructure was required and how such spheres of interaction were overlaid upon more local and land-based interaction spheres. It is possible to approach such matters initially using precious cups of a rather special character, an object type for which renewed study was stimulated by the discovery of a new gold example from Ringlemere, Kent, only 14 km north of Dover (Needham *et al* (eds) 2006).

Precious cups and Early Bronze Age maritime interactions

Only sixteen Early Bronze Age cups of this special character are known. Very few of them are so closely similar to one another as to argue for them coming from the hands of the same craftsman or 'workshop' (Fig 2.1) (Needham *et al* 2006, 54–60). The examples made in gold – numbering seven – have stylistic similarities but present a range of designs and their production may span as much as four centuries. Even the similarity between Ringlemere and Rillaton merits closer scrutiny; although they follow the same basic style, their detailed form and execution is rather different. The Breton cups have their own regional idiosyncrasies: two of the three are made of silver, a raw material not used elsewhere for the type; and two (a different pair) are the only ones of this series to have composite bodies – two parts joined at the carination by rivets. Just two cups are known in amber and they present very different profiles and proportions from one another; the Clandon example respects the predominant biconical form, but that from Hove is almost hemispherical. Amongst the shale series, finds of which come from a restricted area of southern England, four do show more stylistic homogeneity; however, the lost Stoborough cup, suspected also to be of shale, is distinct and more like the Hove amber cup.

On the basis of these inter-comparisons, I have suggested that the precious cups are mainly the products of craftsmen working in their respective regions, although clearly they were equipped with inter-regionally distributed knowledge. The plain silver and gold examples from Brittany and Fritzdorf on the Rhine are likely to have been among the earliest examples (from the nineteenth century BC onwards), but the examples with simple embossing – Ringlemere and Rillaton – need not be appreciably later. Although requiring the mastery of a technically demanding metal-working technique, their embossing is limited to horizontal corrugations. The creators of these early embossed cups probably drew on the technology developed slightly earlier for ornaments in central Britain (Needham 2000b), but I believe both to be products of the south, which was most exposed to the continental influence responsible for this novel cup form. Ultimately the fusion of technology and object type seen in the *embossed* cups spread back across the Channel to the Rhinelands, there producing similar and yet novel variants (Fig 2.1 nos 4, 5 and 7).

Precious cups were not themselves the products of long-distance exchange, even though the materials from which they are fashioned often were, and I have argued that there was something linking these cups beyond simply a desire to emulate other regional elites. The basis of the argument is their distribution which is at the same time far-flung and yet strangely limited (Fig 2.2). There is a strong attraction to coastal lands and the major river of the Rhine, but even so, there are many coastal parts of north-west Europe that have not yielded precious cups. Precious cups have thus been interpreted as having a specialist role relating to an emerging maritime interaction network which operated within a specific zone – the Channel and the southern North Sea including the in-flowing rivers (Needham *et al* 2006, 75–81). But I now wish to go further and convey the importance of the organisational and perceptual infrastructure – the maritory – that linked these particular groups together.

Defining a 'Maritory'

The first important point to make about a maritory is that there need be no prior expectation about its shape and form; just as for territories, the composite and complex cultural picture of any given time will give rise to a historically specific form. In this respect a maritory is a form of 'geographic system' not a geographic region (Rappaport 1969). A geographic system has been defined as '… a set of biological and ecological elements, *their structural relationships, and their functional operation*' (Terrell 1977–8, 63; emphasis mine). Insofar as a maritory is concerned, the core economic and ecological elements are diverse: those of the sea itself (sea resources, tides, currents, navigability), those of the coast (harbourage, estuaries, beaches, navigability) and those of the supporting territories (people, provision for subsistence and vital materials for sea craft etc).

A maritory should not be seen as analogous to a culture zone. Nor need a maritory be a rigidly bounded entity (but this is true also of many early territories). It is unlikely that a maritory would be pre-conceived by the

Figure 2.1 Reconstructed profiles of the Early Bronze Age precious cups of north-west Europe (drawing Stephen Crummy; after Needham et al 2006). 1. Ringlemere, Kent; 2. Rillaton, Cornwall; 3. Fritzdorf, Nordrhein-Westfalen; 4. Gölenkamp, Niedersachsen; 5. Eschenz, Canton Thurgau; 6. Ploumilliau, Côtes d'Armor; 7. No provenance ('South Germany'); 8. Saint-Adrien, Côtes d'Armor; 9. Saint-Fiacre, Morbihan; 10. Clandon Barrow, Dorset; 11. Hove, West Sussex; 12. ?Wiltshire 1; 13. ?Wiltshire 2; 14. Farway 1, Devon; 15. Farway 2, Devon; 16. Stoborough, Dorset.

Gold

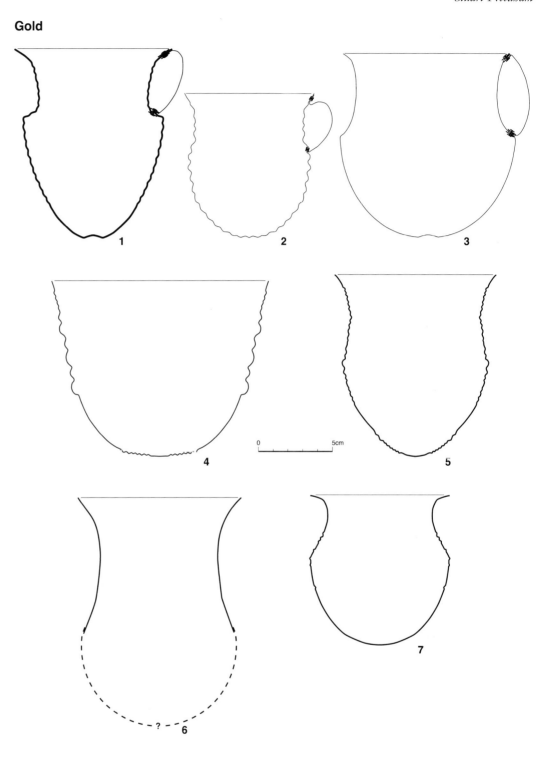

societies concerned; rather it would develop a degree of coherence through a set of shared and reciprocal interests amongst participating communities; geographical delimitation might follow incidentally from this process (Fig 2.3).

It can be seen from this starting definition that a maritory could often have been constituted across a spectrum of different cultures and while those cultures might consequently have experienced a degree of cultural convergence,

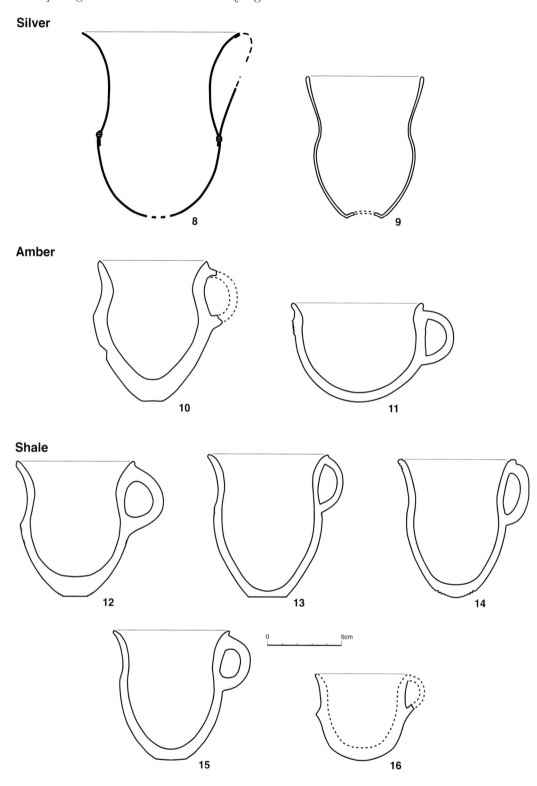

Silver

8

9

Amber

10

11

Shale

12

13

14

0   5cm

15

16

there is no reason to expect the end result to be cultural unification. In terms of Kristiansen and Larsson's recent analysis of Bronze Age societies (2005), a maritory can be viewed as a particular kind of institution, an institution that served specifically for the conduct of certain kinds of interaction across the water. This should be neither elevated above nor wholly divorced from similar institutions controlling land-based interactions, but it inevitably has its

Figure 2.2 Map of recovery of precious cups; for individual findspots see caption to Fig. 1 (drawing Stephen Crummy; after Needham et al 2006). Also shown are the putative sources (ceramic handled cups and embossed sheet metal ornaments) for the style of the cups and technology of the embossed examples.

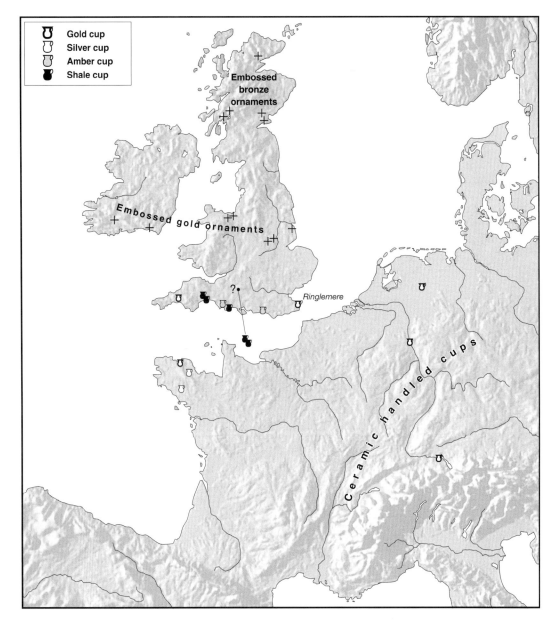

own peculiar infrastructural needs not relevant to land.

In summary, a maritory is a definable zone of privileged or relatively high-flux interaction used for the execution of certain specialist maritime 'exchanges'. Those exchanges may be few or many in kind, highly focussed or diverse – the possible range includes non-local raw materials, exotic artefacts and esoteric knowledge – but also people, for example, marriage partners, adoptees, ambassadors, interns or craftsmen. The relative intensity of such a system may have been in part self-reinforcing since some of the exchanged items and ideas may have been consciously or sub-consciously contrived to facilitate the counter-flow of others. This in turn can help promote a sense of cohesion.

In order to exist, a maritory needs an infrastructure of people and society (Fig 2.4). It requires man-power, specialist craftsmen to produce the vessels of carriage, experienced navigators, those who could read tides and currents and predict weather, and those who could intercede with the relevant gods and spirits. It also required people who had some 'right' in the eyes of society to travel widely; these were not early-day package holidays that anyone could embark on. Among the travellers it was essential to have individuals who had

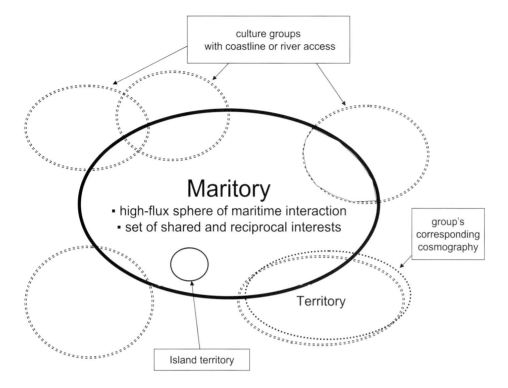

Figure 2.3 Model for the relationship between a maritory and the territories of participating groups. The intersection between a territory and the maritory represents both the physical and metaphysical engagement of the community with the sea and seafaring.

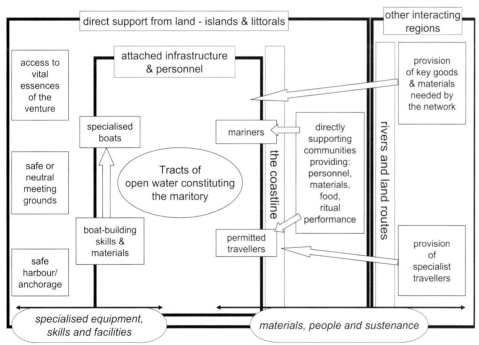

Figure 2.4 The elements of a maritory.

command of foreign languages or a *lingua franca* and knowledge of foreign customs – these too were specialists in their own right (Helms 1988; Van de Noort 2006).

The maritory must of course include some territory, not only for the seafarers themselves to dwell, but also for the supporting cast of the communities that produced food and materials (such as timber) and shelter, and who would offer hospitable reception in whatever circumstances (Sherratt and Sherratt 1998, 337; Kristiansen and Larsson 2005, 28). The support territories will inevitably have littoral or riparian borders, but that does not mean we should expect a ribbon of land of constant width and unchanging contribution to provide the infrastructure. Inland communities can of course be involved in maritime activities and their support, but rarely in isolation from the intervening coastal zones. Maritime symbolism is not the exclusive preserve of 'maritime cultures' and we should not automatically interpret such symbols from inland contexts as being indicative of an actual engagement with the sea (Westerdahl 1994, 266; Clark 2004b, 321).

The vital need for ritual to allow early societies to engage in distant travel is beginning to be well acknowledged in archaeology (*eg* Cunliffe 2001, 9; Chapman and Geary 2004, 455; Van de Noort 2006). From historical times there is the celebrated case of Venice's ritual pact with the sea which was annually reaffirmed in a ceremony. The ritual connection could also reflux such that key icons of travel, such as the ship, were absorbed within broader ritual practices (Ballard *et al* 2003, 392). By adopting some common rituals, groups participating within a maritory could have emphasised that they were part of a union which had a common belief in both the value of the exchange venture and the appropriate way to conduct it. Many elements of ritual are likely to be archaeologically intangible, but specialised artefacts and recurrent practices leaving particular archaeological traces will always be capable of being discerned; the precious cups can be interpreted as one such piece of evidence. The constituent communities 'signed up' to a particular way of engaging with each other and with the forces of the sea – and one outward manifestation of that signing up was the adoption of a specific ritual vessel form. We cannot be sure exactly how the cups were used, whether for libations or to dispense some kind of hallucinogenic or narcotic substance, but their unstable form– incapable of standing unaided upright on a surface – and their construction from rare materials makes it patently clear that they were highly specialised within the cultural contexts in which they occur (Needham *et al* 2006, 69–81).

The cups would have helped service the maritime interaction network by providing the necessary ritual sanctions for engaging in the dangerous and uncertain venture of maritime travel to distant shores, but their role need not have been restricted to this. At the local level

the cups would have come to symbolise the prevailing preoccupations of the constituent communities and their use in other rituals – including occasionally as funeral offerings – would bring special sacred power to those discourses (Needham *et al* 2006, 69–72).

In order to relate the concept of a 'maritory' to that of 'seascape', we need look no further than the relationship of 'territory' to 'landscape'. Seascape provides the overarching concept within which we can appreciate manifold cultural responses to the sea and equally manifold ways of incorporating it in the psyche; it is closely linked to *mare*. A maritory, on the other hand, is a specific tract of sea and its associated cultural components which are interpreted from the archaeological evidence as having a circumscribed historical significance in terms of inter-group interactions.

The Channel/southern North Sea (CSNS) Maritory of the Early Bronze Age

For the period and regions of concern here analysis of wide ranging evidence allows the interpretation of a maritory approximately as shown in Fig 2.5. At its heart are the tracts of sea we know as the Channel and the southern North Sea – so it can be dubbed the CSNS maritory for convenience. Its definition does not of course preclude other axes of contact, either by land or water, but it does attempt to represent a zone of privileged interaction where one particular network operated with its own particular ideological and organisational framework. It is apparent that the maritory thus defined is far from simply the product of geographical determinism; there is no 'logic' to this particular attenuated stretch of sea having a relatively high flux of internal interaction.

A similar geographic entity has been identified in recent years by French scholars working from different material sources. Strong cross-Channel comparisons, once apparent only for certain metalwork, are now emerging also for ceramics, house architecture and even land allotment from the final Early Bronze Age (1750/1700–1500 BC) onwards and have led Cyril Marcigny to envisage 'un vaste complexe technoculturel littoral Manche-mer du Nord (MMN)' (Marcigny and Ghesquiere 2003, 167–168 fig 146). Maréva Gabillot (2005) has argued

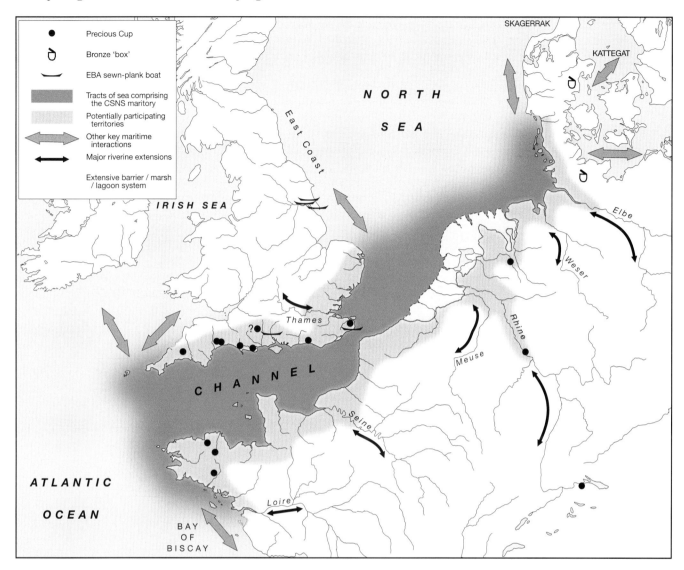

for a similar though slightly larger maritime tract as having supported special interactions through her study of metalwork relationships for the *Bronze Moyen* (*c* 1750/1700–1300 BC). I see the emergence of this interactive system at an earlier stage and, in defining the CSNS maritory, attempt to go beyond just trade or settlement to explain how and why it came about.

The Early Bronze Age CSNS maritory has obvious extension arms in the rivers feeding into it, since passage by boat can continue uninterrupted. The larger tentacles are shown in Fig 2.5, but we should not ignore the potential importance of the many small rivers and streams, such as the Dour (in proximity to the Dover boat) and the Durlock (Ringlemere cup) both in Kent, the Sid in Devon (Farway

cups), or the Trieux in Côtes d'Armor (Saint Adrien cup). The large rivers on the continental side tap deeply into the landmass, a point that has not escaped generations of prehistorians trying to understand inter-regional contacts.

It can be seen that Eschenz, at the head of the Rhine, is something of an outlier in relation to the maritory; so too might be the unprovenanced cup said to be from southern Germany. It is not without significance that these two are typologically the latest in the whole series, and they could represent a transition to precious cups in a wholly different cultural context, for they essentially initiate the sequence of *later* Bronze Age embossed gold vessels in continental Europe (Needham *et al* 2006, 61 fig 30, 62).

Figure 2.5 The Channel/ Southern North Sea maritory of the Early Bronze Age. The larger inflowing rivers are also shown. Shown in addition to precious cups are potentially related bronze lidded 'boxes' from Jutland and Early Bronze Age boat finds.

The role of the islands and near-islands

Of obvious interest in the context of a maritory are islands and prominent peninsulas; the CSNS maritory has a good number, of varied sizes. It is easy to appreciate the distinctive character that island cultures tend to acquire when we see them in a negative-image geographic context as both isolated entities and at the same time bound together by an unusual cultural construct in the form of a maritory (Figs 2.3 and 2.6); island communities can be torn between the need for ties with closest mainland communities and the need to serve a unique and special role within the maritory.

Mike Parker Pearson is one of the latest to have considered the distinctive place of

islands in cultural landscapes; for him they raise 'interesting issues of identity, isolation, connectivity, power and resources' (Parker Pearson 2004, 130). Although by definition they are geographically insulated by sea, they cannot be studied in isolation from the outside world (also Evans 2003, 1–6); indeed, despite their individual character they are often 'the nodes through which sea-faring communities come together and communicate' (Parker Pearson 2004, 129). This role may apply equally to coastal communities and can be one aspect leading to certain unifying elements within a maritory. However, the islands, especially those of small size or lacking ecological diversity, may be prone to being 'more dependent on alliances and support from neighbours than mainland communities' (*ibid*, 129). The islands provide

Figure 2.6 Islands and selected near-islands in the CSNS maritory.

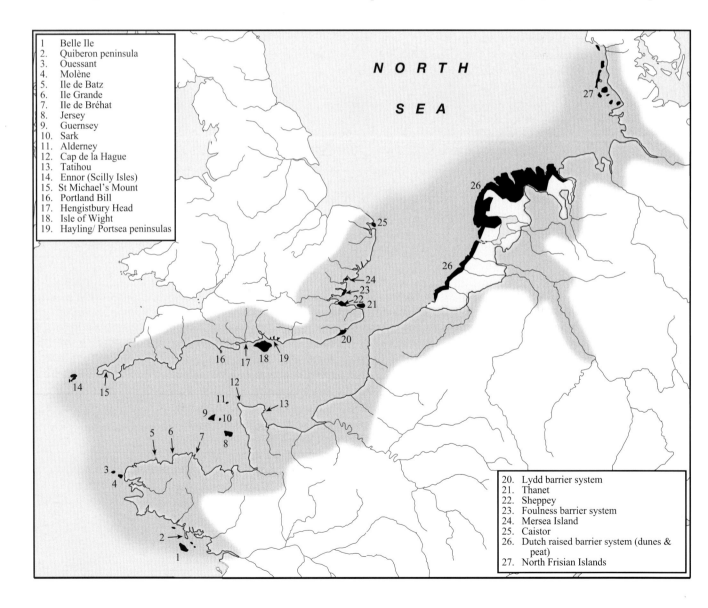

1	Belle Ile
2.	Quiberon peninsula
3.	Ouessant
4.	Molène
5.	Ile de Batz
6.	Ile Grande
7.	Ile de Bréhat
8.	Jersey
9.	Guernsey
10.	Sark
11.	Alderney
12.	Cap de la Hague
13.	Tatihou
14.	Ennor (Scilly Isles)
15.	St Michael's Mount
16.	Portland Bill
17.	Hengistbury Head
18.	Isle of Wight
19.	Hayling/ Portsea peninsulas

20.	Lydd barrier system
21.	Thanet
22.	Sheppey
23.	Foulness barrier system
24.	Mersea Island
25.	Caistor
26.	Dutch raised barrier system (dunes & peat)
27.	North Frisian Islands

a series of useful stepping stones which could at times have been more inherently receptive to sea travellers than the corresponding coastal territories.

One feature of the islands in the CSNS zone and its approaches is that there are no large archipelagos and many are single isles or small groups with one dominant island and tiny satellites; most are close to the mainland (*eg* St Michael's Mount, Wight, Thanet, Ouessant/ Molène, Ile Grande, Bréhat) and some may have been peninsulas in the Bronze Age (notably Tatihou – see below). In fact near-islands are worth considering as cosmologically related on the grounds that they can seem to be more a part of the domain of the sea and all it represents, than of the land (Cunliffe 2001, 10): Portland Bill, Hengistbury Head, Selsey, Cap de la Hague, Quiberon, to name just a few.

The Isle of Thanet, truly an island in the Early Bronze Age, seems to be exceptionally well endowed with burial monuments (Perkins 2004, 76; Parfitt in Needham *et al* 2006, 49), but this is also true of the north-east corner of mainland Kent. In other words, both flanks of the Wantsum Channel were densely occupied by monuments to the dead and it may not be without significance that Ringlemere lies amidst the mainland group just 2km from the Wantsum coast. These monument concentrations seem to have been demarcating a particular land-cum-seascape centred on the Wantsum with its potential special connotations of connectivity, transition and liminality (*cf* Chapman and Geary 2004, 456 – for the Fleet across Spurn Head). A similar emphasis on burial has been suggested for outlying small islands in the Outer Hebrides and the Ouessant/Molène archipelago in the Neolithic (Parker Pearson 2004, 133; Scarre 2002), while Phillips has observed that and the 'public face' of the impressive array of Neolithic cairns on Rousay, Orkney, seems to have been intended to be appreciated from the sea (Phillips 2003, 380).

The Isles of Scilly also seem to have been unusually well endowed with supposed burial monuments, although many examined 'graves' have failed to yield burial remains. There could originally have been as many as 100 cairns, mainly of the 'entrance grave' type; most occupied the larger island of Ennor before partial submergence fragmented it into the archipelago we know today (Thomas 1985, 40–48 and ch. 5; Ashbee 1974, ch. 4; Robinson 2007). However, it is significant for this paper that use of the entrance graves and slab-lined cists seems mainly to date to the second millennium BC (although see Mercer 1986, 57–61, for full discussion of the problem of dating their construction) and, moreover, that this may be the first period of substantial settlement on the Scillies. Settlers are argued to have arrived around 2000 BC from west Penwith, the western tip Cornwall, where a smaller group of comparable tombs are known (Thomas 1985, ch. 4; Mercer 1986, 39 fig 1) – perhaps west Penwith too was a cultural island.

In contrast to the Scillies, the corresponding islands off the westerly promontories of Armorica saw considerable use in the Neolithic (Scarre 2002); this may have been because they lay closer to the mainland. They too have suffered more recent submergence and early in the Neolithic virtually all except Ouessant were united in a single island (Molène – Le Bihan 2001, 20 fig 1; Scarre 2002). Sea-level rise had undoubtedly fragmented this larger island by the Early Bronze Age, at which time Ousessant, the outer and little-changed isle, saw substantial activity at the site of Mez-Notariou. An area of some 2000m^2 has the remains of Early to Middle Bronze Age occupation and this must have originally been more extensive still, for much has evidently been destroyed by later Iron Age structures (Le Bihan 2001, 50–51). Le Bihan stresses the nodal position of Ouessant in relation to the 'economic and cultural currents of history', as well as the tension between aspects of insularity and elements drawn from afar which suggests a certain internationalism or cosmopolitanism (2001, 61). The island's originality stems from the accommodation between these two 'contradictory' factors – an interpretation that could be applied more widely to islands.

Ouessant/Molène and the Scillies both sit in the open sea beyond the tips of substantial west-pointing peninsulas. They form portals to the wide Atlantic beyond the Channel, hence also to Ireland, western Britain and the southern Atlantic seaboard. It is possible that their respective, albeit divergent evidence for significant Early Bronze Age activity reflects the growing importance of sustained maritime interaction and the emergence of the CSNS maritory. Both island clusters have the potential not only to define major cultural thresholds, but also to serve as pivotal points between key links in the maritime chain. Thomas (1984) notes that the chamber plans of the Scillonian tombs are frequently boat-like. It also seems possible that this 'entrance grave' form was inspired by the wedge tombs of western Ireland, where a strong concentration occurs in the region and at the time of the early exploitation of copper sources there (O'Brien 1999).

The Channel Isles, Île Tatihou, Portland Bill, Hengistbury Head and the Isle of Wight not only represent useful 'ports of call' for along-Channel movement, but also form part of a corridor of cross-Channel connections from the Cotentin peninsula to the Dorset/Hampshire coast that would be a natural funnel for traffic in the western Channel in most periods (McGrail 1993; Tomalin 1988; Sherratt 1996). Sherratt has highlighted the beneficial co-alignment of this corridor with rivers penetrating northwards into Wessex and, via inter-fluves, to regions beyond. This is an important geographical conjunction that will at times have become a prominent axis in waterborne communication; it is pertinent to the consideration of inland Wessex below.

The Channel Isles, like Ouessant/Molène well occupied during the Neolithic, are well known for their distinctive cultural elements. For the Beaker period and Early Bronze Age there are insular pot variants and Tomalin suggested that Jersey played a pivotal role in regular cross-Channel connections that resulted in the dissemination of haematite-coated *vases à anses* (Tomalin 1988, 210–212, 208 fig 3). In addition to a copper axe from the Pinnacle, Jersey, the isles have yielded several early bronze flat axes (Kendrick 1928, 60–61; Hawkes 1939, 69; Heather Sebire *pers comm*) some of which are of Hiberno-British rather than Armorican style (Brithdir/Migdale/Killaha assemblage – *c* 2150–2000 BC).

Île Tatihou is today a tiny island off the Cotentin peninsular of Normandy but has yielded remarkable archaeological evidence – a landscape of field boundaries and associated settlement structures all associated with a material assemblage that would be perfectly at home in the Trevisker plus Deverel-Rimbury cultures of southern England (Marcigny and Ghesquiere 2003). Careful analysis of possible coastline changes due to relative sea-level rise and coastal erosion suggests that the 'island',

which even today can be reached on foot at lowest tide, would have been more definitively attached to the mainland in later prehistory (*ibid,* 31). A triple ditch system that cuts SW-NE across the island – perhaps constructed in the Iron Age rather than earlier – suggests the familiar mode of demarcating promontories in this part of the world. The field system went through two phases of remodeling or re-definition, the latest being as late as the final Iron Age. Initial emplacement, however, took place in the period 1750/1700–1500 BC and there are no real signs of earlier occupation.

The geographical importance of Hengistbury Head with its natural protected harbour hardly needs reiterating after Cunliffe's intensive campaign of work there (Cunliffe 1987). For the Early Bronze Age, not only is there the famous internationally connected grave group to mark the entrance to the river Avon, route to the heart of Wessex (Beck and Shennan 1991, 84–85), but the promontory has also yielded an Armorican low-flanged axe, one of only two in Britain (Needham 1979a, 274 fig 9.2). Dating later is an off-shore find made at Southbourne, a little to the west of Hengistbury, a shafthole axe of Sicilian type of around the thirteenth century BC (Needham and Giardino 2008).

The Isle of Wight's main claim to fame in the Early Bronze Age is that it has a disproportionate concentration of Arreton metalwork (Fig 2.7c), three hoards, including the Arreton hoard itself, belonging to the second half of the period concerned here (1750/1700–1500 BC; Northover 2001). Amongst this material are spearheads, mostly tanged, but including some novel socketed forms probably influenced by southern Scandinavian examples (see further below on the significance of spearheads). From around 2000 BC there is the important grave from Gallibury Down containing an Armorican style *vase à anse* now dated to 3632 ± 31 BP (2130–2080, 2040–1880 cal BC; GrA-19055, 19412; BM-2232R; Tomalin 1988) By the Taunton stage of the Middle Bronze Age (*c* 14th century BC), a distinctive palstave form, the Werrar type, was concentrated on the island and may have reflected its identity; the type is also found across the Solent, particularly in neighbouring Hampshire and Dorset (Rowlands 1976, map 6) and occasional examples have been found in northern France (*eg* Gabillot 2003, especially pl. 33 nos 5–6, pl. 34 nos 1–2).

Hayling Island and the flanking peninsulas themselves do not show any prominence in the Early Bronze Age, but it has not escaped notice that two distinctive 'Wessex' burials, amongst other Early Bronze Age burials, were set on Portsdown ridge which has superb command of this landscape of peninsulas and natural harbours (Ashbee 1967; Rudkin 1989). The small lugged 'Food Vessel' from the site (Ashbee 1967, 28–29 fig 5.8) is described as having a dark red surface, possibly a slip, which recalls Tomalin's haematite-coated series of *vases à anse*. Middle Bronze Age metalwork finds manifest in a different way the nodal importance of this coastline. Not only are finds dense but some comprise sizable hoards for the period and include a number of north French palstaves (Rowlands 1976, map 26; O'Connor 1980, 781 map 5, 798 map 22; Lawson 1999, 100 fig 11.5).

The configuration of the coastal plain in this area has in fact changed significantly since the early second millennium BC. Today's series of 'natural' harbours – Portsmouth, Langstone and Chichester – are the result of the more recent flooding of low-lying estuarine basins (Allen and Gardiner 2000). Nevertheless, this whole land-mass would have been laced by a network of creeks suitable for harbourage and limited penetration inland. Detailed survey of Langstone harbour has produced evidence for land-use throughout the second millennium, including a burial ground of the Deverel-Rimbury period, but earlier occupation may have been seasonal (Allen and Gardiner 2000, 205–214).

Another complex coastline with drowned estuaries, extensive salt marshes and (near-) islands is that of Essex; it has seen considerable changes over the past few millennia (Murphy and Brown 1999). In the northern stretches the main pattern is one of coastline retreat in the face of advancing sea level, but islands such as Mersea and Osea have been relatively stable since the Bronze Age (N Brown *pers comm*). In contrast, around the Foulness peninsula the Neolithic coastline appears to have been more inland than today's and by the Early Bronze Age it was extending seaward with the development of 'a complex environment of tidal sand flats, upper tidal silt flats, and occasional beach ridges of sand, gravel and shell with intervening estuaries' (Murphy and Brown 1999, 13). This doubtless included emergent islands through which flowed the small river Roach; on this river lies the Rochford grave, containing amber and gold otherwise very rare in the East Anglian Early Bronze Age (Piggott 1938, 92).

The late Holocene changes to the coastline of the western Netherlands are both more massive in scale and more fully researched. By the Early Bronze Age the coast featured a near continuous barrier system trapping lagoon and marsh systems behind and blocking off the hinterland of slightly elevated sands with intervening alluvial strips (Fig 2.6; Arnoldussen and Fontijn 2006, 290 fig 1). Some of the barrier dunes saw use, for example a barrow of 1800 BC was excavated in the Velserbroek area (van Gijssel and van der Valk 2006, 71), while the much celebrated Voorhout hoard, long appreciated to contain palstaves from the west, was deposited around the 15th century BC behind one of these fringing sand banks (Fontijn this volume; Butler 1963, 51–52 fig 11). This liminal location could well have been ritually strategic, signifying particular links with the maritory and all it embraced.

A parallel for this topographic siting can be seen across the Channel at Lydd where a group (probable hoard) of low-flanged axes of Willerby stage (Period 3) were deposited on the growing shingle bar system projecting far across a wide inlet (Needham 1988); in time the system became the backbone of the Dungeness peninsula. It is easy to see Lydd, with its marsh and quiet waters protected behind the broad shingle bars, as a potential departure point for material in transit towards the Continent, but it could just as much be a 'port of entry' for metal carried by sea routes from the active copper mines in central and north Wales. Again, the act of deposition of the hoard is better explained in terms of propitiatory rites rather than practicalities or happenstance.

Elements of interaction within and beyond the CSNS maritory (Periods 3–4)

Some influential axes of contact flowed out from this Early Bronze Age maritory, not least along the Rhine, where other contact finds may be added to the precious cup evidence (Fig 2.7a–e). Both the hoard from Gaubickelheim, Rheinland-Pfalz, and four graves at Singen,

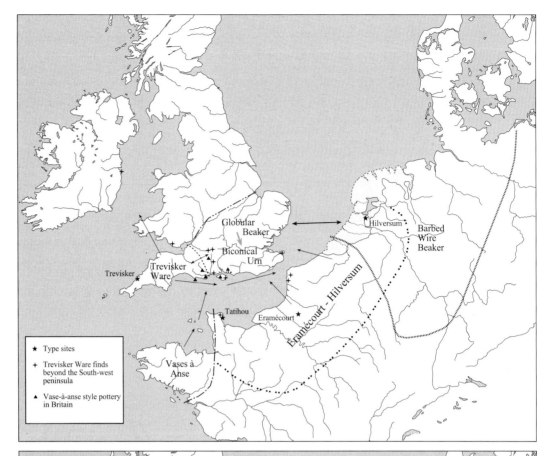

Figure 2.7a Ceramic traditions (c 2000–1500 BC) and evidence for the transfer of ideas and pots within the CSNS maritory.

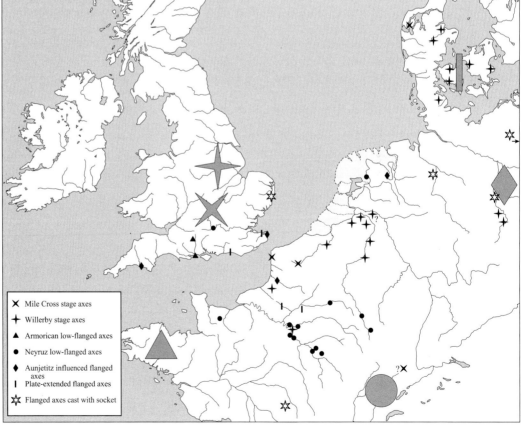

Figure 2.7b Selected bronze axe types (c 2000–1500 BC) within and around the CSNS maritory; black symbols are exported or influenced finds outside their main range; corresponding large grey symbols indicate source regions.

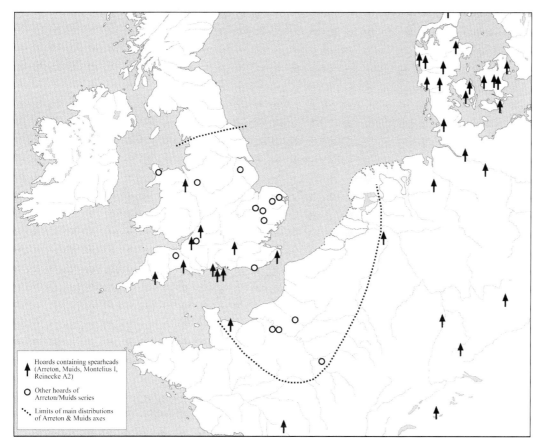

Figure 2.7c Bronze hoards (c 1750/1700–1500 BC) containing spearheads in and around the CSNS maritory, other hoards of Arreton/Muids series and the limits of the main distributions of Arreton and Muids flanged axes.

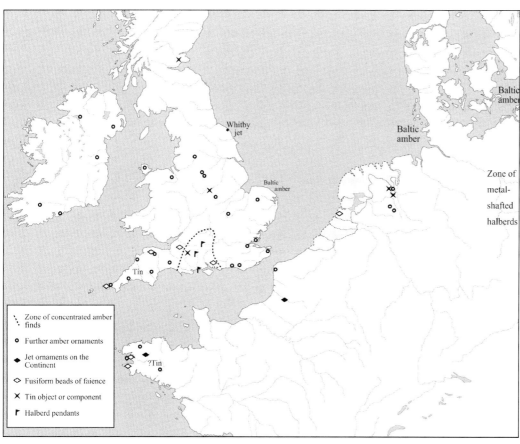

Figure 2.7d Selected ornaments (c 2000–1500 BC) and the likely source areas of their materials or object prototype; the zone of concentrated amber finds also encloses twelve findspots for Whitby jet in southern England.

Figure 2.7e Selected bronze dagger types (c 2000–1500 BC) within and around the CSNS maritory; small symbols are exported or influenced finds; corresponding large grey symbols indicate source regions.

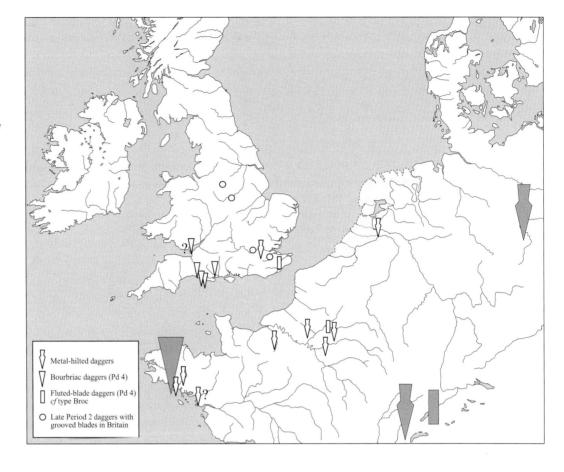

at the head of the Rhine (close to Eschenz), contain Armorico-British inspired daggers (Hundt 1971; Krause 1988). The hoard from Weingarten, Germersheim, in the middle Rhine contains an Arreton style socketed spearhead with a local Langquaid axe (Brandherm 1998). The question arises to what extent should we regard the Rhine, or a substantial part of it, as an integral part of the maritory. This is a perennial problem of definition that recurs for links in other directions, for example in southern Scandinavia, where precious cups may be replaced by equally unusual and highly specialised bronze boxes – only two are known so far, both from Jutland (Fig 2.5; Vandkilde 1988). It has long been appreciated that British or Irish decorated axes occur beyond the amber-rich coasts of Friesland and Jutland, although only a handful are likely to have actually emanated from Britain or Ireland (Fig 2.7b; Megaw and Hardy 1938; Butler 1963; Jockenhövel 2001). And much has also been made in the past of the eastward distribution of south-west peninsular tin, seen in unalloyed form in two of the Dutch finds – Exlooermond

and Bargeroosterveld (*eg* Butler 1963, 204; Sheridan and Shortland 2004).

The Thames would be another obvious route for inland diffusion and this finds some support in a few amber finds from the Upper Thames with the recent addition of a set of amber beads from a burial near Gravesend on the Thames estuary. Flanking the outer reaches of the estuary are the finds from Rochford (Essex) and Ringlemere (Kent). It is possible that an earlier, diminutive low-flanged axe from Tilehurst, Berkshire, is of the central European Neyruz type (Needham 1979a, 274, 277 fig 8.4) and two of the earliest British daggers featuring grooved blades (*c* 2000–1900 BC) are from Aylesford on the Medway, Kent, and Teddington on the Thames in west London (Fig 2.7e). The Thames passage forged a stronger connection with the maritime interaction network after about 1750/1700 BC when Arreton and other metalwork drew upon continental influences and raw material.

Inland Wessex was the recipient of many influences and goods and host to special travellers – pilgrims – and this gave its funerary repertoire an unusually diverse character (Needham 2008). However, this interpretation also makes it especially difficult to assess whether an introduced type came to be produced locally, or was consistently brought in from neighbouring regions or further afield. Just a few types of object will be mentioned here. The Winterbourne Stoke G5 *vase à anse* is a clearly intrusive type, though not necessarily an import from Armorica *per se*; the few other British finds of this type come from the south coast (Tomalin 1988). One of the two Armorican low-flanged axes from Britain comes from a grave at Wilsford G58, near Stonehenge (Needham 1979a, 279 fig 9.2; Annable and Simpson 1964, cat no 213).

Above all, Wessex's engagement with the maritory was concerned with the acquisition of amber. It is remarkable, if we look at the post-2000 BC distribution of amber finds in Britain how strongly represented they are in the far south, and how relatively poorly elsewhere (Fig 2.7d; Needham *et al* 2006, 77 fig 37). It is also noteworthy that there was a powerful draw towards just a few central Wessex foci. The amber used for the spacer-plate necklaces of Period 3 (*c* 1950/1900–1750/1700 BC) was almost certainly brought in as raw material and fashioned locally to judge from the restricted distribution of the necklaces that survive most complete (Beck and Shennan 1991; Woodward 2002).

Another type of particular interest to this discussion is the halberd-pendant – an exotic form made from exotic materials (bronze, gold and amber). Two come from central Wessex graves and a third from the coast beside the mouth of the Avon at Hengistbury (grave group mentioned above). There is no need to doubt their inspiration in metal-bound and metal-hafted halberds of the northern Aunjetitz zone given the evidence that the links were all in place (Piggott 1973, 361; Needham 2000b, 51; *pace* Case 2003, 181); not least there is the unequivocal Hiberno-British axe in the Dieskau 2 hoard in that zone (von Brunn 1959; Butler 1963, pl. Ib). However, perhaps the most significant point is that these halberd imitations in diminutive form were evidently produced at considerable remove from the prototypes. As with the precious cups, the concept of the type has travelled far, whereas the objects themselves were made in the region.

Armorica must also have been a key player

in the CSNS maritory to judge from its three precious cups. Several amber objects occur in the grave at Kernonen close to the north coast, including the closest parallels for the Ringlemere pendant (Briard 1970; Needham *et al* 2006, 40–41). Another fine piece of Breton amber is from St Fiacre, well south in the central uplands, a rich grave group that not only yielded one of the silver cups, but also an imported Rhône type metal-hilted dagger (Needham 2000a, 164 fig 6.6 and 6.18). Just as far-displaced is the spacer-plate bead of Whitby jet found in the Kerguévarec tomb, Finistère (Piggott 1939; Needham 2000a, 178, 188); fresh study of the piece (Alison Sheridan *pers comm*) has confirmed the material and, moreover, shows that it had been modified since being dismantled from its original necklace.

Biconical/fusiform beads of faience have recently been shown by Alison Sheridan to link Armorica with both southern England and the Dutch coast (Sheridan and Shortland 2004, fig 21.9). It is though specifically the faience version of this type that seems to tie in with the CSNS maritory, for examples in amber, gold, lignite and jet are more widely spread in Britain and there are amber parallels in Denmark (*ibid*).

There were undoubtedly also links south-wards towards Iberia (as discussed by Briard 1995) given that Brittany was in an obviously pivotal geographic position for linking two major coastal spheres. However, this does give us a problem in determining the character of the boundary of the CSNS in this sector. One geographical factor in relation to longer-distance maritime links may have been the 'uncongenial coasts' of France south of the Gironde and northern Spain (Cunliffe 2001, 26–29, 43 fig 2.18). A sparser population along this coast would not have precluded interaction coastwise or across the Bay of Biscay, but it may not have sustained such a regular web of interconnections with the result that the southern-coast communities of Armorica established stronger ties with the coastlands extending northwards and into the Channel.

Further east, along the coastlands from Normandy to Belgium, most evidence has traditionally come from metalwork finds, but this is now being increasingly supplemented by ceramics and evidence for round barrows closely comparable to elsewhere within the maritory. Although increasing numbers of ring-ditches (long-ploughed-out barrows) dating to the Early and Middle Bronze Age, have emerged from systematic aerial survey particularly in Picardy and Flanders (Ampe *et al* 1996; Bourgeois and Talon, this volume), few have as yet yielded graves. A rare non-ceramic grave find is an amber V-perforated ornament from Wimereux flanking the Straits of Dover (Blanchet 1984, 95 fig 42; Needham *et al* 2006, 77). The ring-ditches do, however, show that these regions shared highly comparable funerary architecture with Britain and the Low Countries creating an important trans-regional sphere in this respect from early in the second millennium BC. The tumuli of the Armorican Early Bronze Age also relate in terms of their external appearance. It appears that substantial round tumuli (as opposed to tiny mounds over early Beaker burials) emerged first in Armorica and Britain late in the third millennium BC, presumably inspired by the impressive Neolithic round mounds standing in parts of their respective landscapes.

A small but important group of funerary urns with plastic and cord ornament (Fig 2.7a – Eramécourt) forges the same linkages as the tumuli across the Channel and towards the lower Rhine (Blanchet 1984, 101 ff; Billard *et al* 1996; Marcigny *et al* 2005). Ceramic inter-comparisons throughout the maritory will, however, require very close scrutiny, since some elements of style are much more broadly spread across Early Bronze Age western Europe – being found for example in the Rhône culture well to the south. The key question is whether there are stronger ties within the proposed maritory than exist between it and neighbouring 'culture zones'.

The CSNS picture shown in Figure 2.7a is complex and partly diachronic. The Barbed Wire style of decorating Beaker pottery seen in the lower Rhine region and further east is primarily associated with the globular S-profiled shape that is characteristic of the first quarter of the second millennium BC in south-east Britain (Needham 2005, 200). There is then a continuation of cross-sea parallelism as these Beaker styles gave way to Biconical and Hilversum Urns in the second quarter of the millennium. These urn types may actually derive from the Eramécourt series, suspected to have earlier origins. This whole suite of inter-related regional styles extends further to the Trevisker Urns of south-west England and, less obviously, the *vases à anses* of Armorica. The situation is even more complex in Britain where these regional traditions, excepting Trevisker, are overlaid upon a vigorous continuing tradition of Collared Urns found almost throughout the island and yet strangely absent from the near-Continent.

Metalwork of the earlier part of the period under consideration is still rather sparse in northern France and the Low Countries. The bronze objects, even if not actual imports, reflect parent types emanating from different directions, notably Britain and the circum-Alpine zone (Fig 2.7b for axes). It was only in the Muids phase (*Bronze Moyen 1*, equivalent to British period 4) that stocks of metal in circulation seem to have reached a critical threshold allowing much more profligate deposition. There are a good number of flanged axes of a style closely related to the Arreton axes of south-east Britain (Blanchet and Mordant 1987) including some in important hoards which show that the north French valleys including much of the Seine basin were well engaged in the broader CSNS contact zone by the second quarter of the second millennium (Fig 2.7c). Significantly, this is also the stage when southern British metalwork saw a major shift in terms of dominant metal supply, from the low-impurity metal of Willerby stage metalwork perhaps drawn mainly from Welsh copper sources, to the more mixed composition assemblage of Arreton metalwork, some of which (with certain impurities at highish levels) seems to be metal from the Continent, probably with a central European input (Rohl and Needham 1998, 91–93; Northover 2001, 438–439).

Metalwork of this phase (Arreton/Muids/Nordic Period I) presents another interesting phenomenon that spreads across and beyond the maritory – the sudden development of bronze spearheads (hoards containing them are shown in Fig 2.7c). These are amongst the first bronze spearheads anywhere in Europe and it is important to note that it is not the same type throughout this zone. In southern Scandinavia they are socketed forms from the outset (Bagterp type) with a few parallels in central European contexts (Vandkilde 1996, 212 *ff*). A rare find of related spearheads further west at this date occurs in the Maison hoard, Normandy (Briard and Verney 1996).

By far the dominant type in Britain was instead the tanged spearhead, although occasionally modified by the addition of a collar; even the few examples in which the weapon was cast with a socket retain the distinctive style of the Arreton tanged blades, especially when account is taken of their hafted appearance (Needham 1979b).

Occasional spearheads in the British style are widely dispersed, a tanged example comes from Argenton-sur-Creuse, Indre, and socketed ones from Weingarten, Germersheim in the middle Rhine and Sporupland, Zealand (Cordier 1976, 546–547 fig 2.4; Brandherm 1998; Butler 1963, 97 fig 27). Tanged spearheads appear also to have been made in Ireland, but interestingly metalworkers in that island quickly developed their own distinctive socketed type, the end-looped type, which was then distributed back into Britain (Burgess and Cowen 1972).

In relation to the emergence of socketed implements, it is also worth mentioning the rare examples of Early Bronze Age flanged axes which have been cast with a socket (Fig 2.7b). The single known British example from Wangford, Suffolk, is paralleled in northern Europe – Borstel, Kütten and Prettmin – and in a much more ornate example from Lignières, Indre (Butler 1963, 97 fig 27; Gerloff 1975, 154–155; Needham 1979a, 278). There are, however a number of morphological differences between the individual pieces which suggests that few need be products of the same regional tradition.

Space here does not permit citing all relevant material (although more is shown in the accompanying maps), nor any detailed consideration of the relationships of the proposed maritory to neighbouring intensive spheres of sea interaction (Fig 2.5). Around Britain's coasts there was clearly an intensifying interaction sphere down the east coast, all the way from the Moray to East Anglia, which needs at some point to be related to the CSNS maritory. Jet ornaments were one prime concern of that network. Similarly, much was happening around and across the Irish Sea, not least because of the location of key metal sources, as already touched upon earlier in this article.

Conclusion

This is not the place for an extended discussion of the evidence of preceding periods (a summary is provided in Fig 2.8), but it is self-evident that the maritime affairs considered here had a deeper ancestry beginning with the establishment of early Beaker networks in the Channel zone and Lower Rhine from around the middle of the third millennium BC. The expansion of Beaker groups in this part of Europe must have made especially strong use of communication by water, exploiting both coastal and riverine routes, and in this respect as in many others they may have differed from the pre-existing cultural entities. Early Beaker culture gave rise to a new kind of spatial interaction quite unlike that typical of the indigenous territorially based cultures. It had an interest in maintaining long-range networks for both the maintenance of cultural identity and the acquisition of critical materials and knowledge (Clarke 1976; Needham 2005; 2007; Vander Linden 2006) and this necessitated cross-sea contacts on a much more regular basis than hitherto.

By the last quarter of the third millennium, cross-sea links may have fluctuated, but the situation is complex and there are certainly small numbers of axes closely related to British/Irish ones of the Brithdir/Migdale/Killaha stage (*c* 2150–2000 BC) in two main zones of the continental shore (Fig 2.9). Broadly contemporary gold lunulae were also a part of this outward diffusion of Hiberno-British metalwork styles.

It is clear that maritime interactions were nothing new in the early second millennium BC. The key question to conclude this paper then is to what extent might the earlier spheres of preferred maritime interaction be definable as 'maritories'. There is no black-and-white answer to this and it may be that a subtle gradation of scale and scope is what we should expect of cross-sea interactions as they acquired a pivotal position in determining social values.

Two things perhaps elevate the earlier second millennium BC maritory above those interaction networks that existed before. The first is the adoption of the highly specialised ritual artefact – the precious cup; this evidence alone may not be enough since it is entirely possible that other aspects of ritual observance in other systems would be difficult to discern. The second feature, however, is the sheer quantity and diversity of different contact finds

SUMMARY OF MARITIME INTERACTIONS FROM A SOUTHERN BRITISH PERSPECTIVE

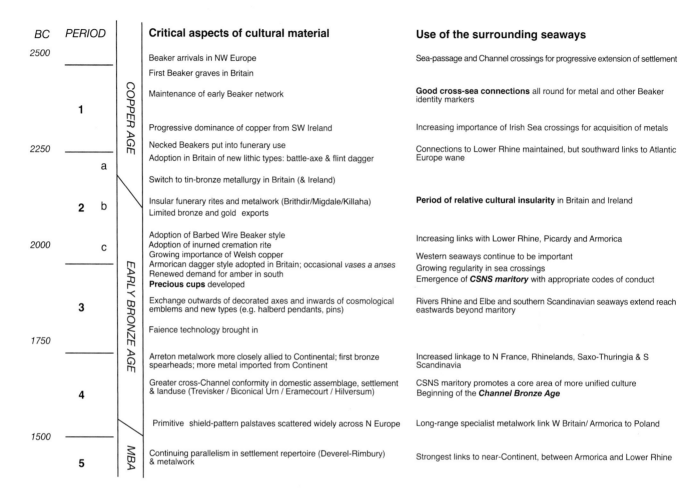

BC	PERIOD			Critical aspects of cultural material	Use of the surrounding seaways
2500				Beaker arrivals in NW Europe	Sea-passage and Channel crossings for progressive extension of settlement
				First Beaker graves in Britain	
	1		COPPER AGE	Maintenance of early Beaker network	**Good cross-sea connections** all round for metal and other Beaker identity markers
				Progressive dominance of copper from SW Ireland	Increasing importance of Irish Sea crossings for acquisition of metals
2250		a		Necked Beakers put into funerary use	Connections to Lower Rhine maintained, but southward links to Atlantic Europe wane
				Adoption in Britain of new lithic types: battle-axe & flint dagger	
				Switch to tin-bronze metallurgy in Britain (& Ireland)	
	2	b		Insular funerary rites and metalwork (Brithdir/Migdale/Killaha)	**Period of relative cultural insularity** in Britain and Ireland
				Limited bronze and gold exports	
2000		c		Adoption of Barbed Wire Beaker style	Increasing links with Lower Rhine, Picardy and Armorica
				Adoption of inurned cremation rite	
				Growing importance of Welsh copper	Western seaways continue to be important
			EARLY BRONZE AGE	Armorican dagger style adopted in Britain; occasional *vases a anses*	Growing regularity in sea crossings
				Renewed demand for amber in south	Emergence of **CSNS maritory** with appropriate codes of conduct
				Precious cups developed	
	3			Exchange outwards of decorated axes and inwards of cosmological emblems and new types (e.g. halberd pendants, pins)	Rivers Rhine and Elbe and southern Scandinavian seaways extend reach eastwards beyond maritory
1750				Faience technology brought in	
				Arreton metalwork more closely allied to Continental; first bronze spearheads; more metal imported from Continent	Increased linkage to N France, Rhinelands, Saxo-Thuringia & S Scandinavia
	4			Greater cross-Channel conformity in domestic assemblage, settlement & landuse (Trevisker / Biconical Urn / Eramecourt / Hilversum)	CSNS maritory promotes a core area of more unified culture Beginning of the **Channel Bronze Age**
1500				Primitive shield-pattern palstaves scattered widely across N Europe	Long-range specialist metalwork link W Britain/ Armorica to Poland
	5		MBA	Continuing parallelism in settlement repertoire (Deverel-Rimbury) & metalwork	Strongest links to near-Continent, between Armorica and Lower Rhine

Figure 2.8 A summary of maritime interactions in the later third and earlier second millennium BC with specific reference to southern Britain.

spread over and beyond the maritory, these involving a range of materials, object types and cultural contexts some of which I have reviewed above. There is then a quantitative leap over what went before in the CSNS zone. Whatever, it is important that we do not automatically translate all evidence for cross-sea contact into a maritory. The key point about a maritory is that it is not the result of opportunistic or purely geographically determined exchanges; it has a particular ideological and organizational infrastructure giving it a measure of constancy to ensure that the participating communities continued to get out of it what they most sought.

Finally, we can take into consideration the evidence for boats in this period, for we witness the development of an entirely new type of seaworthy vessel. With only ten finds so far, it would be incautious to assume that we already have their earliest development. Nevertheless,

there is no doubt that these would have been among the craft that serviced the maritime networks of the earlier second millennium BC (Wright *et al* 2001; van de Noort 2003; 2006). Sturdy though these oak-plank boats were, they were not necessarily more capable of, or reliable for, cross-sea journeys than the skin boats that had probably plied the seaways and coasts for millennia before. This begs the question of what the new sewn-plank construction technique actually signifies in cultural development terms. The answer may well lie less in functionality and more in giving added prestige value. This would link with Helms' consideration (this volume) of such a craft (*sensu* boat) of the high seas also representing a craft of high art; the specialised skills and valuable (labour-demanding) materials incorporated into these boats imbued them with special qualities. It was part of the process of engaging in the new maritime

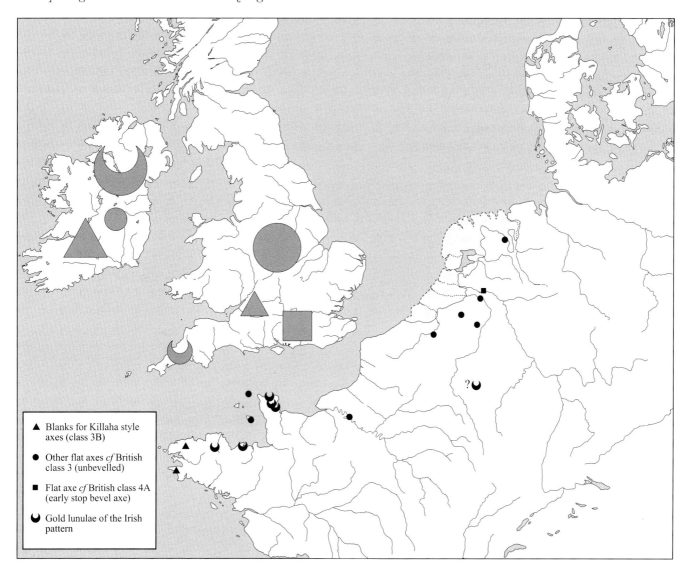

Legend:
▲ Blanks for Killaha style axes (class 3B)
● Other flat axes *cf* British class 3 (unbevelled)
■ Flat axe *cf* British class 4A (early stop bevel axe)
☾ Gold lunulae of the Irish pattern

Figure 2.9 British/Irish types of Period 2 (c 2250–1950 BC) from the Continent: gold lunulae of the Irish pattern and flat bronze axes (Brithdir/ Migdale/Killaha stage); large grey symbols indicate the most likely source areas.

enterprise, of bringing to it a vessel endowed with the right spiritual as well as physical properties. Such a vessel would seem solid and impressive in relation to contemporary boats. It was in all respects a fitting vehicle for the conduct of the most important matter of cosmological acquisition.

On current evidence, therefore, I would see a new emphasis on maritime interactions developing after 2000 BC to a degree that made those interactions central and common concerns in the lands flanking the Channel and its approaches. At first the maritory's main purpose was to provide for varied cosmological needs of the participating groups, but the endurance of the maritime interactive system led to closer and closer ties between some groups. From 1750/1700 BC onwards we

can see clear evidence for more cultural unification, a character which was to persist through the rest of the Bronze Age, albeit with fluctuating territorial coverage. This is the cultural construct I have referred to as the *Channel Bronze Age* (Needham *et al* 2006) and Marcigny as *Manche–Mer du Nord* (Marcigny and Ghesquiere 2003). These in turn are a sub-part of the looser set of cultural similarities often expressed as the *Atlantic Bronze Age* (Oliveira Jorge (ed) 1998; Ruiz-Galvez 1998). Such terms though are only useful if they are attached to thorough analyses of both similarities and differences and how these relate to the particular workings of the interaction system. The CSNS maritory and the Channel Bronze Age are simplifications within a highly dynamic cultural situation with complex overlaying of different cultural entities. However, these terms do have the virtue of emphasising a focal aspect of the cosmologies of the constituent societies – namely that the sea just as much as the land was a topography needing to be physically and conceptually encompassed.

Acknowledgements

My thanks go to the following for sharing with me useful information on their respective areas of study: Stijn Arnoldussen, Nigel Brown, David Fontijn, Jacky Nowakowski, Brendan O'Connor, Keith Parfitt, Heather Sebire, Alison Sheridan, Marc Talon. Gratitude is also due to Stephen Crummy for sharing the illustration work.

List of references

Allen, M and Gardiner, J 2000 *Our Changing Coast: a Survey of the Intertidal Archaeology of Langstone Harbour, Hampshire,* York: Council for British Archaeology Research Report, **124**

Ampe, C, Bourgeois, J, Crombé, P, Fockedey, L, Langohr, R, Meganck, M, Semey, J, van Strydonck, M and Verlaeckt, K 1996 'The circular view: aerial photography and the discovery of Bronze Age funerary monuments in East and West-Flanders (Belgium)', *Germania*, **74**, 45–94

Annable, F and Simpson, D 1964 *Guide Catalogue of the Neolithic and Bronze Age Collections in Devizes Museum,* Devizes: Wiltshire Archaeological and Natural History Society

Arnoldussen, S and Fontijn, D 2006 'Towards familiar landscapes? On the nature and origin of Middle Bronze Age landscapes in the Netherlands', *Proceedings of the Prehistoric Society*, **72**, 289–317

Ashbee, P 1967 'The Wessex grave', in A Corney, 'A prehistoric and Anglo-Saxon burial ground, Ports Down, Portsmouth', *Proceedings of the Hampshire Field Club and Archaeology Society*, **24**, 20–41

Ashbee, P 1974 *Ancient Scilly: from the First Farmers to the Early Christians*, London: David and Charles

Ballard, C, Bradley, R, Nordenborg Myre, L and Wilson, M 2003 'The ship as symbol in the prehistory of Scandinavia and southeast Asia', *World Archaeology*, **35**, 385–403

Beck, C and Shennan, S 1991 *Amber in Prehistoric Britain*, Oxford: Oxbow Books Monograph, **8**

Billard, C, Blanchet, J-C and Talon, M 1996 'Origine et composantes de l'Âge du Bronze Ancien dans le Nord-Ouest de la France', in C Mordant and O Gaiffe (eds), *Cultures et Sociétés du Bronze Ancien en Europe*, Paris: Comité des Travaux Historiques et Scientifiques, 579–601

Blanchet, J-C 1984 *Les Premiers Metallurgistes en Picardie et dans le Nord de la France*, Paris: Mémoires de la *Société préhistorique française*, **17**

Blanchet, J-C and Mordant, C 1987 'Les premières haches à rebords et à butée dans le basin Parisien et le Nord de la France', in J-C Blanchet (ed), *Les Relations entre*

le Continent et les Iles Britanniques à l'Âge du Bronze: Actes du Colloques de Lille, Amiens: Supplément à la Revue Archéologique de Picardie, 89–118

Bradley, R 2000 *An Archaeology of Natural Places*, London: Routledge

Bradley, R and Edmonds, M 1993 *Interpreting the Axe Trade*, Cambridge: Cambridge University Press

Brandherm, D 1998 'Ein Langquaidbeil und eine Lanzenspitze westeuropäischen Typs aus Weingarten, Kr. Germersheim: ein neuer Hortfund der jüngeren Fruhbronzezeit vom nördlichen Oberrhein', *Archäologisches Korrespondenzblatt*, **28**, 47–58

Briard, J 1970 'Un tumulus de Bronze Ancien: Kernonen en Plouvorn (Finistère)', *L'Anthropologie*, **74**, 5–55

Briard, J 1984 *Les Tumulus d'Armorique*, L'Age du Bronze en France, **3**, Paris: Picard

Briard, J 1995 'Les relations entre l'Armorique et la Méditerranée au Chalcolithique et à l'Âge du Bronze', in R Chernorkian (ed), *L'Homme Méditerranéen: mélanges offerts à Gabriel Camps, professeur émérite de l'Université de Provence*, Aix-en-Provence: l'Université de Provence, 403–409

Briard, J and Verney, A 1996 'L'Âge du Bronze Ancien de Bretagne et de Normandie: actualité', in C Mordant and O Gaiffe (eds), *Cultures et Sociétés du Bronze Ancien en Europe*, Paris: Comité des Travaux Historiques et Scientifiques, 565–578

Broodbank, C 1993 'Ulysses without sails: trade, distance, knowledge and power in the early Cyclades', *World Archaeology*, **24**, 315–331

Broodbank, C 2000 *An Island Archaeology of the Early Cyclades*, Cambridge: Cambridge University Press

Burgess, C and Cowen, J 1972 'The Ebnal hoard and Early Bronze Age metal-working traditions', in F Lynch and C Burgess (eds), *Prehistoric Man in Wales and the West: Essays in Honour of Lily F Chitty*, Bath: Adams and Dart, 167–181

Butler, J 1963 'Bronze Age connections across the North Sea: a study in prehistoric trade and industrial relations between the British Isles, the Netherlands, north Germany and Scandinavia, *c* 1700–700 BC', *Palaeohistoria*, **9**

Case, H 2003 'Beaker presence at Wilsford 7', *Wiltshire Archaeological and Natural History Magazine*, **96**, 161–194

Chapman, H and Geary, B 2004 'The social context of seafaring in the Bronze Age revisited', *World Archaeology*, **36**, 452–458

Clark, P (ed) 2004a *The Dover Bronze Age Boat*, Swindon: English Heritage

Clark, P 2004b 'Discussion', in P Clark (ed), *The Dover Bronze Age Boat*, Swindon: English Heritage, 305–322

Clarke, D 1976 'The Beaker network – social and economic models', in J Lanting and J van der Waals (eds), *Glockenbecher Symposium, Oberried 1974*, Bussum/Haarlem: Fibula-van Dishoeck, 459–476

Cooney, G 2003 'Introduction: seeing land from the sea', *World Archaeology*, **35**, 323–328

Cordier, G 1976 'Les civilizations de l'Âge du Bronze dans le Centre-Ouest et les pays de la Loire moyenne', in J Guilaine (ed), *La Préhistoire Française, Tome II Les Civilisations Néolithiques et Protohistoriques de la France*, Paris: Centre National de la Recherche Scientifique, 543–560

Crumlin-Pedersen, O 1996 *Archaeology and the Sea,* Kroon-Voordracht, **18**, Amsterdam: Stichting Nederlands Museum voor Anthropologie en Praehistorie

Cunliffe, B 1987 *Hengistbury Head, Dorset, Volume I: The Prehistoric and Roman Settlement, 3500BC–AD500,* Oxford: Oxford University Committee for Archaeology, Monograph, **13**

Cunliffe, B 2001 *Facing the Ocean: the Atlantic and its Peoples 8000 BC–AD 1500,* Oxford: Oxford University Press

Evans, C 2003 *Power and Island Communities: Excavations at the Wardy Hill Ringwork, Coveney, Ely,* East Anglian Archaeology, **103**, Cambridge: Cambridge Archaeological Unit

Evans, J 1973 'Islands as laboratories of cultural change', in C Renfrew (ed), *The Explanation of Culture Change: Models in Prehistory,* London: Duckworth, 517–520

Gabillot, M 2003 *Dépôts et Production Métallique du Bronze Moyen en France Nord-Occidentale,* Oxford: British Archaeological Reports (International Series), **1174**

Gabillot, M 2005 'Des relations privilègiées entre le Nord-ouest de la France et la Région de l'Elbe au Bronze Moyen', in R Laffineur, J Driessen and E Warmenbol (eds), *L'Âge du Bronze en Europe et en Méditerranée,* Oxford: British Archaeological Reports (International Series), **1337**, 43–53

Gerloff, S 1975 *The Early Bronze Age Daggers in Great Britain and a Reconsideration of the Wessex Culture,* Prähistorische Bronzefunde, **6 (2),** Munich: Beck

Godelier, M 1999 *The Enigma of the Gift,* Chicago: University of Chicago Press, (English translation by N Scott; original French edition 1996)

Hawkes, J 1939 *The Archaeology of the Channel Islands, Volume II: The Bailiwick of Jersey,* Jersey: Société Jersiaise.

Helms, M 1988 *Ulysses' Sail,* Princeton: Princeton University Press.

Helms, M 1993 *Craft and the Kingly Ideal: Art, Trade, and Power,* Austin: University of Texas

Helms, M 1998 *Access to Origins: Affines, Ancestors and Aristocrats,* Austin: University of Texas

Helskog, K 1999 'The shore connection: cognitive landscape and communication with rock carvings in northernmost Europe', *Norwegian Archaeological Review,* **32**, 73–94

Hundt, H-J 1971 'Der Dolchhort von Gau-Bickelheim in Rheinhessen', *Jahrbuch des Römisch-Germanischen Zentralmuseums Mainz,* **18**, 1–50

Hunter, J 1994 '"Maritime Culture": notes from the land', *International Journal of Nautical Archaeology,* **23**, 261–264

Jockenhövel, A 2004 'Von West nach Ost? Zur Genese der Frühbronzezeit Mitteleuropas', in H Roche, E Grogan, J Bradley, J Coles and B Raftery (eds), *From Megaliths to Metal: Essays in Honour of George Eogan,* Oxford: Oxbow Books, 155–167

Kendrick, T 1928 *The Archaeology of the Channel Islands: Volume I: the Bailiwick of Guernsey,* London: Methuen

Krause, R 1988 *Die Endneolithischen und Frühbronzezeitlichen Grabfunde auf der Nordstadtterrasse von Singen am Hohentwiel,* Stuttgart: Landesdenkmalamt Baden-Württemberg

Kristiansen, K and Larsson, T 2005 *The Rise of Bronze Age Society: Travels, Transmissions and Transformations,* Cambridge: Cambridge University Press

Lawson, A 1999 'The Bronze Age hoards of Hampshire',

in A Harding (ed), *Experiment and Design: Archaeological Studies in Honour of John Coles,* Oxford: Oxbow Books, 94–107

Le Bihan, J-P 2001 *Archéologie d'une Île à la pointe de l'Europe: Ouessant. Tome 1, Le Site Archéologique de Mez-Notarou et le Village du Premier Âge du Fer,* Centre de Recherche Archéologique du Finistère/Revue Archéologique de l'Ouest

Lindendauf, A 2003 'The sea as a place of no return in ancient Greece', *World Archaeology,* 35, 416–433

Malinowski, B 1922 *Argonauts of the Western Pacific,* London: Routledge

Marcigny, C and Ghesquiere, E 2003 *L'Île Tatihou (Manche) à l'Âge du Bronze: Habitats et Occupation du Sol,* Documents d'Archéologie Française, **96**, Paris: Maison des Sciences de l'Homme

Marcigny, C, Ghesquiere, E, Clément-Sauleau, S and Verney, A 2005 'L'Âge du Bronze en Basse-Normandie: définition par le mobilier céramique, une première tentative', in J Bourgeois and M Talon (eds), *L'Âge du Bronze du Nord de la France dans son contexte européen,* Paris: Comité des Travaux Historiques et Scientifiques, 303–332

Mauss, M 1970 *The Gift: Forms and Functions of Exchange in Archaic Societies,* London: Cohen and West, (English translation by I Cunnison; original French edition 1923)

McGrail, S 1993 'Prehistoric seafaring in the Channel', in C Scarre and F Healy (eds), *Trade and Exchange in European Prehistory,* Oxford: Oxbow Books Monograph, **33**, 119–210

Megaw, B and Hardy, E 1938 'British decorated axes and their diffusion during the earlier part of the Bronze Age', *Proceedings of the Prehistoric Society,* **4**, 272–307

Mercer, R 1986 'The Neolithic in Cornwall', *Cornish Archaeology,* **25**, 35–80

Murphy, P and Brown, N 1999 'Archaeology of the coastal landscape', in L Green (ed), *The Essex Landscape: in Search of its History,* Chelmsford: Essex County Council, 11–19

Needham, S 1979a 'The extent of foreign influence on Early Bronze Age axe development in southern Britain', in M Ryan (ed), *The Origins of Metallurgy in Atlantic Europe,* Dublin: Stationery Office, 265–293

Needham, S 1979b 'A pair of Early Bronze Age spearheads from Lightwater, Surrey', in C Burgess and D Coombs (eds), *Bronze Age Hoards: Some Finds Old and New,* Oxford: British Archaeological Reports (British Series), 671–640

Needham, S 1988 'A group of Early Bronze Age axes from Lydd', in J Eddison and C Green (eds), *Romney Marsh: Evolution, Occupation, Reclamation,* Oxford: Oxford University Committee for Archaeology Monograph, **24**, 77–82

Needham, S 2000a 'Power pulses across a cultural divide: cosmologically driven exchange between Armorica and Wessex', *Proceedings of the Prehistoric Society,* **66**, 151–207

Needham, S 2000b 'The development of embossed goldwork in Bronze Age Europe', *Antiquaries Journal,* **80**, 27–65

Needham, S 2000c 'The gold and copper metalwork', in G Hughes, *The Lockington Gold Hoard: an Early Bronze Age Barrow Cemetery at Lockington, Leicestershire,* Oxford: Oxbow Books, 23–46

Needham, S 2005 'Transforming Beaker culture in north-west Europe; processes of fusion and fission', *Proceedings of the Prehistoric Society*, **71**, 171–217

Needham, S 2007 'Bronze makes a Bronze Age? Reflections on the implications of selective deposition', in C Burgess, P Topping and F Lynch (eds), *Beyond Stonehenge: Essays on the Bronze Age in Honour of Colin Burgess*, Oxford: Oxbow Books, 278–287

Needham, S and Giardino, C 2008 'From Sicily to Salcombe: a Mediterranean Bronze Age object from British coastal waters', *Antiquity*, **82 (315)**, 60–72

Needham, S 2008 'Exchange, Object Biographies and the Shaping of Identities, 10,000–1,000 BC', in J Pollard (ed), *Prehistoric Britain*, Oxford: Blackwell Studies in Global Archaeology, 310–29

Needham, S, Parfitt, K and Varndell, G (eds) 2006 *The Ringlemere Cup: Precious Cups and the Beginning of the Channel Bronze Age*, London: British Museum Research Publication, **163**

Northover, P 2001 'Bronze Age metalwork of the Isle of Wight', in W Metz, B van Beek and H Steegstra (eds), *PATINA: Essays presented to Jay Jordan Butler on the Occasion of his 80th Birthday*, Gronigen: privately published by Metz, van Beek and Steegstra, 431–448

O'Brien, W 1999 *Sacred Ground: Megalithic Tombs in Coastal South-west Ireland*, Bronze Age Studies, **4**, Galway: National University of Ireland

O'Connor, B 1980 *Cross-Channel Relations in the Later Bronze Age*, Oxford: British Archaeological Reports (International Series), **91**

O'Sullivan, A 2003 'Place, memory and identity among estuarine fishing communities: interpreting the archaeology of early medieval fish weirs', *World Archaeology*, **35**, 449–468

Oliveira-Jorge, S (ed) 1998 *Exista uma Idade do Bronze Atlântico?*, Lisbon: Instituto Português de Archeologia

Pare, C 2000 'Bronze and the Bronze Age', in C Pare (ed), *Metals Make the World Go Round: The Supply and Circulation of Metals in Europe*, Oxford: Oxbow Books, 1–38

Parker Pearson, M 1999 *The Archaeology of Death and Burial*, Stroud: Sutton

Parker Pearson, M 2004 'Island Prehistories: a view of Orkney from South Uist', in J Cherry, C Scarre and S Shennan (eds), *Explaining Social Change: Studies in Honour of Colin Renfrew*, Cambridge: McDonald Institute Monograph, 127–140

Parker, A 2001 'Maritime Landscapes', *Landscapes*, **2**, 22–41

Perkins, D 2004 'Oval barrows on Thanet', in J Cotton and D Field (eds), *Towards a New Stone Age: Aspects of the Neolithic in South-east England*, York: Council for British Archaeology Research Report, **137**, 76–81

Phillips, T 2003 'Seascapes and landscapes in Orkney and northern Scotland', *World Archaeology*, **35**, 371–384

Piggott, S 1938 'The Early Bronze Age in Wessex', *Proceedings of the Prehistoric Society*, **4**, 52–106

Piggott, S 1939 'Further Bronze Age 'dagger graves' in Brittany', *Proceedings of the Prehistoric Society*, **5**, 193–195

Piggott, S 1973 *A History of Wiltshire, Volume 1 part 2*, London: Victoria History of the Counties of England

Raban, J 1999 *Passage to Juneau: a Sea and its Meanings*, London: Picador

Rappaport, R 1969 'Some suggestions concerning concept and method in ecological anthropology', in D Dames (ed), *Contributions to Anthropology: Ecological Essays*, National Museums of Canada Bulletin, **230**, Anthropology Series, **86**, 184–188

Robb, J 2001 'Island identities: ritual, travel and the creation of difference in Neolithic Malta', *European Journal of Archaeology*, **4**, 175–202

Robinson, G 2007 'Journeys through the seascapes of Scilly', in V Cummings and R Johnston (eds), *Prehistoric Journeys*, Oxford: Oxbow Books, 110–120

Rohl, B and Needham, S 1998 *The Circulation of Metal in the British Bronze Age: the Application of Lead Isotope Analysis*, London: British Museum Occasional Paper, **102**

Rowlands, M 1976 *The Production and Distribution of Metalwork in the Middle Bronze Age in Southern Britain*, Oxford: British Archaeological Reports (British Series), **31**

Rudkin, D 1989 'Excavations at Southwick Hill crossroads, Portsdown, Portsmouth', *Proceedings of the Hampshire Field Club and Archaeological Society*, **45**, 5–12

Ruiz-Gálvez Priego, M 1998 *La Europa Atlántica en la Edad del Bronce: Un Viaje a los Raíces de la Europa Occidental*, Barcelona: Crítica

Scarre, C 2002 'A pattern of islands: the Neolithic monuments of north-west Brittany', *European Journal of Archaeology*, **5**, 24–41

Scarre, C and Healy, F (eds) 1993 *Trade and Exchange in European Prehistory*, Oxford: Oxbow Books Monograph, **33**

Sheridan, A and Shortland, A 2004 '"…beads which have given rise to so much dogmatism, controversy and rash speculation": faience in Early Bronze Age Britain and Ireland', in I Shepherd and G Barclay (eds), *Scotland in Ancient Europe: the Neolithic and Early Bronze Age of Scotland in their European Context*, Edinburgh: Society of Antiquaries of Scotland, 263–279

Sherratt, A 1996 'Why Wessex? The Avon route and river transport in later British prehistory', *Oxford Journal of Archaeology*, **15**, 211–234

Sherratt, A and Sherratt, S 1998 'Small worlds: interaction and identity in the ancient Mediterranean', in E Cline and D Harris-Cline (eds), *The Aegean and the Orient in the Second Millennium*, Liège: Aegaeum, **18**, 329–342

Terrell, J 1977–8 'Geographic systems and human diversity in the North Solomons', *World Archaeology*, **9**, 62–81

Thomas, C 1985 *Exploration of a Drowned Landscape: Archaeology and History of the Isles of Scilly*, London: Batsford

Tomalin, D 1988 'Armorican vases à anses and their occurrence in southern Britain', *Proceedings of the Prehistoric Society*, **54**, 203–221

Van de Noort, R 2003 'An ancient seascape: the social context of seafaring in the Early Bronze Age', *World Archaeology*, **35**, 404–415

Van de Noort, R 2006 'Argonauts of the North Sea – a social maritime archaeology for the 2nd millennium BC', *Proceedings of the Prehistoric Society*, **72**, 267–287

Van Gijssel, K and van der Valk, B 2006 'Shaped by water, ice and wind: the genesis of the Netherlands', in L Kooijmans, P van den Broeke, H Fokkens and A van

Gijn (eds), *The Prehistory of the Netherlands*, Amsterdam: Amsterdam University Press, 45–74

Vander Linden, M 2006 *Le Phénomène Campaniforme dans l'Europe du 3ème millénaire avant notre ère*, Oxford: British Archaeological Reports (International Series), **1470**

Vandkilde, H 1988 'A Late Neolithic hoard with objects of bronze and gold from Skeldal, Central Jutland', *Journal of Danish Archaeology*, **7**, 115–135

Vandkilde, H 1996 *From Stone to Bronze: the Metalwork of the Late Neolithic and Earliest Bronze Age in Denmark*, Åarhus: Jutland Archaeological Society Publications, **32**

von Brunn, W 1959 Die *Hortfunde der frühen Bronzezeit aus Sachsen-Anhalt, Sachsen und Thüringen*, Berlin: Deutsche Akademie der Wissenschaften zu Berlin Schriften der Sektion für Vor- und Frühgeschichte, Band 7

Westerdahl, C 1994 'Maritime cultures and ship types: brief comments on the significance of maritime archaeology', *International Journal of Nautical Archaeology*, **23**, 265–270

Woodward, A 2000 *British Barrows, A Matter of Life and Death*, Stroud: Tempus

Woodward, A 2002 'Beads and Beakers: heirlooms and relics in the British Early Bronze Age', *Antiquity*, **76 (294)**, 1040–1047

Wright, E 1990 *The Ferriby Boats: Seacraft of the Bronze Age*, London: Routledge

Wright, E, Hedges, R, Bayliss, A and Van de Noort, R 2001 'New AMS radiocarbon dates for the North Ferriby boats – a contribution to dating prehistoric seafaring in north-western Europe', *Antiquity*, **75 (290)**, 726–734

3. From Picardy to Flanders: Transmanche connections in the Bronze Age

Jean Bourgeois and Marc Talon

Introduction

North-western France (generally speaking Normandy and Picardy) and Flanders (both provinces of East and West Flanders in Belgium) are characterised by quite different research traditions, even different ways of interpreting the archaeological record.

French researchers, for instance, have looked to the east (continental Europe) and the west (Southern England), whilst in Flanders relations with the north (the Netherlands) have been emphasised and the role of continental Europe generally viewed in a different way. As an example, for the Middle Bronze Age, French archaeologists have stressed the importance of the Eramecourt-group, while Flemish and Dutch archaeologists concentrated on Hilversum traditions. The same goes for later periods (the Rhin-Suisse-France Orientale (RSFO) culture versus the Urnfield culture for example).

During a conference in Lille organised in 2000 by the Comité des Travaux Historique et Scientifiques (CTHS), it appeared clear that there were many ways to combine information from both sides of the modern border (Bourgeois and Talon 2005). Even more, the importance of the relations between the continent and the British Isles became obvious.

This paper aims to analyse these relations and present a possible model of explanation.

Recent developments in archaeological research in Northern France and Flanders must be stressed. First, large scale excavations, especially in Northern France and to a lesser extent in Flanders have yielded a lot of information about settlements as well as funerary sites, though the data is quite different from period to period and from area to area.

Secondly, the impact of aerial photography on archaeology is well known and accepted. However, research by Roger Agache in the 1960s and 1970s in Picardy focused much more on the Roman period. Recently, the data gathered by Agache have been re-analysed from a Bronze Age point of view (by Marc Talon and latterly Sébastien Toron). In Flanders, aerial research by Ghent University from the 1980s on has allowed a much better understanding of the Bronze Age occupation of both East and West Flanders.

Finally, it should be stressed that new dating techniques (especially radiocarbon dating of cremated bone) have opened completely new horizons in both Northern France and Flanders. More traditional radiocarbon dating based on charcoal (on the Flemish barrows for instance) has also yielded a lot of new information.

The purpose of this paper is to review some recent results, though not taking metal artefacts fully into account. We will try to review the similarities and differences between both areas and consider the position of this part of Europe in relation to the British Isles. Finally, an attempt will be made to propose a chronological sequence valuable for both Northern France and Flanders.

Chronology

There is a lot of debate concerning the chronological framework of the late Neolithic and the Bronze Age in Northern France and Flanders. For the sake of this paper and in relation to what is suggested in the Netherlands, we would like to consider traditionally the Early Bronze in Flanders and Northern France to be dated between 2000 and 1800 cal BC (3650–3450 BP); the Middle Bronze Age is subdivided in two phases (Middle Bronze Age A, between 1800 and 1500 cal BC (3450–3300 BP)) and Middle Bronze Age B, between 1500 and 1100 cal BC (3300–2900 BP); major changes seem to appear in the Late Bronze Age, between 1100 and 800 cal BC (2900–2600 BP; Arnoldussen and Fontijn 2006; Fokkens 2005a; 2005b; Fig 3.1).

Funerary practices in the Bronze Age

One of the most characteristic features of the Early and Middle Bronze Age landscape of Northern France and Flanders is the presence of a great many barrows. Most of them have been discovered by aerial photography, but also through extensive fieldwork.

In the valley of the Somme in northern France and on the sandy soils of both East

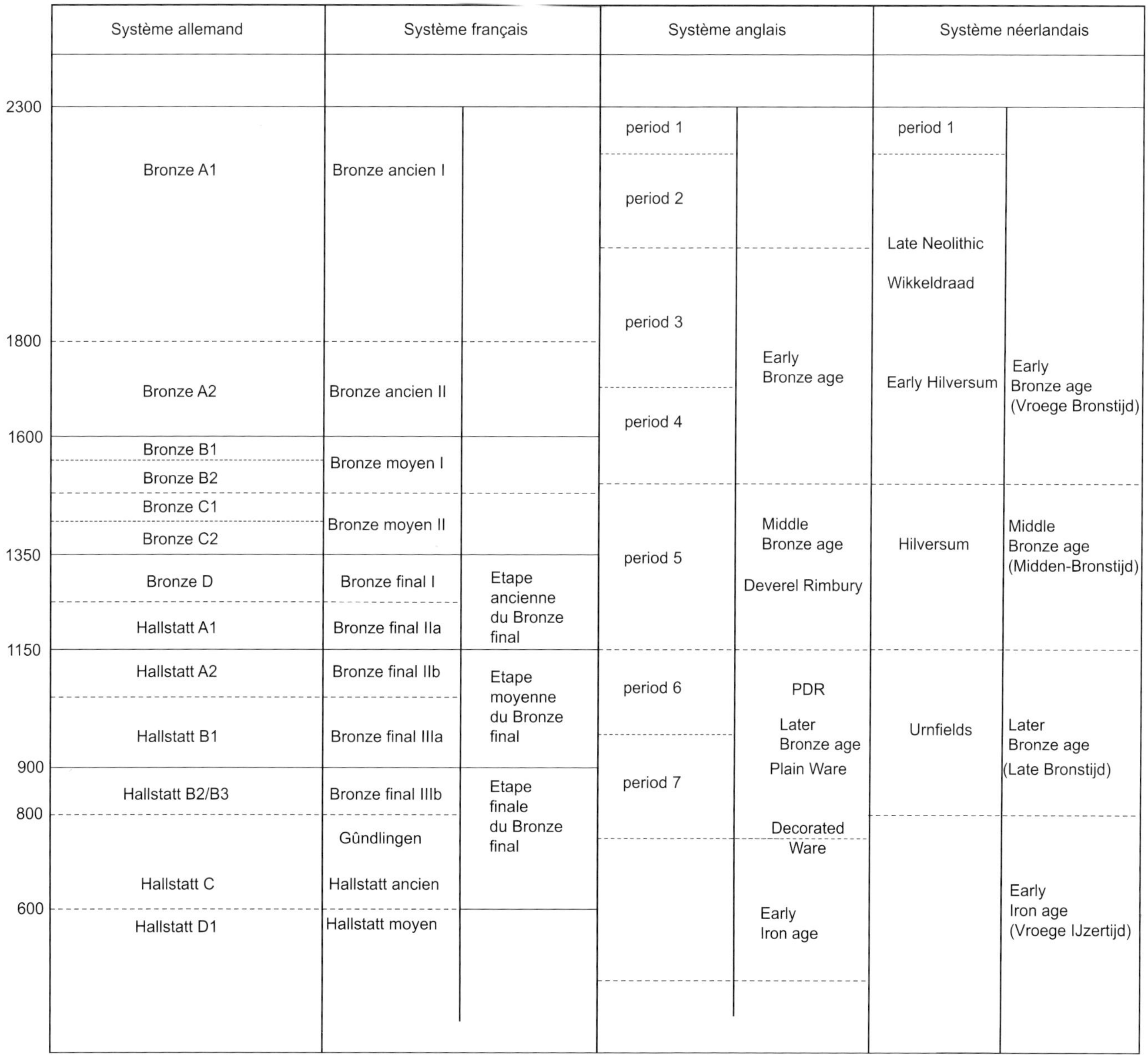

Figure 3.1 Chronological table of the Bronze Age in the British Isles and on the continent (after (Arnoldussen and Fontijn 2006; Blanchet 1984; Fokkens 2005b)

	Système allemand	Système français		Système anglais		Système néerlandais	
2300				period 1		period 1	
	Bronze A1	Bronze ancien I		period 2			
						Late Neolithic	
						Wikkeldraad	
				period 3			
1800					Early Bronze age	Early Hilversum	Early Bronze age (Vroege Bronstijd)
	Bronze A2	Bronze ancien II		period 4			
1600	Bronze B1	Bronze moyen I					
	Bronze B2						
	Bronze C1	Bronze moyen II			Middle Bronze age	Hilversum	Middle Bronze age (Midden-Bronstijd)
	Bronze C2			period 5			
1350	Bronze D	Bronze final I	Etape ancienne du Bronze final		Deverel Rimbury		
	Hallstatt A1	Bronze final IIa					
1150	Hallstatt A2	Bronze final IIb	Etape moyenne du Bronze final	period 6	PDR	Urnfields	Later Bronze age (Late Bronstijd)
	Hallstatt B1	Bronze final IIIa			Later Bronze age		
900	Hallstatt B2/B3	Bronze final IIIb	Etape finale du Bronze final	period 7	Plain Ware		
800		Gûndlingen			Decorated Ware		
	Hallstatt C	Hallstatt ancien					Early Iron age (Vroege IJzertijd)
600	Hallstatt D1	Hallstatt moyen			Early Iron age		

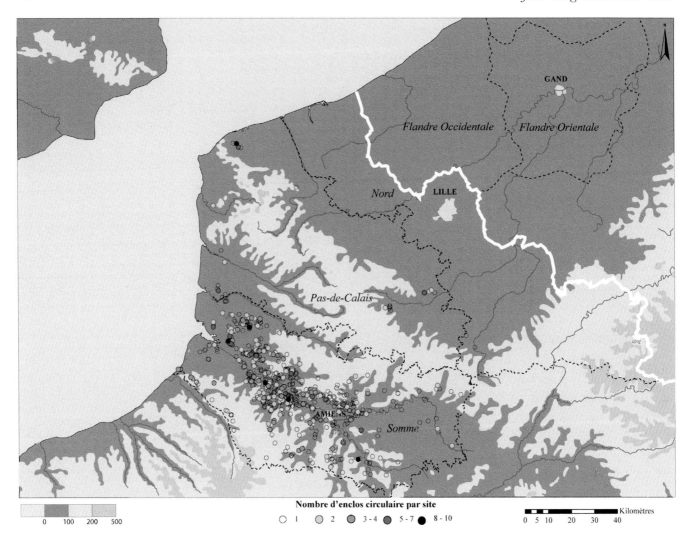

Nombre d'enclos circulaire par site

○ 1   ◐ 2   ● 3 - 4   ● 5 - 7   ● 8 - 10

*Figure 3.2 Map of
the circular structures
discovered by Roger Agache
during aerial surveys in
the Somme Valley. Each
dot corresponds to a
single cemetery, generally
consisting of several
enclosures or barrows
(Toron 2005)*

and West Flanders large concentrations of these barrows are known (Figs 3.2 and 3.3; Toron 2005; Ampe *et al* 1996; Bourgeois and Cherretté 2005a; 2005b). They can be related to barrows in Central Belgium (south of Brussels; Fourny and Van Assche 1993), the eastern part of Flanders and the south of the Netherlands (Theunissen 1999; Van Impe and Beex 1977); the phenomenon is clearly part of an Atlantic tradition.

They are apparently scattered over the whole area and make use of the shallow micro-topography to become more prominent. Some areas present a huge concentration of these burial places; in these cases, there is a burial site every one or two kilometres (Fig 3.4). There is no doubt that these burial places were not contemporaneous, but they clearly reveal intense occupation of the area in the Early and Middle Bronze Age.

The barrows seem to be organised in small graveyards (3 to 5 barrows), generally in an alignment but sometimes in clusters. These barrow mounds are mostly not preserved, but thanks to excavation there are hints of a large mound covering one or more burials and surrounded by ditches. In most cases a single ditch defines the barrow area, but in some 10 percent of cases one can suggest the presence of two (or very occasionally three) concentric ditches. Excavation shows that these multiple ditches can be contemporaneous or alternatively due to the fact that the barrow was rebuilt.

At the time of writing, the oldest known examples date back to the late Neolithic or Early Bronze Age (as at Deinze, Ursel and Evergem in East Flanders; Ampe *et al* 1996), but the zenith of the erection of such barrows may clearly be placed in the period around 3300 BP. In

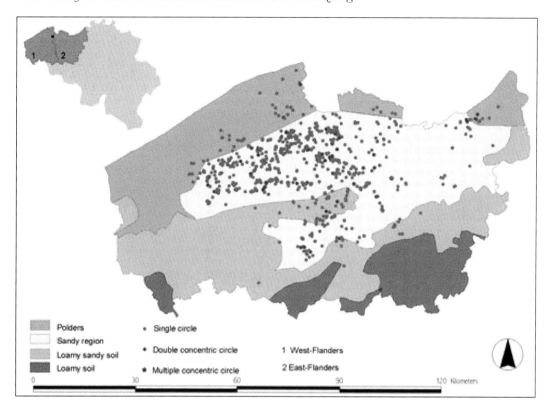

Figure 3.3 Map of the circular structures discovered by the Ghent University team during aerial survey in East- and West-Flanders. Each dot corresponds to one single structure

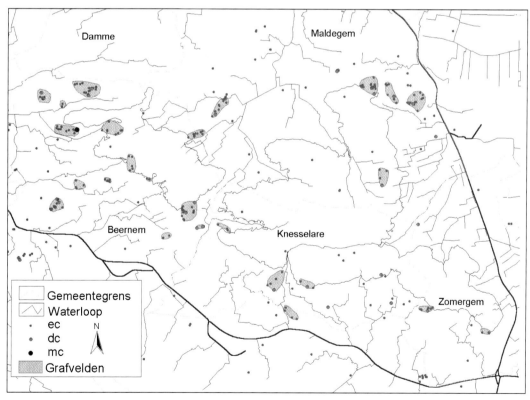

Figure 3.4 Detail of a densely occupied area in East-Flanders. In cases like this, the landscape is obviously dominated by the presence of barrows and mounds

calibrated dates, most of the excavated barrows can be dated between 1800 and 1500/1400 cal BC. After that date, we can suggest that (almost) no new barrows were erected, but that ancient barrows were probably reused. In fact, the archaeological data clearly shows that these burial places were still 'used' in the landscape till at least the Roman period. The examples of Conchil-le-Temple (Picardy; Piningre 1990), Fresnes-les-Montauban (Nord-Pas-de-Calais; Desfossés and Masson 2000), Oedelem and Waardamme (both in West Flanders; Ampe *et al* 1996) are clear (Fig 3.5).

Although there is a strong argument that most barrows were erected before 1500/1400 BC and can be related to the Hilversum culture, there is also some evidence that suggests a more recent date. Some urns discovered in the Renaix area (on the hill tops of the Flemish Ardennes in East Flanders) yielded some pottery with clear Deverel-Rimbury components, which allows us to date these barrows in the early second part of the Middle Bronze Age in Flanders. The same seems to go for sites in France, as at Compiègne 'Carrefour d'Aumont' (Oise; Blanchet 1984).

As the barrow mounds generally do not survive, the burials themselves are often poorly preserved. In the few cases where some information remained, cremation seemed to be the traditional practice, and most tombs were quite poor. In the best cases, only one urn was used.

In several instances the urn was deposited in an inverted position, as at Ruien and Ronse/ Renaix in East Flanders (De Laet 1982; Fourny 1985), Fresnes-les-Montauban and Vitry-en-Artois in Nord-Pas-de-Calais (Desfossés and Masson 2000; Azagury and Demolon 1990) and Rue, Crouy and Eramecourt in Picardy (Buchez and Talon 2005; Breart et Fagnart 1982; Blanchet 1984; *see also* Fig 3.15). This tradition may also be observed in the Netherlands (as at Breda; Koot *et al* 2004).

It is interesting to note that the phenomenon of Bronze Age round barrows does not appear with the same intensity in Normandy. Whether this is related to the level of research in that area is not very clear.

For the second part of the Middle Bronze Age and the Late Bronze Age, the situation in France has changed radically in the last few years. In Normandy and Northern France several graveyards have recently been identified, for example in Thourotte (Picardy; Billand and Talon 2000) and Malleville-sur-le-Bec (Haute Normandie; Mare 2005; Fig 3.6). They consist of quite small burial places with a concentration of small pits containing part of the pyre (ashes, charcoal and some burned

bone). Recent research by Isabelle Le Goff, Estelle Pinard and Ghislaine Billand makes it clear that these pits have to be considered as cremation pits or burials (Le Goff *et al* forthcoming). Analysis of the cremated bones left in the graves suggests that these were the tombs of adults, male and female, and even children. These first cemeteries are probably related to a family group and demonstrate an evolution in the funerary practices of the period, as it appears that all members of the community were involved, in contrast to earlier times when only a few people had access to a monumental burial.

In almost all cases, the burials did not contain any objects, but sieving of the grave content has recovered some small pottery sherds and occasionally fragments of ornaments. Amongst these the most astonishing are the so-called 'hair rings'. These objects were considered to mark the transition from Bronze Age to Iron Age, but recent dating of the associated cremated bone now allows us to place these objects in the Late Bronze Age (Billand and Talon 2007).

Obviously, these burial places replaced the earlier barrow graveyards.

These small family cemeteries have some similarities with burial places in Flanders, though differences are also very clear (Bourgeois and Cherretté 2005b; Warmenbol 1991). From at least 1100 cal BC onwards, urnfields begin to appear in Flanders. In some cases, they are clearly larger than the burial places in France. In Destelbergen and Temse-Veldmolenwijk in East Flanders for example, over 100 burials may be counted (De Laet *et al* 1986; 1958). There are also some cases where smaller graveyards may be observed. The burial places of Temse-Velle, Velzeke-Provinciebaan (much disturbed by later Roman occupation) and Aalter in East Flanders yielded between 20 and 40 burials at most (De Laet *et al* 1958; De Mulder 1994; Fig 3.7). Another difference with France is that these burial places contain cremation pits (as in France), but also quite a number of urngraves and some '*Knochenlager*' or 'bone beds' (as at Destelbergen and Velzeke; De Laet *et al* 1958; De Mulder 1994). It is not yet clear whether the different types of graves represent chronological development, social differentiation or some other aspect of Bronze Age society.

Another major difference with the graveyards of earlier periods is that the burial places

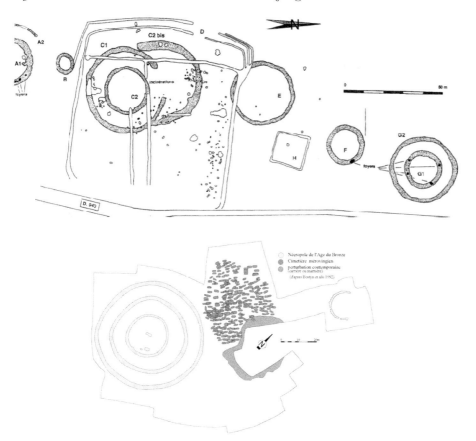

Figure 3.5 Four large excavations of burial places with barrows and later structures. 1. Conchil-le-Temple, 2. Fréthun, 3. Oedelem, 4. Waardamme

OEDELEM-WULFSBERGE

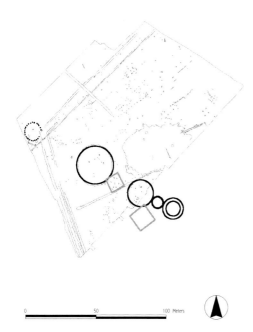

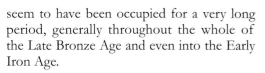

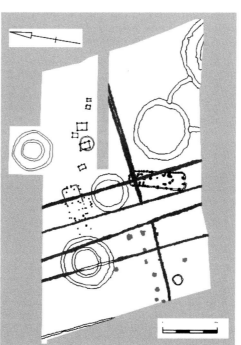

seem to have been occupied for a very long period, generally throughout the whole of the Late Bronze Age and even into the Early Iron Age.

Settlements in the Bronze Age

As early as the 1960s, there was general agreement concerning the existence of round

*Figure 3.6 Plan of the
Thourotte necropolis
(Billand and Talon 2000)*

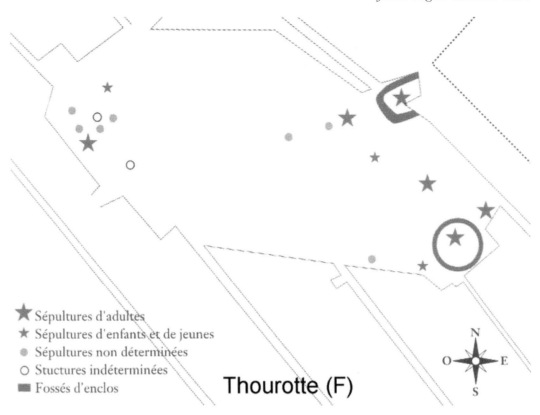

★ Sépultures d'adultes
★ Sépultures d'enfants et de jeunes
⊛ Sépultures non déterminées
○ Stuctures indéterminées
▬ Fossés d'enclos

Thourotte (F)

Figure 3.6 Plan of the Thourotte necropolis (Billand and Talon 2000)

houses on the continent, especially in the Netherlands. They were seen as ultimate proof of migrations from the British Isles and of the close relations between the peoples living either side of the Strait of Pas-de-Calais and the southern North Sea. Recent research has demonstrated that these structures are perhaps better interpreted as animal enclosures (Roymans and Fokkens 1991a; 1991b; Theunissen 1999).

New excavations in Northern France and Normandy, however, have revealed a large number of round houses of this type dating to the Early and Middle Bronze Age. In Normandy, round houses with posts are known, as for example at Tatihou (Marcigny and Ghesquière 2003) and St-Vigor-d'Ymonville (Lepaumier *et al* 2005). Round houses are also common in the Middle Bronze Age in Northern France at Roeux and Étaples in Pas-de-Calais (Desfossés *et al* 2000; Desfossés 2000) and Seclin and Erre, Nord (Révillion *et al* 1994; Leroy-Langevin and Sys 2004; Fig 3.8). These quite simple constructions of the Early and Middle Bronze Age have parallels with examples from Southern England; they are followed by a large number of examples with

more structured plans, sometimes with a porch, as at Malleville-sur-le-Bec (Haute Normandie; Mare 2005) and Cahagnes (Basse Normandie; Jahier 2005; Fig 3.9).

In Northern France there are no known examples of Late Bronze Age round houses, however. This might be due to the use in this area of a particular building technique, using stone foundations laid directly on the ground surface; such a system is not easy to observe on most archaeological sites except where palaeo-soils are preserved. Where this is the case, as at the settlements of Catenoy and Choisy-au-Bac in Picardy (Blanchet 1984), rectangular houses 6–8m long and 4–5m wide have been identified (Fig 3.10).

Further north, in Flanders, though inform-ation about settlements is very scarce, we would perceive a closer connection with the Netherlands, where the large three-aisled house, sometimes with rounded ends is well documented (Arnoldussen and Fontijn 2006; Roymans and Fokkens 1991a; 1991b; Fig 3.11). An example of this type of house has been found at Maldegem-Burkel in West Flanders (Crombé and Bourgeois 1993; Fig 3.12). Recent analysis of the data has showed that

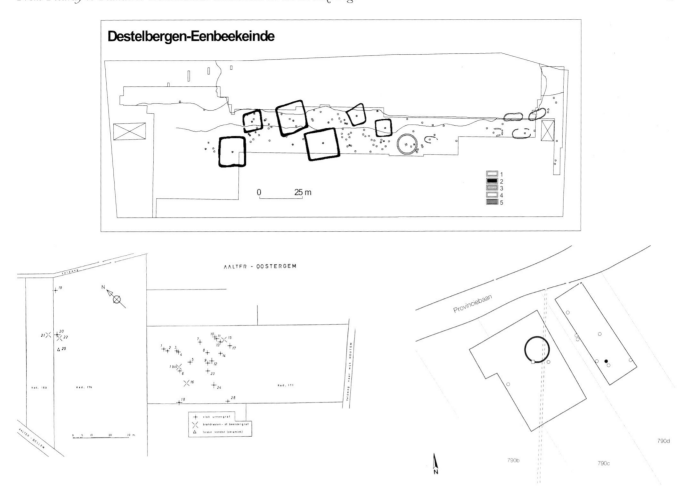

these houses should be dated to the second part of the Middle Bronze Age (Bourgeois and Arnoldussen 2006).

Two-aisled houses dating to the late Bronze Age have been discovered in Flanders as well as in the Netherlands (Arnoldussen and Fontijn 2006). Two- or three-aisled small buildings are known in Northern France, as at Beautot (Seine Maritime; Rougier 1998; Fig 3.13) where a Late Bronze Age rural settlement contained a two-aisled house measuring 13m by 7m. This settlement also revealed several secondary buildings with 6 or 8 posts. The same two-aisled house type is also known from East Flanders, for example at Sint-Denijs-Westrem and Sint-Gillis-Waas (Bourgeois 1991; Fig 3.14). They are remarkably shorter than the houses of the Middle Bronze Age.

Obviously, the architecture of these houses in the (Early and Middle) Bronze Age shows clear differences between Northern France and Flanders, especially when we consider the round houses on one side and the large three-aisled houses on the other. However, new excavations will be necessary to clarify this situation and to provide more information about domestic architecture in the Bronze Age.

In the Early and Middle Bronze Age, as well as in the first part of the Late Bronze Age in Northern France (before 1100 cal BC), the traditional settlement structure was characterised by isolated farms. As they occupy just a small portion of the landscape, they are quite difficult to discover. Furthermore, in most cases there are no refuse pits or ditches, which of course makes the discovery of such settlements very difficult. However, when considering the settlement evidence, one should stress the presence, from the Middle Bronze Age onwards, of some larger enclosed farms, as at Nonant and Mondeville (Basse Normandie; Chancerel *et al* 2006; Marcigny 2005b). Their resemblance to the later '*fermes indigènes*' is obvious. In addition, these sites

Figure 3.7 Plans of Late Bronze Age burial places in Flanders. 1. Destelbergen, 2. Aalter, 3. Velzeke.

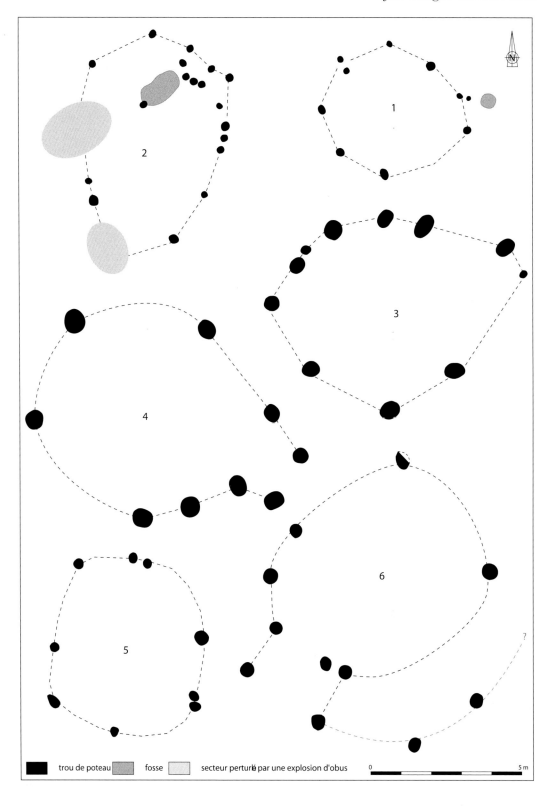

trou de poteau   fosse   secteur perturbé par une explosion d'obus   0   5 m

are characterised by the presence of a field system with ditches, revealing the existence of a structured landscape (for example at Tatihou in Basse Normandie; Marcigny and Ghesquière 2003). Similar field systems are known in England from the end of the Middle Bronze Age (Needham 1996). However, at the time of writing this type of landscape is not known in the northern parts of France or in Flanders, where the oldest example of a really structured landscape dates to the Early Iron Age, at Sint-Gillis-Waas (East Flanders).

In the Late Bronze Age, alongside the isolated farms, the first small agglomerated settlements begin to appear. In some cases it is possible to describe them as small villages, as at Cahagnes (Basse Normandie; Jahier 2005), Malleville-sur-le-Bec (Haute Normandie; Mare 2005), Choisy-au-Bac (Picardy; Blanchet 1984) and Osly-Courtil (Picardy; Le Guen 2005). They are characterised by a quite strict spatial organisation of the settlement, the density of domestic features, diversity in modes of production, the presence of food storage facilities and their close spatial relation with ritual or funeral monuments. Some of these sites seem to yield traces of agricultural activities and were perhaps able to produce surpluses, as suggested by the large granaries at Cahagnes and Osly-Courtil, or the faunal elements revealing a preference for pigs at Choisy-au-Bac. Metallurgical activity has been observed at some settlements but this is clearly more frequent at fortified sites, such as Fort-Harrouard (Centre; Mohen and Bailloud 1987), Quiévrecourt (Haute Normandie; Beurion and Billard 2005), Catenoy (Picardy; Blanchet and Talon 1987) and Saint-Pierre-en-Chastres (Picardy; Blanchet 1984). However, some sites of the '*éperon barré*'-type were occupied during the Late Bronze Age in Normandy (as at Soumont-Saint-Quentin), but on the whole fortified sites seem to be abandoned in northern France as well as in southern England.

Though superficially similar, these 'villages' and fortified settlements do not necessarily possess the same hierarchical or funactional relationships across the region. Indeed, these sites are not all contemporaneous and are not necessarily part of the same cultural area; the fortified sites of the Oise area, settled (chronologically and spatially) in a border area between the Atlantic and the North-Alpine area, do not have the same function as the fortified sites in Normandy.

It is also worth noting that an exceptional number of bronze hoards dating to the end of the Late Bronze Age have been discovered in the middle part of the Oise valley (Blanchet 2001). This coincides with the presence of fortified sites with metallurgical activity, as

at Saint-Pierre-en-Chastres, Catenoy and Choisy-au-Bac. In North-western France, again in Picardy, several hoards have also been discovered in the area around Amiens, as at the eponymous site of Le Plainseau (Blanchet 1984). However, because of the heavy in-

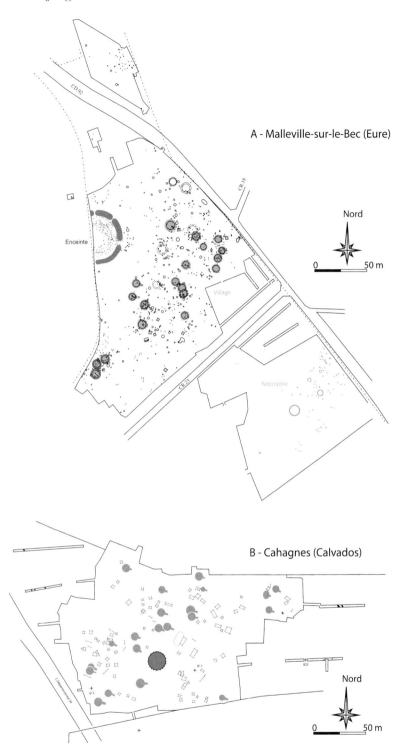

A - Malleville-sur-le-Bec (Eure)

Nord

0   50 m

B - Cahagnes (Calvados)

Nord

0   50 m

Figure 3.9 Plans of the sites of Malleville (Mare 2005) and Cahagnes (Jahier 2005)

CHOISY-AU-BAC (Oise)
Le Confluent

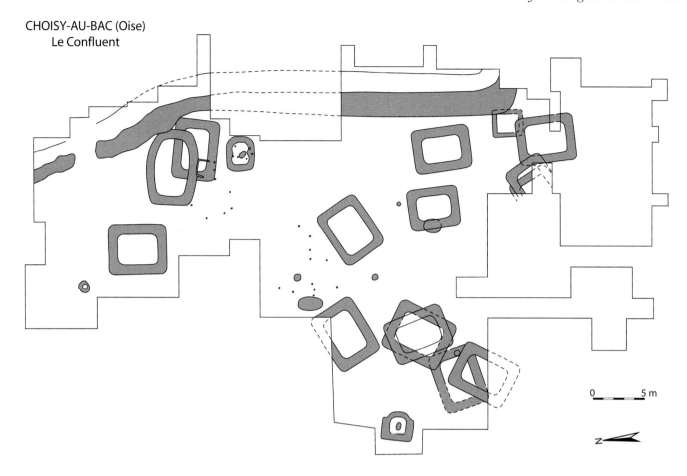

0 ____ 5 m

Figure 3.10 Plan of the Late Bronze Age/Early Iron Age site of Choisy-au-Bac (Blanchet 1984)

dustrialisation of this area, metallurgical installations or fortified sites have not yet been discovered there. Evidence for metallurgical activity does exist in Normandy, at Fort-Harrouard and Quiévrecourt; both sites are dated to the middle phase of the Late Bronze Age but at present there is no evidence suggesting the same activity took place during the transition from the Bronze Age to the Iron Age.

More to the West, as early as the Early and Middle Bronze Age, fortified enclosures set on plateaux begin to appear, as at Étaples (Nord-Pas-de-Calais; Desfossés 2000). They might represent the predecessors of later enclosures of ring fort-type, as identified in excavations at Malleville-sur-le-Bec (Haute Normandie; Mare 2005) or Cagny (Basse Normandie; Marcigny 2005a) or observed by aerial photography in the Caen area (some ten examples; Jean Desloges, *pers comm*) and the Somme-valley (six examples; Buchez and Talon 2005). The enclosure of Malleville-sur-le-Bec is morphologically and chronologically comparable to the ring fort at Springfield, Essex in south-east England

(Buckley and Hedges 1987). These sites are then in turn comparable to the British ring forts of Mill Hill in Deal (Kent; Champion 1980), Mucking South and North Ring (Essex; Jones and Bond 1980) and Thwing (Yorkshire; Manby 1980).

It is still quite difficult today to determine the role of these ring forts in the spatial organisation and structure of the area. It is only possible to observe that they can, as they do in England, play different roles; as ritual enclosures, fortified strongholds or aristocratic farms.

It seems that these ring forts have been observed only in the area of the Manche-Mer du Nord group and that they were abandoned during the transition from the Bronze Age to the Iron Age, a period when the fortifications on higher locations were once again occupied.

There are presently no comparable ring forts recorded in Flanders.

Material culture: ceramic

Though there is little information available

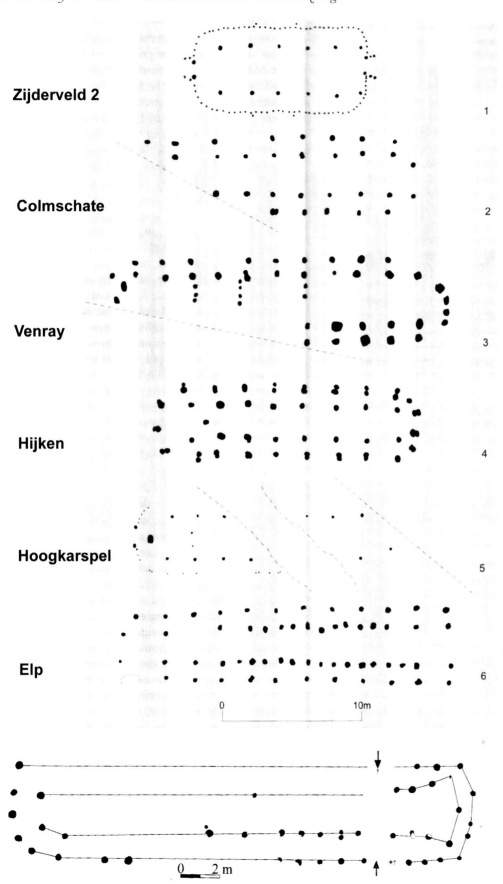

Zijderveld 2

Colmschate

Venray

Hijken

Hoogkarspel

Elp

0   10m

0   2 m

Figure 3.11 Middle Bronze Age houses in the Netherlands (Arnoldussen and Fontijn 2006)

Figure 3.12 Plan of the Middle Bronze Age house of Maldegem (Crombé and Bourgeois 1993).

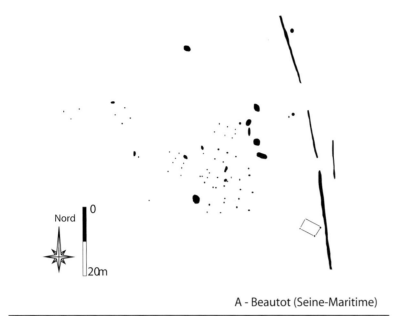

A - Beautot (Seine-Maritime)

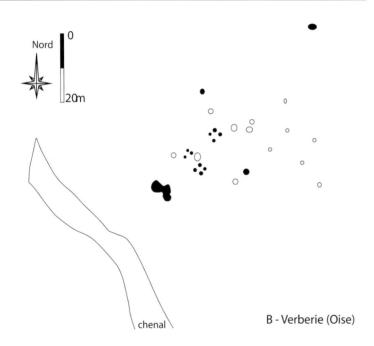

B - Verberie (Oise)

Figure 3.13 Plan of the Late Bronze Age sites of Beautot and Verberie (Rougier 1998; Pinard et al 2000)

for the Early and the Middle Bronze Age, it is currently possible to identify three different ceramic groups, broadly following each other in time, and possibly also partially overlapping chronologically.

The first group corresponds to urns with plastic decoration ('Urnes à décor plastique') with heavy flint or (oyster) shell temper. Quite often there is an applied 'cordon' (or other decoration) in the form of a horseshoe. Some of these vases are decorated with cord impressions, and occasionally this decoration

is also present on the lip. Vases of this type have been discovered in funerary contexts in Flanders at Weelde (Van Impe and Beex 1977), Ruien (De Laet 1982; Fig 3.15, 3), Fréthun (Nord-Pas-de-Calais; Bostyn *et al* 1992; Fig 3.15, 1) and in domestic contexts at Dentergem (West Flanders; Warmenbol 1990), Roeselare (West Flanders; Goderis 2001), Étaples (Nord-Pas-de-Calais; Desfossés 2000), Marquise (Nord-Pas-de-Calais), Hardelot (Nord-Pas-de-Calais), Monchy-Lagache (Picardy; Buchez and Talon 2005; Fig 3.15, 9), Compiègne 'Le Fond Pernant' (Picardy; Blanchet 1984), La Croix-Saint-Ouen 'Le Prieuré' and 'la Station d'Epuration' (Picardy; Billard *et al* 1996) and Bazoches-Les-Bray (Ile de France; Gouge and Peake 2005; Fig 3.15, 2). The radiocarbon dates available for this first group, defined by Blanchet (Blanchet 1984) as the '*groupe des Urnes à décor plastique*' (GDU) are unsatisfying; the hypotheses suggested during a colloquium held at Clermont-Ferrand (Billard *et al* 1996) cannot be assessed or confirmed. It is however quite assured that this group can be dated to the Early Bronze Age A1 and partly also A2, which would then be related to Stuart Needham's Period 3 (2050–1700 cal BC; Needham 1996; Needham *et al* 1997).

A second group could be considered as a variant or an evolution of the first group. These biconical urns with everted rims are not decorated with a cord, but do have a plastic element, quite often in the form of a horseshoe as in the first group. This urn type, often discovered in funerary contexts, has been dubbed the '*Eramecourt*' group by Jean-Claude Blanchet (1984). To the list of examples cited in his book, one may add the vases discovered in funerary contexts at Rebaix (Hainaut; Cammaert *et al* 1996), Vitry-en-Artois (Nord-Pas-de-Calais; Azagury and Demolon 1990; Fig 3.15, 7), Fresnes-les-Montauban (Nord-Pas-de-Calais; Desfossés and Masson 2000; Fig 3.15, 5–6) and Rue (Picardy; Buchez and Talon 2005), together with other finds at Villeneuve-d'Ascq (Nord-Pas-de-Calais; Quérel 2002; Fig 3.15, 8), Loeuilly and Le Translay (Picardy; Buchez and Talon 2005).

In Blanchet's definition, the Eramecourt group is a funerary facies spanning the Early and Middle Bronze Age. In fact, as confirmed by radiocarbon dates on charcoal and cremated bones, it is characteristic of the later part of the Early Bronze Age and the earlier part of

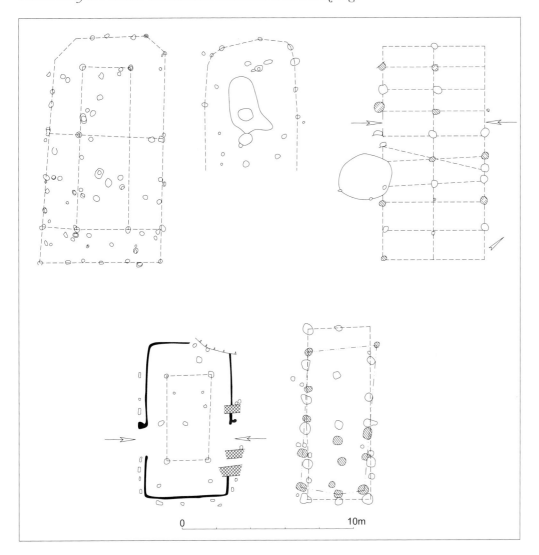

Figure 3.14 Plans of Late Bronze Age houses in Sint-Denijs-Westrem and Sint-Gillis-Waas (Bourgeois 1991)

the Middle Bronze Age, prior to 1500 cal BC. Its start could be correlated to Bronze A2 and the end of Wessex I, extending into Bronze B or Wessex II and the Hilversum-Drakenstein phase, or Needham's Period 4 (1700–1500 cal BC; Needham 1996).

A third group is characterised by simple forms with plastic decoration, cylindrical form and strait or inverted rims; quite often cylindrical clay loom weights are discovered in the same contexts. These forms are characteristic of the Deverel-Rimbury complex. Study of collections on the continent allow us to identify this type of pottery from Belgium to Normandy, even as far as the confluence of Seine and Yonne on the border between Île de France and Burgundy, as attested by the funerary urns of Varesnes (Ile de France; Gouge and Peake 2005; Fig 3.16, 23–25).

In Belgium, the urns of Ronse-Renaix (East Flanders; Fourny 1985; Fig 3.16, 1–3) are obvious examples; others come from non-funerary contexts in the same area, like those from Braffe (Hainaut; Henton and Demarez 2005; Fig 3.16, 4) and from Roeux (Nord-Pas-de-Calais; Desoddés *et al* 2000; Fig 3.16, 5–8), Étaples (Nord-Pas-de-Calais; Desfossés 2000), Wiencourt-L'Equipée (Picardy; Buches and Talon 2005; Fig 3.16, 9–11), Compiègne 'Carrefour d'Aumont' (Picardy ; Blanchet 2004; Fig 3.16, 12) and Cuiry-les-Chaudardes (Picardy; Letterlé 1982; Fig 3.16, 13). These small assemblages are complemented by larger ones from Normandy at Tatihou, Nonant and Mondeville (Marcigny *et al* 2005; 2007; Fig 3.16, 14–16, 17–19 and 20–22).

The Deverel-Rimbury complex corresponds to the Middle Bronze Age and the beginning

*Figure 3.15 Early and
Middle Bronze Age
pottery; 1, Fréthun (Bostyn
et al 1992); 2, Bazoches-
les-Bray (Gouge and Peake
2005); 3–4, Ruien (De
Laet 1982); 5–6, Fresnes-
les-Montauban (Desfossés
and Masson 2000); 7,
Vitry-en-Artois (Azagury
and Demolon 1990); 8,
Villeneuve d'Asq (Quérel
2002); 9, Monchy-Lagache
(Buchez and Talon 2005)*

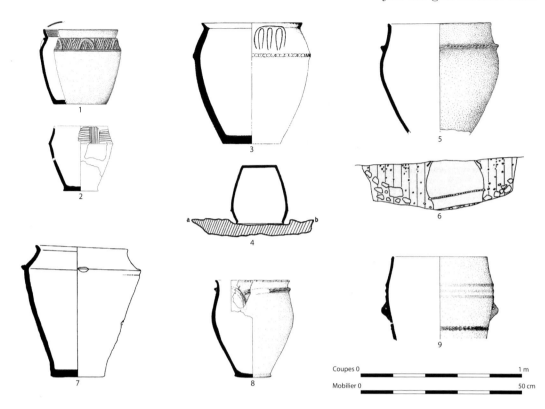

of the Late Bronze Age on the continent and is attributed to Needham's Period 5 (1500–1150 cal BC); in the British Isles, this group is related to the Trevisker group in western England, the Ardleigh group in the east and the bucket urns group in the north (Needham 1996). Deverel-Rimbury ceramics have been found in both funerary and domestic contexts, in contrast to what one generally finds in the Early and Middle Bronze Age.

In north-western France, which belongs to the cultural community of the Channel–North Sea (Manche-Mer du Nord or MMN, a term suggested by Cyril Marcigny and Emmanuel Ghesquière (2003)), the pottery of the group of urns with plastic decoration seems to be seen in continuation of the Gord group of the final Neolithic (Billard *et al* 1996). This MMN group extends up to the central part of the Paris Basin (Gouge and Peake 2005) and corresponds to the Hilversum group in Belgium and the Netherlands (Bourgeois and Cherretté 2004; 2005b; Fokkens 2005b). Though most of the discoveries of the Early and Middle Bronze Age are found in funerary contexts, some settlements attributed to the beginning of the Late Bronze Age have yielded pottery of the Deverel-Rimbury type

(Desfossés 2000; Letterlé 1982; Marcigny *et al* 2005). On the continent, these settlements are characterised by the presence of round houses (see above). One can, as for Southern England (Bradley 1994; Ellison 1980), attribute the first family graveyards to the same chronological horizon to the end of the Middle Bronze Age and the beginning of the Late Bronze Age (Blanchet and Talon 2005; Gaudefroy and Le Goff 2004).

The middle part of the Late Bronze Age (BFIIb–IIIa or Hal A2–B1) sees an extension to the West and the coastal area of the North Alpine zone characterised by RSFO pottery. For many years, this type of pottery, with its easily-identifiable profiles, fabrics and decoration, was used as a chronological marker for the period; a single pottery fragment was enough to date the site where it was found. Now, however, one has to admit that associated metal objects appeared to be largely of Atlantic types. This might suggest that the more atypical pottery found at these sites might or must correspond to pottery of the Atlantic type (Brun 1998).

Cyrille Billard, when publishing the ceramics of Lingreville in 1995 (Billard *et al* 1995) compared them to the Plain ware type of the

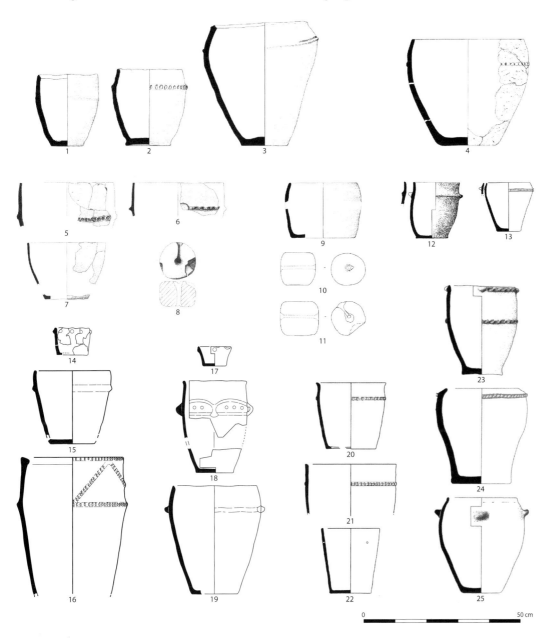

Figure 3.16 'Deverel-Rimbury' pottery from the Continent; 1–3, Ronse-Renaix (Fourny 1985); 4, Braffe (Henton and Demarez 2005); 5–8, Rouex (Desfossés et al 2000); 9–11, Wiencourt-L'Equipée (Buchez and Talon 2005); 12, Compiègne "Carrefour d'Aumont" (Blanchet 1984); 13, Cuiry-les-Chaudardes (Letterlé 1982); 14–16, 17–19, 20–22, Tatihou, Nonant and Mondeville (Marcigny at al 2005); 23–25, Varesnes (Gouge and Peake 2005)

Late Bronze Age, based on John Barrett's work (Barrett 1980); he also drew our attention to a site on the Anglo-Norman island of Aurigny that was dated into the Early Iron Age (Wilson 1984). Continuing on the other hand the work of Patrice Brun on Fort Harrouard (Brun 1998) he also identified potentially Atlantic pottery on the RSFO sites of Quiévrecourt, Fort-Harrouard and Catenoy (Beurion and Billard 2005). These works have allowed us to establish the periodisation of ceramic traditions in Normandy (Marcigny *et al* 2005).

Stuart Needham's Period 6 (1150–950 cal BC) is illustrated by metal objects of the Wilburton phase and late Deverel Rimbury and Post Deverel Rimbury (PDR) pottery. To this period belong phases 2 and 3 of the fortified site of Rams Hill (Needham and Ambers 1994), in addition to the initial phase of the Thwing ring fort (Yorkshire; Manby 1980) and the end of the Reading Business Park site (Berkshire; Moore and Jennings 1992). The pottery related to this phase is however badly documented (Marcigny and Talon forthcoming; Fig 3.17). The profiles are rounder and show more variety than

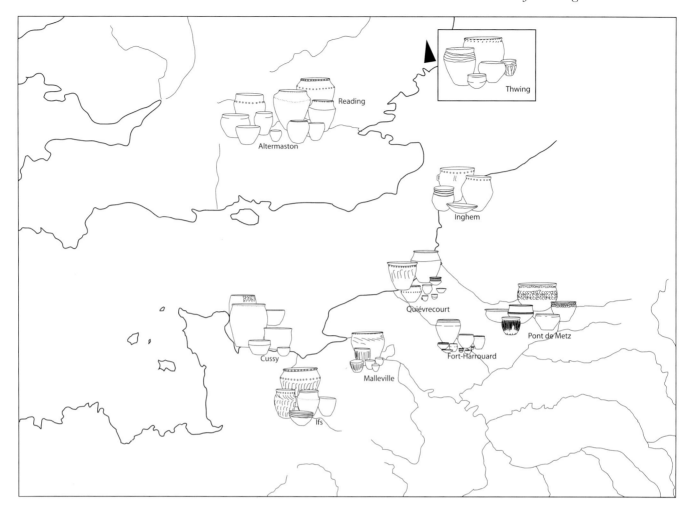

Figure 3.17 'Plain Ware' comparisons across the Channel (computer graphic by E Ghesquière and C Marcigny, Inrap; Marcigny and Talon forthcoming): Altermaston (Bradley et al 1980); Reading (Moore and Jennings 1992), Cussy (Marcigny and Ghesquière 1998); Ifs (Le Goff 2001), Malleville-sur-le-Bec (Mare 2005); Quiévrecourt (Beurion et Billard 2005), Fort Harrouard (Brun 1998); Pont de Metz (Buchez and Talon 2005); Inghem (Piningre 2005)

in previous periods (including vases with S-shaped profiles, divergent necks, small tronconical pots and so on). These forms are mostly undecorated and often bear traces produced by fingers that give the impression that they were not carefully produced. In England, this pottery is called 'plain ware'. There are in France several sites that have produced pottery with the same characteristics, allowing us to date them to the same period; Cussy and Ifs in Normandy (Marcigny and Ghesquière 1998; Le Goff 2001), Malleville-sur-le-Bec (Haute Normandie; Mare 2005), Quiévrecourt (Haute Normandie; Beurion and Billard 2005), Pont-de-Metz (Picardy; Buchez and Talon 2005), Inghem pit 43 (Nord-Pas-de-Calais; Piningre 2005) and Fort-Harrouard (Centre; a selection of the pottery is in Brun 1998).

This chronological attribution is confirmed by the discovery, on the same sites, of some pottery presenting influences from the North

Alpine complex and thus constituting a link between groups of the coastal areas and the heart of the continent.

Finally, Needham's Period 7 (950–800 cal BC; Needham 2007), corresponds to the metallic horizon of Ewart Park. This period is known by Post Deverel Rimbury pottery of the plain ware type, in full continuation of the preceding phase. At about 800 cal BC however, the 'decorated ware' as defined by John Barrett (1980) appears. Recent excavations have identified a large number of sites with this ceramic type; most of the stratigraphic sequence of Runnymede Bridge (Surrey; Needham 1991), the ring forts of Mucking and Springfield (Essex; Jones and Bond 1980; Buckley and Hedges 1987), the site of Potterne (Wiltshire; Lawson 2000; 1994), and several others. During this period, the pottery is less diversified than in the earlier plain ware phase. The high forms especially are more segmented and often decorated by finger-tip impressions

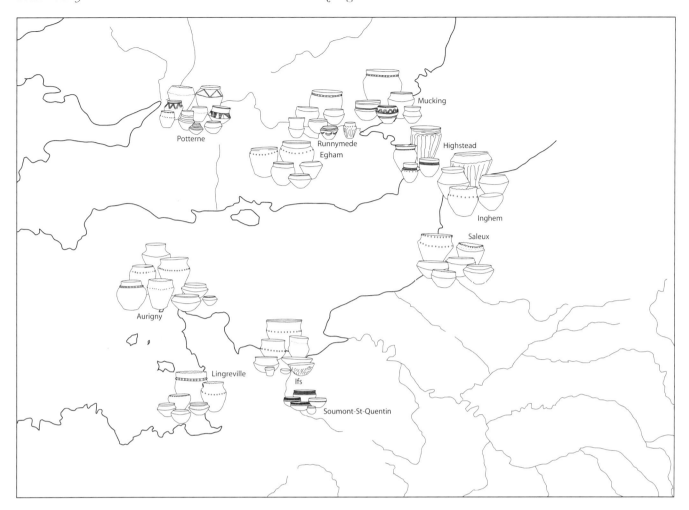

on the shoulder and the rim. In France, there are a number of comparable sites, though some of them seem to have been wrongly dated to the early La Tène period, for reasons of the remarkable similarity in the ceramic corpus. From west to east, one can mention the sites of Lingreville (Basse Normandie; Billard *et al* 1995), Ifs (Basse Normandie; Le Goff unpublished), Soumont-Saint-Quentin (Basse Normandie; Van Den Bossche 2007), Saleux (Picardy; Buchez and Talon 2005) and Inghem pit 2 (Nord-Pas-de-Calais; Piningre 2005). Looking at the map of these sites, one can observe the stylistic homogeneity of these, though some elements, as in Potterne, seem to announce the beginning of the Iron Age (Marcigny and Talon forthcoming; Fig 3.18).

The Earliest Iron Age (800–600 cal BC; Needham 2007) is characterised by the Llyn Fawr metallic phase. From a ceramic point of view, the period is distinguished from the previous one by more decorated pottery,

with incised lines and finger-tip impressions. Parallels with the French coastal area seem to disappear; here, a more continental style dominates.

Conclusion

The development of preventive archaeology and other collective research in France and Flanders during the last ten years or so has allowed us to define and identify, for the Bronze Age, the cultural attribution of populations from Normandy to Flanders and to consider them as one and the same entity, one which is to be found on both sides of the Channel and the North Sea and is related to the Atlantic complex.

These convergences were already known from the study of metallic material culture but appear now to gain increasing importance as we combine information about the pottery, the architecture, the evolution of settlements and

Figure 3.18 'Decorated Ware' comparisons across the Channel (computer graphic by E Ghesquière and C Marcigny, Inrap; Marcigny and Talon forthcoming): Potterne (Lawson 2000); Runnymede Bridge (Needham 1991); Egham (O'Connnel 1986); Mucking (Bond 1988), Highstead (Bennett et al 2007); Aurigny (Wilson 1984); Lingreville (Billard et al 1995); Ifs (Le Goff 2005); Soumont-Saint-Quentin (Van Den Bosshe 2007); Saleux (Buchez et Talon 2005); Inghem (Piningre 2005)

the development of field systems and funerary rituals. It becomes more and more obvious that both areas are part of the same economic network and share the same cultural identity. The discovery of the Dover boat provides us a perfect tool for the regular exchanges around this economic basin peopled and animated by the Manche group (Clark 2004).

List of references

Ampe, C, Bourgeois, J, Crombé, P, Fockedey, L, Langohr, R, Meganck, M, Semey, J, Van Strydonck, M and Verlaeckt, K 1996 'The circular view: Aerial photography and the discovery of Bronze Age funerary monuments in East- and West-Flanders (Belgium)', *Germania*, **74**, 45–94

Arnoldussen, S and Fontijn, D 2006 'Towards Familiar Landscapes? On the Nature and Origin of Middle Bronze Age Landscapes in the Netherlands', *Proceedings of the Prehistoric Society*, **72**, 289–317

Azagury, I and Demolon, P 1990 'Vitry-en-Artois (Pas-de-Calais), Les Colombiers', in *Les enclos funéraires de l'âge du Bronze dans le Nord/Pas-de-Calais,* (Catalogue de l'Exposition Décembre 1990–Mars 1991), Lille-Arras-Boulogne-Douai: Cahiers de Préhistoire du Nord, **8**, 54–58

Barrett, J 1980 'The pottery of the Later Bronze Age in Lowland England', *Proceedings of the Prehistoric Society*, **46**, 297–319

Bennett, P, Couldrey, P and Macpherson-Grant, N 2007 *Highstead near Chislet, Kent: Excavations 1975–1977*, The Archaeology of Canterbury, New Series, **4**, Canterbury: Canterbury Archaeological Trust

Beurion, C and Billard, C 2005 'L'occupation de l'âge du bronze final du site de Quièvrecourt 'l'Hôpital' (Seine Maritime)', in J Bourgeois and M Talon (eds), *L'âge du Bronze du Nord-Ouest de la France dans le contexte européen occidental: nouvelles découvertes et propositions de périodisation, actes de la table ronde tenue dans le cadre du 125ème Congrès national des sociétés historiques et scientifiques, Lille, 2000, Pré- et Protohistoire*, Éditions du Comité des Travaux Historique et Scientifiques et l'Association pour la Promotion des Recherches sur l'Âge du Bronze, 269–286

Billand, G and Talon, M 2000 *Nécropoles de l'âge du bronze: Rue (Somme) et Thourotte (Oise)*, Amiens: Plaquettes Archéologie en Picardie

Billand, G and Talon, M 2007 'Apport du Bronze Age Study Group au vieillissement des 'hair rings' dans le Nord de la France', in C Burgess, P Topping and F Lynch (eds), *Beyond Stonehenge Essays on the Bronze Age in honour of Colin Burgess*, Oxford: Oxbow Books, 342–351

Billard, C, Blanchet, J-C and Talon, M 1996 'Origine et composantes de l'âge du Bronze ancien dans le Nord-Ouest de la France', in C Mordant and O Gaiffe (eds), *Cultures et sociétés du Bronze ancien en Europe: 117e congrès national des sociétés historiques et scientifiques, 1992*, Paris: Éditions du Comité des Travaux Historique et Scientifiques, 579–601

Billard, C, Clet-Pellerin, M and Lautridou, J-P 1995 'Un site protohistorique littoral dans le havre de la Vanlée à Lingreville et Bricqueville-sur-mer (Manche)', *Revue Archéologique de l'Ouest*, **12**, 73–110

Blanchet, J-C 1984 *Les premiers métallurgistes en Picardie et dans le Nord de la France: Chalcolithique, Age du Bronze et Début du Premier Age du Fer*, Mémoire de la *Société préhistorique française*, **17**, Châlons-sur-Marne

Blanchet, J-C and Talon, M 2005 'L'âge du Bronze dans la moyenne vallée de l'Oise: apports récents', in J Bourgeois and M Talon (eds), *L'âge du Bronze du Nord-Ouest de la France dans le contexte européen occidental: nouvelles découvertes et propositions de périodisation, actes de la table ronde tenue dans le cadre du 125ème Congrès national des sociétés historiques et scientifiques, Lille, 2000, Pré- et Protohistoire*, Éditions du Comité des Travaux Historique et Scientifiques et l'Association pour la Promotion des Recherches sur l'Âge du Bronze, 232–273

Blanchet, J-C 2001 'Nouveaux dépôts de la transition Âge du Bronze final/début de l'Âge du Fer dans le contexte de la vallée moyenne de l'Oise', in C-T La Roux (ed), *Du monde des chasseurs à celui des métallurgistes: Changements technologiques et bouleversements humains de l'Armorique aux marges européennes, des prémices de la néolithisation à l'entrée dans l'Histoire. Hommages scientifiques à la mémoire de Jean L'Helgouac'h et mélanges offerts à Jacques Briard*, Revue Archéologique de l'Ouest, **9**, Rennes, 171–180

Blanchet, J-C and Talon, M 1987 'L'éperon barré du 'Camp César' à Catenoy (Oise), à l'âge du Bronze final – premiers résultats', in J-C Blanchet (ed), *Les relations entre le continent et les îles britanniques a l'âge du Bronze: Actes du colloque de Lille dans le cadre du 22ème congrès préhistorique de France*, Amiens: Supplément a la Revue Archéologique de Picardie, 189–210

Bostyn, F, Blancquaert, G and Lanchon, Y 1992 'Un enclos triple du Bronze ancien à Frethun (Pas-de-Calais)', *Bulletin de la Société préhistorique française*, **89**, 393–412

Bourgeois, J 1991 'Nederzettingen uit de late bronstijd en de vroege ijzertijd in westelijk België: Sint-Denijs-Westrem en Sint-Gillis-Waas', in H Fokkens and N Roymans (eds), *Nederzettingen uit de bronstijd en de vroege ijzertijd in de Lage Landen*, Nederlandse Archeologische Rapporten, **13**, Amersfoort, 171–179

Bourgeois, J and Cherretté, B 2005a 'Evolution of Burial Places in Western Flanders in the Bronze and Iron Age', in L Šmejda and J Turek (eds), *Spatial Analysis of Funerary Areas*, Plzen: University of West Bohemia

Bourgeois, J and Cherretté, B 2005b 'L'Âge du Bronze et le Premier Âge du Fer dans les Flandres occidentale et orientale (Belgique): un état de la question', in J Bourgeois and M Talon (eds), *L'âge du Bronze du Nord-Ouest de la France dans le contexte européen occidental: nouvelles découvertes et propositions de périodisation, actes de la table ronde tenue dans le cadre du 125ème Congrès national des sociétés historiques et scientifiques, Lille, 2000, Pré- et Protohistoire*, Paris: Éditions du Comité des Travaux Historique et Scientifiques et l'Association pour la Promotion des Recherches sur l'Âge du Bronze, 43–81

Bourgeois, J and Talon, M 2005 *L'Âge du bronze dans le nord de la France dans son contexte européen, Actes du colloque de Lille, 2000,* Actes des Congrès nationaux des sociétés historiques et scientifiques, 125e Lille, Paris: Comité des Travaux Historique et Scientifiques et l'Association pour la Promotion des Recherches sur l'Âge du Bronze

Bourgeois, Q and Arnoldussen, S 2006 'Expressing monumentality: some observations on the dating of Dutch Bronze Age barrows and houses', *Lunula: Archaeologia Protohistorica*, **14**, 13–25

Bradley, R 1994 *The social foundations of prehistoric Britain*, London and New York: Longman

Brun, P 1998 'Le complexe culturel atlantique: entre le cristal et la fumée', in S Jorge (ed), *Existe una edade do Bronze Atlântico?*, Lisbon: Instituto Português de Arqueologia, 40–51

Buchez, N and Talon, M 2005 'L'âge du Bronze dans le bassin de la Somme, bilan et périodisation du mobilier céramique', in J Bourgeois and M Talon (eds), *L'âge du Bronze du Nord-Ouest de la France dans le contexte européen occidental: nouvelles découvertes et propositions de périodisation, actes de la table ronde tenue dans le cadre du 125ème Congrès national des sociétés historiques et scientifiques, Lille, 2000, Pré- et Protohistoire*, Lille: Éditions du Comité des Travaux Historique et Scientifiques et l'Association pour la Promotion des Recherches sur l'Âge du Bronze, 159–188

Buckley, D and Hedges, J 1987 *The Late Bronze Age and Saxon settlements at Springfield Lyons, Essex: an interim report*, Chelmsford: Essex County Council Occasional Paper, **5**

Cammaert, L, Clarys, B, Van Assche, M, Gailly, O, Bloch, N and Mathieu, S 1996 'Un ensemble funéraire de l'âge du bronze ancien/moyen à Rebaix 'Couture-Saint-Vaast' (Ath, Ht)', *Lunula: Archaeologia Protohistorica*, **4**, 12–15

Champion, T 1980 'Settlement and environment in later Bronze Age Kent', in J Barrett and R Bradley (eds), *Settlement and society in the British later Bronze Age*, British Archaeological Reports (British series), Oxford, 223–246

Chancerel, A, Marcigny, C and San Juan, G 2006 'La double enceinte de l'âge du Bronze moyen de la ZI sud (Mondeville, Grentheville)', in A Chancerel, C Marcigny and E Ghesquière (eds), *Le plateau de Mondeville (Calvados), du Néolithique à l'âge du Bronze*, Paris: Documents d'Archéologie Française (DAF), 140–172

Clark, P 2004 *The Dover Bronze Age Boat in Context: Society and water transport in prehistoric Europe*, Oxford: Oxbow Books

Crombé, P and Bourgeois, J 1993 'Een midden-bronstijd nederzetting te Maldegem-Burkel (O–Vl): resultaten van de opgravingscampagne 1992', *Archeologisch Jaarboek Gent 1992*, 35–48

De Laet, S 1982 *La Belgique d'avant les Romains*, Wetteren: Editions Universa

De Laet, S, Nenquin, J and Spitaels, P 1958 *Contributions à l'étude de la civilisation des champs d'urnes en Flandre*, Dissertationes Archaeologicae Gandenses, **IV**, Brugge: De Tempel

De Laet, SJ, Thoen, H and Bourgeois, J 1986 *Les fouilles du Séminaire d'Archéologie de la Rijksuniversiteit te Gent à Destelbergen-Eenbeekeinde et l'histoire la plus ancienne de la région de Gent (Gand) I La période préhistorique*, Dissertationes Archaeologicae Gandenses, **XXIII**, Brugge: De Tempel

De Mulder, G 1994 'Aspects of the funeral ritual in the Late Bronze age and the Early Iron age in the western part of the Flemish region', *Helinium*, **34**, 94–133

Desfossés, Y 2000 *Archéologie préventive en vallée de Canche, les sites protohistoriques fouillés dans le cadre de la réalisation de l'autoroute A16*, Nord-Ouest Archéologie, **11**, Berck-sur-Mer

Desfossés, Y, Martial, E and Vallin, L 2000 'Le site d'habitat du Bronze moyen du 'Château d'eau' à Roeux (Pas-de-Calais)', in *Habitats et nécropoles à l'âge du Bronze sur le transmanche et le TGV nord, Bulletin de la Société préhistorique française*, Paris: *Société préhistorique française*, 59–107

Desfossés, Y and Masson, B 2000 'Les enclos funéraires du Motel à Fresnes-les-Montauban (Pas-de-Calais)', *Habitats et nécropoles à l'âge du Bronze sur le transmanche et le TGV nord, Bulletin de la Société préhistorique française*, Travaux **1**, Paris: *Société préhistorique française*, 19–58

Ellison, A 1980 'Deverel-Rimbury urn cemeteries: the evidence for social organisation', in J Barrett and R Bradley (ed), *Settlement and Society in the British Later Bronze Age*, British Archaeological Reports (British Series), **83**, Oxford, 115–126

Fokkens, H 2005a 'Le début de l'âge du Bronze aux Pays-Bas et l'horizon Hilversum ancien', in J Bourgeois and M Talon (eds), *L'âge du Bronze du nord de la France dans son contexte européen*, Actes des Congrès nationaux des sociétés historiques et scientifiques, 125e Lille, Paris: Comité des Travaux Historique et Scientifiques et l'Association pour la Promotion des Recherches sur l'Âge du Bronze

Fokkens, H 2005b 'Le début de l'âge du Bronze aux Pays-Bas et l'horizon Hilversum ancien', in J Bourgeois and M Talon (eds), *L'âge du Bronze du Nord-Ouest de la France dans le contexte européen occidental: nouvelles découvertes et propositions de périodisation, actes de la table ronde tenue dans le cadre du 125ème Congrès national des sociétés historiques et scientifiques, Lille, 2000, Pré- et Protohistoire*, Paris: Éditions du Comité des Travaux Historique et Scientifiques et l'Association pour la Promotion des Recherches sur l'Âge du Bronze

Fourny, M 1985 'Le 'Muziekberg' à Renaix: Nouvelle contribution à l'étude de la civilisation de Hilversum/Drakenstein (âge du bronze ancien/moyen). Examen des anciennes collections du Musée du Ce', *Vie Archéologique*, **5**, 41–68

Fourny, M and Van Assche, M 1993 'Les tombelles protohistoriques du Bois de la Houssière (Braine-le-Comte, Hennuyères et Ronquières Hainaut): Monuments classés', *Amphora*, **71–72**, 2–39

Gaudefroy, S and Le Goff, I 2004 'La nécropole du début du Bronze final de Verneuil-en-Halatte (Oise)', *Revue Archéologique de Picardie*, 19–32

Goderis, J 2001 'Vondsten uit de midden-bronstijd te Roeselare (W–Vl)', *Lunula: Archaeologia Protohistorica*, **IX**, 11–16

Gouge, P and Peake, R 2005 'Aux marges du Bronze atlantique, sites et chronologies de la région du confluent Seine-Yonne', in J Bourgeois and M Talon (eds), *L'âge du Bronze du Nord-Ouest de la France dans le contexte européen occidental: nouvelles découvertes et propositions de périodisation, actes de la table ronde tenue dans le cadre du 125ème Congrès national des sociétés historiques et scientifiques, Lille, 2000, Pré- et Protohistoire*, Paris: Éditions du Comité des Travaux Historique et Scientifiques et l'Association pour la Promotion des Recherches sur l'Âge du Bronze, 333–359

Henton, A and Demarez, L 2005 'L'âge du Bronze en Hainaut belge', in J Bourgeois and M Talon (eds), *L'âge du Bronze du Nord-Ouest de la France dans le contexte européen occidental: nouvelles découvertes et propositions de périodisation, actes de la table ronde tenue dans le cadre du 125ème Congrès national des sociétés historiques et scientifiques, Lille, 2000, Pré- et Protohistoire*: Éditions du Comité des Travaux Historique et Scientifiques et l'Association pour la Promotion des Recherches sur l'Âge du Bronze, 83–101

Jahier, I 2005 'Le village de Cahagnes (Calvados)', in C Marcigny, C Colonna, E Ghesquière and G Verron (eds), *La Normandie à l'aube de l'histoire, les découvertes archéologiques de l'âge du Bronze 2300–800 av J-C*, Paris: Somogy Éditions d'art, 50–51

Jones, M and Bond, D 1980 'Later Bronze Age settlement at Mucking, Essex', in J Barrett and R Bradley (eds), *Settlement and society in the British later Bronze Age*, British Archaeological Reports (British Series), **83**, Oxford, 471–482

Koot, C and Berkvens, R (eds) 2004 *Bredase akkers eeuwenoud. 4000 jaar bewoningsgeschiedenis op de rand van zand en klei*, Rapportage Archeologische Monumentenzorg, **102**, ErfgoedStudie, **1**, Breda: Gemeente Breda

Lawson, A-J 2000 *Potterne 1982–5: Animal husbandry in Later Prehistoric Wiltshire*, Wessex Archaeology report, **17**, Salisbury: Wessex Archaeology

Lawson, AJ 1994 'Potterne, Wiltshire', in A Fitzpatrick and E Morris (eds), *The Iron Age in Wessex: Recent Work*, Salisbury: Wessex Archaeology

Le Goff, E 2001 'Ifs, ZAC Object' Ifs sud', in *Bilan Scientifique de la région Basse-Normandie 2000*, Direction Régionale des Affaires Cilturelles de Basse-Normandie, Service Régionale de l'Archéologie, Ministère de la Culture et de la Francophonie, Direction de Patrimoine, Sou-direction à l'archéologie, 40–42

Le Goff, I, Billand, G, Delrieu, F, Le Guen, P, Lepaumier, H, Henton, A and Pinard, E forthcoming 'Forme de sites et des gestes funéraires à la transition Bronze/Fer entre Escaut et Orne', in *Le Nord-ouest du Bassin parisien à la fin de l'âge du Bronze et au début de l'âge du Bronze et au début de l'âge du Fer Identités et influences Actes de la table ronde de Rouen 2005*, Revue Archéologique de l'Ouest

Le Guen, M and Auxiette, G 2005 'Apport récent sur la transition âge du Bronze-âge du Fer dans la vallée de l'Aisne, Osly-Courtil 'La Terre Saint-Mard ' (Aisne): Processus de différenciation de l'habitat au cours du Bronze final', in G Auxiette and F Malrain (eds), *Hommages à Claudine Pommepuy*, Revue Archéologique de Picardie, **22**, 141–161

Lepaumier, H, Marcigny, C and Ghesquière, E 2005 'L'architecture des habitats protohistoriques de Normandie: quelques exemples de la fin du IIIème millénaire au début du second âge du Fer', in O Buchsenschutz and C Mordant (eds), *Architectures protohistoriques en Europe occidentale du néolithique final à l'âge du Fer,* Actes du 127ème congrès des Comité des Travaux Historique et Scientifiques, Nancy, 15–20 avril 2002, Paris: Éditions du Comité des Travaux Historique et Scientifiques, 231–264

Leroy-Langlois, E and Sys, D 2004 *Escaudain-Erre (Nord): Fouilles préventives*, Service archéologique du Douasis

Letterlé, F 1982 'Un site de l'âge du Bronze à Cuiry-les-Chaudardes (Aisne)', in *Vallée de l'Aisne: cinq années de fouilles protohistoriques,* Numéro spécial de la Revue Archéologique de Picardie, **1**, 175–185

Manby, T 1980 'Bronze Age settlement in Eastern Yorkshire', in J Barrett and R Bradley (eds), *Settlement and society in the British later Bronze Age* , British Archaeological Reports (British Series), **83**, Oxford, 307–370

Marcigny, C 2005a 'L'âge du Bronze dans la Hague: un état de la documentation disponible', in C Marcigny and E Ghesquière (eds), *Archéologie, histoire et anthropologie de la presqu'île de La Hague (Manche): Première année de recherche 2005*, Tourlaville: Le Tourp, Imprimerie Artistiques Lecaux, 93–110

Marcigny, C 2005b 'Une ferme de l'âge du Bronze à Nonant (Calvados)', in C Marcigny, C Colonna, E Ghesquière and G Verron (eds), *La Normandie à l'aube de l'histoire, les découvertes archéologiques de l'âge du Bronze 2300–800 av J-C*, Paris: Somogy Éditions d'art, 48–49

Marcigny, C and Ghesquière, E 1998 'L'habitat Bronze final de Cussy 'La Pointe' (Calvados)', *Revue Archéologique de l'Ouest*, **15**, 39–58

Marcigny, C and Ghesquière, E 2003 *L'Île de Tatihou à l'âge du Bronze (Manche) Habitats et occupation du sol*, Document d'Archéologie Française, **96**, Paris: Éditions de la Maison des Sciences de l'Homme

Marcigny, C, Ghesquière, E, Clement-Sauleau, S and Vernay, A 2005 'L'âge du Bronze en Basse-Normandie: définition par le mobilier céramique, une première tentative', in J Bourgeois and M Talon (eds), *L'âge du Bronze du Nord-Ouest de la France dans le contexte européen occidental. nouvelles découvertes et propositions de périodisation, actes de la table ronde tenue dans le cadre du 125ème Congrès national des sociétés historiques et scientifiques, Lille, 2000, Pré- et Protohistoire*, Paris: Éditions du Comité des Travaux Historique et Scientifiques et l'Association pour la Promotion des Recherches sur l'Âge du Bronze, 302–332

Marcigny, C, Ghesquiere, E and Kinnes, I 2007 'Bronze Age cross channel relations. The Lower-Normandy (France) example: ceramic chronology and first reflections', in C Burgess, P Topping and F Lynch (eds), *Beyond Stonehenge: Essays on the Bronze Age in honour of Colin Burgess*, Oxford: Oxbow Books, 255–267

Marcigny, C and Talon, M forthcoming 'Sur les rives de la Manche: Qu'en est il du passage de l'âge du Bronze à l'âge du Fer?', in *De l'âge du Fer (X–VIIème siècle av. J-C)*, Actes du colloque international APRAB-AFEAF de St-Romain-en-Gall 2005, Revue Archéologique de l'Est

Mare, E 2005 'Le village de Malleville-sur-le-Bec (Eure)', in C Marcigny, C Colonna, E Ghesquière and G Verron (eds), *La Normandie à l'aube de l'histoire, les découvertes archéologiques de l'âge du Bronze 2300–800 av J-C*, Paris: Somogy Éditions d'art, 52–53

Mohen, J-P and Bailloud, G 1987 *La vie quotidienne: Les fouilles du Fort-Harrouard*, L'âge du Bronze en France, **4**, Paris: Picard

Moore, J and Jennings, D 1992 *Reading Business Park: a Bronze Age Landscape*, Thames Valley Landscapes: the Kennet Valley, **1**, Oxford: Oxford Archaeological Unit

Needham, S 1991 *Excavation and Salvage at Runnymede Bridge (1978)*, London: British Museum Press

Needham, S 1996 'Chronology and Periodisation in the

British Bronze Age', in K Randsborg (ed), *Absolute Chronology, Archaeological Europe 2500–500 BC, Acta Archaeologica*, **67**, 121–140

Needham, S 2007 '800 BC, The Great Divide', in C Haselgrove and R Pope (eds), *The Earlier Iron Age in Britain and the near Continent*, Oxford: Oxbow Books, 39–63

Needham, S and Ambers, J 1994 'Redating Rams Hill and reconsidering Bronze Age enclosure', *Proceedings of the Prehistoric Society*, **60**, 225–243

Needham, S, Bronk Ramsey, C, Coombs, D, Cartwright, C and Pettitt, P 1997 'An Independent Chronology for British Bronze Age Metalwork: The Results of the Oxford Radiocarbon Accelerator Programme', *Archaeological Journal*, **154**, 55–107

Pinard, E, Alexandre, S, Billand, G, Simon, F and Vanhille, G 2000 'Verberie "Les Gâts" et "La Plaine d'Herneuse". Les occupations du Bronze ancien à La Tène ancienne', in *Programme de surveillance et d'étude archéologique des sablières de la moyenne vallée de l'Oise: rapport d'activité 1999*, Service régional de l'archéologie de Picardie, 45–94

Piningre, J-F 1990 'La nécropole de l'âge du Bronze de Conchil-le-Temple (Pas-de-Calais)', *Cahiers de Préhistoire du Nord*, **8**, 79–89

Piningre, J-F 2005 'Un habitat de la fin de l'âge du Bronze: le site d'Inghem (Pas-de-Calais)', in J Bourgeois and M Talon (eds), *L'âge du Bronze du Nord-Ouest de la France dans le contexte européen occidental: nouvelles découvertes et propositions de périodisation, actes de la table ronde tenue dans le cadre du 125ème Congrès national des sociétés historiques et scientifiques, Lille, 2000, Pré- et Protohistoire*, Paris: Éditions du Comité des Travaux Historique et Scientifiques et l'Association pour la Promotion des Recherches sur l'Âge du Bronze, 137–158

Quérel, P 2002 *Villeneuve d'Ascq, Parc Scientifique de la Haute Borne*, Archéologie en Nord-Pas-de-Calais, **2**

Révillion, S, Bouche, K and Wozny, L 1994 'La partie agricole d'une grande exploitation rurale d'époque romaine: le gisement des 'Hauts de Clauwiers', Seclin (Nord)', *Revue du Nord*, **76**, 99–146

Rougier, R 1998 'Deux nouveaux sites du Bronze final à Beautot et Criquetot-sur-Ouville (Seine-Maritime)', in X Delestre and A Woodcock (eds), *Actes de la table-ronde*

archéologique, Dieppe, 17–18 septembre 1996*, Proximus, **2**, Sotteville-lès-Rouen: Association pour la promotion de l'archéologie en Haute-Normandie, 17–22

Roymans, N and Fokkens, H 1991a 'Een overzicht van veertig jaar nederzettingsonderzoek in de Lage Landen', in N Roymans and H Fokkens (eds), *Nederzettingen uit de bronstijd en de vroege ijzertijd in de Lage Landen*, Amersfoort: Nederlandse Archeologische Rapporten, **13**, 1–20

Roymans, N and Fokkens, H (eds) 1991b *Nederzettingen uit de bronstijd en de vroege ijzertijd in de Lage landen*, Amersfoort: Nederlandse Archeologische Rapporten, **13**

Sys, D and Leroy-Langevin, E 2004 *Escaudain-Erre (Nord). Fouilles préventives: Document Final de Synthèse*, Service archéologique du Douaisis

Theunissen, L 1999 *Midden-bronstijdsamenlevingen in het zuiden van de Lage Landen Een evaluatie van het begrip 'Hilversum-cultuur'*, Leiden: University of Leiden

Toron, S 2005 *Les enclos circulaires du Bronze ancien et moyen aux marges septentrionales du complexe atlantique*, Lille: Université de Lille 3

Van Den Bossche, B 2007 'Le mobilier céramique du Bronze final et du début du premier âge du Fer du Mont-Joly à Soumont-Saint-Quentin (Calvados): nouvelles données', *Bulletin de la Société préhistorique française*, **104**, 147–170

Van Impe, L and Beex, G 1977 *Grafheuvels uit de vroege en midden bronstijd te Weelde*, Archaeologia Belgica, **193**, Brussels

Warmenbol, E 1990 'De bronstijd en -nijverheid in West-Vlaanderen: een status quaestionis', *Westvlaamse Archaeologica*, **6**, 33–48

Warmenbol, E 1991 'Le Bronze Final Atlantique entre Côte et Escaut', In C Chevillot and A Coffyn (eds), *L'Âge du Bronze Atlantique: ses faciès, de l'Écosse à l'Andalousie et leurs relations avec le Bronze continental et la Méditerranée*, Actes du 1er Colloque du Parc archéologique de Beynac, 1er au 10 septembre 1990, Beynac-et-Cazenac: Association des Musées du Sarladais, 89–110

Wilson, K 1984 'Excavation of an Iron Age A site at Les Huguettes, Alderney', *Reports and Transactions of the Société Guernesiaise*, **21**, 393–427

4. British immigrants killed abroad in the seventies: The rise and fall of a Dutch culture

Liesbeth Theunissen

Introduction

This paper is an evaluation of a Dutch archaeological culture, the Hilversum culture. This evaluation was carried out as a PhD research in the last millennium (Theunissen 1999). On request of the organiser of the Dover conference the author went into the subject again and rediscovered the beauty of historial thought. Her PhD study in that time was not just a matter of studying the material culture and the prehistoric societies it represented; it also had a clear historical dimension, as part of a story in which archaeologist themselves have a starring role.

The Hilversum culture is a concept from the 1950s, spawned by the ideas, thoughts and interpretations of a small group of British and Dutch archaeologists who influenced and inspired each other through their contacts across the North Sea.

This paper focuses on their story. Where did the ideas and concepts come from? Who influenced who in the archaeological world back then? What were these personal relationships that spanned the North Sea? What was the 'rise' and 'fall' of the Hilversum culture? Is it an old-fashioned concept, only used as a reminder of the archaeologists of the 1950s on whose shoulders we stand or does it still have value in present-day archaeology?

Development of the culture concept

For the very first notion of the Hilversum culture we must go back to 1925, to Vere Gordon Childe (1892–1957) and the develop-ment of the general culture concept. Of course Childe needs no introduction. Born in Sydney, Australia, he was a man of many talents, including an excellent visual memory and a flair for languages (Green 1981). He was also a very bad driver and scared of dogs. In 1914 he went to study archaeology in Oxford. After graduating he made many tours of Europe, visiting a host of excavations and museums, including those in the Netherlands (Trigger 1980).

He wrote two books presenting the data that he collected during his travels. *The Dawn of European Civilisation* (1925) presents an overview of European prehistory up to the beginning of the Bronze Age. In this book he used a basic concept of archaeological culture drawn from Gustaf Kossina. Kossina, a German archaeologist, was the first to develop the concept of an archaeological culture. With his good command of German, Childe was one of the few to adopt his theory.

Childe combined Kossina's culture concept with Montelius' chronology and with the theory that technological skills had spread into Europe from the Near East. In his second book, *The Danube in Prehistory*, he gave the first clear definition of an archaeological culture;

'We find certain types of remains – pots, implements, ornaments, burial rites, house forms – constantly recurring together. Such a complex of regular associated traits we shall term a 'cultural group' or just a culture. We assume that such a complex is the material expression of what would today be called a "people".' (Childe 1929)

Like Kossina, Childe was not only interested in the study of archaeological cultures as a collection of characteristics, but equally as a source of knowledge about life in the past. Changes in material culture were explained by diffusion and migration – by external factors, in other words.

A Dutch counterpart: Albert Egges van Giffen

Meanwhile, on the other side of the North Sea, another archaeologist was interested in Kossina's culture concept. That archaeologist was Albert Egges van Giffen (1884–1973), founder of modern archaeological research in the Netherlands and of the Biological-Archaeological Institute in Groningen (Fig 4.1). Van Giffen had an international reputation, thanks to his book *Die Bauart der Einzelgräber* (1930) and his fame as an excavator and inventor of the quadrant method. He was in regular contact with Childe in the late 1920s. The two men corresponded and also met during their travels and at conferences.

In the 1920s and 1930s, most of the information for reconstructing the past came from barrow excavations. Like Childe, Van Giffen believed that burial rites were deeply-rooted. The fact that they were both sons of preachers might have had something to do with it. Both Childe and Van Giffen regarded grave rituals as a useful angle from which to trace different cultural groups. His contacts

with Childe probably made Van Giffen aware of the direct parallels between the Netherlands and England; in 1930 he pointed out the clear similarities between the pottery from the Drakenstein barrow in Lage Vuursche and the cinerary urns found in England. In the late Thirties he published a series of articles summarising more similarities between English and Dutch grave rituals – parallels which Childe had undoubtedly pointed out (Van Giffen 1938). One interesting detail is that the two men communicated in German until well into the war, as Van Giffen's command of English was not very good.

In the early post-war period Van Giffen presented his culture concept in the form of a 'culturcel streekdiagram', translated as a regional archaeology survey, which was a new concept. His basic principle was 'to investigate a region systematically and over a long period for remains of lost cultures and their members. This gave insight into the rise and fall of successive civilisational phenomena' (Van Giffen 1947). Migration was *the* most important explanatory model for the appearance of new cultural elements in the archaeological database. Van Giffen naturally passed these ideas on to his students, a new generation of archaeologists who were quite familiar with terms such as continuity, discontinuity and migration.

The emerge of the Hilversum Culture: the inventor

One of those students was Willem Glasbergen (1923–1979). Glasbergen is *the* man behind the term 'Hilversum culture'. It was with him that the Hilversum culture truly began to emerge. Glasbergen was born the son of a flower bulb grower in Noordwijk, near Leiden, in the 'geest' region of sandy soils between the dunes and the polder (Fig 4.2). From an early age he was interested in the past and in archaeology. As a grammar school student he helped with the excavations of the famous Roman *castellum* at Valkenburg. The centre of this village near Leiden had been severely damaged by bombing in May 1940, during the invasion of the Netherlands. So it was temporarily clear of buildings and accessible to archaeologists. The bombing in fact made a dream come true for Van Giffen, who had been longing to dig there since 1914 – not for

Figure 4.1 Portrait of Albert Egges van Giffen [photo archive Groninger Museum, Groningen]

Figure 4.2 Willem Glasbergen recording a Wessex biconical urn [private collection]

loved to tell stories full of puns and allusions. His children called Van Giffen 'Uncle Ab'. Glasbergen was eventually buried beside Van Giffen at the cemetery in Diever. This relationship is fascinating; a unique student-master, friend and father-figure relationship that lasted for decades, continuing even after death. After graduation, Willem Glasbergen began his PhD research, a study of grave rituals based on Bronze-Age grave monuments in Brabant.

The emerge of the Hilversum culture: the archaeological evidence

In 1948 Glasbergen focused on the barrows between the hamlets of Toterfout and Halve Mijl, to the southwest of Eindhoven, which were threatened by land reclamation work. The institute in Groningen was quick to react, and Van Giffen sent Glasbergen to carry out the investigations. Glasbergen went to Brabant in 1948 to head the research team, and was awarded his doctorate six years later for his thesis based on the results.

His thesis, entitled *Barrow Excavations in the Eight Beatitudes*, is unique in the fact that it was the first thesis in the Netherlands to be published in English (Glasbergen 1954). It reflects the many contacts he had made during his research, particularly with English archaeologists. Glasbergen had discussed pottery and the barrows with timber circles with Christopher Hawkes, Gerald Dunning and Humphrey Case.

The development of the term 'Hilversum culture' began in 1950 when the primary urn was found in barrow 1B at Toterfout-Halve Mijl (Fig 4.3). Until that time, these large, coarsely tempered urns were known as 'Deverel' pottery, because of their similarity to the pottery W.A. Miles had discovered in the Deverel barrow in Dorset in 1825. Lord Abercromby classified these pots as 'Deverel-Rimbury' in 1912, because of their resemblance to the pottery from the flat grave at Rimbury.

In 1938, Dutch archaeologist Bursch assumed that the Deverel urns could be chronologically positioned at the transition from the Bronze Age to the Iron Age. The typological similarity between the English Deverel-Rimbury urns and the coarsely tempered pots from mainland Europe led to the assumption that there had been a direct

nothing was his nickname 'the little digger'. He therefore eagerly grasped the opportunity to launch an archaeological investigation there. It may sound somewhat crude, but without the German attack on the Netherlands in 1940, the extensive archaeological investigation of the *castellum* in the heart of Valkenburg would never have been possible.

In July 1941, schoolboy Glasbergen, who lived in the next village, wandered into the excavation pits at Valkenburg, and after a year became Van Giffen's assistant. This first contact with the great Van Giffen determined the rest of Willem Glasbergen's life. He soon grew very close to Van Giffen and, after the war, went to study archaeology with him in Groningen. Glasbergen moved into a room in Van Giffen's home. He later married Mrs Van Giffen's niece. In the 1950s he succeeded Van Giffen as professor at the University of Amsterdam, and in the 1960s took over a great deal of his research.

The lives and academic careers of these two men were thus closely intertwined. Van Giffen was a dominant figure, who demanded as much of his staff as he did of himself, managing on four hours' sleep a night. Glasbergen, also a dominant man, linguistically-inclined,

cultural relationship between England and the continent around 800 BC.

The term 'Deverel pottery' remained in use until the urn from Toterfout was dated. First, another student of Van Giffen's and friend of Glasbergen, Tjalling Waterbolk, produced a relative dating on the basis of pollen analysis. A few years later, in 1952, an absolute dating was made when a charcoal sample from the Toterfout urn was among the first to be dated using the C14 method. The result – 3450 ± 100 BP – confirmed the results of Waterbolk's research, and led to the rapid acceptance of the C14 method.

The Toterfout urn changed the existing view. This kind of pottery, decorated with cord impressions, seemed to been much older than previously thought. It strongly resembles British urns and seemed to be linked with the later continental urns of the Deverel type. Glasbergen concluded that the Deverel type must also have 'devolved' from the older type, which he called pottery of the Hilversum type. Glasbergen had come to this conclusion after heated discussions during a visit to Christopher Hawkes in Oxford. Hawkes had written a retrospective entitled *Deverel-Rimbury pottery in Britain and its implications*. The work had never been published, however. A discussion one night about the origins of the Dutch Deverel culture and related objects led to a short joint paper in which the authors called for the term 'Drakenstein pottery' to be used in place of 'Deverel urn'. The Hilversum pots decorated with cord impressions and cordon bore a strong resemblance to the Wessex Biconical Urns found in southern England. The Hilversum pottery was thought to have been brought to the sandy soils of the Netherlands by English invaders. The Drakenstein pottery, a degenerate version of the Hilversum pottery without cord decoration, was thought to be a local product.

Glasbergen saw British origins not only in the pottery, but also in the grave monuments. The urn from Toterfout came from what we call a *ringwalheuvel* – a barrow with bank and ditch – which in his eyes strongly resembled the English disc and bell barrows. His mentor Van Giffen had indeed already pointed out this similarity before the Second World War. The early dating of the urn of Toterfout also placed the barrow with bank and ditch early in the Middle Bronze Age. Pollen analysis

Figure 4.3 Urn of Toterfout [Groninger Instituut voor Archeologie]

Figure 4.4 Bronze chisel from De Zwartenberg barrow [RACM]

had already shown that the barrow of this type at Toterfout was contemporaneous with the De Zwartenberg barrow with bank and ditch at Hoogeloon, in the centre of which a bronze chisel had been found (Fig 4.4). What is more, Glasbergen had noticed that these barrows occurred in a specific region – Dutch and Belgian Kempen – which was also the distribution area of another type of barrow; the barrow with a paired post circle. He believed that the assumed structure of the post circle, with lintels and an entrance was probably derived from the trilithons of Stonehenge.

In line with the thinking of archaeologists at that time, the appearance of these new cultural characteristics was attributed to the arrival of a new population group. Glasbergen believed that the motive for this migration was the trade in bronze. This explanation was based largely on the known bronze hoard of Voorhout. Found in 1907, it consisted of 16 palstaves, a chisel and two flanged axes. The bronzes appeared to come from Wales, and were interpreted as the stock of a travelling bronzecaster.

Glasbergen regarded the carriers of the Hilversum culture as tradesmen from the wealthy Wessex culture who had crossed over to the continent. Small groups of colonists had arrived in the Netherlands around 1500 BC, where they forged peaceful contacts with the indigenous population. The immigrants settled mainly in the North Brabant and Belgian Kempen region. The fact that relations were peaceful was evidenced by the secondary interments in the large barrows with bank and ditch. Members of the indigenous population were buried in Drakenstein urns in the same barrows where the first generation of colonists had been buried in Hilversum urns.

By around 1956, when the term first began to appear in publications, the Hilversum culture had truly arrived. It was defined on the basis of the culture-historical framework common at the time and based on a number of new elements in the archaeological material culture. And it was explained by the arrival of British migrants. Glasbergen's theory – which he provocatively called 'The Toterfout urn and the reformation of the British Bronze Age' in his inaugural lecture – set English archaeologists thinking (Glasbergen 1957).

An English answer

Jay Butler (1923) and Isobel Smith (1912–2005) were the first to respond. They had visited the Netherlands in summer 1951 with John Alexander, at the invitation of Pieter Glazema, director of the State Service for Archaeological Investigations, as the ROB was then known. It was to be a kind of work experience visit.

Butler, Smith and Alexander were all study-ing with Childe at the Institute of Archaeology in London. Childe was a conscientious lecturer who was highly knowledgeable in many areas. As a teacher he could be hard to understand, as he often mumbled. His students had difficulty keeping up with his nimble wit, but once they had absorbed the knowledge, they often discovered inspiring ideas behind the mental leaps. Jay Butler and Isobel Smith embarked on their PhD studies after graduation, both of them inspired by their supervisor Gordon Childe. Jay Jordan Butler, who was born in

America, began with a study of the North European bronzes. Isobel Foster Smith, a Canadian, turned her attention to the pottery.

In 1956 they jointly published a paper in which Butler described the razors and Smith the urns with cordon (Butler and Smith 1956). The early dating of the Toterfout urn had shifted these two British material categories from the Late Bronze Age to the Middle Bronze Age.

One important object examined in the paper, entitled *Razors, Urns and the British Middle Bronze Age*, was the razor from Drouwen. This was part of an exceptionally rich grave that Van Giffen had discovered in 1927 between the four post traces of a mortuary house – a notable find in Dutch archaeology. Four years after this discovery, Childe visited the Provincial Museum in Assen. He was struck by the razor, a type that the British had placed in the Late Bronze Age, while the other objects from the grave were older. Childe wrote to Van Giffen asking for more information about the context. If it was a closed find, it would mean a Middle Bronze Age dating. And this indeed turned out to be the case. This find, combined with the Toterfout urn, must have inspired Childe to put two of his students to work exploring the implications of an earlier dating. And that was indeed the outcome of both studies. Butler concluded from his investigation of the razors that a dating in the Middle Bronze Age was most likely. Smith drew the same conclusion from her work on the pottery.

Both continued with their individual studies. Jay Butler decided to move to the Netherlands in 1957, to lecture on the Bronze Age in Groningen, and later also in Amsterdam. In 1963 he defended his thesis, *Bronze Age connections across the North Sea* (Butler 1963). Isobel Smith was writing her doctoral thesis on English Neolithic ceramics when in 1955 Alexander Keiller died, leaving 15 years of intensive excavation at Avebury unanalysed and unpublished. His widow Gabrielle was determined to see the work finished. Within weeks of completing her PhD in 1956, Smith was housed at Avebury and entrusted with the task. Despite this new challenge in Avebury, in 1961 Isobel Smith published a new reconstruction model for the British Bronze Age. She compared the find complexes of the Wessex and Hilversum cultures in a paper entitled *An essay towards the reformation of the*

British Bronze Age. Smith concluded that an English pottery group – the Wessex Biconical Urns – could be identified as the forerunner of the Hilversum pottery. This type had only a limited geographical distribution in southern England, and had been dated to *c* 3400 BP on the basis of the grave gifts. Many elements of the decoration showed clear similarities with the Hilversum group. But other elements also occurred on both sides of the North Sea, including bone pins and segmented bone beads that have been interpreted as imitation faïence. In 1961, she wrote of the Exloo necklace; 'It is a reasonable conjecture that the famous necklace found at Exloo arrived from England in the pocket of a Hilversum immigrant' (Smith 1961).

The last building stone

Until the late 1950s the definition of the Hilversum culture was based largely on the characteristics of the pottery and the grave monuments. While settlement complexes and ground plans had been found in the western and northern Netherlands in the early 1950s and early 1960s, it was not until 1965 that the first such features were found in the central and southern Netherlands. In that year, the ground plans of round houses were found in the riverine area, near to the village of Zijderveld.

These round to oval structures differed sharply from the dozens of three-aisled ground plans of farmhouses found in the northern Netherlands, but showed clear parallels with the settlements at Itford Hill and Cock Hill in southern England. Research on British settlements had concluded that round was the only shape used for houses there. And it was these round houses at Zijderveld, and also at Dodewaard, that I re-examined for my PhD studies. A rather bureaucratic exercise, because it was thirty years after discovery, but still. These round to oval ground plans confirmed Glasbergens theory; these were the houses of British immigrants.

The 'fall' of the Hilversum culture

By the early 1960s the term 'Hilversum culture' had become common in the archaeological world. This rapid acceptance resulted from a number of circumstances. Glasbergen had written a textbook with a Belgian archaeologist from Ghent, S.J. de Laet, in which they devoted many pages to the Hilversum culture (Fig 4.5; De Laet and Glasbergen 1959). The book gave a detailed summary of Dutch and Belgian prehistory, and for many years was a standard text for students. Glasbergen lectured for many years as professor at the University of Amsterdam, introducing the concept to his students, and launching a series of excavations of Middle Bronze Age remains.

The late 1960s saw the appearance of two important Bronze Age publications in the

Figure 4.5 De Laet and Glasbergen in the dolmen of Weris [private collection]

Netherlands. In 1968 Glasbergen gave a talk about the Hilversum and Drakenstein pottery at the general meeting of the Dutch Society of Arts and Sciences, in which he summarised all the archaeological arguments (Glasbergen 1968). A year later, Butler's popular book 'Nederland in de bronstijd' was published, presenting the Hilversum culture and the migration theory to a wider audience (Butler 1969).

It was around that time – in the late 1960s and early 1970s – that a growing scepticism began to emerge about migration as an explanatory model. A new generation of archaeologists critically re-examined Childe's culture concept, undermining the models of diffusion and migration. Cracks began to appear in the culture-historical paradigm. The impact of the New Archaeology was soon felt, although the break between the old culture historians and the New Archaeologists was not as radical as it was in the United States and Britain. The Dutch research tradition still clearly bore the mark of Van Giffen, giving it its own unique character; strongly empirical studies in which scientific methods such as C14 dating and pollen analysis had been applied from an early stage.

Two young archaeologists headed the field. Leendert Louwe Kooijmans drew into question the assumption that British immigrants had brought the Hilversum culture to the Netherlands. Given the similarities in the Late Neolithic pottery, he espoused the theory of indigenous local development. Diderik van der Waals found the assumption that 'a find complex equals a social tradition equals a people' to be untenable. Those two young critics made that the original excitement about the Hilversum culture died down.

In the mid-seventies the concept of the Hilversum culture as an invasion culture slowly but surely began to lose ground. The old idea of the English migrants faded over the years, although a odd lost British migrant did show up in books for the wider public in the early 1980s. Archaeologists became more and more convinced that archaeological cultures do not represent actual social units, but are our own constructs. The culture concept was stripped of all ethnic implications; an archaeological 'culture' was no longer equated with the material expression of a single people. As a result, migration and diffusion were no longer adequate explanations of change.

The Hilversum culture nowadays

Nowadays our knowledge of the past has increased tremendously. Many settlement sites from the Middle Bronze Age have been excavated over the past thirty years; more than three hundred house plans are now known in the Netherlands. Nevertheless, the term Hilversum culture continues to be used to this day, though nowadays more in a descriptive sense to refer to Early and Middle Bronze Age remains in the southern Low Countries (Louwe Kooijmans *et al* 2005). After all, certain characteristic remains – visible largely in the grave ritual – remain an archaeological reality (Theunissen 1999; Lanting and Van der Plicht 2001/2002). The find complexes that Glasbergen used for his definition are still unique, in both a temporal sense – they are a new phenomenon – and a spatial sense, being distributed over a very limited area. Hilversum pottery, barrows with bank and ditch, barrows with paired post circles, urns filled with cremation remains are found repeatedly, and virtually exclusively.

Only the round houses cannot be determined in an archaeological sense. My re-analysis of the excavation drawings from Zijderveld and Dodewaard led me to dismiss them as a myth. What it boils down to is that the round houses were recognised in excavation pits with a high density of features. And sometimes not until after the excavation, at the drawing table, when it was no longer possible to verify their existence in the field on the basis of identical infill, cross section and depth. I also found very few similarities with the English round houses. Besides the excavation campaigns at Zijderveld and Dodewaard yielded very convincing ground plans of three-aisled farm houses. The conclusion was therefore that, though there may have been round structures in the Bronze Age, their existence has never been convincingly proved yet.

We can continue to use the term Hilversum culture for this collection of unique complexes – the pottery with rope impressions, the barrows with bank and ditch and so on. The Hilversum culture as a unique archaeological culture with its core in the southern Netherlands and Flanders, where all the features occur in combination. Despite these unique characteristics, the Hilversum culture is also part of the extensive Northern European

Bronze Age tradition characterised by long farmhouses and barrow burials in general. In this way, the term 'Hilversum culture' can be defined in social terms, as referring to the societies responsible for the characteristic remains. These communities are not to be seen as isolated units, but as societies with widely branched social networks and long-range contacts, across the North Sea. The recent study of the necklace of Exloo revealed one of the latest ideas; the most probable provenance of the necklace is Southern England (Haveman and Sheridan 2005/2006). The Wessex-Hilversum connection could well have been the mechanism for the transmission of the Exloo necklace from England to the Netherlands. So more than forty years after Isobel Smith's hypothesis, we could say that the necklace can still be seen as an evidence of long-distance contacts across the North Sea. The British immigrants were killed in the seventies, but the Bronze Age contacts are still strong.

List of references

Butler, J 1963 *Bronze Age connections across the North Sea*, Palaeohistoria, **9**, 1–286

Butler, J 1969 *Nederland in de bronstijd*, Haarlem: Fibula

Butler, J and Smith, I 1956 *Razors, urns, and the British Middle Bronze Age*, Twelfth Annual Report of the University of London Institute of Archaeology, 20–52.

Childe, V 1929 *The Danube in Prehistory*, Oxford: Oxford University Press

Giffen, A 1930 *Die Bauart der Einzelgräber: Beitrag zur Kenntnis der ällteren individuellen Grabhügelstrukturen in den Niederlanden*, Leipzig: Mannus Bibliothek

Giffen, A 1938 'Continental bell or disc-barrows in Holland with special reference to tumulus I at Rielsche Hoefke', *Proceedings of the Prehistoric Society*, **4**, 258–271

Giffen, A 1947 *Oudheidkundige perspectieven in het bijzonder ten aanzien van de Vaderlandsch Prae- en Protohistorie. Rede uitgesproken naar aanleiding van de aanvaarding van het ambt van buitengewoon hoogleeraar aan de Universiteit van Amsterdam op maandag 3 februari 1947*, Groningen.

Glasbergen, W 1954 *Barrow excavations in the Eight Beatitudes: The Bronze Age cemetery between Toterfout and Halve Mijl, North Brabant*, Groningen/Djakarta: Wolters

Glasbergen, W 1957 *De urn van Toterfout en de reformatie van de Britse bronstijd*, Groningen (bijdragen tot de studie van het Brabants heem 8)

Glasbergen, W 1968 *Nogmaals HVS/DKS*, Haarlem (Haarlemse voordrachten 28)

Green, S 1981 *Prehistorian: A Biography of V Gordon Childe*, Bradford-on-Avon: Moonraker Press

Haveman, E and Sheridan, J A 2005/2006 'The Exloo necklace: new light on an old find', *Palaeohistoria*, **47/48**, 101–139

Laet de, S and Glasbergen, W 1959 *De voorgeschiedenis der Lage Landen*, Groningen: Wolters

Lanting, J and Van der Plicht, J 2001/2002 'De 14C-chronology van de Nederlandse pre- en protohistorie. IV: bronstijd en vroege ijzertijd', *Palaeohistoria*, **43/44**, 117–262

Louwe Kooijmans, L, Van den Broeke, P, Fokkens, H and Van Gijn, A 2005 *The prehistory of the Netherlands*, Amsterdam: Amsterdam University Press

Smith, I 1961 'An essay towards the reformation of the British Bronze Age', *Helinium*, **1**, 97–118

Theunissen, L 1999 *Midden-Bronstijdsamenlevingen in het zuiden van de Lage Landen: Een evaluatie van het begrip 'Hilversum-cultuur'*, Leiden: University of Leiden

Trigger, B 1980 *Gordon Childe: Revolutions in archaeology*, London: Thames and Hudson

Trigger, B 1989 *A history of archeological thought*, Cambridge: Cambridge University Press

5. The Canche Estuary (Pas-de-Calais, France) from the early Bronze Age to the *emporium* of Quentovic: A traditional landing place between south-east England and the continent

Michel Philippe

The Quentovic *emporium* was founded in the Canche Estuary sometime in the 6th century AD. It was the hub of an active maritime trading world, and one of the busiest ports of the Merovingian kingdom of Neustria, and later the Carolingian Empire. It traded with other centres of the same type along the Friesian coasts, such as Dorestad at the mouth of the Rhine, and ports in the British Isles like Hamwic and Lundenwic. During the 7th century AD, it lay on the main route taken by travellers from the island of Britain to Rome, and was also one of the main customs posts for these states. A study of contemporary writings reveals that this port was the counterpart of Dorestad (Lebecq 1991); goods and travellers, moving westwards and towards central Europe, *en route* for the Atlantic and Mediterranean worlds, had to pass through Quentovic, whereas those moving eastwards had to travel via Dorestad. These two ports were thus closely linked by the Strait of Dover which acted as a sort of dividing line.

One may discern, through the earliest writings, that these ports were part of a system of sea routes, themselves connecting with river and road networks, which were the primary means of transporting goods and people (Lebecq 1994).

In prehistoric Europe also, particularly since the beginning of the Bronze Age and the rapid growth of metal circulation, exchange relations involved cultural contacts (Clark 2004a). These exchange relations imply that there were regular landing places to which port facilities were attached, which should probably be imagined as natural beaching points. They were no doubt well-known to navigators and linked to each other through routes that were carefully memorised by sailors.

In societies that had no form of writing, the current state of archaeology does not yet permit a precise study of the historical geography of the traditional maritime routes around the Strait of Dover. Despite this limitation, imposed by the lack of documentation, it seems possible, as an initial approach, to look at the numerous pieces of evidence recovered from the estuary of the River Canche and to identify it as a strategic hub for one of these routes, a traditional-landing place for people and cargoes. Its foundation dates back at least to the prehistoric navigators of the Bronze Age.

The aim of this text is to present the data on the basis of which I can advance this suggestion, and to explore a few hypotheses that could explain why this estuary was involved in cross-Channel contact for such a long time. Space does not allow an exhaustive review of all sites and evidence from the estuary; I will simply present the sites that provide evidence

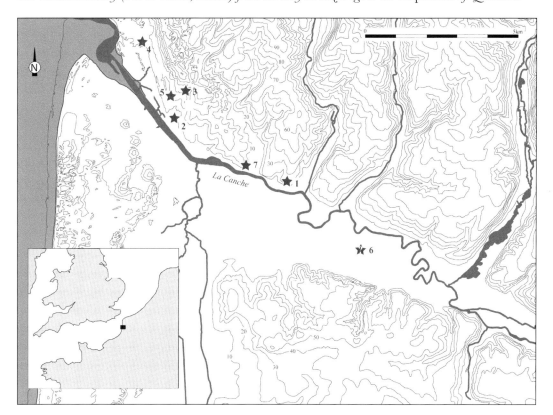

Figure 5.1 Location of the sites mentioned in the text: 1 – Étaples, 'Mont-Bagarre'; 2 – Étaples, 'Bel-Air'; 3 – Étaples, 'La Pièce-à-Liards'; 4 – Beach sites ; 5 – Étaples, north vicus; 6 – Quentovic (presumed location); 7 – Étaples, 'Les Sablins'

for the continuous role of trading place for the River Canche (Fig 5.1).

The early and middle Bronze Ages: the first port?

A significant complex of Bronze Age dwellings, the result of at least five hundred years of continuous occupation starting from the beginning of the early Bronze Age, was revealed during construction of a motorway in 1992 at the hill of 'Mont-Bagarre' near Étaples (Desfossés 2000a).

The first inhabitants settled here between the twentieth and eighteenth centuries BC on a promontory overlooking the river, slightly upstream of the river mouth. A very large oval enclosure was constructed, (Fig 5.2), its ditch over one hundred metres in diameter, but less than one and a half metres deep. It had three points of exit/entry, and its ditch was lined with an internal bank made from upcast spoil. Its role marking a territorial boundary is evident, however. It seems to affirm the possession of the territory by the group that inhabited it. Perhaps it was also used as a sheepfold? Did it have some sort of ritual status? At any event,

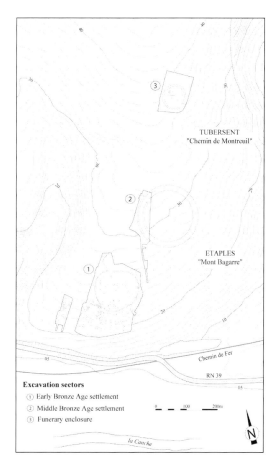

TUBERSENT
"Chemin de Montreuil"

ETAPLES
"Mont Bagarre"

Excavation sectors
① Early Bronze Age settlement
② Middle Bronze Age settlement
③ Funerary enclosure

Figure 5.2 Étaples 'Mont-Bagarre'; site plan showing the areas of excavation and distribution of features (after Desfossés 2000a, modified)

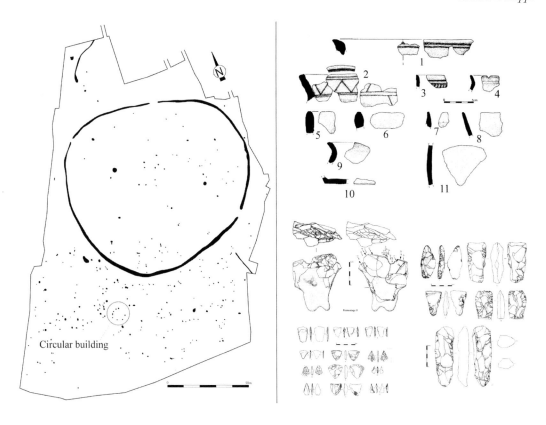

Circular building

it did not appear to play a defensive role as its associated settlement lay outside it, as can be deduced from the post-holes, ditches and granaries to the south and south-west of the enclosure ditch and bank.

Among the excavated structures there was a group of post-holes that may be identified as at least one building, a circular structure reminiscent of the British building tradition. Despite their generally poor condition, certain pottery sherds show many similarities with contemporary British pots of the 'Collared urns – Primary Series' and the complex of 'Food Vessels' (Desfossés 2000a, 39–40), for example Fig 5.3 No. 2, with a simple cord decoration impressed along the edge of the rim.

These characteristics appear to be in a more overtly British tradition than that of nearby sites, which often display mixed influences, as at Fréthun 'Les Rietz', excavated during the Eurotunnel construction (Bostyn *et al* 1990). This triple funerary enclosure produced an urn decorated with chevrons made by using impressed cord on the upper part – the British influence – though it's S-shaped profile is very different to that of English vessels, as are its

four arched handles, typical of continental influence.

Due to soil truncation and later disturbances, we know little of quotidian life in the Étaples 'Mont-Bagarre' village; the abundant assemblage of lithic tools attest to the important role of this resource, whilst an (unpublished) piece of bronze casting waste provides evidence for metallurgy and the discovery of three loom weights for weaving.

A few hundred years later, on the cusp of the early and middle Bronze Ages, between the nineteenth and sixteenth centuries BC, this first site was abandoned. The population moved higher up the hill, where a new and perfectly circular ditch was dug. The new enclosure, measuring a hundred thirty metres in diameter, was much more pronounced in size than its predecessor. Its ditch was three and a half metres wide on average, and its depth often exceeded two metres. Here again, upcast from the ditch was used to create an embankment on the inside edge of the ditch.

This new accommodation experienced a phase of expansion between the 17th and 15th centuries BC. This time, rather than moving away, the occupants preferred to dig

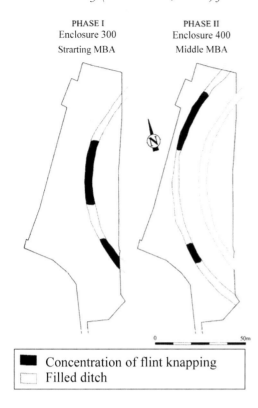

PHASE I
Enclosure 300
Strarting MBA

PHASE II
Enclosure 400
Middle MBA

■ Concentration of flint knapping
☐ Filled ditch

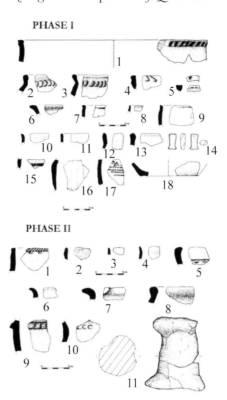

PHASE I

PHASE II

Figure 5.4a Étaples 'Mont-Bagarre'; plan showing the development of the northern (middle Bronze Age) enclosure. The original enclosure ditch (Phase I; Enclosure 300) was infilled and a larger, concentric ditch constructed (Phase II; Enclosure 400) Figure 5.4b Ceramic material associated with the two phases of the northern (middle Bronze Age) enclosure (after Desfossés 2000a, modified)

another ditch around the previous one, which was then infilled. The new enclosure reached a diameter of a hundred sixty metres, and was somewhat wider than its predecessor (4m). After this expansion, occupation of the interior continued and covered the area previously occupied by the first ditch.

Here again, the pottery reveals British traditions; the finger-tip impressions cordons (for example, Fig 5.4 Phase I, Nos 2–4; Phase II, No. 9) lie alongside examples with cord impressed decorations, reminiscent of the Deverel Rimbury culture (Desfossés 2004a, 39–40).

The position of these two concentric enclosures at the edge of the excavation area meant that it was not possible to observe more than 10 per cent of their internal area (nearly 17,000 m² for the second enclosure). It is thus difficult to determine precisely the nature of occupation. Several factors however allow us to assume a domestic function for the settlement; the diversity of ceramic forms, the abundance and composition of the flint tool assemblage, indicators of craft industry (a briquetage pillar used for salt production; a perforated stone weight from a balance) and of domestic construction (cob).

A huge ring ditch with an unbroken diameter of sixty metres was associated with one of the later two villages, lying some 300m to the north. Numerous indications, including an absence of the recutting of the ditch and the quantity and composition of material discovered, indicates that this was a funerary enclosure, surrounding a now completely levelled mound.

So, during the early and middle Bronze Ages, the Estuary of River Canche was occupied by a large settlement, dominated by a monumental enclosure. Material left by its occupants indicates a close relationship with the British Isles. What type of relationship was this? Is the similarity between the pottery from Étaples and the English material due to the passage of pots, potters or style? The site was too badly eroded to provide an answer to this question, although an analysis of the clay from which the sherds were made, which remains to be performed, might provide more clues.

At any event, and whether or not the occupants were colonists who had arrived from Great Britain (which is the interpretation preferred by Yves Desfossés; 2004b), this settlement suggests that the Canche estuary almost certainly played a major strategic role in the routes across the Channel around the

Figure 5.5 The Boulonnais and its hinterland (map by Brigitte Van Vliet-Lanoë)

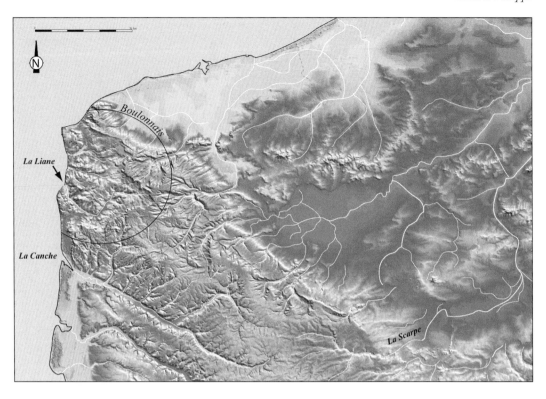

Strait in the context of a busy trade between the coastal settlements of the Continent and the British Isles. The exchanges, which involved most of the Channel Coasts and the North Sea, are revealed in a number of ways (Bourgeois and Talon 2005), including architectural similarities in funerary enclosures and dwellings, similarity of pottery styles and decoration and finds from the sea floor (whether they be from shipwrecks or deliberately deposited; Samson 2006). The British boats from this period, and particularly the Dover boat (Clark 2004b), constitute magnificent evidence of the type of vessel used.

This leads us to the geographic factors which, above any other consideration, no doubt governed the choice of this estuary. The architectural design of these fluvio-maritime boats is adapted to the particular environment of the coastal and riverine context of Northern Europe, where the relations between coastal maritime space and river space are often considered in terms of complementarity and of continuity *via* a full lagoon estuary at the mouth of many rivers (Pomey and Rieth, 2005). Moreover, it is probable that the first occupants who selected the site as their usual landing-place had analysed the course and navigability

of the waterway as a means of exploring the interior. This constituted a natural way through the dense primal forest (although it had thinned considerably since the start of the Neolithic), as well as a practical transport solution for equipment and goods.

Let us look at the topography of the continental part of the Strait and the first portion of the Atlantic seaway on the basis of this supposition (Fig 5.5).

The area closest to the English coast is the 'Boulonnais'. It consists of an eroded anticline caused by the forces of Alpine compression, whose Mesozoic chalk covering was eroded after its uplift (Van Vliet-Lanoë *et al* 1998). The inlier is edged to the south and east by a chalky *cuesta* which is nearly hundred metres higher than the enclosed hills of clay. This unusual relief restricts the flow of water, which is enclosed in the inlier, thus creating a basin isolated from other local valleys by a steep slope.

The River Liane, which is the first navigable river to offer itself to navigators moving through the Strait towards the Atlantic, is not a good route for penetrating the hinterland because it is very short, for the reasons described above. Trying to move inland by boat along this route would involve a complicated portage.

That is not the case with the River Canche, which would have been the second estuary encountered by navigators, and which gave access to a waterway deep enough to be navigable. This river allows penetration of the interior for a distance of more than 80km, where it reaches the junction with the river basins of the Scarpe and the Escaut.

No doubt this geographical factor, perfectly conformed to the required criteria, contributed to the choice of site.

In any case, it should be noted that other settlements showing a similar tradition have been found along this river route. There is the necropolis of Fresnes lès Montauban (Desfossés and Masson 2000) which shows at the end of the early Bronze Age the emergence of finger-tip decoration and the presence of a pottery vessel of a very similar shape to that of the British 'bucket urns'. The ceramics of the nearby middle Bronze Age site of Rœux (Desfossés *et al* 2000) have even more markedly similar characteristics, due to the presence of large cylindrical vases, the preponderance of finger-tip decoration and the existence of cylindrical weights which are very similar to those found in the Deverel-Rimbury complex. In addition, two small oval houses were excavated that are very similar in size and arrangement of post-holes to numerous British examples.

On the other side of the relief created by the Boulonnais, on the border of the plain of Flanders, numerous finds (such as funerary enclosures and gold necklaces), suggests the existence of a similar settlement, possibly included in this system.

For this reason, Yves Desfossés has suggested that the Mont-Bagarre settlement at Étaples could have been a bridgehead destined for the colonisation of the continental hinterland (Desfossés 2000b; Desfossés and Philippe 2002). Whether this assumption is confirmed or not in the future, the evidence from Étaples shows that between the 20th and 15th centuries BC the estuary of the Canche played a role not dissimilar to that which it would take in the early Middle Ages. We cannot, of course, necessarily connect the choice of the former with the existence of the latter. We should now examine the evidence which may make it possible to suggest the

continuity of this role through the times which separate them.

From the late Bronze Age to the Roman conquest: continuity of the phenomenon?

At around 1300 BC the site of Mont-Bagarre was abandoned, a time when indications of the island traditions disappeared from the region, which was re-occupied by Continental groups from the RSFO (Rhin-Suisse-France Orientale) complex (Blanchet 1984).

The late Bronze Age settlement moved from the hill of Bagarre to the mouth of the estuary. This site, at Étaples 'Bel-Air', was discovered in the 1960s (Fig 5.1; Mariette 1970). The excavations, performed entirely by hand, only recognised the site through soundings. From what can be gleaned from the few items that were published and the resumption of fieldwork currently in progress, it would appear to have been a substantial settlement.

Its eventual abandonment was probably the result of changes in the coastline and the river courses due to geodynamic variations (Meurisse 2004; Van Vliet-Lanoë *et al* 2004).

Towards the end of the early Iron Age, domestic occupation seems to stay around the entrance of the estuary. This is indicated by the discovery of an early Iron Age cemetery at 'La Pièce à Liards', sited on a rise on the plateau that dominates the bay, which was probably used for the leaders of the community. It was revealed during the construction of a new district to the north of Étaples in 2003 (Fig 5.1; Henton 2005). A square ditch surrounded enclosed this small necropolis that contained twelve tombs, of which nine had been covered in wooden cladding (Fig 5.6). Three individuals had been buried with rich grave goods. Two of them wore necklaces that combined elements of bronze and a perishable material, possibly leather, which appear to be, in the current state of knowledge, unknown elsewhere. Another wore a bronze brooch whose parallels seem be limited to Ireland and Wales (Fig 5.7), whilst numerous amber beads recovered from the thorax indicated that they had been buried in decorated garments which suggests some contact with northern or central Europe.

The limited number of graves in the necropolis, the fact that the tombs were covered in cladding and the ornamentation

Figure 5.6 Étaples 'La-Pièce-à-Liards'; site plan showing the relationship between the original (early Iron Age) cemetery and subsequent (late Iron Age) enclosures (after Henton in preparation)

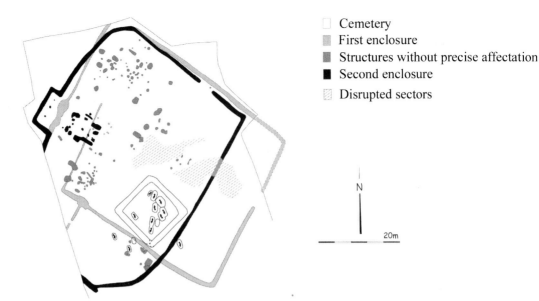

☐ Cemetery
▨ First enclosure
▨ Structures without precise affectation
■ Second enclosure
▨ Disrupted sectors

N

20m

Figure 5.7 A bronze brooch from Étaples 'La-Pièce-à-Liards' (after Henton in preparation)

accompanying the bodies are all indications of the high status of the deceased. Since this has been studied at numerous other sites, it is widely held that the ruling classes of the early Iron Age built their fortune and power on the control of trade, particularly between northern Europe and the Mediterranean area. Even though the study of this site is still in progress, we can advance the possibility that this cemetery indicates the existence of a trading post perhaps run by the deceased, which was no doubt linked to contacts across the English Channel (as suggested by the brooch).

After the cemetery ceased to be used for burial (we have no knowledge of the settlement linked to it), a large village was built at the foot of the hill in about the 4th century BC (the middle La Tène period). It was excavated on the beach of St Gabriel in the 1960s (Fig 5.1; Mariette 1972). As at the excavations at Étaples 'Bel-Air', the site was only recognised through soundings, though the quantity and extent of

material recovered suggests it was extensive. The site seems to have remained occupied until the Roman conquest.

The rise on the plateau on which the necropolis was sited ('La Pièce à Liards') was reoccupied by the inhabitants of this beach settlement on the cusp of the 2nd and 1st centuries BC (Fig 5.6). A small group of structures were surrounded by a roughly rectangular ditch, which also enclosed and respected the earlier necropolis, running along its south-western side. For a reason which escapes us, this enclosure was soon replaced by a new ditch of the same type, but slightly offset from it. This also enclosed and respected the necropolis, running along its south-eastern side. The necropolis was still visible and recognisable some 300 years after its creation, and clearly had some significance to those who built the enclosures. Perhaps the enclosures and associated structures were not typical settlements, but rather places of worship (Henton in preparation).

After the Roman conquest, the siting of regional ports underwent a fundamental change. The Liane estuary, which hitherto seems to have been sparsely occupied, became the site of the continental military port of the *Classis Britannica*. The town of Boulogne (*Bononia-Gesoriacum*), headquarters of the military administration, developed in parallel as a trading centre and became the main customs post of the Dover Strait. Paved roads connected it to Thérouanne (*Taruenna*), capital

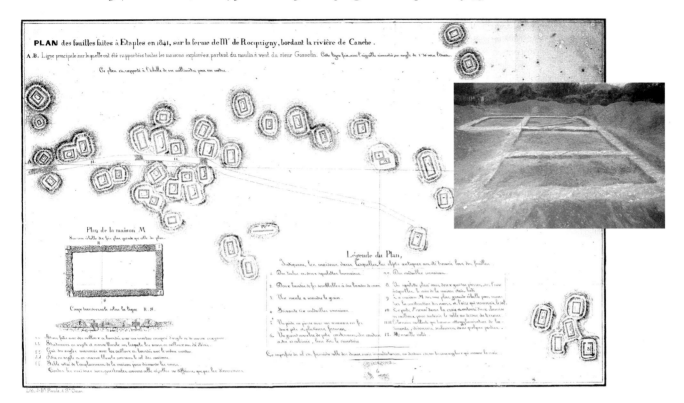

city of the *Civitas Morinorum*, and to Amiens (*Samarobriva Ambionorum*), one of the largest urban centres of the northern Empire.

The Canche estuary remained occupied during the Roman period by a dense and extensive settlement that spread along the road to Boulogne, in the same area of the earlier settlements (Philippe 2004). A large sector of it was excavated in 1841–42, but almost all the data and material then recovered has since been dispersed (Marguet 1841; Cousin 1842). After 1964, the southern part of this settlement was excavated at the time of the construction of the 'Blanc-Pavé' and 'Bergeries' districts (Couppé 1972). This possible *vicus* consisted of more than 120 buildings and adjoining structures (courtyards, streets, wells, etc.), with foundations of chalk and sandstone, and with wattle and daub walls (Fig 5.8).

The age of the most extensive excavations makes the interpretation of detail of this settlement difficult; complementary to Boulogne, it no doubt formed part of the trade networks of the Strait. We do not know the exact site of its port, which could have been a simple boat hard on the beach. Perhaps during the Later Empire, this site was supplemented by a military installation; certain elements collected at the site of the castle of Étaples at the time of the nineteenth century excavations seem to indicate the existence of buildings and a necropolis here (Souquet 1865). The distribution of military places known on the British coast in the vicinity of the Strait shows that Dover, seat of the *Classis Britannica*, was surrounded of a network of forts, separated by 20 to 30km (*Lemanis*-Lympne, in the south; *Rutuplae*-Ritchborough and *Regulbium*-Reculver in the north; Ordnance Survey 1956). It seems plausible that a similar network might exist around Boulogne, continental seat of the fleet. The estuary of Canche, about 30 km to the south of Boulogne, could, accordingly, have constituted an important strategic point.

However, the amount of material that this *vicus* has produced is considerable (Delmaire 1994). Over 15,000 Roman coins have been found, from at least ten hoards. In addition there are more than 10,000 brooches, numerous tools, evidence of fishing (anchors, needles for mending fishnets, fish-hooks) and evidence of cosmetics and jewellery. The excavations also collected an important quantity of ceramics, including several vessels of 'Black Burnished Ware', a British import (Clotuche 1998).

Let us consider a particular coin hoard, on display in Quentovic Museum. It was uncovered in 1964 when the current road to

Figure 5.8 The ancient vicus of Étaples; plan of the 1841–1842 excavations (after Cousin 1842). Inset: photograph of a large building with chalk foundations at Étaples 'Blanc-Pavé' (photo: Jean Couppé)

Boulogne was being widened (Giard 1965; Delmaire and Couppé 1988), and consists of almost 4,000 silver coins dating from the 3rd century AD, minted in Rome, Milan, Antioch and Cologne. None of the coins show signs of deterioration due to their having been in circulation. An excavation carried out following this discovery showed that this deposit was placed in the foundations of a building (Couppé 1965). Judging by its composition, it was probably payment for a large commercial transaction rather than the hoarding of official coinage by an individual. This makes it possible to suggest that even if the main commercial route across the Strait had undeniably moved to Boulogne in antiquity, trade still thrived in the Bay of the River Canche. The number of coin hoards recovered (around ten or so), reinforces this impression, especially as the routine explanation of coin hoards as a response to catastrophic events like war and invasion is no longer widely accepted, allowing alternative possibilities such as economic and commercial operations as their *raison d'être* (Delmaire 1995).

Evidence for this period is more fragmentary than for earlier times, because no domestic settlement has been the subject of modern, exhaustive excavation. If the little evidence we do have does not allow detailed interpretation, they however make it possible to posit the continuity of occupation and its peripheral technical elements in the estuary. The high social status of the people of the First Iron Age, and the remote geographical references of the ornaments with which they were associated, suggests the maintenance of an establishment dedicated to trade between British Isles and the continent. The importance of the later Roman settlement and the quantity of coin hoards found in it insufflate a concept of permanence.

The end of Roman rule: a return to the Canche

The situation would, once more, change fundamentally after the fall of the Roman Empire. With the arrival of new political masters, the economic and political basis of the region suffered a radical change. For the Germanic groups who came to dominate the Western European area, the north seas played a vital role, similar to that assigned to the Mediterranean sea by the civilisations of Antiquity.

In this context of intense commercial and diplomatic activity, the Canche Estuary regained its regional supremacy in links with Great Britain following the establishment of the *emporium* of Quentovic, discussed above. After the decline of the Roman *vicus* at Étaples, which started in the last quarter of the 3rd century AD and ended with its disappearance in the early 4th century, the *emporium* was installed further upstream on the left bank of the river.

The re-establishment of the Canche Estuary as the major regional port for maritime trade, at the end of what was merely an interregnum of a few hundred years, seems to point another important factor that would also explain the role played by this area throughout history. It is that of shipbuilding.

The port of Boulogne seems to have been an *ex-nihilo* creation, preceded by no other known settlement. What was the important event that permitted – or caused – the choice of this site, in view of the fact that it was restricted to the period of Roman occupation? Numerous criteria probably played a role, such as the ability to build paved roads, which in part facilitated movement away from the *cuesta*-bound coast and out of the Boulonnais. At the same time, as the dominance of Boulogne was limited to the Roman period, we must surely consider the introduction of ships from the Mediterranean tradition (one trireme at least is attested in Boulogne by an *ex-voto*), which were unsuited to the lagoon-like estuaries of the region or for beaching. The Liane estuary, which cuts through more solid geology than the chalky soil of Artois, would make it much easier to build a port with quays.

This is probably not the only reason for the change of site. From what we understand, the vessels of the Roman tradition were more seaworthy than those of the local inhabitants (Pomey and Rieth 2005); their keels enabled them to brave stronger winds and sail in more extreme weather. Whether before or after the Empire, local ships, adapted to inland waterways and lagoons, were by nature of their system of propulsion and steering less manœuvrable and capable at most of using a cross-wind. They were thus much more at the mercy of the vagaries of current and wind.

The English Channel at the Strait of Dover

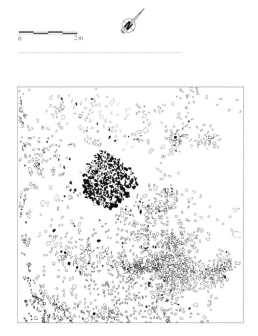

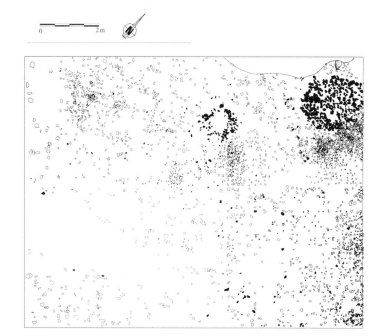

is a shallow corridor, through which huge masses of water and sediments are transported, just like an estuarine river. The speed of the current increases as the gap narrows, creating a significant flow which, dependant on the time of day, pulls either towards the Channel or the North Sea. The currents at high tide (flowing towards the North Sea) are stronger than at low tide (flowing in the opposite direction). Thus a ship sailing from the Canche Estuary at high tide would be carried towards the Hampshire or Kent coasts for up to six hours. If leaving from the Thames Estuary at low tide, it would borne towards the Friesian or northern French coasts; however, if a ship sailed at high tide from Cap Gris-nez or its immediate surroundings, it would tend to be taken northwards, out on to the high sea.

For this reason, it would appear that the Canche Estuary was highly suited to take advantage of the currents in the Strait, in addition to providing a suitable environment for beaching such vessels, as noted for the ships of the later Middle Ages by Michel Rouche (1977). Using their knowledge of the currents, sailors of all periods seem to have found just the right balance between the constraints created by topography and level of contemporary seamanship at the mouth of the River Canche.

A Neolithic foundation?

At what moment and by whom was this choice first made? In the current state of knowledge, it can be attributed at least to the early Bronze Age. Yet the existence in the estuary of dense Neolithic occupation may suggest an earlier date.

This Neolithic settlement of Étaples, 'Les Sablins', appears to have covered a total area of about 45 hectares. It no doubt consisted of a village with peripheral industrial areas which are evidenced by numerous flint knapping spots and hearths (Fig 5.9), as well as a dense concentration of stakes-holes discovered in 2006 that are still quite a puzzle.

The largest part of the site had only just been identified when the land was allocated for industrial development in 1970, though an area where the occupation deposits were in an excellent state of preservation, including a well preserved paleosol, was protected as an archaeological 'reservation'. Numerous excavations have been conducted since (Hurtrelle and Piningre 1976; 1979; Piningre *et al* 1991; Philippe *et al* 2006).

The first occupants were probably drawn to this place by its exceptional situation; near fertile land on a headland at the edge of sea. It was, moreover, located near a source of flint of a rare quality in the area. There were three phases of occupation. The lowest

Figure 5.9 Étaples 'Les Sablins'; site plans showing the distribution of Neolithic burnt stone (white) and knapped flint (black) (after Hurtrelle and Piningre 1976)

has been dated to around 4700 cal BC by radiocarbon dating, and belongs to the Cerny culture (Néolithique moyen I); the intermediate phase last year produced a sherd of Chasséo-Michelsberg pottery (Néolithique moyen II), whilst the upper phase produced bell-shaped pottery sherds (attributable to the Néolithique final).

If the challenge of the current excavations consists mainly in characterising the type of occupation of each phase, the general issue surrounding the estuary, as I have described it, is not absent from our preoccupations. Many criteria show us that since the beginning of the 4th millennium BC, the sea has not constituted an obstacle to relations, even over long distances (Cunliffe 2002). I am thinking particularly of the spread of stones axes from the Alps to Scotland and Ireland (Pétrequin *et al* 2005), or of the spread of megalithic architecture which has shown that there were direct connections between the coasts of Portugal, Brittany and Ireland, evidence which is again reinforced by the distribution of the first Beaker (Campaniforme) pottery (Salanova 2000).

It is thus possible to imagine that the Neolithic inhabitants of the Canche estuary were in contact with their contemporaries in south-east England, especially since the Dover boat has shown, through the technological advancement of its construction, that the tradition of boat-building extends far back in time, even if we do not know the type of vessel then used.

Conclusion

The possibility of a cross-Channel port in the Canche Estuary during the Neolithic must remain speculation until more concrete evidence emerges from the excavations at 'Les Sablins', where we have been working for only a short time. For now, it is the seamen of the early Bronze Age – the contemporaries of the Dover boat – are those who must be credited with opening up a sea route that seems to have remained active for more than 3,000 years.

Whoever these pioneers were, this very special estuary deserves the description of a 'hub' of the maritime route across the Strait, even though much remains to be done to fill in the outlines presented here.

We have surveyed the various factors that may be behind this; the physical geography of the coast and its hinterland, the architecture of the sea vessels employed, and the relationship with the marine currents and prevailing winds around the Strait. These various combined factors seem to me to have created the right conditions for the first inhabitants to have considered the local geography of the Canche in their search for a permanent base for maritime connections across the Strait and this is what ultimately dictated their choice.

Acknowledgement

Thank you to Peter Clark for his kind help in the translation of this paper.

List of references

Blanchet, J 1984 *Les premiers métallurgistes en Picardie et dans le Nord de la France*, Mémoires de la *Société préhistorique française*, **17**, Paris

Bostyn, F, Blancquaert, G and Lanchon, Y 1990 'L'enclos triple de Fréthun «Les Rietz»', *Cahiers de Préhistoire du Nord*, **8**, 37–46

Bourgeois, J and Talon, M (eds) 2005 *L'âge du Bronze du Nord la France dans son contexte Européen: Hommage à Jacques Briard*, Actes du 125e Congrès National des Sociétés Historiques et Scientifiques, section pré- et protohistoire, archéologie, Lille, 2000

Clark, P (ed) 2004a *The Dover Bronze age boat in context – Society and water transport in prehistoric Europe*, Oxford: Oxbow Books

Clark, P (ed) 2004b *The Dover Bronze Age boat*, with illustrations by Caroline Caldwell, London: English Heritage

Clotuche, R 1998 *Étaples: «La Garennière» Rapport préliminaire de fouille de sauvetage urgent, 1997*, Association pour les Fouilles Archéologiques Nationales and the Service Régional d'Archéologie Nord-Pas-de-Calais

Couppé, J 1965 *Rapport d'intervention sur le bâtiment ayant livré le trésor: Rapport de fouilles archéologiques*, Étaples: Société Quentovic

Couppé, J 1972 'Le Gallo-romain à Étaples', *Quentovic*, **11**, *Collections du musée d'Étaples et notes historiques*, 16–24

Cousin, L 1842 'Rapport sur les fouilles archéologiques faites par le Comité de Boulogne à Étaples en 1842', *Bulletin de la Société des Antiquaires de la Morinie*, **6**, 1841–1843, 47–64

Cunliffe, B 2002 'People of the sea', *British Archaeology*, **63**, 12–17

Delmaire, R (ed) 1994 *Le Pas-de-Calais*, Carte archéologique de la Gaule, Pré-inventaire archéologique, Académie des Inscriptions et des Belles-Lettres, Association pour les Fouilles Archéologiques Nationales, Maison des Sciences de l'Homme, Paris

Delmaire, R 1995 'Les enfouissements monétaires, témoignages d'insécurité?', *Revue du Nord-Archéologie*, **77** (313), 21–26

Delmaire, R and Couppé, J 1988 'Un lot du trésor trouvé à Étaples en 1964', *Trésors Monétaires*, **10**, 55–57

Desfossés, Y (ed) 2000a *Archéologie Préventive en Vallée de Canche: Les sites protohistoriques fouilles dans le cadre de la réalisation de l'autoroute A16*, Nord-Ouest Archéologie, **11**, Berck-sur-Mer: Centre de Recherches Archéologiques et de Diffusion Culturelle

Desfossés, Y 2000b 'L'apport des sites d'Etaples-Tubersent et de La Calotterie' in Y Desfossés (ed), *Archéologie Préventive en Vallée de Canche: Les sites protohistoriques fouilles dans le cadre de la réalisation de l'autoroute A16*, Nord-Ouest Archéologie, **11**, Berck-sur-Mer: Centre de Recherches Archéologiques et de Diffusion Culturelle, 185–187

Desfossés, Y and Masson, B 2000 'Les enclos funéraires du «Motel» à Fresnes-Lès-Montauban (Pas-de-Calais)', in J-C Blanchet (ed), *Habitats et nécropoles de l'Age du Bronze sur le Transmanche et le TGV Nord, Bulletin de la Société préhistorique française* (Etudes et Travaux), **89** (10–12), Travaux 1, 303–342

Desfossés, Y and Philippe, M 2002 'Angleterre et France à l'Age du Bronze – Les Contacts Transmanche', *Archéologia*, **391**, 46–57

Desfossés, Y, Martial, E and Vallin, L 2000 'Le site d'habitat du Bronze moyen du « Château d'Eau» à Roeux (Pas-de-Calais)', in J-C Blanchet (ed), *Habitats et nécropoles de l'Age du Bronze sur le Transmanche et le TGV Nord, Bulletin de la Société préhistorique française* (Etudes et Travaux), **89** (10–12), Travaux 1, 344–391

Dilly, G 1988 'Découvertes côtières et marines sur la Côte d'Opale', *Nord-Ouest Archéologie*, **1**, 25–32

Gallois, J and Couppé, J 1977 'Découvertes gallo-romaines au nord et à l'est d'Étaples', *Bulletin de la Commission Départementale des Monuments Historiques du Pas-de-Calais*, **10** (2), 65–72

Geoffroy, J-F 1994a 'Étaples: Fouille d'un quartier d'habitat rural secondaire', *Revue du Nord-Archéologie*, **76** (308), 147–153

Giard, J-B 1965 'Le trésor d'Étaples', *Revue Numismatique*, (6ᵉ série), **7**, 206–224

Henton, A 2005 'Étaples – «La Pièce à Liards»', *Bilan Scientifique Régional Nord-Pas-de-Calais 1994*, Ministère de la Culture et de la Communication, 145–148

Henton, in preparation *Étaples – «La Pièce à Liards»: Rapport de fouilles*, Institut National de Recherches Archéologiques Preventives

Hurtrelle, J and Piningre, J 1976 'Le site néolithique des Sablins à Étaples (Pas-de-Calais): premiers résultats', *Septentrion*, **6**, 46–57

Hurtrelle, J and Piningre, J 1979 'Les ateliers de taille du silex à Étaples', *Archéologia*, **137**, 36–40

Lebecq, S 1991 'Pour une histoire parallèle de Quentovic et de Dorestad', in J-M Duvosquel and A Dierkens (eds), *Villes et campagnes dans l'Occident medieval: Mélanges Georges Despy*, Bruxelles-Liège, 415–428

Lebecq, S 1994 'Entre Manche et mer du Nord, entre Grande-Bretagne et continent, les relations à travers le détroit dans les premiers siècles médiévaux', in S Curveiller and A Lottin (eds), *Les champs relationnels en Europe du Nord et du Nord-ouest des origines à la fin du Premier Empire*, Calais: La Municipalité de Calais, 29–43

Marguet, H 1841 'Rapport sur les fouilles faites en 1841 à Étaples, lu à la séance publique du 20 décembre 1841', *Bulletin de la Société des Antiquaires de la Morinie*, **6**, 1841–1843, 191–215

Mariette, H 1970 'Préhistoire de la Côte d'Opale, du mésolithique à la conquête romaine', *Septentrion*, **5–6**, 90–96

Mariette, H 1972 'Un site protohistorique de production du sel à Étaples (Pas-de-Calais)', *Congrès Préhistorique de France, XIXè session, Auvergne, 1969*, Paris: Centre National de la Recherche Scientifique, 284–292

Meurisse, M 2004 'Evolution du littoral Picard durant l'Holocène', *Sucellus*, **55**, 17–31

Munaut, A 1989 'Analyse palynologique de structures datant des IIIe et IVe s.s, observées à Étaples «Blanc-Pavé» (Pas-de-Calais)', in I Sidera (ed), *Une agglomération secondaire romaine en secteur rural: Rapport de fouilles archéologiques*, Association pour les Fouilles Archéologiques Nationales and the Service Régional d'Archéologie Nord-Pas-de-Calais, annexe 1

Ordnance Survey 1956 *Map of Roman Britain*, 3rd edition, Chessington: Ordnance Survey

Petrequin, P, Errera, M, Cassen, S, Billand, G, Colas, C, Marechal, D, Prodeo, F and Vangele, F 2005 'Des Alpes italiennes à l'Atlantique au Ve millénaire – Les quatre grandes haches polies de Vendeuil et Maizy (Aisne), Brenouille (Oise)', in G Auxiette and F Malrain (eds), *Hommages à Claudine Pommepuy*, Revue Archéologique de Picardie, numéro special, **22**, 75–104

Philippe, M 2004 'L'occupation du territoire d'Étaples (Pas-de-Calais) durant l'Antiquité gallo-romaine – un état des connaissances après deux siècles de fouilles et de trouvailles', *Sucellus*, **55**, 32–50

Philippe, M, Meurisse, M, March, R and Rassart, V 2006 *Fouilles archéologiques et études morphosédimentaires du site d'Étaples, 'Les Sablins' (Pas-de-Calais): Rapport de fouille, janvier 2006*, Service Régional de L'archéologie Nord-Pas-de-Calais

Piningre, J, Bostyn, F, Couppe, J, Constantin, C and Delibrias, G 1991 'L'atelier de taille du silex des Sablins à Étaples (Pas-de-Calais)', *Gallia Préhistoire*, **33**, 83–135

Pomey, P and Rieth, E 2005 *L'Archéologie navale*, Paris: Éditions Errance

Rouche, M 1977 'Les Saxons et les origines de Quentovic', *Revue du Nord – Archéologie*, **235**, 457–478

Salanova, L 2000 *La Question du Campaniforme en France et en les Ile Anglo-Normandes: Production, Chronologie et Rôles d'un Standard Céramique*, Paris: *Société préhistorique française*/ Comité des Travaux Historiques et Scientifiques

Samson, A 2006 'Offshore finds from the Bronze Age in North-Western Europe: The Shipwreck Scenario revisited', *Oxford Journal of Archaeology*, **25(4)**, 371–388

Souquet, G 1865 'Rapport sur des fouilles faites au château d'Étaples en 1864', *Bulletin de la Comité des Antiquités Départementales du Pas-du-Calais*, **2**, 270–274

Van Vliet-Lanoë, B, Gandouin, E and Meurisse, M 2004 'Evolution des niveaux marins quaternaires dans le nord de la France: données nouvelles et mise au point', *Sucellus*, **55**, 1–16

Van Vliet-Lanoë, B, Mansy, J, Margerel, J, Vidier, J, Lamarche, J and Everaest, M 1998 'Le Pas-de-Calais, un détroit cénozoïque à ouvertures multiples', *Comptes Rendus de l'Académie des Sciences, Série 2, Sciences de la terre et des planètes*, **326**, (10), Paris, 729–736

6. Looking forward: maritime contacts in the first millennium BC

Barry Cunliffe

It is abundantly clear, from even a cursory survey of the prehistoric material culture found in coastal regions of Britain and the adjacent Continent, that the sea provided a ready means of communication and that people, sharing knowledge, beliefs and material culture, made extensive use of the relative ease of mobility which the water provided. By the end of the second millennium BC substantial plank-built vessels were being constructed as the dramatic discoveries in the Humber estuary and at Dover bear witness (Wright 1900; van de Noort *et al* 1999; Clark 2004) and it is clear from shipwreck sites at Dover and Salcombe (Muckelroy 1981) that cargoes of scrap bronze were being transported across the Channel. Indeed the many artefacts of Continental type or inspiration, found in Britain throughout the Late Bronze Age and Early Iron Age (O'Connor 1980; Cunliffe 2005, 446–84), leave little doubt that networks of maritime exchange were in lively use. By the Late Iron Age these networks had come into much sharper focus as foreign items of exchange, such as Gallo-Belgic coins, Armorican pottery, north Italian wine-drinking equipment and Mediterranean-produced wine amphorae, were transported from the Continent and fed into the local British networks (Cunliffe 1982; 2005; Cunliffe and de Jersey 1998). By this time it is possible to identify some of the British ports through which these exchanges were articulated – places such as Mount Batten (Cunliffe 1988), Portland (Taylor 2001), Poole Harbour (Markey *et al* 2002) and Hengistbury (Cunliffe 1987) and others may be suspected,

for example a port somewhere in the estuary of the river Arun (Cunliffe and de Jersey 1998, 106). The evidence is such that there can be little doubt that the seaways around the coasts of Britain were alive with traffic.

Taking a very broad perspective we can offer the generalisation that Britain engaged in two major European systems – an Atlantic System and a Continental System (Fig 6.1) which, over the last five millennia, have contributed to the very different cultural characteristics displayed by east-facing and west-facing Britain. We have considered elsewhere the Atlantic System in its

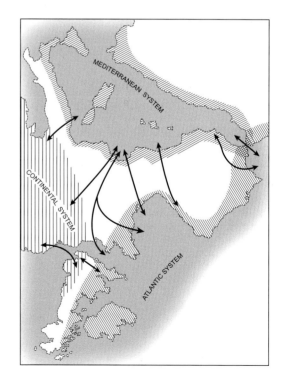

Figure 6.1 The maritime systems of western Europe

longue durée (Cunliffe 2001a). Nothing more will be said of it in this paper where the emphasis will be on the Continental System within the restricted time frame from the middle of the second to the end of the first millennia BC. To propose two systems is, of course, something of an oversimplification particularly since the English Channel spans both and is, in itself, a subsystem. For our purposes, therefore, we will consider the southern North Sea and the eastern Channel together as our principal zone of focus.

Maritime capability in the first millennium

There is little direct archaeological evidence of maritime technology in the region in the first millennium BC, with the exception of the iron anchor and anchor chain found at Bulbury in Dorset (Cunliffe 1972), but classical texts give some insight into the two styles of vessel in use. Plank-built boats of the first century BC are vividly described in a famous passage by Julius Caesar in his account of the Venetic fleet which he encountered (and destroyed) in the Bay of Morbihan. The vessels were solidly built and high sided with square rigged sails of raw hide – vessels capable of withstanding the rigours of the Atlantic (*BG* III, 13). Schematic representations of such vessels are found on coins of Cunobelin (Cunliffe 2001a, fig 3.6) suggesting that the type was widespread and indeed the famous Roman-period wrecks from St Peter Port, Guernsey (Rule and Monaghan 1993) and Blackfriars in London (Marsden 1994) were constructed in the same tradition – a tradition generally referred to as Romano-Celtic. These sturdy vessels presumably evolved locally in Atlantic/North Sea waters from the assured plank-boat technology manifest in the Ferriby and Dover boats. We can only hope that future discoveries will bring to light tangible evidence to help us trace the intermediate stages in the development.

The second tradition – the skin boat – probably long pre-dated the development of the plank boat. Plank boats needed efficient bronze axes and adzes for their construction, while skin boats, composed only of hides and bent small-wood, relied on simpler technologies in place already in Mesolithic times. The earliest evidence we have of skin boats in British waters dates to the late fourth or early third century BC. It survives in the work of the first century AD writer, Pliny the Elder, who mentions the Britons' use of 'boats of wicker covered with sewn hides' (*Nat. Hist.* 4.104). Pliny credits his source as Timaeus of Tauromenium (*c* 356–270 BC) – a compiler who relied heavily on the writings of the Massilliot traveller, Pytheas. Pytheas circumnavigated Britain about 320 BC and may well have observed skin boats in action off the Cornish peninsula (Cunliffe 2001b, 74–7). Julius Caesar had also noted boats of this kind when he was in Britain in 55 and 54 BC. Some years later, campaigning in Spain, he ordered similar vessels to be built. 'The keels and ribs were made of light wood; the rest of the hulk was made of woven withies covered with hides' (*Bello Civili* 1.54). The appearance of such craft is suggested by the famous gold model found at Broighter in Co. Derry, Ireland dating to the first century BC. It represents a large vessel with seating for seven rowers and was provided with a square cross rigged sail and a steering oar. Clearly these were quite substantial vessels.

The evidence, disparate though it is, is sufficient to suggest that the seaways around Britain were busy with sea-going vessels, built either of planks or of hides, robust enough to be capable of carrying men and cargoes across the open water on a sustained basis. The sail, first evident in the first century BC, would have greatly facilitated these voyages. When the sail was first introduced into the region is impossible yet to say but one possibility is that it was the expansion of Phoenician influence into the Atlantic coastal waters of North Africa and Iberia in the eighth century BC that first demonstrated to indigenous boat builders the benefits of the fixed mast.

The seas of Belgica and Armorica

This, somewhat anachronistic, subtitle conveniently describes the geographical region which concerns us in this paper embracing as it does the English Channel and the southern North Sea from the longitude of Ushant and Land's End to the latitude of the Humber and the Frisian Islands. The phrase in fact comes from the command given to the Menapian sailor, Carausius, in AD 285 who was charged to 'rid the seas of Belgica and Armorica' of the Frankish and Saxon pirates then disrupting

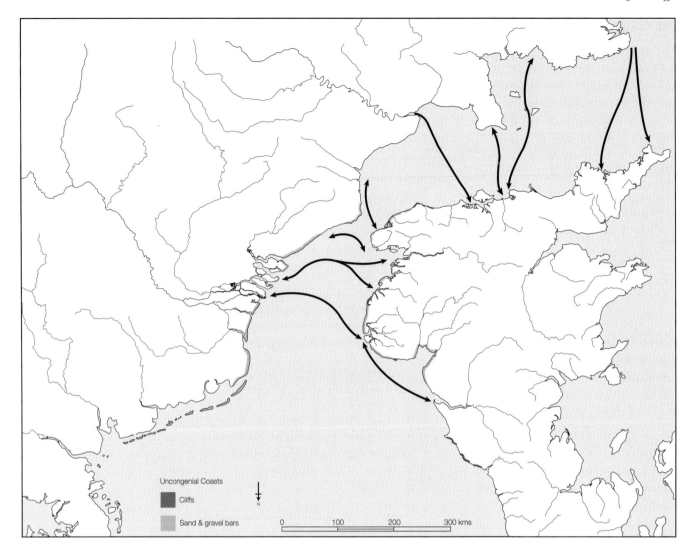

Figure 6.2 The major sea routes linking southern Britain to the Continent emphasising the constraints of coastlines in the North Sea. Coastlines have been adjusted to reflect the situation in the mid-first millennium BC

the maritime networks linking the province of Britannia to the Continent. His broadly defined theatre of operations was evidently regarded as a cohesive geographical continuum.

This is not the place to discuss in detail the complexities of navigation across this stretch of water conditioned by variations in tides, currents and wind patterns. Suffice it to say that the potential crossings are many and well within the navigational capabilities of seafarers at the time. The situation in the Channel has been analysed in useful detail by McGrail (1983). The southern North Sea has received less specialist attention but the map (Fig 6.2) gives some idea of the most likely routes to have been used. The map has been adjusted to account for changes in coastal topography and attempts to give a picture of the coastline in the mid-first millennium BC. A point that needs

to be stressed is that much of the Continental coast would have been relatively uncongenial to shipping at the time in that it was fringed by extensive coastal dunes backed by expanses of marsh and peat bog. Only the great estuaries of the Rhine, Maas and Schelde would have provided the havens and protected landfalls sought by seafarers. The British coast, too, was fringed by coastal barriers but the Thames, the Essex rivers and the now largely silted great estuary of the Yare/Waveney on the Norfolk coast offered congenial points of entry.

The easiest maritime routes tend to focus on the narrowing, southern part of the North Sea, and, as the archaeological evidence shows, it was here that the networks of contact were at their most intense. We should not, however, overlook the possibility of much longer, open sea, crossings further to the north using the method of latitude sailing that was so effective in Viking and later times.

In addition to open sea sailing out of sight of land, there would also have been much coastal movement, relying on techniques of pilotage rather than navigation. Cabotage voyages of this kind provided a faster and much safer way to transport goods from one part of Britain to another compared with overland routes. We will return to this theme again below (p. 88–91).

The situation in the Middle and Late Bronze Age

It has long been recognised that active networks of contact were maintained between Britain and the Continent in the late second and early first millennia BC – a contact manifest in the transport of bronze implements (O'Connor 1980; Muckelroy 1981). A previous generation of scholars led principally by J J Butler (1963) had argued for population movements between the Low Countries and the south-east of Britain to account for similarities in ceramic development between the Hilversum-Drakenstein tradition of the Continent and the Deverel-Rimbury tradition of Britain, but in the anti-invasionist mood of the 1960s and 70s interpretations involving large-scale population mobility were generally rejected in favour of contact for purposes of trade.

More recently a number of large-scale excavations in the coastal zone of north-western France have presented an abundance of new settlement evidence which shows that the settlements of this region share many of the characteristics of the Deverel-Rimbury and post-Deverel-Rimbury settlements of south-eastern England. Settlements such as L'île Tatihou (Manche), dating to the second half of the second millennium, with its farmstead set between small square 'Celtic fields' have produced an assemblage of pottery closely similar to that of contemporary Deverel-Rimbury settlements on the opposite coasts of Dorset and Hampshire (Marcigny and Ghesquière 2003). Even more impressive is the Late Bronze Age village covering some 4.5 ha at Malleville-sur-le-bec (Eure) comprising a number of circular houses occupying a hill slope between a circular ring fort and a barrow cemetery. The ring fort matches in plan and construction the ring forts of south-eastern

Britain (summarised with references in Cunliffe 2005, 39–42). The pottery recovered from the settlement can be directly compared to the post-Deverel-Rimbury tradition of southern Britain (Marcigny *et al* 2005, 52–3, 57). These are just two examples chosen from a growing corpus of settlements, many of them with roundhouses indistinguishable from the British tradition of roundhouse building. So similar is the culture on both sides of the Channel that Cyril Marcigny has chosen to refer to it as *composante culturelle Manche-Mer-du-Nord* (Fig 6.3; Marcigny *et al* 2002).

The new settlement evidence from the coastal regions of northern France provides a much fuller cultural context against which to understand the trans-shipment of bronzes. The totality of the evidence now available leaves little doubt that cultural contact between the two facing shore lines and their hinterlands must have been intense and sustained far beyond the level of simple 'trade'. The exchange of bronzes is best seen as one of the more archaeologically-visible manifestations in a system of complex social interactions which bound the communities of the facing territories tightly together allowing the exchange of beliefs and values as well as technologies and artefacts. Within these networks of mobility

Figure 6.3 The maritime culture of the Channel/southern North Sea zone in the late second millennium BC. After Marcigny et al 2002

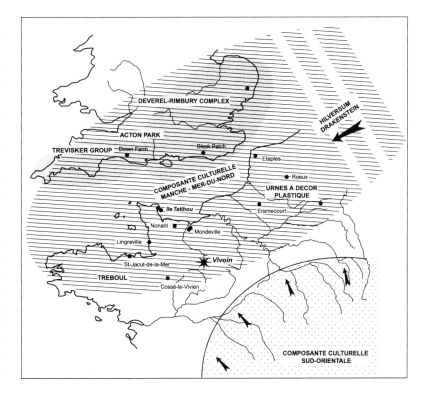

it is highly likely that small-scale movements of people took place in the context of intermarriages contrived to maintain social cohesion.

As Needham (this volume, p. 12) has so vividly demonstrated, the Channel and southern North Sea were already criss-crossed by networks of interaction as early as 2000 BC. It is tempting to suggest that it was the development of plank-built vessels capable of taking to the open sea that facilitated these movements. By the middle of the second millennium the cultural similarities on either side of the sea had developed to such an extent that shipbuilding and seafaring must by now have been widely practised throughout the maritime communities.

The Early Iron Age: 800–500 BC

The pattern of contact, once established in the Middle–Late Bronze Age, continued throughout the Early Iron Age (*c* 800–500 BC) and is demonstrated by a variety of direct archaeological evidence. At an elite level the Hallstatt C sword of Gundlingen type and the associated winged chapes provide a good example. The swords are distributed widely in Britain and Ireland and on the Continent (Cunliffe 2005, 447–52). While there has been much debate about the origins of the type it is now widely believed that the Gundlingen sword was an Atlantic development, first produced somewhere in the southern North Sea region, quite possibly in south-eastern Britain. The wide distribution of these swords reflects networks of elite exchange embracing Britain, Ireland, northern France, the Low Countries and beyond. The pattern of sword distribution, which favours the southern North Sea and Channel axes, echoes earlier elite networks represented by the distribution of gold 'hair rings' and Ballintober-type swords of the Late Bronze Age (Eogan 1994).

Elite exchange of the Hallstatt period is further reflected in distributions, in Britain, of horse gear belonging to categories widely known in western and west central Europe (Cunliffe 2005, 448–53). The simplest explanation for the appearance of these artefacts in the British archaeological record is that horses, decked out in their finery, were the actual item of exchange. Nor should we forget the comparatively large number of Hallstatt brooches found in Britain

(Cunliffe 2005, 458–61). Though none has yet been recovered from a sound archaeological context, a percentage of them, at least, are likely to have been contemporary imports. It is quite likely that they were brought into Britain on the dress of women arriving in the islands to sustain alliances through marriages.

The brooches span the period from the eighth to sixth centuries. The sixth century also sees the appearance in southern Britain of a dagger type closely modelled on Continental daggers of Hallstatt D date (Jope 1961). Some British manufactured types found their way to the Continent.

Viewing the metalwork overall it is fair to say that from the beginning of the eighth century to the end of the sixth century Britain and the Continent were bound by networks of exchange which seem to have focused on the southern North Sea region; thereafter the quantity of goods transported significantly diminished.

Against this background we must briefly consider other aspects of material culture. Broad similarities in ceramic styles continue between the eastern region of Britain and the Low Countries. This is particularly true of the Darmsden-Linton styles of East Anglia, the Highstead-Dollands Moor of Kent and the various regional styles identified along the coastal regions of Belgium and Holland (Cunliffe 2005, 102–3 and figs 5.4, A:13 and A:14; van Heeringen 1989). While the similarities are not extensive they are sufficient, both at a general level and in terms of specific detail, to show that the two regions must have maintained a level of contact over time. Another item of material culture shared between the two regions (though extending over a broader chronological range) is the triangular loom weight (Wilhelmi 1977). Taken together the evidence strongly suggests that the contacts established in the mid-Bronze Age continued to be maintained throughout the Early Iron Age.

The Middle Iron Age: 500–150 BC

The diminution in the quantity of recognisable items of elite exchange found in Britain during the Middle Iron Age gives the impression that the intensity of transmarine contact may have slackened during this period – an impression strengthened by the development of a distinct regionality among the communities of southern Britain. That said, there is ample evidence that a level of contact was maintained in particular in the Channel zone. This is demonstrated most dramatically by the very close similarities in pottery styles and technology between Kent and the adjacent Continent. We may refer to this as the Southern North Sea Cultural zone. The Kentish assemblage (the Highstead-Dollands Moor style) includes rusticated wares (*eclaboussée*) and painted wares closely similar to pottery from Belgium and northern France dating from the mid-sixth to the end of the fifth centuries. In Kent the most extensive of the published assemblages comes from Highstead (Bennett *et al* 2007). Contemporary Continental material is conveniently brought together in Hurtrelle *et al* 1989; Leman-Delerive 1984; Cahen-Delhaye and Maes 1991; and Bourgeois 1991.

The coarse-ware tradition shared by communities on the two sides of the Channel covered extensive territories while the painted wares were of far more limited distribution and, on the Continent, show distinct regional concentrations (Fig 6.4). Painted wares are so far recorded from five sites in Kent: Castle Hill, Folkestone; Sarre, Thanet; Whitfield, Dover; Highstead, Chislet; and Dollands Moor. The forms and styles of decoration can be most closely paralleled in the Pas de Calais and Belgium. Insufficient scientific analysis has yet been undertaken to show whether the British painted wares were imported or locally made but at the very least they imply that the communities of Kent were in close contact with their nearest Continental neighbours in the sixth and fifth centuries.

The burial rites practised on the two sides of the Channel–southern North Sea divide make an interesting comparison. At first sight there appear to be considerable variations (Fig 6.5). Several discrete zones of inhumation or cremation burial can be distinguished but over considerable areas in south-eastern Britain, northern France and Belgium careful burial of this kind is unknown. It is, however, precisely in these territories that what have been referred to as 'pit burials' occur. The type is well known in Britain (Whimster 1981, 198–225; Cunliffe 1992). The Continental material appears to be no less extensive but has not yet been brought together in a synthesis. This is not the place to discuss 'pit burials' in any detail. Suffice it to say

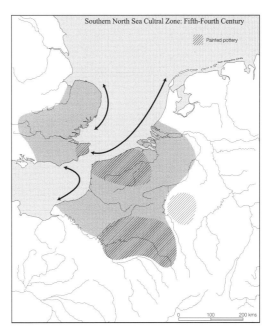

Figure 6.4 Aspects of pottery styles in the fifth–fourth centuries BC. Based on Hurtrelle et al 1989 with details added

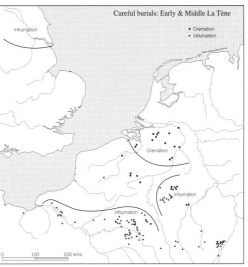

Figure 6.5 Careful burial in the Early and Middle La Tène. Based on Hurtrelle et al 1989

that bodies or parts of bodies placed in pits are one aspect of a complex pattern of disposal which most likely involves excarnation as one stage in the *rite de passage* of death. The burial evidence, therefore, suggests that a considerable part of southern Britain, northern France and the Low Countries shared a common burial rite. The zones where careful inhumation and careful interred cremation were practised were largely peripheral to the 'excarnation region' occupying the interfaces between the Southern North Sea Cultural zone and adjacent territories. This observation has interesting implications for the definition of territorial boundaries but cannot be pursued further here.

A further theme that needs to be addressed

*Figure 6.6 (right)
La Tène influence
on Britain. After
Cunliffe 2001a,
fig 8.12*

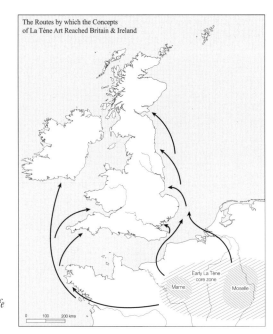

*Figure 6.7 (below)
Distribution of early
Gallo-Belgic coins in
Britain. After Cunliffe
2005, fig 6.2*

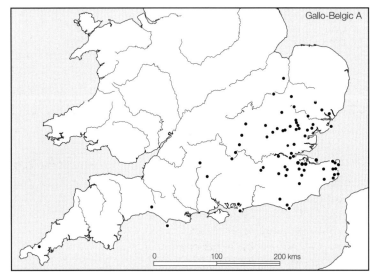

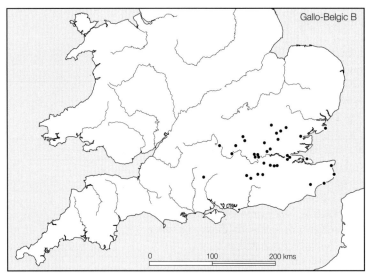

is the processes by which the concepts and values of La Tène 'art' reached Britain. La Tène art styles developed during the fifth century in a broad zone stretching across west central Europe, with innovating centres concentrated in the Marne and Moselle regions, fringing the Southern North Sea Cultural zone (Fig 6.6). Items of elite metalwork produced in the La Tène centres would have passed by exchange through the adjacent territories using existing networks. One axis can be posited along the Loire by means of which elite items reached Armorica and the Atlantic network (Cunliffe 2000) thence to west of Britain and probably Ireland. Other axes, using the Seine, Somme and Rhine, would have linked to the Channel–southern North Sea networks. By these routes La Tène 'values' as well as artefacts reached the east of Britain giving rise to indigenous craft schools of which the Witham–Wandsworth–Torrs school was the most inventive (Jope 2000, 53–72). The exact mechanisms by which the flow of elite goods, the technical skills involved in their production and the belief systems in which they were embedded reached Britain are beyond recovery. But given the long-established networks of interaction which had bound the east of Britain to the Continent for more than a millennium, the spread of La Tène cultural attributes required no new initiatives – cultural exchanges of this kind were part of an established tradition.

The Late Iron Age: 150 BC–AD 50

In the latter part of the second century BC a new artefact type – the coin – developed in north-western Europe ultimately from Mediterranean prototypes. The coins of this early period were mostly gold staters stamped with distinctive motifs characteristic of the minting authority. As items of high value they served to articulate networks of social obligation. Coins, then, provide a ready source of evidence for demonstrating the existence and the extent of social networks. The earliest coins to be manufactured in the Channel–southern North Sea zone were minted in northern France in the second half of the second century BC. They are traditionally called Gallo-Belgic A and Gallo-Belgic B and are thought to be types issued by the Belgic tribes, the Ambiani and the Caletes. The distribution of the coins in Britain (Fig 6.7) leaves little doubt that the axis of contact through which they passed focused on the Thames estuary. A slightly later type, Gallo-Belgic C, possibly minted by the Suessiones, has much the same distribution but there is now some additional emphasis on the Sussex coast. Although it has been traditional to regard the coins as reflecting an entirely new phenomenon, when seen against the deep-time background sketched above it becomes clear that the coins are simply continuing to make archaeologically visible the long-established networks of interaction; they are another surrogate for social intercourse between the maritime communities.

In the middle of the first century BC cross-Channel interactions are mentioned for the first time in classical literature. In his *Commentaries* on the Gallic War Julius Caesar offers two relevant insights. He records that Britons had served in most of the Gallic Wars (*BG* IV, 20, 1) and that King Diviciacus of the Suessiones 'had control not only over a large area of this region [northern Gaul] but also of Britain' (*BG* II, 4, 7). Both references reflect the social obligations which existed between Britain and the Continent; a Gaulish king could claim the allegiance of British kings and British troops were sent to Gaul to support their allies in the war against Roman aggression. The coins add further to the picture. A massive issue, Gallo-Belgic E, is thought to have been minted to 'fund' the Gallic resistance. Large numbers found their way to Britain perhaps as a reward for military services. The distribution again favours the Thames valley, the Essex and Suffolk rivers and the Sussex coast.

Various interpretations have been offered of the Gallo-Belgic coin distributions. Some writers (Hawkes 1968; Rodwell 1976) saw them as the result of successive waves of immigrants. Given what we now know of the *longue durée* of cross-Channel contact this seems unlikely and it is simpler to see the successive inflows of coins minted in Belgic Gaul as a reflection of continuing patterns of interaction between communities bound by traditional ties of social obligation.

The possibility that some small-scale population movements may have taken place at this time should not, however, be overlooked. British fighting men leaving to take part in the Gallic Wars constituted one such movement. Caesar also refers to an immigration of 'Belgae' who settled in the 'maritime regions' of Britain

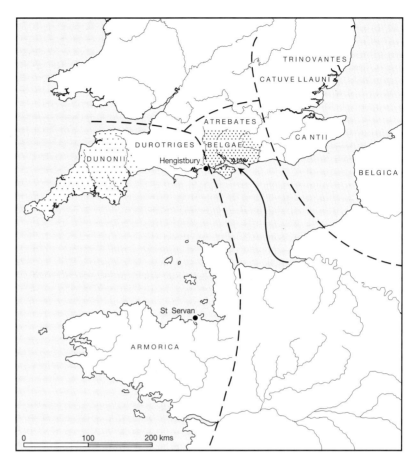

following a period of raiding some time in the recent past. There has been much debate about this event since 1890 when Arthur Evans suggested that the Belgae settled in Kent, Essex and Hertfordshire (Evans 1890). The idea was restated in much more detail by Hawkes and Dunning (1931) but has come under criticism. An alternative view (Cunliffe 1984) is that the settlement took place in the Solent region where, under later Roman administration, the Belgae were said to be located, with Winchester as their capital (Fig 6.8). A Solent landfall would have lain sufficiently beyond the traditional zone of social interaction not to have disrupted existing alliances.

Further west still a different network of interaction can be detected in the archaeological evidence representing direct sea journeys from the north coasts of Armorica and the south coasts of south-western Britain. Hengistbury Head on Christchurch Harbour in Dorset served as a major port of entry in the first half of the first century BC with Poole Harbour taking over later. This system has been discussed in considerable detail elsewhere (Cunliffe 1987;

Figure 6.8 Spheres of influence in the first century BC

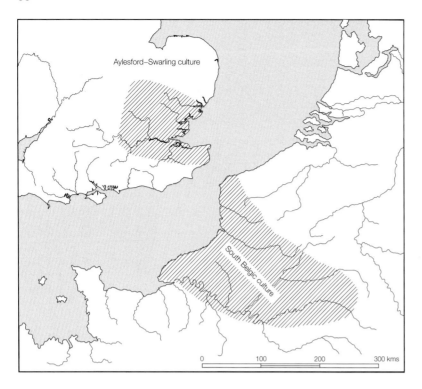

the network of social interactions between Britain and the Continent in the decades before the heavy hand of Rome began to impose entirely new economic networks predicated on the maintenance of Empire.

Coastal waters

In the discussion above we have been concerned to summarise the archaeological evidence for the maritime networks linking Britain and the adjacent Continent. We should not, however, overlook cabotage which is likely to have been intensely practised in British and Continental waters. To what extent the cabotage and transmaritime systems were interconnected it is difficult to say but the possibility that they may have been largely separate, involving quite different vessels and techniques of sailing, should at least be borne in mind.

Evidence for cabotage though widely scattered in the archaeological literature has not been brought together in any systematic manner; here all we can do is to present a few examples.

In a seminal paper, which initiated a major reconsideration of the British Iron Age, Roy Hodson drew attention to similarities existing between the fine-ware pottery of the Earliest Iron Age found around the south and east coasts of Britain (Hodson 1960). Subsequent detailed characterisation of these ceramic assemblages (Cunliffe 2005, 87–124) gave further emphasis to this observation. Four distinct *style-zones* can be identified, Kimmeridge-Caburn, Highstead 2, West Harling-Fengate and Staple Howe, all sharing in common a preference for small finely made bowls with sharp shoulder angles and the use of applied cordons sometimes with 'herringbone' slashing. The distribution of these style-zones is strikingly coastal (Fig 6.10) and is best explained by supposing that maritime contact was maintained, presumably in short-haul journeys, along the entire coastal zone between Yorkshire and Dorset. We can only speculate on what commodities may have been carried – Kimmeridge shale, Whitby jet and east coast amber may all have featured alongside a range of perishables. A distinctive pottery vessel found at Darmsden in Suffolk (Cunliffe 1968, fig 4 no. 2), made in a hard black sandy ware coated externally with iron oxide slip and decorated with impressed circlets

Figure 6.9 Zones sharing similar cultural characteristics in the late first century BC

Cunliffe and de Jersey 1998) and is strictly beyond the limits of this paper. Its relevance to the present discussion lies in the fact that the Solent region seems to have been a no-man's-land between the two existing exchange networks. It would therefore have been an appropriate landfall for the 'Belgic' settlers.

In the last 90 years between Caesar's expeditions to Britain in 55 and 54 BC and the invasion of Claudius in AD 43 the pattern of maritime interactions continued, and if anything intensified, between the communities of north-western Gaul and the greater Thames valley region embracing Kent, Essex and Hertfordshire. Gaul was now under Roman control but even so indigenous culture continued to develop largely undisturbed at least until the early decades of the first century AD by which time Romanisation was well under way. In northern Gaul a *South Belgic culture* can be distinguished, characterised by a distinctive range of wheel-made pottery, extensive use of cremation burial and an elite system reflected in elaborate burials containing Roman wine amphorae and wine-drinking equipment. The same cultural elements were widely adopted by the tribes of south-eastern Britain and can be distinguished as the *Aylesford-Swarling culture* (Fig 6.9; Cunliffe 2005, 151–9). In this map we see the final manifestation of

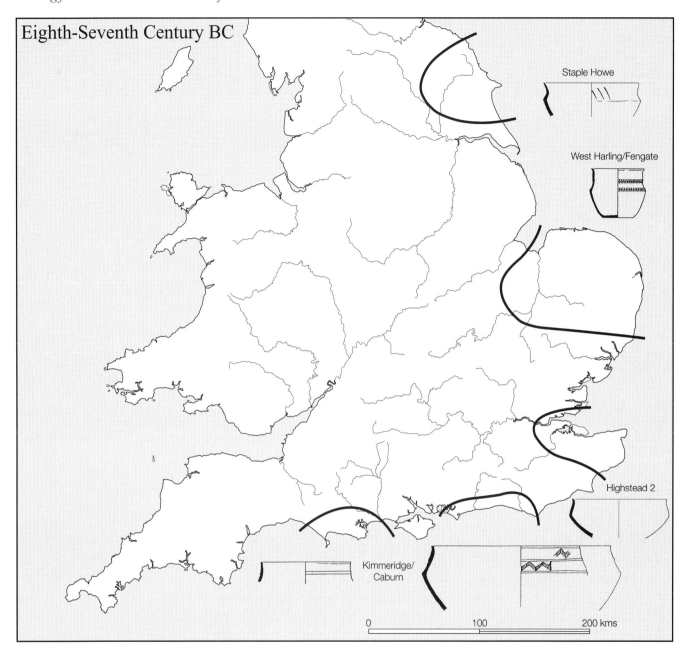

and stab-filled pendent triangles, is highly characteristic of the Early All Cannings Cross pottery of Wessex. Perhaps it was used to carry a Dorset delicacy to Suffolk!

In the second century BC direct evidence of long-shore exchange is provided by the coastal distribution of distinctive South Western Decorated Wares made in gabbroic clay from the Lizard Peninsula in Cornwall (Peacock 1969; Harrard 2003). The distribution (Fig 6.11) suggests maritime portage along the south and east coasts at least as far as Heybridge

in Essex, and along the north Cornish coast to the Severn estuary.

By the beginning of the first century BC the south-western coastal network articulated with cross-Channel traffic at the port-of-trade at Hengistbury Head (Fig 6.12). Here there is evidence of tin ore from Cornwall, silver-rich copper ore from the Callington region of Devon, silver-rich lead from the Mendips and pottery from Devon. These commodities were no doubt transported to Hengistbury because it was known to be the port-of-trade with direct

Figure 6.10 Ceramic styles in coastal regions in the eighth and seventh centuries

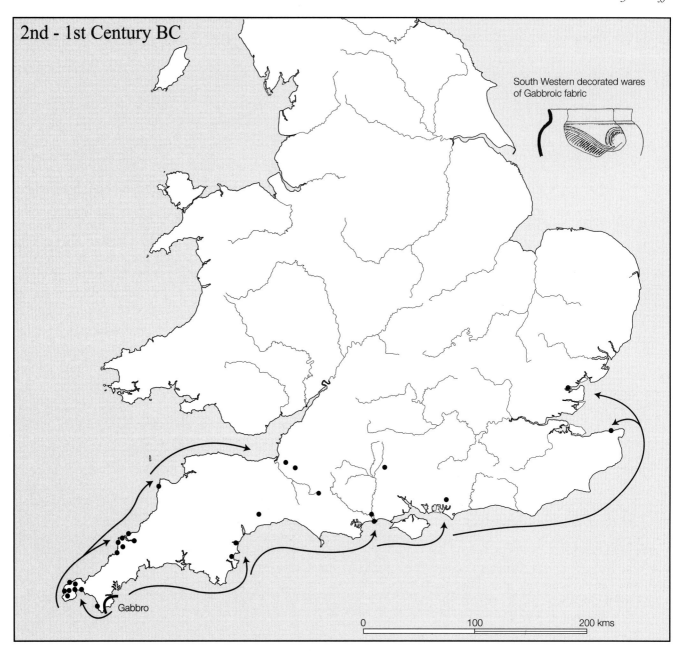

2nd - 1st Century BC

South Western decorated wares
of Gabbroic fabric

Gabbro

0   100   200 kms

Figure 6.11 Distribution of gabbroic South Western Decorated Wares in relation to possible coastal routes

maritime links to Armorica and a place where exotic goods were available.

The first century BC saw the development, in southern and eastern Britain, of a number of ceramic style-zones each characterised by a range of decorated vessels. One pottery type, common to the coastal zone, was the large globular-bodied jar with everted rim, decorated on the shoulder by a zone of arcs or arcs and swags impressed into the leather-hard body of the vessels, usually with a roulette wheel, before firing. These highly recognisable types

are found at Hengistbury, along the Sussex coast, on both sides of the Thames estuary and in Lincolnshire (Fig 6.13). Once more it is the coastal distribution that stands out. While the fabrics indicate that the vessels were probably locally made and were not the result of trade in pottery, the adoption of this highly distinctive motif to decorate the equally distinctive globular form hints at shared values among the coastal communities. What this means in actual terms is difficult to say but it could be simply that the form and decorative motif

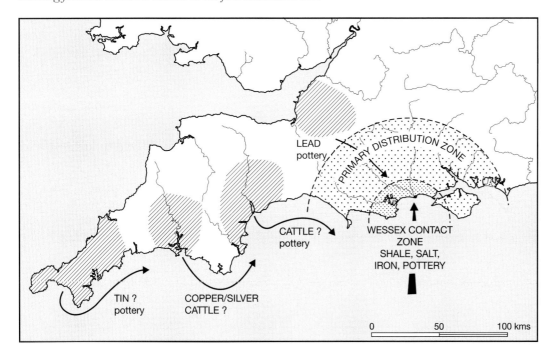

Figure 6.12 South-western Britain. The coastal routes in relation to the port-of-trade at Hengistbury Head and the cross-Channel network

were adopted as indicators of the contents of the vessels.

Ceramics with closely similar arc motifs are also known on sites around the Armorican coast and further afield along the north coast of Iberia between A Coruña (Galicia) and Gijón (Asturias) where it has been suggested to be an aspect of a unified maritime culture extending along the Atlantic seaways in the first century BC and early first century AD (González-Ruibal 2004).

The significance of cabotage has received scant attention in the past. Sufficient will have been said above to indicate something of its extent and importance in south-eastern Britain in the first millennium BC. The locations of havens and ports necessary to support the system have barely been mentioned. Clearly, there is much work to be done in this area.

The sea in the longue durée

This brief overview of the maritime inter-actions between south-eastern Britain and the Continent in the late second and first millennia BC has shown something of the richness of the database and of the complexity of the subject. One thing is abundantly clear – the sea was no obstacle to movement. Indeed it could be said that the sea facilitated and encouraged contact. Movement on water would have been quicker, and probably safer, than movement by land.

In the second half of the second millennium a remarkable cultural similarity had developed between communities facing each other across the English Channel and southern North Sea. Such similarities can only have come about as the result of intensive and sustained communication. Thereafter the networks continued to function maintaining a high level of mobility. In the later first millennium the greater range of archaeological and textual evidence which becomes available allows a more nuanced picture to emerge suggesting specific axes of communication and hinting at the different subsystems in operation fuelled by different imperatives. There may also have been periods when maritime contact slackened for a while. Clearly there is far more work to be done in refining the picture. Yet standing back from the detail there can be little doubt that throughout later prehistory the British seas would have been alive with sea-going vessels.

List of references

Bennett, P, Couldrey, P and Macpherson-Grant, N 2007 *Excavations at Highstead, near Chislet, Kent 1975–77*, Canterbury

Bourgeois, J 1991 'Céramique peinte de La Tène ancienne dans le bassin de l'Escaut Belge', in *La céramique peinte celtique dans son contexte Européen*, Mémoire de la Société Archéologique Champenoise, **5**, Reims, 75–82

Butler, J 1963 *Bronze Age Connections Across the North Sea*, Palaeohistoria, **9**, Groningen: J B Wolters

Cahen-Delhaye, A and Maes, L 1991 La céramique peinte

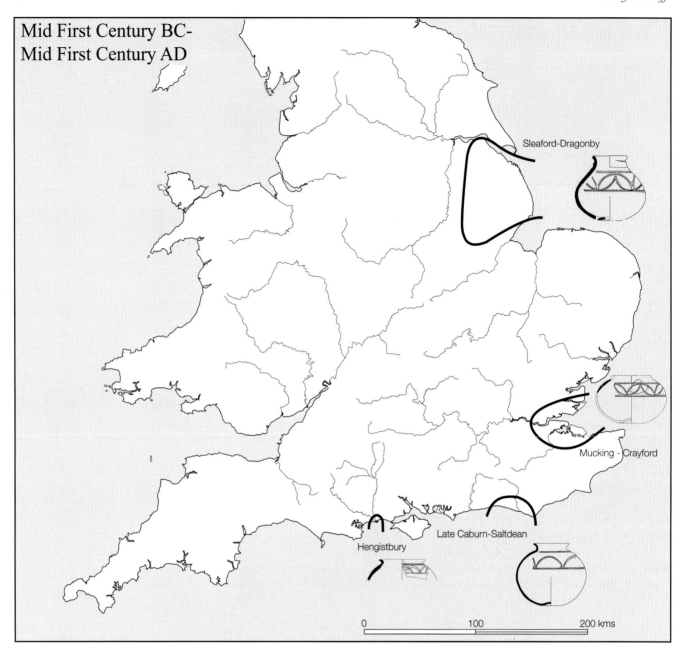

Sleaford-Dragonby

Mucking - Crayford

Late Caburn-Saltdean

Hengistbury

0   100   200 kms

*Figure 6.13 Maritime-
zone ceramics in the late
first century BC and early
first century AD*

de La Tène I en Belgique, in *La céramique peinte celtique
dans son contexte Européen*, Mémoire de la Société
Archéologique Champenoise, **5**, Reims, 65–74

Clark, P (ed) 2004 *The Dover Bronze Age Boat*, Swindon:
English Heritage

Cunliffe, B 1968 'Early Pre-Roman Iron Age Communities
in Eastern England', *Antiquaries Journal*, **48**, 175–91

Cunliffe, B 1972 'The Late Iron Age metalwork from
Bulbury, Dorset', *Antiquaries Journal*, **52**, 293–308

Cunliffe, B 1982 'Britain, the Veneti and beyond', *Oxford
Journal of Archaeology*, **1(1)**, 39–68

Cunliffe, B 1984 'Relations between Britain and Gaul in
the first century BC and early first century AD', in
S Macready and F H Thompson (eds), *Cross-Channel
Trade between Gaul and Britain in the Pre-Roman Iron*

Age, Society of Antiquaries Occasional Paper, **4**,
London, 3–23

Cunliffe, B 1987 *Hengistbury Head, Dorset. Vol 1: Prehistoric
and Roman Settlement 3500 BC–AD 500*, Oxford
University Committee for Archaeology Monograph,
13, Oxford

Cunliffe, B 1988 *Mount Batten, Plymouth. A Prehistoric
and Roman Port*, Oxford University Committee for
Archaeology Monograph, **26**, Oxford

Cunliffe, B 1992 'Pits, preconceptions and propitiation
in the British Iron Age', *Oxford Journal of Archaeology*,
11(1), 69–83

Cunliffe, B 2000 'Brittany and the Atlantic rim in the
later first millennium BC', *Oxford Journal of Archaeology*,
19(4), 367–86

Cunliffe, B 2001a *Facing the ocean. The Atlantic and its peoples*, Oxford: Oxford University Press

Cunliffe, B 2001b *The extraordinary voyage of Pytheas the Greek*, London: Allen Lane

Cunliffe, B 2005 *Iron Age Communities in Britain* (4th edition), London: Routledge

Cunliffe, B and de Jersey, P 1998 *Armorica and Britain: Cross-Channel relationships in the late first millennium BC*, Oxford University Committee for Archaeology Monograph, **45**, Oxford

Eogan, G 1994 *The Accomplished Art. Gold and Gold-working in Britain and Ireland during the Bronze Age*, Oxford: Oxbow Books

Evans, A J 1890 'On a Late-Celtic urn-field at Aylesford, Kent', *Archaeologia*, **52**, 315–88

González-Ruibal, A 2004 'Facing two seas: Mediterranean and Atlantic contacts in the north-west of Iberia in the first millennium BC', *Oxford Journal of Archaeology*, **23(3)**, 287–317

Harrard, L 2003 *The production and trade of prehistoric ceramics in Cornwall*, Unpublished DPhil thesis, University of Oxford

Hawkes, C F C 1968 'New Thoughts on the Belgae', *Antiquity*, **42 (165)**, 6–16

Hawkes, C F C and Dunning, G C 1931 'The Belgae in Gaul and Britain', *Archaeological Journal*, **87**, 150–335

Hodson, F R 1960 'Reflections on the 'ABC' of the British Iron Age', *Antiquity*, **34 (134)**, 138–40

Hurtrelle, J, Monchy, E, Roger, F, Rossignol, P and Villes, A 1989 *Les débuts du second âge du fer dans le Nord de la France*, Givenchy-en-Gohelle: Gauheria

Jope, E M 1961 'Daggers of the Early Iron Age in Britain', *Proceedings of the Prehistoric Society*, **27**, 307–43

Jope, E M 2000 *Early Celtic Art in the British Isles*, Oxford: Clarendon Press

Leman-Delerive, G 1984 'Céramique Laténienne domestique de la région Lilloise (Nord)', *Gallia*, **42**, 79–95

Marcigny, C and Ghesquière, E 2003 *L'île Tatihou à l'âge du Bronze (Manche), habitats et occupation du sol*, Documents d'Archéologie Française, **96**, Paris: Éditions de la Maison des sciences de l'homme

Marcigny, C, Aubry, B, Verney, A, Vacher, S and Thooris, C 2002 'Découvertes récentes de l'âge du Bronze moyen dans le Département de la Sarthe (Pays-de-la-Loire)', *Revue archéologique de l'Ouest*, **19**, 7–13

Marcigny, C, Colonna, C, Ghesquière, E and Verron, G 2005 *La Normandie. À L'aube de l'histoire*, Paris

Markey, M, Wilkes, E and Darvill, T 2002 'Poole Harbour: An Iron Age Port', *Current Archaeology*, **181**, 7–11

Marsden, P 1994 *Ships of the Port of London: First to Eleventh Centuries AD*, London: English Heritage

McGrail, S 1983 'Cross-Channel seamanship and navigation in the late 1st millennium BC', *Oxford Journal of Archaeology*, **7(1)**, 35–46

Muckelroy, K 1981 'Middle Bronze Age trade between Britain and Europe; a maritime perspective', *Proceedings of the Prehistoric Society*, **47**, 275–97

O'Connor, B 1980 *Cross-Channel relations in the Later Bronze Age*, British Archaeological Reports International Series, **91**, Oxford

Peacock, D 1969 'A contribution to the study of Glastonbury ware from south-western Britain', *Antiquaries Journal*, **49**, 41–61

Rodwell, W J 1976 'Coinage, oppida and the rise of Belgic power in south-eastern Britain', in B Cunliffe and T Rowley (eds), *Oppida: The Beginnings of Urbanism in Barbarian Europe*, British Archaeological Reports Supplementary Series, **11**, Oxford, 181–367

Rule, M and Monaghan, J 1993 *A Gallo-Roman Trading Vessel from Guernsey*, St Peter Port: Guernsey Museums and Galleries

Taylor, J 2001 'The Isle of Portland: an Iron Age port-of-trade', *Oxford Journal of Archaeology*, **20(1)**, 187–205

van de Noort, R, Middleton, R, Foxton, A and Bayliss, A 1999 'The 'Kilnsea-boat' and some implications from the discovery of England's oldest plank boat remains', *Antiquity*, **73 (279)**, 131–5

van Heeringen, R M 1989 'The Iron Age in the Western Netherlands. V: Synthesis', *ROB*, **39**, 157–265

Whimster, R 1981 *Burial Practices in Iron Age Britain*, British Archaeological Reports British Series, **90**, Oxford

Wilhelmi, K 1977 'Zur Funktion und Verbreitung dreieckiger Tongewichte der Eisenzeit', *Germania*, **55**, 179–84

Wright, E 1990 *The Ferriby boats: Seacraft of the Bronze Age*, London: Routledge

7. Copper mining and metal production at the beginning of the British Bronze Age

Simon Timberlake

From stone to metal

As the technological revolution underlying the change from stone to metal gathered pace in southern Europe at the beginning of the third millennium BC, the necessary precursor for the development of an indigenous metallurgy here in Britain, a mental geological map of these islands, was probably already in existence.

Locally within upland areas this body of knowledge would have included a familiarity with the subtleties of the texture and properties of potentially useful igneous, contact metamorphic and volcanic rocks, as well as the concept of following beds, horizons and veins across the landscape, perhaps even the recognition of displacements (or faults). This ability to undertake prospection through subtle visual assessment of the rock exposure and by sampling (flaking or crushing of rocks and minerals) will have been as relevant to the identification of a suitable rock type from which to make axe rough-outs high up on the slopes of the Langdale Pikes (Cumbria), Mynydd Rhiw or Graig Llwyd (North Wales), as it would be to the task of recognising the underground beds of floorstone flint within the mine shafts at Grimes Graves or on Hambledon Hill. Of equal importance would have been a knowledge of the range of coloured or metallic-looking minerals present within a landscape of quartz and other mineral vein outcrops distributed across areas of upland Britain. These would have been important from the earliest times as sources of pigment, although clues as to where to look for this evidence are now only just beginning to emerge. Examples of this early interest in minerals is suggested by the discovery of Mesolithic camp sites which seem to coincide with areas of malachite and azurite extraction on Alderley Edge (Timberlake and Prag 2005). There are also finds of stone hammers within old iron mines which suggest early, perhaps pre-Bronze Age iron ochre extraction in the Forest of Dean (J Wright *pers comm*; Strasburger 2001). More recently several third and fourth millennium BC radiocarbon dates have been obtained from investigations of the earliest outcrop extraction or the working of the scree debris on Copa Hill, Cwmystwyth (Timberlake 2003). All this implies pre-metallurgical interest in these minerals and an earlier surviving history of extraction linked to at least some of these sites.

The apparent inaccessibility and marginal location of some of the Late Neolithic axe quarries (*ie* Scafell Pike, Rathlin Island, Co. Antrim and Lambay Island, Dublin (Cooney 2005)) attests to the contemporary familiarity with the natural (geological) landscape as well as to the existence of a much greater area of rock exposure prior to the mid-2nd millennium BC enroachment of blanket peat across the upland areas of Western Britain and Atlantic Ireland (Tinsley and Grigson 1981). This westerly distribution of Neolithic axe factory sites and their sometimes near-coastal locations is perhaps being echoed by the later distribution of Early Bronze Age metal mines. This similarity, however, may be more apparent than real. As we shall see, the maritime link, though not always fully explicable, has much stronger links with the discovery, extraction and first use of metal ores than it does with the manufacture of stone axes.

By the time copper metallurgy reached Britain, re-awakening an interest in our own mineral deposits, the techniques of underground mining were already well developed. We see this in the multiple shaft flint mines, some of which were still being worked at Grimes Graves during the Late Neolithic/Early Bronze Age using antler picks and hammer stones (Barber *et al* 1999). Meanwhile the techniques of hard-rock mining using well-directed fire-setting and stone tools had been used for hundreds of years within the axe quarry sites at Langdale (Claris and Quartermaine 1989). Such a scenario must have been the backdrop to the first exploitation of metallic ores at the end of the third millennium. The very earliest mining would have been associated with surface exposures of secondary (oxidised) copper minerals which had formed on upstanding quartz veins, on limestone cliff outcrops, or within the post-glacially developed iron gossans which might then have capped the massive sulphide deposits such as found on Parys Mountain in Anglesey (Dewey and Eastwood 1925). Given their familiarity with rock types, shallow mining and quarrying, it is very difficult to share the sceptical approach adopted by Briggs concerning the likelihood and difficulties of primary extraction of metal ores in prehistory (1988; 2003).

Although the few dates which are available for the working of the Graig Lwyd axe factory place this firmly in the Later Neolithic (Williams and Davidson 1998), it is not entirely inconceivable that there remains some continuity or overlap between this operation and the extraction of malachite for pigment (and later copper ore) on the Great Ormes Head, the limestone headland which lies immediately opposite the quarries on the other side of the Conway Estuary. The potential within this area for continuity in the mining/quarrying tradition was also noted by Edmonds (2004). There is some parallel to be found in the extended production (though at a much reduced level) of smaller Group VI axes well into the Early Bronze Age in Cumbria. This latter activity however may just represent the re-grinding and polishing of worn or broken axes rather than any continuity in stone axe production side by side with that

of metal. The flip side of all this could mean that the presence of an active and functioning stone axe industry within North Wales and Antrim might actually have delayed the onset of metallurgy within these areas, reflecting a certain 'lack of enthusiasm' in metal on the part of those controlling stone axe production (O'Brien 1999).

In fact, a measure of co-existence between stone axe and early metalworking traditions is perhaps best seen in Ireland. O'Brien (2004) commented upon a denser concentration in the observed distribution pattern of late 3rd millennium Irish copper axes in the Antrim area close to the porcellanite (Group IX) quarries of Tievebulliagh and Rathlin Island. Perhaps the presence of these Lough Ravel and other metal axes apparently derived from ores mined at Ross Island could be seen as part of an exchange mechanism, one of metal ousting stone, or the trading of equally desirable but quite different prestige items. Meanwhile in south-west Ireland close to the source of these ores there is another equally interesting but just as ambiguous indicator of this cross-over relationship. In 1853 a cache of twelve polished stone axes was found buried within a peat-filled Mount Gabriel-type primitive mine at Ballyrisode on the Mizen peninsula. The chamber in which these were found has recently been re-excavated (O'Brien 2003), the results of this suggesting that the deposition of these axes was contemporary with the stone mining hammers and samples of copper ore and that this assemblage dated to the fully developed Early Bronze Age, *c* 1853–1619 cal BC. These chipped and worn axes may have been curated items, either placed here as a votive deposit, perhaps in exchange for the metal removed, or else deposited for later retrieval. This evidence seems to suggest that the decline in demand for stone axes was a gradual and uneven process, one which could have been dependent upon the rate at which metal became valuable to individual communities across Britain and Ireland (Smith 1979). Either way, the caching of these and other hoards of stone axes seems to represent the turning point and final supersedence of stone tools by metal early in the 2nd millennium BC.

It is not difficult to see why the properties of metal such as lustre, strength and lack of brittleness were desirable, as would have been the ability to hammer-harden and easily sharpen blades, to melt down objects and recycle them, to mix and add to the metal, to cast this into new and interesting shapes, and to harden it through alloying. The mercurial and versatile nature of this material would have been magical in comparison to stone, yet it was this very changeability which ensured its anonymity as the number of different sources of metal grew.

A comparison drawn between the stone-axe factories of the Late Neolithic and the metal-producing sites of the Early Bronze Age (primitive mines and smelting sites) suggests a number of differences in status (Timberlake 1992a; 2002a). Yet on a physical level there are many similarities. Both axe quarries and mines are frequently to be found at elevated and isolated locations surrounded by waste tips and scree, more often than not with little or nothing in the way of associated settlement or working areas which contain pottery or other culturally or chronologically identifiable artefacts. However this parallel seems to falter when one looks at the regional importance of these sites. The grouping of henge monuments and stone circles during the later Neolithic in North Wales and Cumbria has been linked to the prestige, economic and symbolic importance of major axe factory sites such as Graig Llwyd and Langdale (Houlder 1976; Burl 1976). The regional distribution of such monuments has also been shown to coincide with the principle distribution areas of stone axe groups (Bradley 1984). No good correlation has yet been made, however, between Bronze Age mines and the distribution of Bronze Age monuments. South-west Ireland has many Bronze age monuments, although the distribution bears no obvious relationship to that of the known mines, except perhaps that wedge tombs appear to concentrate in west and south-west Cork within the same general area as the Mount Gabriel-type mines (O'Brien 1994). However, Mid-Wales with the greatest number of potential mining sites, has a rather moderate distribution of Bronze Age monuments, whilst the much larger production centre based on the Great Orme appears to have an even less clear-cut relationship with contemporary sites. Further links in the chain may yet be forged, but for the present the contrast remains. Axe-factory sites appear to have a relatively high status, whilst copper mining sites apparently do not. This being so, might such a difference

have something to do with changes in society, or could it just be something to do with the nature of the product?

During the later Neolithic the axes traded from different axe-factory sites would have been instantly recognisable by discerning consumers, and moreover would be easily identifiable with their original sources. It seems possible therefore that such objects fabricated from natural stone possessing prestige, economic, and perhaps even a magical value would confer a similar status upon the sites and territories where these were produced. No such relationship, however, would have been possible between a copper or bronze axe and the mine or mines which contributed the metal. Even the bronze smiths themselves may have been unaware of where the metal used in a particular axe had originated. If anything, the discernable relationship would have been between (a) the unique style of axe manufacture and (b) the recognisable industry which produced it (eg Brithdir, Willerby or Acton Park). In some cases this may not have been local or even regionally close to the actual sources of the metal used.

It was the discovery and excavation of some of these Early Bronze Age mines in Britain and Ireland during the late 1980s and 1990s which changed our perceptions concerning the first production and use of indigenous metal (Fig 7.1).

The earliest mining in Ireland: the beginnings of an indigenous metalworking tradition

The re-discovery of the ancient copper mine at Ross Island on the shores of Lough Killarney (Ireland) followed by its excavation between 1992 and 1996 seems to have provided us with at least some of the evidence we were looking for concerning the origins of an indigenous metallurgy in these islands (O'Brien 2004). The existence of this rich deposit of easily mined arsenical copper ore linked to the archaeological evidence for Copper Age–Early Bronze Age mining (2400–1800 BC) and a 'mining camp' settlement associated with Bell Beaker pottery and possible smelting pits fits well with the known data already provided us by compositional analyses of Irish and British metalwork. This had clearly indicated a south-west Irish source for the earliest Type

A metal (consisting of copper containing between 0.67–2 per cent arsenic impurity along with traces of antimony and silver), a view first held by Coghlan and Case (1957; Case 1966) then re-iterated and developed by Northover (1980b; 1982; 1999). Recent work carried out on the lead isotope analysis of British Bronze Age metalwork appears to confirm the strong correlation between Type A Copper Age metal (or lead isotope type IMP-LI-1) in circulation between 2500 and 2100 BC and the composition of the *fahlerz* tennantite (arsenical copper sulphide) ores from Ross I (Rohl and Needham 1998). More detailed work on the ore bodies and mineralisation of this deposit has identified two distinct types of ore (Ixer and Budd 1998); epigenetic veins of chalcopyrite-tennantite ore in limestones from the Western Mine (cave-like galleries associated with the excavated site), and a strata-bound chalcopyrite-tennantite ore intimately mixed with galena (lead) and sphalerite (zinc) associated with the now flooded Blue Hole workings. Ore samples from the latter have been recognised within some of the 'furnace pits' excavated within the Beaker mining camp, implying that it was this rather more complex deposit which was being worked during the main phase of operation of the mine. Indeed, the lead isotope ratios associated with Type A metal appears to form a closer match with the ores from the Blue Hole deposit than they do with the ores from the Western Mine (O'Brien 1999).

It is thought that smelting would have been undertaken at or close to the mine, although finds of metal here are limited to a small copper slab (ingot?) and a single droplet of raw copper, and some copper matte. Meanwhile the complete absence of tuyere debris/blow-pipe tips, crucibles or slag has been explained by there once having been furnaces much closer to the lake shore (O'Brien 2004), an alternative explanation for this being the use of slag-free smelting technique (Craddock 1995). To prove the possibilities of the latter suggestion an experimental smelting of *fahlerz* ore was undertaken by O'Brien and his colleagues using reconstructions of the furnace pits. This met with qualified success producing copper prills and a small amount of slag/clinker waste (O'Brien 2004). Whatever the method, it appears that there was a well-developed sulphide metallurgy being practised

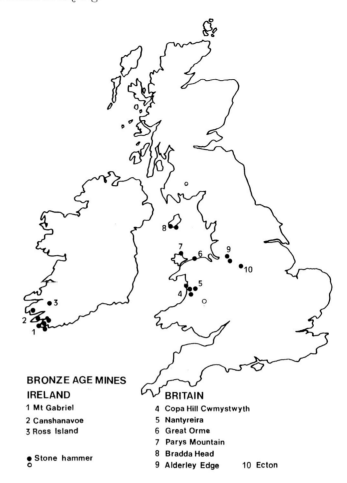

BRONZE AGE MINES
IRELAND
1 Mt Gabriel
2 Canshanavoe
3 Ross Island

● Stone hammer
○

BRITAIN
4 Copa Hill Cwmystwyth
5 Nantyreira
6 Great Orme
7 Parys Mountain
8 Bradda Head
9 Alderley Edge   10 Ecton

Figure 7.1 Bronze Age mining in the British Isles

here during the Copper Age–Early Bronze Age. Seemingly this was a characteristic of the later continental Beaker tradition, perhaps with connections to France (O'Brien 1999) or the alpine areas of Europe. Ross Island may not have been the earliest source of copper used in Ireland (the Castletownroche thick-butted axes may be Early Beaker or pre-Beaker and made of imported or local metal), or for that matter the only source of Irish *fahlerz* ore, yet it does provide us with one of the clearest links we have between an ore and a metal in circulation prior to the melting pot of the Early Bronze Age.

In Britain the introduction of Type A axes and halberds superseded the earliest metalwork of continental origin such as that found associated with Early Beaker burials such as at Radley Hill, Oxfordshire (Northover 1999). However, within 200 years of this we find metal of similar composition prominent within the Scottish Migdale tradition (*c* 2100–1900 BC). Originally thought to represent the exploitation of a rather similar British or Scottish *fahlerz* ore, this is now thought to be the result of the re-distribution of Irish metal entering the north of Britain via Antrim, in contraflow to the Bell Beaker material entering Southern Britain from the continent (Needham 2006). Although small-scale indigenous Copper Age production using locally sourced arsenical copper ores may be hinted at by the composition of axes such as those from the Moel Arthur hoard, we do seem to be looking at the contemporary Brithdir/Mile Cross metalwork (2150–1900 BC) for evidence of the first mixing of Irish and British metal in Southern Britain. During this period we witness the production of what is probably the first British tin bronze, almost certainly using an alluvial tin ore from the south-west of England.

Given the start of the mixing and first alloy-ing of metal, the task of matching metalwork with ore sources from this point onwards becomes increasingly difficult. Interestingly there is radiogenic lead within some of the copper metal used, a fact which may indicate the use of ores from Devon and Cornwall, but alongside this there is a very distinct change in metal impurity composition. This changes from the high-Nickel Bell Beaker metal common to Southern Britain which is associated with an Early Beaker Atlantic continental tradition based on carbonate metallurgy with its origins in Iberia, to what Needham (2002) refers to as low-Nickel Bell Beaker metal (0.1 per cent Ni), a composition which may be wholly or partly produced from British copper ores. The distribution pattern of this new type of metal within South-Central Britain falls off sharply northwards, suggesting amongst other options a possible origin in Wales. Welsh chalcopyrite and the oxidised ores formed from the weathering of this mineral which contain low levels of arsenic and nickel in amounts similar to those present within Northover's Group B4 (Northover 1980b) may yet prove to be suitable source ores for some of this low-Ni BB metal.

Within British metalwork the Type A impurity pattern continues well into the Early Bronze Age (Rohl and Needham 1998), the final cut-off level for this being around 1800 BC, a date which seems to correspond to the exhaustion of the easily mineable shallow ore at Ross Island and the flooding of the Blue Hole workings as a result of rising lake levels (O'Brien 2004). This inundation may have been a response to the climatic down-turn of the early 2nd millennium BC, an event which also affected the upland mine of Copa Hill, Cwmystwyth in West Wales. It is interesting to speculate therefore on the effects of both natural and anthropogenically induced environmental change alongside those of economic and social change on the overall level of early mining and prospecting activity within the British Isles.

There seems little doubt that it was the introduction of larger amounts of Irish metal into Britain, coupled with its variable supply, which encouraged local prospection for and small-scale mining of Welsh and other copper ores. This assumption appears to be supported by the very earliest dates we have of 2100 BC or before for three of the later 2nd millennium mid-Wales mines (Timberlake forthcoming). Clearer still is the general up-turn in prospection which seems to have followed the final abandonment of Ross Island mine. Whilst it is quite difficult to pin-point any date for certain within a radiocarbon dated chronology, the existing calibrated dates we have for already excavated sites would seem to indicate that what we are witnessing is large numbers of primitive mines appearing around, or just after, 1850 BC.

In south-west Ireland three Mount Gabriel-type mines have been located on the Beara Peninsula (Canshanavoe, Crumpane and Toreen) whilst eight sites including the Mount Gabriel complex (31 mines) and Derrycarhoon have been identified on the Mizzen Peninsula, Co. Cork. Of these, five within the Goleen area have now been excavated (Carrigacat and Milleen, Calloras Oughter, Boulysallagh, Ballyrisode and Toormore). Others are implied, such as by reference to the 'Dane's workings' on Horse Island and elsewhere (O'Brien 2003). Most however appear to be relatively short-lived trials or mines worked during a well-defined 400 year period (the last around 1400 BC). These small fire-set drift workings exploited low-grade copper bed deposits consisting of disseminated sulphides (bornite and chalcocite) and carbonates similar to those found on Mount Gabriel (O'Brien 1994). Individual mines may have produced on average 100 kg or less of metal from 30–100 tonnes of mined rock before becoming flooded, abandoned, then rapidly covered by peat. Whether or not the much richer veins of copper ore (bornite) outcropping along the coastline of the Beara Peninsula mined on an industrial scale during the 19th century AD (Williams 1991) were first targeted by Bronze Age prospectors in preference to the much poorer copper beds inland remains a moot point (O'Brien 1996) Unfortunately no such evidence survives, either of the vein or the coastal copper-bed workings, yet the association of these prospection territories with coastal locations remains; all of the sites lying within a few kilometres of the sea, from the beaches of which cobbles were collected for use as tools within the mines (O'Brien 1994).

The catalogue of radiocarbon dates for Bronze Age mines within the British Isles makes no distinction at all between the dates for this phase of prospection in SW Ireland and that on the mainland of Britain. Quite possibly there was none. If anything, we may have slightly earlier dates for Wales, yet clearly much of this prospection was simultaneous, sampling a variety of different geological environments ranging from massive volcanogenic sulphides (pyrite) ore bodies to Triassic Red Bed deposits. Despite this apparent randomness of exploitation, we can still get some idea of the routes taken along this greater 'prospection path' as those in search of metal, or with an interest in it, made their way across the British Isles. What we begin to see here are indications of island hopping, a link to coastlines, coastal promontories and seaward-facing mountains, such as along the western seaboard of Wales and then along the large river valleys and plains into Central England – in short a maritime link from west to east across the Irish Sea (Fig 7.2).

The Irish Sea connection: territorial links with copper, tin and gold

The Isle of Man, an island rich in Beaker and Early Bronze Age remains and one of the principle stopping-off points for the earliest seafarers between Ireland and Britain, was also on the route along which some of the first metallurgists travelled. We can see this in the evidence (though still undated) for prehistoric prospection around the southern tip of the island, such as on the Langness peninsula where hammer stones associated with an area of copper mineralisation were found during fieldwalking in 1999 (Doonan and Eley 2000),

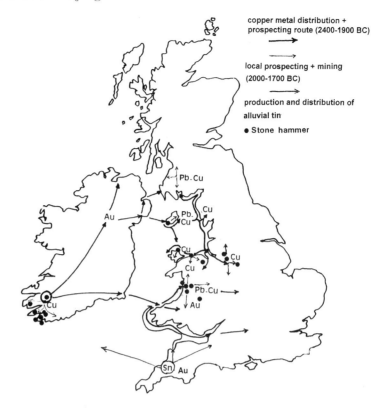

Figure 7.2 The 'metal prospection route' 2400–1700 BC; one interpretation

whilst to the west of here, similar tools made of basalt beach cobbles were recovered from North Bradda Head in 1998 (Doonan and Hunt 1999) and from South Bradda Head in 1987 (Pickin and Worthington 1989). Adjacent to the natural harbour of Port Erin, South Bradda forms a prominent headland which faces west and looks out across the Irish Sea, the visibly copper-stained cliffs here being associated with a rich lode containing chalcopyrite, secondary minerals, and quartz described by Lamplugh in 1903 as being 'amongst the most spectacular displays of quartz veining in Europe' (Fig 7.3). The presence of mineral here can still be seen far out to sea, much as it would have been in antiquity as the Neolithic and Bronze Age peoples crossed in their plank boats or *curraghs* from Ireland. The presence of this 'metal route' seems all the clearer when we examine the Copper Age/Early Bronze Age metalwork from the island which shows affinities with both Irish and early Welsh and Scottish (Migdale) axes, along with the mixing (or recycling) of Ross Island metal with copper from other sources (Davey et al 1999).

The position of the Isle of Man becomes all the more striking when we compare it with the metalliferous coastline of SW England

Figure 7.3 The copper lodes of Bradda Head, Isle of Man; the presence of these veins would have been visible far out to sea (photograph D Kenkins)

(Cornwall), an area rich in easily exploitable copper ores (including native copper, carbonates, arsenates and copper sulphides) but with no evidence of prehistoric mining (Craddock and Craddock 1996; Sharpe 1997), Irish type-A metal axes or halberds, or indeed any substantial Early Beaker presence. Indeed there is very little Copper Age metalwork from Cornwall or Devon, and none of this seems likely to be local (Northover 1999). Rohl and Needham (1998) tentatively suggest SW England as a possible source of the radiogenic copper ores responsible for the IMP-LI2 metal, but there are few analyses, and no clear links with local metalwork. What we do have however is an Irish 'influence from afar' in the Harlyn Bay gold lunulae (2300–2000 BC), objects which appear to be made from local alluvial gold (Penhallurick 1997) in the Kerry lunulae style. This may be evidence of an interest in metallurgy amongst emerging entrepreneurial groups, but at the same time a dominance of the old lineages which resisted change (Pearce 1983; O'Brien 1994). Alternatively this could be seen as a response to the continuation of a locally viable stone axe tradition (O'Brien 1999), or quite simply a disinterest in mining in a landscape where the focus of wealth was agricultural. The latter seems credible when one considers the amount of land under cultivation within the mineral-rich granite uplands of the South-West during the Early Bronze Age (Herring 1997). Yet another reason might be the presence of alluvial gold and tin, both more valuable and easier to extract than copper ore, the latter in the form of an almost unlimited deposit of high grade cassiterite gravel. Prehistoric workings may have been located in the Carnon, Pentewan, and Fal valleys and around Bodmin Moor and Penwith. From all of these tin gravels has come considerable artefactual evience of Bronze Age activity; this includes possible mining tools such as antler picks. Unfortunately most of these objects were discovered and disturbed by later tin streaming works (Penhallurick 1986; 1997).

Gold production here could never have held sway with that undertaken in Ireland at the end of the third/beginning of the second millennium BC, yet control of this tin resource may have commanded a much more significant economic leverage. The extent of this influence will have depended upon the level of cross-Channel exchange then taking place with Brittany, another potentially important tin producer with clear influences in Wessex (Penhalurick 1986). O'Brien emphasises the links between Atlantic France (Brittany), Britain and Ireland in the context of the transference of Beaker traditions and metallurgical knowledge (O'Brien 1994; 2004), yet the actual contacts forged this way may have been relatively short-lived or intermittent. More long-standing perhaps would have been the renewable agreements made between distinct regional groups of metalworkers and pastoralists who undertook mining on a periodic basis within their grazing territories, as well as with those chiefdoms controlling the strategic resources and rich agricultural landscapes of the henge territories of Wessex and Cornwall. Thus Cornish tin may have become a much more prestigious and valued object by virtue of the control exerted on its production and distribution; access to it only being possible through the act of alloying this with a metal produced outside of the production area (Timberlake 2002a). Agreements may also have been made on the reciprocal exchange of finished metal objects, and on limits the level of production and the amounts of re-cycling permitted. Consensus on the latter may have helped to control or standardise the composition of metal.

Whilst this might help to explain the absence of Copper Age/Early Bronze Age copper mining within the South-West, a situation implied by the complete absence of stone mining hammers at any of the lode exposures examined (Timberlake 1992a, Budd and Gale 1994; Sharpe 1997), it really doesn't help us much with the reasons why we find no evidence for this within some of the other copper-rich areas of the UK such as North Wales (Snowdonia), the Lake District and parts of Southern Scotland (Timberlake 1992a). Some finds of hammer stones are known from areas of Cumbrian mining such as around Coniston (King 1996; Lund 2001), yet these appear to be neither the right size or type for mining tools, and still more importantly, none have been found at the actual mine sites themselves. Although there are references to 'pre-Roman' stone mining tools found within old workings in the Leadhills (Wilson 1921), a single surviving example of an Alderley Edge-type grooved stone mining hammer found at or close to the Wanlockhead Mine in the 1930s is probably the only artefactual evidence for Bronze Age-type prospection or mining from the whole of Scotland (*info* John Pickin 2001).

Beaker metallurgist/prospectors within Wales and England

The mines of the Isle of Man, the North Wales coast (Great Orme and Parys Mountain), Mid-Wales, Alderley Edge and Ecton stand alone in Britain as being on the 'metal route', a network linking Ireland with Southern Britain. The fact is this matches quite closely the route of the 'Beaker Folk Penetration' first mapped by Lal Chitty and Christopher Hawkes more than 60 years ago; one which linked East Anglia, the Peak District and the Cheshire Plain with North Wales and Anglesey, another branch cutting across the middle of Wales to the Dovey Valley and the coast of Ceredigion (Varley 1964). Of course in this case the movement is shown going the other way, yet it is the gross similarity in the overall pattern which emphasises the use of the same well-worn paths! Burl (1976) makes the link between the movement of Beaker peoples and/or their influence into Wales and the presence of stone circles in Pembrokeshire. Alongside this was the abundant evidence of

burials (settlement) and of course Early Bronze Age bluestone extraction in the Preselis, the evidence for which has been confirmed by recent excavations on Carn Menyn (Darvill *et al* 2005). Significantly Burl suggested a link between the Preselis, bluestone and Beaker Period metal prospectors travelling by boat down the coastline of Wales and around the headlands of Pembrokeshire. Other possible links between Wessex and Wales have been suggested by isotope studies carried out on the bones of the 'Amesbury Archer' and 'Boscome Bowmen' burials (*see* Fitzpatrick this volume). The isotope data obtained from the latter skeletons suggested that they may have lived for at least part of their adult lives within the Lower Palaeozoic lands of Wales. Whether hunters, begetters of bluestone or metallurgists their presence here may have acted as a conduit, catalyst or source of economic motivation for the earliest exploitation of copper.

The presence of hunting groups passing through these mineral landscapes is suggested in the mid-Wales area by the considerable numbers of Beaker-type barb and tang flint arrowheads (over 70) found on the Plynlimon moorlands around Llyn Bugeilyn in Montgomeryshire (Peate 1925a; Peate 1925b; Savory 1980; CPAT SMR 2002), all of them apparently as single chance finds which suggests loss during hunting expeditions. Many were described as being of 'Irish affinity', a type rare in Britain but with many parallels in Co. Antrim, Co. Down and Co. Mayo (Peate 1928). In fact the actual distribution of these arrowheads within the uplands is a good deal wider than this, with find spots ranging from Dylife to Cwmystwyth (as suggested by the numbers of unreported finds), many of which seem to be associated with sheltered moorland areas encircling natural tarns, perhaps woodland clearings where red deer once congregated. The presence of and exploitation of these animals is indicated by finds of antler in the Early Bronze Age mines such as on Copa Hill (Cwmystwyth). It is believed that between 100–300 antler tools may have been consumed during the working of the latter mine alone (Timberlake 2003).

It seems unlikely, given what we now know of the better studied mines such as Copa Hill and the Great Orme, that Beaker metallurgists were ever directly involved in their working. This activity was probably the role of the pastoralists who had traditional grazing rights within these areas; marginal peoples on marginal lands who might nevertheless have related and traded directly with these Beaker hunters and metalworkers who passed through their territories. The trade of metal or ore was simply the means by which these subsistence peoples could enter into the exchange economy (*see* Shennan 1999; Timberlake 2003). To some extent the Beaker incomers may also have remained on the outside of most established territory-holding lineal groups (Parker Pearson 1993) thus their presence within the upland grazing and hunting landscapes of Wales would not be altogether surprising, even though little in the way of associated artefacts or burial monuments survive within the areas of these mines. Most likely the 'Beaker' connection with these early mines may have been limited to the first wave of prospection *c* 2200–1900 BC, the role of middle-men and metallurgists being replaced by others during the main period of copper production (1900–1600 BC). We should be aware that apart from the huts and settlement and pottery found at Ross Island which date to an early stage in this tradition, there are few examples of direct Beaker-type association with these sites. However, a quick examination of what evidence there is from Wales and Cheshire (Alderley Edge) might be useful here.

Radiocarbon dates of *c* 2400 BC as well as thumb-nail flint scrapers were obtained from an early mine pit-working on Engine Vein, Alderley Edge in 1998 (Timberlake and Prag 2005). However, the possibility of contamination with material derived from the sides of these pits (such as the inclusion of Mesolithic flintwork) puts any dates earlier than 1900 BC into question. Also of relevance was the find of an axe-hammer re-used as a mining implement nearby at Pillar Mine (Pickin 2005). In this case there was no evidence that the original implement was of Beaker type, or that it was contemporary with the mining. In addition, no known Beaker monuments or groups of finds are associated with the site, or even with its immediate vicinity. Nevertheless, there does seem to be a concentration of Early Bronze Age stone axe-hammer finds in the Alderley Edge/Macclesfield area with several examples from the Edge (Timberlake and Prag 2005). Roe (1979) suggested that there might be a connection between these and copper

mining, though it is possible in the case of Pillar Mine that we are simply looking at the re-use of a residual and broken implement. The discovery of a complete Beaker-type axe-hammer within the 'old workings' of a copper mine in Co. Cork may provide better evidence of an association with mining (Simpson 1990). From Britain we have a vague record for the discovery underground of a 'perforated stone implement' within the workings of the Trecastell Lead Mine near Conwy, North Wales (Davies 1937), whilst the collections of the Manx Museum contain an axe-hammer from the Foxdale mine on the Isle of Man (Pickin 1990). What we are less certain about here is the relevance of their context.

In North Wales there appear to be no dateable finds or sites of Beaker Age directly associated with the prehistoric mines of Parys Mountain and the Great Orme, although we do find monuments of Beaker Age including henges along the North Wales coast, and plenty more in Anglesey.

The Banc Tynddol disc, lunulae and the exploitation of alluvial gold

By far the most interesting and likely Beaker connection with mining is to be found in mid-Wales. At Banc Tynddol, Cwmystwyth, an apparently now empty though clearly disturbed Beaker grave was found during the excavation of an Early Medieval lead smelting bole located at the foot of the Comet Lode mineral vein, the top of which was worked at the very beginning of the Bronze Age (Timberlake 2004a). Given the paucity of prehistoric monuments in the vicinity it seems quite possible that the two sites were in some way connected. From the grave came the single find of a centrally perforated gold foil disc decorated with a repoussé ornamentation (see Fig 7.4) undertaken in the classic Early Beaker style, *c* 2500–2100 BC (Timberlake 2002b). Whilst this shows certain similarities with Breton, Scottish and Northern English examples, by far the greatest number of similar discs come from Ireland, in particular from the wedge tomb territories of Co. Cork and Kerry linked with the Mount Gabriel-type 'primitive mines' (Fig 7.5; O'Brien 1994; 2004).

In Ireland there is a sharp distinction between the distribution of discs and that of the gold lunulae, the latter linked instead

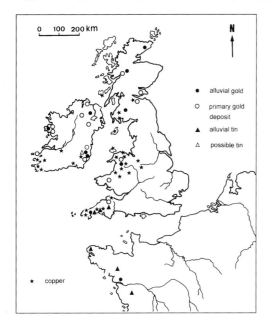

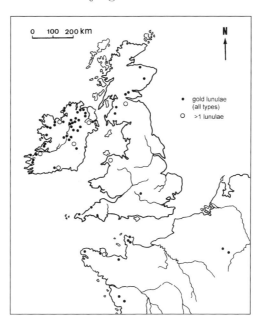

Figure 7.4 (left) Mineral deposits of the British Isles and Northern France; gold, copper and tin occurrences

Figure 7.5 (right) The distribution of Copper Age–Early Bronze Age gold lunulae within the British Isles and Northern France (modified after Taylor 1994)

Figure 7.6 (below) The distribution of Beaker and Early Bronze Age gold foil ornaments within the British Isles and Northern France (modified after Taylor 1994)

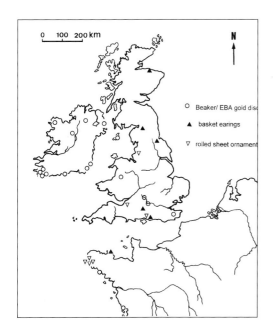

to henge monument territories and finds of Beaker pottery and settlement, and perhaps also the rich arsenical copper deposits of Central Kerry (Fig 7.5). This observation led O'Brien (2004) to speculate upon the contrasting but vying control between the two different areas. In this model he suggested the Mount Gabriel mines would have been under local tribal control, the occurrence of gold discs being symbolic of a less dominant but contemporary 'Beaker inspired' style, one linked perhaps to the very margins of

their cultural and economic influence. Might the Banc Tynddol disc be part of the same phenomenon? Its discovery at Cwmystwyth might provide us with a link to Ireland and also a Beaker-influenced local tradition rather than to a background of direct control exercised by a mining elite and practising metallurgists. The analysis of this gold is also consistent with it being of Irish origin, although it should be said how difficult it is to distinguish between natural unalloyed alluvial gold from Irish and British sources.

The current consensus of opinion is that alluvial gold was being worked in the Wicklow Mountains and perhaps also around Croagh Patrick, Co. Mayo and elsewhere in the centre of Ireland as early as 2200 BC (Taylor 1994; O'Brien 2004; BBC 2006). The possibilities of former occurrences of alluvial gold are greater still based on what we now know of the widespread distribution of gold-bearing rocks (McArdle *et al* 1987; and *see* Fig 7.4). It is interesting therefore to look at the distribution of gold lunulae finds within the British Isles, for it is these rather than the gold discs (Fig 7.6) which reasonably accurately demarcate the gold-producing territories. We see this in Ireland where the sheer numbers and clusters of finds suggest local production, but in Britain where finds of classical or provincial type lunulae are rare, the correspondence with known alluvial gold deposits is even more striking. The Cornish examples from Harlyn

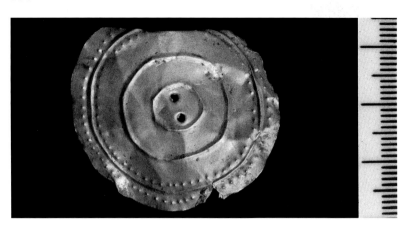

Figure 7.7 The Banc Tynddol gold disc, Copa Hill, Cwmystwyth (reproduced with the permission of the National Museum of Wales, Cardiff)

Bay and St. Juliot contain gold with traces of tin suggestive of a local alluvial source, the Ladock and the Carnon Valley having produced significant nuggets of gold within recent historic times (Penhallurick 1986). In North Wales the findspot of the Llanllyfni lunula near Dolbenmaen (Savory 1980) lies within 20 km of the Dolgellau goldfield, whilst in the Southern Uplands and North-Eastern Scotland gold lunulae have been found within moderate distances of alluvial gold deposits such as the Leadhills and Helmsdale in Sutherland. The trading or long-distance exchange of these worn and possibly heirloom artefacts may not in fact have been the norm, though local manufacture, use, concealment and burial perhaps was.

However, as with the earliest copper axes, the distribution of Beaker gold discs may imply the existence of some sort of exchange route between Ireland and Britain, perhaps via the Isle of Man, with deposition in the Thames valley and then a cross-Channel link to Brittany. The latter may also have been a gold-producing region during the Copper/ Early Bronze Age, whilst to the south of here we have similar gold artefacts being produced on the Atlantic seaboard of Iberia. Taylor notes this link between the discs and Irish gold sources, but also with the copper mining areas of SW Ireland (Taylor 1994). Interestingly, the Ballyvourney disc found near Mount Gabriel showed certain similarities to Banc Tynddol; in this the cross was absent and instead was replaced by concentric circles, the latter suggesting continuity with discs of a similar style found along coastal Iberia and France. It was even suggested that this emblem may have been a recognisable badge worn by somebody representing mining or metallurgical

interests (Taylor 1994, 46). Within Britain, the questionably earlier basket earings and rolled sheet ornament types of gold work appear to be associated with 3rd millennium Beaker burials which have a predominantly Wessex and NE England distribution, and once again, a possible link with henge territories. In this respect at least the Banc Tynddol gold disc is both interesting and unusual; in its form, size and composition this shows strong similarities with the Southern Irish gold foil discs, yet the simpler style of ornament consisting of alternating circular lines and rings of punctations is much rarer amongst the discs but common in the earlier basket earings. These latter artefacts are characteristically British and uniquely associated with Early Beaker burials.

The first miners in Wales

Does the above evidence provide us with any clues concerning an earlier presence of Beaker metalworkers and mineral prospectors travelling west into the mid-Wales *c* 2400–2200 BC, or does it suggest a later influx around 2000 BC? If the latter is the case, then this prospection phase would have post-dated the Copper Age/Early Bronze Age decline in mining at Ross Island but could coincide with the period of 'primitive mine' prospection around the coastline of SW Ireland (O'Brien 1994, 1996). The answer to this may or may not lie in a number of recently obtained third millennium BC radiocarbon dates obtained from the earliest workings on Copa Hill, Tyn y Fron and Erglodd, all of which are located in Ceredigion, mid-Wales (Timberlake 2008 *forthcoming*). These workings appear to considerably pre-date the exploitation of the Mount Gabriel-type mines, suggesting at least the presence of an earlier Irish or non-Irish influenced prospection here in Wales which coincided with the height of Copper Age copper production in Ireland. With this in mind it is interesting perhaps that a copper halberd made of A1 (Irish 'Ross Island type' metal) was found 'near a copper-mine at Pontrhydygroes' (close to Cwmystwyth) sometime during the nineteenth century (Savory 1980; Briggs 1994). We know little of the circumstances of the find, yet it does seem to provide us with another metalwork link between these early Welsh mines and Ireland, moreover one that could also be contemporary with the Banc Tynddol find.

Although we may be looking at a phenomenon which appears at the end of the Irish Copper Age, the widespread prospection for metal, of which Cwmystwyth is part of, hails of what has been previously referred to as the 'Early Bronze Age copper rush'; an event which may relate more to a perceived shortage and to local opportunistic exploitation rather than to any sort of significant production. However, the period 1800–1650 BC seems to represent the acme of this first phase of prospection and exploitation of copper ores in Britain; one that is pretty much centred on Wales.

Early Bronze Age mines of the North Wales coast: Parys Mountain and the Great Orme

At least 20 'primitive mines' associated with stone hammers and/or bone or antler tools have now been identified in Wales, with two the largest situated along the North Wales coast (Fig 7.8). On Parys Mountain (Amlwch, NE Anglesey) chalcopyrite veins of the Carreg-y-Doll and North Discovery Lodes (which may or may not have contained copper sulphides, sulphates, oxides or even native copper at surface) were being worked at outcrop close to the summit of the mountain as early as 1900 BC (Timberlake 1990; Jenkins 1995). These mines soon developed into what appear to have been opencast inclined drifts driven into the veins (Timberlake 2002c), the latter excavated by means of firesetting and the use of stone mauls through the hard quartz-veined rocks reaching depths of up to 20–30 m below surface (Jenkins 1995), this perhaps over a 100–150 year period (Jenkins 2002). Sedimentation and waterlogging within the iron ochre-rich clays at the base of these ancient stopes has ensured the preservation of organic material including bracken, acorns, wood and charcoal (Mighall and Jenkins *pers comm*). These occur in the silts which lie sandwiched in between layers of slumped-in or backfilled spoil, the latter dumped or else washed back down from surface. However, no evidence for the processing or smelting of ores has been recognized within this, or within the mine tips examined at surface (Timberlake 1990); much of the area is now covered with thousands of tonnes of nineteenth century

mine spoil. The source of the cobbles used in the mines seems to be the rocky coastline just a few kilometres distant. This may also have been the location for the original discovery of copper ores, stone hammers having been reported from an old 'Roman Level' discovered in 1872 during the working of a small trial for copper at Pant y Gaseg on the sea cliffs near Bull Bay west of Amlwch (Mining Journal 1872). Today the site is open but no evidence of early working is visible.

Despite their similar situation buried beneath thousands of tonnes of modern mine spoil, the workings on the Great Orme's Head, Llandudno (less than 30 km east of Parys Mountain) present a quite different geological picture (Figs 7.9a–7.9b). Here sub-parallel veins carrying chalcopyrite, which show near-surface alteration to the oxidised minerals malachite, azurite and limonite, were mined from the Early Bronze Age onwards (Lewis 1990). The presence of caves or karstic solution hollows within the limestone enabled primitive style mining to be carried out to depths of 70 metres below the surface without the problems of flooding (Timberlake 2002c). The soft dolomitised limestone beds beneath the Pyllau Valley, close to the summit of this steep-sided Carboniferous Limestone headland, could easily be quarried away to expose and work the discontinuous vertical veins of copper mineral as well as the clay wayboards and mudstones which contained thin seams of redeposited malachite and azurite (James 1988; Lewis 1990; Timberlake 2002c). The true extent of this early opencast

Figure 7.8 Bronze Age mines and finds of stone mining hammers in Wales

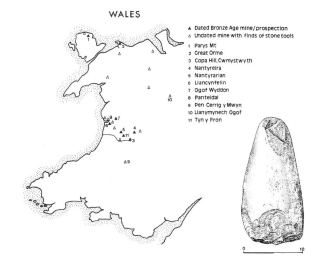

WALES

▲ Dated Bronze Age mine/prospection
△ Undated mine with finds of stone tools

1 Parys Mt
2 Great Orme
3 Copa Hill, Cwmystwyth
4 Nantyreira
5 Nantyrarian
6 Llancynfelin
7 Ogof Wyddon
8 Panteidal
9 Pen Cerrig y Mwyn
10 Llanymynech Ogof
11 Tyn y Fron

Figure 7.9a (above) The Great Orme Bronze Age opencast workings, Pyllau Valley, Great Orme Head, Llandudno in 1990 (photograph S Timberlake)

Figure 7.9b (right) A cache of bone and stone mining tools deposited within a worked cavity in the side of the Great Orme opencast (photograph S Timberlake)

mine workings consisting of up to 6.5 km of passage were discovered. (Lewis 1990; 1996). Modern miners first broke into these sealed and partially backfilled caverns in 1831, and again in 1849 (Stanley 1850) during the course of deep mining from shafts.

More than 15 radiocarbon dates have now been obtained from the Great Orme. These have come from charcoal used in firesetting and from lighting splints as well as from simple scraper and pick tools fabricated from domestic animal bone; the latter were recovered from amongst thousands of other fragments of bone, much of it food waste, distributed alongside the mauls within the backfilled galleries and stopes (Lewis 1996; James 1988; David; 1998; 1999; 2000; 2001). The dates range from around 1800 BC to about 600 BC, most of these being Early-Middle Bronze Age, with the Middle-Late Bronze Age dates generally confined to the deepest workings. A single Medieval date was obtained from prehistoric mine spoil which had been removed from the mine to Ffynnon Galchog (Lewis 1996), one of many natural springs on the sides of the limestone headland used for the washing of ore. This processing or re-processing of the waste to extract malachite took place either during the Bronze Age, as suggested by Ottaway and Wager (2000), or it involved a later re-working, something which is suggested by local legend at Ffynnon Rhufeiniog ('Roman Well'). Nevertheless, the height of Early Bronze Age production on the Great Orme seems to equate with the period 1700–1500 BC. This would seem to match with the suggestion of Rohl and Needham (1998) that the slightly radiogenic ore of the Great Orme could be responsible for the distinctive lead isotope composition present within the Arreton (bronze) metalwork assemblage of the British Bronze Age. However, it is important to remember that the Great Orme is unique both in terms of its size as well as its continuity of mining into the Middle Bronze Age. Production from this mine post-1400 BC probably provided much of the copper used in Acton Park metalwork, an industry with a very distinct regional basis in North Wales (Rohl and Needham 1998; Northover 1982).

Against this back-drop of the Great Orme as a significant player in British Early-Middle Bronze Age copper production we should consider the position of the more numerous,

from which about 28400 tonnes of rock was removed in antiquity was only revealed following archaeological excavation (Dutton and Fasham 1994) and subsequently clearance carried out during the early 1990s as part of a plan to open it up as a tourist attraction; currently Europe's only Bronze Age Mine open to the public. Whilst clearing underground passages accessible from the sides and bottom of the opencast a network of Bronze Age

yet smaller Early Bronze Age mines and trials in Wales. The origins of many pre-date the Orme, yet are eclipsed by it. Most however have provided us with some insight into this period of transformation and exploitation of the upland landscape, the technology of primitive mining, and at least some of the reasons for their abandonment. In fact the largest known group of these sites in Britain is to be found within the Central Wales Orefield, all of them linked to surface or shallow outcrops of copper ore (chalcopyrite) associated with what were predominantly lead-zinc sulphide lodes (Fig 7.10).

The Early Bronze Age mines of mid-Wales

At least 12 mines have been identified within an area ranging from north of the Dovey (Panteidal and Balkan Hill) southwards to the Ystwyth Valley (Cwmystwyth), and eastwards beyond Plynlimon to the headwaters of the River Severn (Nantyreira and Nantyricket Mines). The last three sites are to be found within the uplands above the 400m contour and are amongst the most isolated locations for mining in Wales. Pretty much all of the mines listed have now been investigated, whilst most have also been archaeologically excavated and radiocarbon dated (see Table 7.1). The latter has involved the sampling of burnt wood (charcoal), wooden artefacts, mining timbers, antler tools, and the primary deposited short-lived organics (twigs/leaves) which overlie the earliest mining sediments.

An examination of the geographical distribution of these Early Bronze Age mines and trials within the Central Wales orefield shows a nucleated pattern which doesn't particularly relate to the distribution of copper mineralisation. Whilst all of these early worked sites appear to have near-surface showings of copper, some of the richer deposits such as at Dylife, Esgairfraith, Gwestyn and Guefron show no indications of having been touched. This is particularly surprising at Guefron Mine where the ores are partly oxidised and malachite is abundant (Bick 1977).

Instead there appear to be a number of common factors to the location of Bronze Age mines/trials within these five 'prehistoric prospection areas' (Fig 7.10). This seems to include an association with lodes to be found

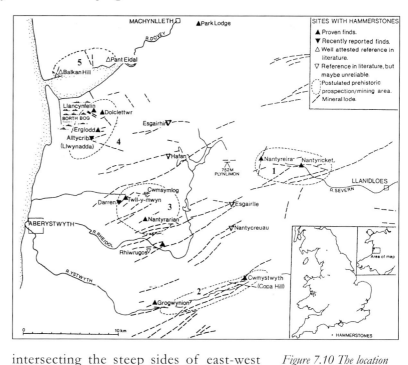

Figure 7.10 The location of Early Bronze Age mines and prospection areas (Areas 1–5) around Plynlimon in the Central Wales Mining Field

intersecting the steep sides of east-west river valleys, with mineral veins that outcrop around the margins of buried land surfaces such as Borth Bog (Prospection Area 4), with prominent white quartz or rusty brown ankerite veins, with visible iron-stained outcrops (some of which may also have had coatings of copper, lead, zinc and manganese oxides/carbonates precipitated from springs issuing on the faults), and finally with the discovery of 'tumblers' of galena and well mineralised vein-rock present within the beds of streams or else in scree below the mineral outcrops (Timberlake 2002c). However, there must be other factors as well, probably those relating to land-use, ancient de-afforestation and erosion.

Attempts have been made to try and link cycles of increased alluviation and silting-up of river systems in Britain during the Neolithic and Early Bronze Age to climate deterioration enhanced by the effects of woodland clearance and agriculture taking place throughout the upland areas of Britain (Macklin and Lewin 2003). In this case one of the first environmental disasters to hit the uplands of Plynlimon may have resulted from the sporadic burning and felling of woodland in order to make space for pasture. This de-afforestation would have led to the inadvertent hushing of the hillsides, and as a result, the first discovery of workable ores (Timberlake 2002a). These various groupings of mines referred to as 'prospection

mine	location	finds/ C14 date	discovery/ excavation	references	date range (2 sigma)
Balkan Hill	Aberdovey	-	mined 1823	Bowen & Gresham 1963; Pickin 1990	Bronze Age?
Panteidal	Aberdovey	mauls, 30m opencast, 'water races	discovered 1899; surveyed/trenched 1996	*Mining Journal* 1899; Timberlake 2008 *(forthcoming)*	Bronze Age?
Park Lodge (Ogof Wyddon)	Machynlleth	mauls, opencast, tip, charcoal (C14)	discovered 1856; trench excavation 1997	RCAHM(W 1911; Timberlake & Mason 1997	1890–1630 Cal BC
Llancynfelin	Trer-ddol	3 sites: Site A (Borth Bog) 44 mauls, mortar, C14 charcoal	mined 1800s; trenched 1992, peat core 2003	Bick 1976; Timberlake 1992b, 1995, 2002c	1745–1645 Cal BC
Pwll Roman	Tre-Taliesin	west edge of Borth Bog: mauls	mined 1852; surveyed 2004	Timberlake 2004c	Bronze Age?
Erglodd	Talybont	NW edge Borth Bog: mauls, charcoal (C14)	mined 1800s; surveyed/trenched 2005	*Mining Journal* 1869; Hughes 1981; Timberlake 2006 *(forthcoming)*	2340–2130 Cal BC
Twll y mwyn (Cwm Darren	Penrhyncoch	>50m long opencast, mauls, charcoal (C14)	discovered 1744; surveyed/trenched 2005	Lewis Morris (1744) in Bick & Davies 1994; Timberlake 2006 *(forthcoming)*	1910–1700 Cal BC
Nantyrarian	Goginan	opencast, tip and mauls, charcoal (C14)	discovered 1866; surveyed/trenched 1992	*Cambrian Arch. Ass.*1866; Williams 1866; Timberlake 1992b, 1995, 2002c	1885–1735 Cal BC
Tyn y fron	Cwmrheidol	opencast, tip (track section), mauls, charcoal (C14)	discovered 1744, mined 1900s; surveyed/trenched 1996	Smyth 1848; Bick & Davies 1994; Timberlake 1996, 2002c	2135–1885 Cal BC
Nantyreira (Snowbrook)	Plynlimon	opencast >50m, mauls, mortar, charcoal (C14)	discovered 1859; dug 1937, trenched 1988	Jones 1922; Davies 1937; Timberlake 1990	1856–1610 Cal BC
Nantyricket	Plynlimon (River Severn)	opencast, tip, mauls	discovered 1800s	Jones 1922; Davies 1937; Timberlake 1990	Bronze Age?
Grogwynion	Pontrhydygroes	maul	1987	Thorburn 1990	Bronze Age?
Copa Hill (Comet Lode Opencast)	Cwmystwyth	opencast 10m+ deep and tips; mauls, antler tools, wooden launder, withies; wood, charcoal (C14)	discovered 1813; tips trenched 1930s and 1986, excavated 1989–1999	Smyth 1848; Jones 1922; Davies 1947; Timberlake 1987, 2003	X 25 C14 dates : approx. range 2100–1500 BC

Table 7.1 Dated and undated Bronze Age mining and prospecting sites in Central Wales

areas' might thus relate to quite specific woodland clearances undertaken within the grazing territories tenured by particular groups of pastoralists. It was probably these groups who opportunistically prospected for copper ore, thereafter engaging in mining seasonally as part of their annual transhumance cycle. The latter lifestyle will have involved the yearly movement of animals from the coastal lowlands up to the summer pastures. During the course of this migration the pastoralist miners would have been able to bring fresh supplies of rounded beach pebbles up to the mines on the backs of their animals, whilst at the same time using brushwood from the gradual and continuing clearance of the valley-side scrub oak woodland for fire setting.

Copa Hill: a case study of an Early Bronze Age mine

After almost 20 years of excavation and fieldwork the Comet Lode Opencast on Copa Hill (Cwmystwyth) is probably the best known and understood of the 17 identified Bronze Age metal mines in Britain. Here we are looking at a relatively undisturbed Early Bronze Age trench mine which remains intact within its upland setting, fortuitously preserved on account of its location on the brow of the hill and the rapidly accumulated peat infill and waterlogging of the opencast. In more recent times the partial drainage of this 40m long, 5–10m wide and over 10m deep opencast resulting from the driving of a shaft rise up into its base sometime during the late 18th–early 19th century has been similarly providential; this has enabled modern archaeological excavation to be carried out to depths of over 8m free of the problems of water. As such we are dealing with a happy coincidence. This is not to detract from the immense logistical problems associated with such a project, such as the undertaking of archaeology at this depth using shored sections, and the carrying of all materials and equipment up to site by foot, a steep climb of over 200 metres from the valley floor. This 10 year programme of excavations (1989–1999) provided the first in-depth study of a British Bronze Age mining site (Timberlake 2003).

Archaeological excavations undertaken against the north wall of the opencast in 1989–1990 uncovered a 'cave-like' prehistoric mine gallery complete with stone tool-marks preserved in its roof and the remains of fireset hearth and small caches of stone tools underneath (Fig 7.11). Subsequent excavations carried out within the front to middle part of the opencast revealed a great depth of accumulated scree, silt, re-deposited (slumped) tip, organic silt and up to 3m of mossy peat overlying backfilled timber and mine spoil resting upon thin deposits of Early Bronze Age mine sediments (Fig 7.12). These were draped over an emerging rock landscape of pillars and ledges left in between a series of thin worked-out veins. Effectively these sections through the middle of the opencast provided a comprehensive record of the use, abandonment and infill of this working dating from about 950 BC to 1800 AD; in the base of this working could be seen a peat of Early Bronze Age date which had formed *in situ* within the waterlogged bottoms of the already abandoned veins. This layer was being deposited whilst other areas of the mine were still being worked. Into it both tooled and burnt timber had been thrown along with abandoned sections of mine launder and wooden stemples. Evidence for rock cut ledges and steps descending into the deeper parts of the working suggest that these and the stemples rather than log ladders may have been used to gain access into the mine.

The most important discovery followed the excavation of a working area at the front of the opencast. Here a rock-cut channel up to 2m wide had been cut with a level to slightly dip-

Figure 7.11 (above) Bronze Age mining gallery with stone tool-marks preserved in its roof, Comet Lode Opencast, Copa Hill, Cwmstwyth (photograph P Craddock)

Figure 7.12 (left) Rock platforms within the Comet Lode Opencast emerging from beneath metres of peat infill following deep excavation in 1993 (photograph S Timberlake)

ping floor to assist in the removal of water from the mine. Mining sediments deposited in this area remained partially waterlogged, preserving a host of organic materials. This included fragments of twisted hazel (withy) rope, parts of a broken withy handle which once held a hammer stone, fragments of a basket thrown onto a fire but only half-burnt, the worn and broken ends of picks and a hammer fabricated from red deer antler, and finally a unique 5

Figure 7.13 (right) Part of a four thousand year old alder wood launder lying in situ within the entrance to the prehistoric mine on Copa Hill, Cwmstwyth in 1994 (photograph S Timberlake)

Figure 7.14 (a) (right) A discarded antler pick/hammer, (b) (below) a fragment of basketry rope and (c) (far right) hazel withies including the two halves of a broken handle which held a hammer stone (photographs by S Timberlake)

manufacture were still visible on its sides. This launder may once have formed part of a series of gutters tapping spring water and channelling it away from the deeper workings – perhaps one of the earliest examples of mine drainage known. An alternative, though possibly an additional function of this may have been to wash the crushed ore, separating the lighter copper (malachite and/or chalcopyrite) from the denser lead (galena). Certainly the evidence is that crushing was taking place within this area and that alternating lead-rich and copper-rich waterlain sediments were being deposited.

It seems that much of this ore was being crushed by hand on the tips outside of the mine using broken flat-sided stone hammers as anvils and small crushing stones. In this fashion the copper ore could be separated from the lead by eye and a large part of the galena discarded. An excavated vein of this can be seen in the floor of the entrance area to the mine still with a stone chisel jammed into it and large lumps of lead ore discarded either side (Fig 7.15). It appears that the miners may have been chasing it hoping that it would bunch out and lead to some pockets of copper. More

metre long split and hollowed out alder log used as a gutter or launder to carry away water from the inside of the mine (Figs 7.13–7.14). The launder has been radiocarbon dated to between 2400 and 1750 BC, suggesting an already long history of use in the mine before the date of its final abandonment around 1600 BC. We found the launder still *in situ* supported at the either end to take a flow of water out of the mine. On closer inspection, the cut marks of the flat copper or bronze axes used in its

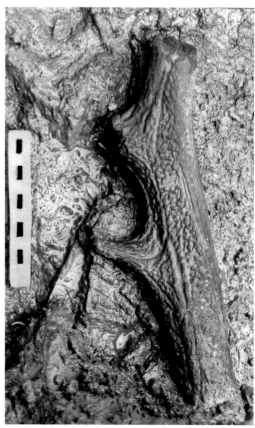

revealing was our micro-excavation of a single square metre of the surface of the mine tip at a point where a former crushing platform had been identified. The evidence that this was where the ore had been crushed was present in the form of finely crushed fragments of mineral and vein rock (< 5mm). Amongst these were large numbers of small (< 2mm) grains of iron oxide (goethite). Some of these were later sectioned, polished, and looked at under reflected light. Surprisingly most showed fresh unoxidised cores of chalcopyrite, suggesting that this was the mineral that the miners were trying to recover for processing, either for the sulphides or for oxidised minerals with which it was associated (Mighall *et al* 2000; Timberlake 2002c). Of course this provided an explanation for the apparent absence of copper ore despite the high concentration of dissolved copper analysed within the sediments and tips (Jenkins and Timberlake 1987).

During the Bronze Age mining was probably only ever carried out on a seasonal basis, something which is suggested by the presence of leaves and nuts on cut hazel branches brought up to site as well as by the presence

of an excess amount of freshly collected stone tool material, the latter being an indicator of repeated, though not necessarily well organised or regular mining campaigns (see Craddock 1995 regarding the Woman meteorite). Of course this approach would have made mining in the deeper parts prone to flooding difficult, hence one of the functions of the wooden launders. It seems likely that on occasions considerable de-watering of the bottoms would sometimes have been necessary; for example using skin bags for baling and perhaps also the cutting of narrow channels through the rock at lower levels.

The radiocarbon dates suggest that the main period of mining took place over just a one to two hundred year period (1750–1950 BC). However the earliest dates for prospection (in this case the digging of ore) begin around 2000–2100 BC, the location for this being the foot of the outcropping vein (now beneath the Lateral Tip) where minor trials and sampling of the vein seems to have been undertaken fairly early on (Timberlake 2004b).

The end of mining

The Comet Lode Opencast seems to have been abandoned as a result of flooding linked to the growth of the blanket peat above the mine, perhaps a result of tree clearance and/or climatic change. Another contributory factor could have been the exhaustion of the more easily won oxidised ores associated with sulphides in the upper part of this complex of

Figure 7.15 A small lead vein excavated in the search for copper ore. This was found surrounded by lumps of discarded galena, whilst a stone chisel remains firmly wedged across it (photograph S Timberlake)

veins forming the lode outcrop. The copper content of these veins appears to hold out at depth, but these are all of un-oxidised chalcopyrite, an ore which was probably not worked on its own until the later historic period.

Given what we know or suspect of this piecemeal low-key exploitation of minerals during the Early Bronze Age a relatively minor environmental impact from the actual mining (post-original woodland clearance) is not entirely unexpected. This is borne out by several recent palaeo-environmental studies. At Cwmystwyth pollen cores and monoliths taken from the surrounding blanket peat show small declines in oak (the main timber and fuel wood used in the mine) as well as a geochemical signature resulting from lead/copper pollution which clearly relates to the period of Bronze Age mining. Whilst detectable, the scale of this fluctuation in tree pollen is very minor, something which suggests neither manage-ment (coppicing) nor wholesale clearance, but instead low-intensity grazing which has helped maintain a mixture of open woodland and grassland. Nevertheless, the perpetuation of these cleared areas could have been one of the factors responsible for the gradually encroaching blanket bog and increasingly wet conditions in the mine (Mighall and Chambers 1993a; 1993b; Mighall *et al* 2002). This flooding led to its final abandonment around 1600 BC. Just as the environmental effects of land use led to the discovery of these sites, it also contributed to their final demise.

How much copper?

We can only hazard a guess at the amount of copper ore that was mined from the Comet Lode Opencast during the Bronze Age. Given the low grade of the primary ore (at 20–25 per cent copper) and its variable distribution with good ore being less than 1 per cent of the rock extracted, coupled with a minimum recovery rate of 30–40 per cent after hand-picking and crushing (much less if the miners were gravity separating oxidised ores from the sulphides using water), we might be looking at a production of only 50+ tonnes of copper ore over a period of several hundred years. If we then take into account other factors such as the knowledge of smelting being quite basic, and the process inefficient, what then should

we be expecting of this sort of operation in which perhaps only a small proportion of the copper actually present could ever have been recovered? Our original estimates were between 2–4 tonnes of copper metal (Timberlake 1990) and 1–2 tonnes of copper metal (Timberlake 2003) over the lifetime of the mine. On reflection it seems that the actual recovery of metal could have been a lot less.

The mysteries of smelting and copper production – the role of mines, miners and metalworkers during the Early Bronze Age

As we have no direct evidence for smelting at or close to any of the known mines, we can only presume that the ore was being smelted at the permanent settlements, or else was traded on in the form of ore concentrate to itinerant metalworkers. With plenty of pasture available, summer would have been the slack time of year, enabling mining to be undertaken communally, an activity engaged in by at least part of each family group (Timberlake 2002a; 2003). Thus it would have been to temporary settlements or shepherding camps (such as might once have existed on the floor of the Ystwyth Valley below Copa Hill) that the initial products of mining, perhaps as little as one small bag of hand-picked, crushed and concentrated ore per day, would have been brought during the few months of residence within the area (Timberlake 2002a). In fact the mining of ore may simply have been a means by which these relatively low-status subsistence farmers could enter into the exchange economy. Shennan (1999) refers to a slightly more sophisticated form of this in his socio-economic study of the Bronze Age miners/metalworkers at the mining settlement of Klingleberg in the Mitterburg of Austria. Yet within the uplands of Wales the production of the actual metal itself may have seemed an altogether less important goal; rather it would have been the contacts and exchanges negotiated with metallurgists passing through the area, first Beaker-type metalworkers and then later on other elites, which provided these miner/pastoralists with their first metal objects.

The ability to exchange ore concentrate for finished metal would have given those who mined the mineral and who had ancestral rights to the land in which this was found a distinct advantage over their neighbours. However, not having either the skills or the will to produce metal or to control its distribution meant that an elite or power base could not develop as a result. We see this, or the lack of it, within the mining territories of mid-Wales, and pretty much the same thing also along the North Wales coast close to the 'production centre' of the Great Orme. There is no clustering of significant monuments centred upon the mines or their immediate hinterland, and this despite the fact that the Plynlimon area is a moderately busy landscape at the beginning of the second millennium BC. Even more significant is the relative paucity of contemporary metalwork within these areas. As Briggs pointed out (1983; 1994) there seems to be no evidence for any fall-off in distribution away from the presumed 'production zones', in terms of artefact findspots. This contrasts with the pattern for stone implements in the Neolithic and perhaps also with gold objects in Ireland during the Copper/Early Bronze Age. With copper and bronze however this lack of correlation is repeated across the whole of Britain in terms of the distribution of objects or ingots, a situation which persists at least until Late Iron Age and Roman times. The role of the itinerant metalworkers plus the active recycling of metal are the probably the main reasons for this cloak of invisibility.

It is difficult to try and model the movement of metalworkers in and out of these mineral landscapes given the almost complete lack of evidence for settlement, smelting or metal-working hearths of this period. What we should endeavour to remember however is the potential complexity of these metal pathways, particular where this involves a multitude of different sources of manufactured metal and ores (many of which remain unknown) and a diverse production base of itinerant smiths, most of whom will be working on a quite small-scale at temporary smelting and melting hearths, mixing ores as well as alloying and re-melting metal. Perhaps it is not surprising therefore that following the 'first great copper rush' into Britain it would have been almost as difficult for a Bronze Age smith to be certain of the source of his metal as it is for us to now to try and determine it on the basis of trace metal composition and lead isotope analysis.

With the latter we are dealing not only with the cross-over in the plots for the British lead isotope fields but also the knowledge that from 1900BC onwards we are probably dealing with both the intentional or inadvertent blending of copper through the gradual incorporation of scrap and also the melting together of primary ingot (Timberlake 2005). That is not to say that there aren't circumstances where we think we can find a reasonable match between individual pieces of metalwork and the composition of a known ore source.

During the Wessex I (Bush Barrow) phase of the Wessex culture we begin to see the emergence of a powerful elite occupying the chalk lands of Wiltshire around Stonehenge, and as a result the production of fine metal-work including sheet gold ornaments, bronze daggers and decorated/undecorated low-flanged flat bronze axes which reaches its peak between 1800–1600 BC. Not surprisingly this period corresponds with the peak in mining activity and also the highest level of new prospection witnessed within the known mining areas of Britain. At the same time the metalwork compositions identified in this Willerby (or IMP-LI6 type) assemblage indicate a variety of possible sources, amongst them metal with generally low impurity levels suggesting an unmixed composition, some of which may have a Central Wales origin. In particular there are several objects from the Lydd and West Overton grave groups that are naturally high in lead and which show a good match with the lead isotope ratios and galena/chalcopyrite ores from Copa Hill (Rohl and Needham 1998). Either this reflects a suddenly much larger output or it is the result of smelting and metalwork production taking place much closer to the mine.

Smelting

A rare example of small scale local smelting was discovered and partially excavated at Pen Trwyn on the Great Orme in 1998. The latter site had suffered very extensively from erosion, and what now remains in the way of smelting debris (crushed fayalitic slag and copper prills) could have been derived from the single smelt of a small bowl or shaft furnace (Chapman 1997). An Early-Middle Bronze Age date (1675–1500 cal BC) was obtained from a small charcoal-rich feature associated with the metalworking debris following excavation (Jones 1999). The latter had evidently been crushed to try and extract the metal prills; something which suggested that this process did not produce a proper slag. The analysis of these prills indicated the smelting of chalcopyrite (Northover *pers comm*), perhaps the partially oxidised chalcopyrite-malachite ore that is typical of the Great Orme lodes (Timberlake 2002c). Despite the paucity of evidence this site has provided us with our only indication of the Early Bronze

Figure 7.16a (right) Experiments in primitive copper smelting undertaken by Birkbeck College MA students at Butser Iron Age Farm in 2006; the reconstruction of the roasting of chalcopyrite (photograph S Timberlake)

Figure 7.16b (below) The casting of a flat axe within an open clay mould using copper smelted from a malachite ore, Butser Iron Age Farm (photograph S Timberlake)

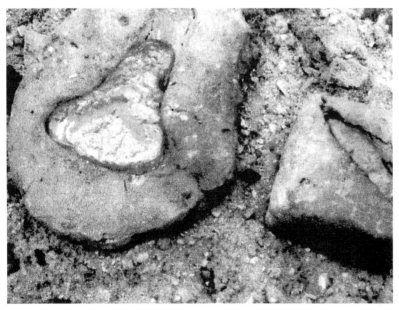

Age smelting process. However, another route to understanding this is through experimental archaeo-metallugy (Figs 7.16a–7.16b).

Work undertaken using simple hearths has demonstrated that when dominated by carbonates, copper ores can be relatively easily smelted using small earth shaft or bowl furnaces with crucibles, it being perfectly possible for the relatively unskilled or non-specialist person(s) to make all the tools needed for this on the spot (Timberlake 2005, 2007). Cassiterite (tin ore) can be smelted at temperatures of around 1000°C in a bowl hearth whilst tin and copper ores can be co-smelted to make bronze or else the metals melted and alloyed together in a crucible between 1100°–1200°C. The whole process to the stage of making moulds and casting flat axes and small daggers can be carried out in less than a week, supporting the concept of the itinerant smith and smelting at campsite settlements. In contrast to this, the smelting of chalcopyrite would have been much more difficult task, the repeated roasting of the ore then smelting of this with a flux over a much longer period at a higher temperature might mean that at least some of the process was carried out close to the mine. To date very little success has been achieved experimentally using these primitive types of furnace (Timberlake 2007; Craddock *et al* 2007). As a result this process is almost inconceivable in the absence of a more sophisticated shaft furnace smelting technology, one that we don't believe reached Britain until at least the Late Bronze Age (Timberlake 2007). It seems that here, as is often the case in these discussion, we are left with many more questions than answers.

Great Orme and the British copper supply in the Middle-Late Bronze Age

With the exception of the Great Orme, the exhaustion, flooding and abandonment of mines in Ireland, Wales and England at the end of the Early Bronze Age (*c* 1500 BC) was pretty much a universal event. Despite additional comparisons drawn between the lead isotope and trace element compositions present within Middle–Late Bronze Age metalwork and those of the ores of Central Wales and Alderley Edge (Rohl and Needham 1998) there is no archaeological evidence whatsoever to suggest that any of these mines were still operating. The new ore sources may be British, but their specific identity and whereabouts continues to remains a mystery.

The addition of lead to bronze from Acton Park times onwards (perhaps intentionally as a means to improve the flow properties of the alloy for more sophisticated castings such as palstaves, looped spearheads and later socketed axes (Tylecote 1986) has meant that lead isotope data from here on begins to relate more to the mined lead ores such as galena than to the lead impurities associated with the copper ores malachite and chalcopyrite. Because of this we begin to recognise the signature for Mendip ore in the heavily leaded Wilburton bronze swords of the Late Bronze Age. In the case of the Acton Park metalwork, an industry which has its origins in NE Wales (Northover 1982), the lead may have a separate or common origin to the copper. The metal of the principal isotopic group (IMP-LI9) corresponds well with a Great Orme source. Although lead is rare in this deposit (being confined to a single vein of galena) the level of correspondence between the Acton Park metalwork signature and the copper and lead ores from here is good. However, a similar but much more plentiful lead source is also present within what is essentially the same Carboniferous Limestone-hosted orefield of Denbighshire and Flintshire. This may indicate the separate mining of lead as early as the beginning of the Middle Bronze Age.

The radiocarbon-dated chronology (Lewis 1996) obtained from the Great Orme mine suggests a second phase of underground working between 1550–1400 BC (the period of the Arreton-Acton Park metalwork assemblage), and then a third phase between 1400–1200 BC (Taunton-Penard); the latter phase overlapping the second but nevertheless indicating a distinct shift in the calibrated range. The chronology suggests that mining continued at least on some level to the end of the Wilburton phase, *c* 1000 BC. However, there does appear to be a very distinct break at the beginning of the Iron Age, a phenomenon which might relate to the sudden halt in reliance on bronze tools. Prior to this event, at the very end of the Bronze Age (*ie* the Ewart Park metalwork phase) the recycling of Wilburton bronze is followed by the import of scrap, ingot, and finished metalwork items from the continent (*see* Rohl and Needham 1998). This will have reduced demand for what may then have already been regarded as a slightly inferior and certainly harder to win British metal.

Perhaps even at the beginning of the Middle Bronze Age scrap metal and/or ingot began to arrive from the across the Channel. We may be seeing this as early as the date of construction of the Dover boat (1500–1400 BC), yet by the time of the Langdon Bay and Salcombe wrecks (1300–1150 BC) such scrap cargoes might have been quite common. These imports of metal would probably have been a response to an increase in demand which could not be met internally; a supplement to the variable and not always predictable output from the British mines as well as to the volume of recycled metal already in circulation.

Resolving the metalwork enigma: comparing estimates of Bronze Age production and consumption

A great deal is known about the archaeology and whereabouts of mining sites and also much about the composition of metalwork, yet little attempt has ever been made to both qualitatively and quantitatively link up the two different sets of data. In particular there is a big gap in knowledge concerning the actual amount of Bronze Age metalwork in circulation at any given point in time, and the different contributions to this supply in terms of newly mined, imported and recycled metal. Needless to say one is never going to be able to get this exactly right, but at least some idea of the correct proportions and order of magnitude of production and consumption would be helpful in order to be able to model, perhaps for the first time, the use and circulation of metal in the British Bronze Age. It never ceases to amaze me that whilst on the one hand vast tonnages are sometimes quoted as estimates of production from these Bronze Age mines (*ie* 1769 tonnes of copper metal from the Great Orme alone (Randall 1995)), calculations concerning the actual quantities of metalwork either recovered or made from this metal tend to fall at the other end of the spectrum altogether (*eg* 0.75 tonnes for the combined metal content of *all* recorded Early Bronze age axes from Ireland, with the suggestion that no more than 2 tonnes of metal may have been used in their manufacture (Flanagan 1979)). A study to try and address this imbalance is long overdue and is well worthy of somebody's PhD research. However, until that point is reached, some sort of provisional revision of these figures seems to be appropriate. This revision takes the shape of an informed guess, an attempt to re-assess or downsize previous estimates for the mined production of copper (metal) from Britain and Ireland based on our knowledge of the limitations of primitive mining, ore recovery, and smelting efficiency rather than on any sort of modern assessment of the ratios between the rock moved, the amount of ore present and the maximum amount of metal which can be recovered.

This revised figure of 51.5 tonnes of copper metal from all the known Bronze Age mines in Britain and Ireland is broken down to its constituent parts in Table 7.2. Table 7.3 provides estimates for the production of metal in Britain and Ireland between the Copper Age and Middle Bronze Age. As one can see the calculations based only on estimates from *known* mines suggest a higher production during the Early Bronze Age than during the Middle Bronze Age (although for Britain the situation is the reverse). Clearly this has implications for any model which seeks to

explain the apparent rise in metal consumption and deposition.

The task of gathering data on the amounts of Bronze Age metalwork held in British museum collections and in private hands is enormous, particularly if one also had to try and sensibly assess what still lies buried, what has been lost, or more relevantly what has been recycled. However, in order to begin this process a pilot assessment has been undertaken based on existing published data such as the *Guide Catalogue of the Bronze Age Collections within the National Museum of Wales* (Savory 1980), the *Catalogue of Prehistory Accessions in the Local and County Museums of Wales and Other Collections* (Figgis 1999), finds reported within issues of *Archaeology in Wales* (1982–2005), and the *Treasure Annual Reports* of the Portable Antiquities Scheme (1998–2004). Wherever possible published weights of objects have been used, but otherwise these are calculated based on average weights for different artefacts (*eg* 400g for a Migdale axe). The results of this are shown in Table 7.4. The small combined weights may seem surprising, but are not entirely unexpected. What has to be added to this though are the estimates of the number of unreported finds, the missing hoards (*see* Northover this volume), plus a calculation of

Table 7.2 Maximum and (revised) minimum estimates for production of metal from known Irish, Welsh and English mines during the Bronze Age

	Mine	Maximum estimates of production	Revised minimum estimate (range)	Approx. figures	TOTAL
Ireland	Ross Island	500 tons[1]	<20 tons	15 tons	
	Mt.Gabriel mines	146 tons[2] 1.5–26.5 tons[3]	1–3 tons	1.75 tons	
	all other mines (Mizzen & Beara penisula)	227 tons[2]	1 ton	1 ton	
					17.75 tons
Wales	Great Orme	885–1769 tons[4] 175 tons[5]	<30 tons	25 tons	
	Parys Mt.		1–4 tons[6]	2 tons	
	Copa Hill	2–4 tons[7]	1–2 tons	1.5 tons	
	all other mid-Wales mines	4–6 tons[7]	< 4 tons	3 tons	
					31.5 tons
England	Alderley Edge		1–2 tons[6]	1.5 tons	
	Mottram St. Andrew		< 300 kg[6]	< 300 kg	
	Ecton		< 500 kg[6]	< 500 kg	2.3 tons
					51.55 tons

[1] Northover in O'Brien 2004 (p.537-538); [2] Jackson 1980; [3] O'Brien 1994; [4] Randall 1995 (unpbl. MSc); [5] Lewis 1996 (unpubl. MPhil); [6] author's estimates only; [7] Timberlake 2003

Table 7.3 Estimates of the production of copper metal from mines in Ireland and Britain from the Copper Age to the Middle Bronze Age

	Ireland	Britain	TOTAL
Copper Age	7 tons	1 ton	8 tons
Early Bronze Age	9.5 tons	14 tons	23.5 tons
Middle Bronze Age	1 ton	18.8 tons	19.8 tons

	Museum collections	Known private collections	Estimated collection (additional)	Recycled (missing hoards)	Remaining unexcavated / lost(x20 ?)	TOTAL (estimate)
Copper Age	5.6 kg [8][9]	?	4 kg	?	200 kg	209 kg
Early Bronze Age	32.1 kg [8][9]	4.2 kg [9]	30 kg	?	1320 kg	1.38 tons
Mid Bronze Age	72.7 kg [8][9]	5.5 kg [9]	60 kg	50 kg [10]	3760 kg	3.95 tons

[8] Savory 1980; [9] Figgis 1999; [10] Northover see this vol.

Table 7.4 Known and estimated quantities of copper within copper and bronze artefacts from Wales between the Copper Age and Middle Bronze Age.

	Welsh metalwork	British metalwork (x10)	British mine production	Recycled metal	Imported Irish metal	Imported continental metal
Copper Age	0.21 ton	2.1 tons	1 ton		2 tons?	1 ton?
Early Bronze Age	1.38 ton	13.8 tons	14 tons	2 tons?	3 tons?	
Mid Bronze Age	3.95 ton	39.5 tons	17.8 tons	16 tons?		10 tons?

Table 7.5 A comparison between estimated quantities of British metalwork and the amounts of metal produced from British mines, from recycled sources, and through the import of metal from Ireland and Europe.

existing but as yet undiscovered metalwork. The latter calculation (x20) is perhaps not un-generous given the likely association of future finds with already known archaeological monuments. A total of 1.38 tonnes of copper present within Early Bronze Age metalwork is a figure which might well have been arrived at imperfectly, but which is probably realistic nevertheless, at least in terms of it being the right order of magnitude. However, this figure doesn't take into account the amount of metal which is recycled and which then ends up re-circulated within the metal pool of the Middle Bronze Age.

The final tabulated calculation is perhaps the most interesting (Table 7.5). In the absence of proper data gathering at this stage the estimate for the total volume of British metalwork is at about 10x the Welsh figures. This takes into account both land mass ratios and known relative densities in metalwork distribution. When we bring into the equation estimates of the amount of recycling taking place during the Early Bronze Age and Middle Bronze Age periods and compare this with estimates for mine production and the import of Irish and Continental copper we finish up with some interesting observations. Our figures seem to suggest that at the beginning of the metal-using period there is almost twice as much copper being produced or imported into Britain than we can account for in the form of metalwork consumption. During the Early Bronze Age however there seems to be some sort of parity; metalwork production increases to the level of copper production then probably exceeds it with some recycled and imported

metal. However, ever larger amounts of this production becomes recycled and this is eventually re-circulated into Middle Bronze Age metal as the demand for metalwork gradually outstrips domestic supply. This shortfall is taken up by the import of scrap and metal ingot from the continent. Ten tonnes of metal is a stab in the dark, but at least this figure provides something to model with. If for instance we assume that a Langdon Bay-type metal cargo might contain *up to* 150 kilos of bronze, then we would be looking at a requirement for 67 cargoes of continental metal over a one to two hundred year period. Typically the weight of metal scrap carried by individual vessels like the Dover Boat may have been a lot less. However, by the beginning of the Late Bronze Age this trade would probably have increased dramatically, with there being evidence for considerable amounts of disposable metal yet very little in the way of indigenous mining.

Concluding comments

It is useful to reflect upon the thread of continuity which links the earliest Beaker inspired dissemination of metallurgical know-ledge from Atlantic Europe into Ireland and Britain in the 3rd millennium BC, and the arrival on these shores of the first cross-Channel ferries with their cargoes of scrap bronze towards the end of the 2nd millennium BC. We have seen the importance of this maritime connection in the earliest trade in metal axes between Ireland and the west of Britain, as well as in the shortest crossings and coast-hugging routes which could have led to the discovery and exploitation of the copper deposits on the Isle of Man, those of the North Wales coast (Parys Mountain and the Great Ormes Head) and the mines around the Dovey Estuary in mid-Wales. This same 'metal route' may have encompassed the alluvial gold deposits of the Wicklow Mountains, Co. Mayo, Wales, Scotland and the gold and alluvial tin deposits of Cornwall all of which are closely connected to the sea by rivers and their estuaries. The first miners in Wales were probably pastoralists who brought their animals and supplies of stone tools from the coast up to the mines during the summer months, these becoming all but abandoned by the end of the Early Bronze Age. Only the naturally well-drained, rich and easy to work mines of the Great Orme continued to be mined through into the Middle Bronze Age, with most of the activity ceasing around 1000 BC. Here we see the independence of the British mines losing out to the more abundant and guaranteed availability of European metal.

Acknowledgements

I would like to acknowledge the help and support of my colleagues in the Early Mines Research Group in the excavation of the mining sites and in providing useful commentary on these ideas. In particular Brenda Craddock, who has produced most of the graphics used in this paper. The many different grant-awarding bodies who have helped fund these archaeological projects over the last 20 years are too numerous to mention here, however the National Museum of Wales stands out for its consistent long-term support of this work.

List of references

Barber, M, Field, D and Topping, P 1999 *The Neolithic Flint Mines of England*, English Heritage (Royal Commission Historic Monuments for England) 95pp

BBC/OU/Open 2.net/landscapemysteries/prog 1 2006 *In Search of Irish Gold* (Croagh Patrick)

Bick, D 1976 *The Old Metal Mines of Mid-Wales Part 3: Cardiganshire-north of Goginan*, The Pound House, Newent, Glos

Bick, D 1977 *The Old Metal Mines of Mid-Wales Part 4: West Montgomeryshire*. The Pound House, Newent, Glos

Bowen, E and Gresham, C 1967 *History of Merioneth* Volume 1, p.55 (quote from R. Fenton's *'Tours in Wales 1804–1813'* re-published as a Supplement in *Archaeologia Cambrensis* (1917))

Bradley, R 1984 *The Social Foundations of Prehistoric Britain*, London and New York: Longman Archaeology Series

Briggs, C S 1983 'Copper mining at Mt.Gabriel, County Cork: Bronze Age bonanza or post-famine fiasco?', *Proceedings of Prehistoric Society*, **49**, 317333

Briggs, C S 1988 'The location and recognition of metal ores in Pre-Roman and Roman Britain and their contemporary exploitation', in J Ellis-Jones (ed), *Acta of British School in Athens Centenary Conference on Ancient Mining and Metallurgy*, Bangor: University College of North Wales, 106–114.

Briggs, C S 1994 'The Bronze Age', in J Davies and D Kirby (eds), *Cardiganshire County History Volume 1: From the Earliest Times to the Coming of the Normans*, Cardiff: Cardiganshire Antiquarian Society and Royal Commission for Ancient and Historical Monuments for Wales, 26–218

Briggs, C.S. 2003 'A Strategy for Raw Materials in Welsh Archaeology', in C Briggs (ed), *Towards a Research Agenda for Welsh Archaeology*, Oxford: British Archaeological Reports (British Series), **343**, 201–212

Budd, P and Gale, D 1994 'Archaeological survey of an early mineworking at Wheal Coates near St Agnes, Cornwall', *Cornish Archaeology*, **33**, 14–21

Burl, A 1976 *The Stone Circles of the British Isles*, Newhaven and London: Yale University Press

Cambrian Archaeological Association 1866 'Temporary Museum at Machynlleth (hammers, wedges and buckering stones from Blaendyffryn Mine)', *Archaeologia Cambrensis*, August 1866, 544–545

Case, H 1966 'Were Beaker People the first metallurgists in Ireland?', *Palaeohistoria*, **12**, 141–177

Chapman, D 1997 'Great Orme smelting site, Llandudno', *Archaeology in Wales*, **37**, 56–57

Claris, P and Quartermain, J 1989 'The Neolithic Quarries and Axe-Factory Sites of Great Langdale and Scafell Pike', *Proceedings of the Prehistoric Society*, **55**, 1–26

Coghlan, H and Case, H 1957 'Early Metallurgy of Copper in Britain and Ireland', *Proceedings of the Prehistoric Society*, **23**, 19–23

Cooney, G 2005 'Stereo Porphyry: Quarrying and Deposition on Lambay Island, Ireland', in P Topping and M Lynott (eds), *The Cultural Landscape of Prehistoric Mines*, Oxford: Oxbow Books, 14–30

CPAT (Clwyd Powys Archaeological Trust) Sites and Monuments Record 2002 – flint arrowheads from Llyn Bugeilyn, Powys

Craddock, B and Craddock, P 1996 'The Beginnings of Metallurgy in South-West Britain: Hypotheses and Evidence', in P Newman (ed), *The Archaeology of Mining and Metallurgy in South-West Britain: Papers presented at the conference held at Seale-Hayne College, Newton Abbot, Devon, on the 12th to 14th April, 1996, Mining History: Bulletin of the Peak District Mines Historical Society*, **13** (2), 52–63

Craddock, P 1995 *Early Metal Mining and Production*, Edinburgh: Edinburgh University Press

Craddock, P, Meeks, N and Timberlake, S 2007 'On the Edge of Success: The scientific examination of the products of the Early Mines Research Group smelting experiments', in S La Niece, D Hook, and P Craddock (eds), *Metals and Mines: Studies in Archaeometallurgy*, London: Archetype Publications/British Museum, 37–46

Darvill, T, Evans, D, Fyfe, R and Wainwright, G

2005 'Strumble-Preseli Ancient Communities and Environment Study (SPACES): Fourth Report 2005', *Archaeology in Wales*, **45**, 17–25

Davey, J, Northover, P, O'Connor, B and Woodcock, J 1999 'Bronze Age Metallurgy on the Isle of Man: A Symposium', in P Davey (ed), *Recent Archaeological Research on the Isle of Man*, Oxford: British Archaeological Reports (British Series), **278**, 39–60

David, G 1998' Great Orme Bronze-Age Mine, Llandudno', *Archaeology in Wales*, **38**, 94–95

David, G 1999 'Great Orme Bronze-Age Mine, Llandudno', *Archaeology in Wales*, **39**, 78–79

David, G 2000 'Great Orme Bronze-Age Mine, Llandudno',. *Archaeology in Wales*, **40**, 73–75

David, G 2001 'Great Orme Bronze-Age Mine, Llandudno', *Archaeology in Wales*, **41**, 118–119

Davies, O 1937 'Mining Sites in Wales', *Report of the Annual Meeting of the British Association for the Advancement of Science – Section 4 (1937)*, 1–3 and 301–303

Davies, O 1938 'Ancient Mines in Montgomeryshire', *Montgomeryshire Collections*, **45**, 55–60 and 152–157

Davies, O 1947 'Cwm Ystwyth Mines', *Archaeologia Cambrensis*, **100**, 61–66

Dewey, H and Eastwood, T 1925 *Copper Ores of the Midlands, Wales, the Lake District and the Isle of Man*, *Memoirs* of the Geological Survey Special Reports, **30**, London

Doonan, R and Eley, T 2000 'The Langness Ancient Mining Survey', in T Darvill, (ed), *Billown Neolithic Landscape Project, Isle of Man: 5th Report 1999*, Bournemouth University School of Conservation Sciences Research Report, **7**, Bournemouth and Douglas: Manx Natural Heritage, 45–53

Doonan, R and Hunt, A 1999 'Assessing the research potential for prehistoric mining and metallurgy on the Isle of Man' in T Darvill, (ed), *Billown Neolithic Landscape Project, Isle of Man: 5th Report 1999*, Bournemouth University School of Conservation Sciences Research Report, **7**, Bournemouth and Douglas: Manx Natural Heritage, 64–69

Dutton, L and Fasham, P 1994 'Prehistoric Copper Mining on the Great Orme, Llandudno, Gwynnedd', *Proceedings of the Prehistoric Society*, **60**, 245–286

Edmonds, M 2004 *The Langdales – Landscape and Prehistory in a Lakeland Valley*, Tempus

Figgis, M 1999 *Welsh Prehistory catalogue accessions in museums in Wales and elsewhere*, Machynlleth, Powys: Atelier Productions

Flanagan, L 1979 'Industrial resources, production and distribution in earlier Bronze Age Ireland', in M Ryan (ed), *The Origins of Metallurgy in Atlantic Europe*, Proceedings of the Fifth Atlantic Colloquium, Dublin, 145–163

Herring, P 1997 'The prehistoric landscape of Cornwall and west Devon: economic and social contexts for metallurgy', in P Budd and D Gale (eds), *Prehistoric Extractive Metallurgy in Cornwall*, Truro: Cornwall County Council, 19–22

Houlder, C 1976 'Stone Axes and Henge Monuments', in G Boon and J Lewis (eds), *Welsh Antiquity*, Cardiff: National Museum of Wales, 55–62

Hughes, S 1981 *Ancient Mining in Mid Wales*, unpublished MA Thesis, University of Manchester

Ixer, R and Budd, P 1998 'The Mineralogy of Bronze Age Copper Ores from the British Isles: implications of the composition of early metalwork', *Oxford Journal of Archaeology*, **17**, 15–41

James, D 1988 'Prehistoric copper mining on the Great Orme's Head', in J Ellis-Jones (ed), *Aspects of Ancient Mining and Metallurgy, Acta of a British School at Athens Centenary Conference, Bangor, North Wales, 1986*, Bangor: University College of North Wales, 115–121

Jenkins, D 1995 'Mynydd Parys Copper Mines', *Archaeology in Wales*, **35**, 35–37

Jenkins, D 2002 *Potential investigations on Mynydd Parys, October 2002: C14 dates*, unpublished report

Jenkins, D and Timberlake, S 1987 *Geo-archaeological research into prehistoric mining for copper in Wales*, unpublished report to the Leverhulme Trust, University of Wales, Bangor

Jones, O 1922 *Lead and Zinc. The Mining District of North Cardiganshire and West Montgomeryshire: Memoirs of the Geological Survey: Special Reports on the Mineral Resources of Great Britain*, **20**, London

Jones, S 1999 'Great Orme Bronze-Age Smelting Site, Llandudno', *Archaeology in Wales*, **39**, 79

King, A 1996 'Note on a stone find from Lake Windermere', *Transactions of the Cumberland and Westmorland Antiquarian and Archaeological Society*, (second series), **96**, 227–228

Lewis, A 1990 'Underground exploration of the Great Orme Copper Mines', in P Crew and S Crew (eds), *Early Mining in the British Isles: Proceedings of the Early Mining Workshop at Plas Tan y Bwlch, Snowdonia National Park Study Centre, 17–19 November 1989*, Plas Tan y Bwlch Occasional Paper, **1**, 5–10

Lewis, A 1996 *Prehistoric Mining at the Great Orme: Criteria for the identification of early mining*, unpublished MPhil Thesis, University of Wales, Bangor

Lund, J 2001 *The re-discovery of two stone hammers from Coniston, Cumbria*, typescript report deposited in National Trust offices, Ambleside

Macklin, M and Lewis, J 2003 'River sediments, great floods and centennial-scale Holocene climate change', *Journal of Quaternary Science*, **18** (2), 101–105

McArdle *et al* 1987

Mighall, T and Chambers, F 1993a 'The environmental impact of prehistoric mining at Copa Hill, Cwmystwyth, Wales', *The Holocene*, **3**, 260–264

Mighall, T and Chambers, F 1993b 'Early mining and metalworking: its impact on the environment', *Journal of the Historical Metallurgy Society*, **27**(2), 71–78

Mighall, T, Abrahams, P, Grattan, J, Hayes, D, Timberlake, S and Forsyth, S 2002 'Geochemical evidence for atmospheric pollution derived from prehistoric copper mining at Copa Hill, Cwmystwyth, mid-Wales, UK', *Science of the Total Environment*, **282**, 69–80

Mighall, T, Timberlake, S, Grattan, J, and Forsyth, S 2000 'Bronze Age Lead Mining at Copa Hill, Cwmystwyth – fact or fantasy?', *Historical Metallurgy*, **34** (1), 1–12

Mining Journal 1869 'Mining past and present in Cardiganshire (Penpompren Mines, Talybont)', *Mining Journal*, **39** (1763), 400

Morris, L 1746 '*An account of the Lead and Silver Mines in the King's Manor called Cwmmwd y Perveth*', in D Bick and P Davies, P (eds), *Lewis Morris and the Cardiganshire Mines*, Cardiff: National Library of Wales

Needham, S 2002 'Analytical implications for Beaker metallurgy in North-West Europe', in M Bartelheim, E Pernicka and R Krause, *The Beginnings of Metallurgy in the Old World*, Forschungen zur Archaeometrie und Altertumswissenschaft, **1**, Rahden, Westfalia: Institut fur Archaometrie, Freiberg, Verlag Marie Leidorf Gmbh, 99–134

Needham, S 2006 'Migdale-Marnoch: sunburst of Scottish metallurgy', in I Shepherd and G Barclay (eds), *Scotland in Ancient Europe: The Neolithic and Early Bronze Age of Scotland in their European Context*, Edinburgh: Society of Antiquaries of Scotland, 217–245

Northover, J P 1980a 'Bronze in the British Bronze Age', in W Oddy (ed), *Aspects of Early Metallurgy*, London: British Museum Occasional Paper, **17**, 63–70

Northover, J P 1980b 'The Analysis of Welsh Bronze-Age Metalwork', in H Savory, *Guide Catalogue of the Bronze Age Collections*, National Museum of Wales, Cardiff, 229–243

Northover, J P 1982 'The exploration and long distance movement of bronze in Bronze Age and Early Iron Age Europe', *Bulletin of the Institute of Archaeology*, **19**, 45–72

Northover, J P 1999 'The earliest metalwork in Southern Britain', in A Hauptman, E Pernicka, T Rehren and U Yalcin (eds), *The Beginnings of Metallurgy, Proceedings of the International Symposium, April 1995*, Der Anschnitt Beihift, **9**, Bochum, 211–226

O'Brien, W 1994 *Mount Gabriel – Bronze Age Mining in Ireland*, Galway University Press

O'Brien, W 1996 *Bronze Age Copper Mining in Britain and Ireland*, Shire Archaeology, **71**

O'Brien, W 1999 'Resource Availability and metal supply in the insular Bronze Age', in A Hauptman, E Pernicka, T Rehren and U Yalcin (eds), *The Beginnings of Metallurgy, Proceedings of the International Symposium, April 1995*, Der Anschnitt Beihift, **9**, Bochum, 227–235

O'Brien, W 2003 'The Bronze Age copper mines of the Goleen area, Co.Cork', *Proceedings of the Royal Irish Academy*, **103C** (2), 13–59

O'Brien, W 2004 *Ross Island – Mining, Metal and Society in Early Ireland*, Bronze Age Studies, **6**, Galway: National University of Ireland

Ottaway, B and Wager, E 2000 'Ffynnon Rufeinig, Great Orme, Llandudno', *Archaeology in Wales*, **40**, 73

Parker-Pearson, M 1993 *Bronze Age Britain*, London: Batsford/English Heritage

Pearce, S 1983 *The Bronze Age Metalwork of South-Western Britain*, Oxford: British Archaeological Reports (British Series), **120**

Peate, I 1925a 'Arrow-heads from Bugeilyn', *Archaeologia Cambrensis*, **80** (1), 196–202

Peate, I 1925b 'Arrow-heads from Bugeilyn', *Archaeologia Cambrensis*, **80** (2), 415–416

Peate, I 1928 'More arrow-heads from Bugeilyn', *Archaeologia Cambrensis*, **83** (2), 344–345

Penhallurick, R 1986 *Tin in Antiquity*, London: Institute of Metals

Penhallurick, R 1997 'The evidence for prehistoric mining in Cornwall', in P Budd and D Gale (eds), *Prehistoric Extractive Metallurgy in Cornwall*, Truro: Cornwall County Council, 23–31

Pickin, J 1990 'Stone Tools and Early Metal Mining in England and Wales', in P Crew and S Crew (eds), *Early Mining in the British Isles. Proceedings of the Early Mining Workshop at Plas Tan y Bwlch, Snowdonia National Park*

Study Centre, 17–19 November 1989, Plas Tan y Bwlch Occasional Paper, **1**, 39–42

Pickin, J 2005 'A Bronze Age axe-hammer from the Alderley Edge copper mines', appendix in S Timberlake, 'Stone Mining Tools from Alderley Edge', in S Timberlake and A Prag (eds), *The Archaeology of Alderley Edge – Survey, Excavation and Experiment in an Ancient Mining Landscape*, British Archaeological Reports (British Series), **396**, 75–78

Pickin, J and Worthington, T 1989 'Prehistoric mining hammers from Bradda Head, Isle of Man', *Bulletin of the Peak District Mines Historical Society*, **10** (5), 274–275

Randall, M 1995 *Estimates of Bronze Age Copper Production at Great Orme*, unpublished MSc Thesis, University of London

Roe, F 1967 'The Battle-Axes, Mace Heads and Axe Hammers from South-West Scotland', *Transactions of the Dumfries and Galloway Natural History Society*, **44**, 57–80

Roe, F 1979 'Typology of stone implements with shaft holes, in T McK Clough and W Cummins (eds), *Stone Axe Studies vol I*, Council for British Archaeology Research Report, **23**, London: Council for British Archaeology, 23–48

Rohl, B and Needham, S 1998 *The circulation of metal in the British Bronze Age: the application of lead isotope analysis*, London: British Museum Occasional Paper, **102**

Royal Commission Ancient and Historical Monuments in Wales 1911 Ogof Widdon. *An Inventory of the Ancient Monuments in Montgomeryshire* no. 923, p.180

Savory, H 1980 *Guide Catalogue of the Bronze Age Collections*, Cardiff: National Museum of Wales

Sharpe, A 1997 'Smoke but no fire, or the mysterious case of the missing miner', in P Budd and D Gale (eds), *Prehistoric Extractive Metallurgy in Cornwall*, Truro: Cornwall County Council, 35–40

Shennan, S 1999 'Cost, benefit and value in the organization of Early European copper production', *Antiquity*, **73 (280)**, 352–365

Simpson, D 1990 'A stone battle-axe from Co. Cork', *Journal of the Cork Historical and Archaeological Society*, **95**, 168

Smith, I 1979 'The Chronology of British Stone Implements', in T McKClough, T.H. and Cummins, W.A. (eds.) *Stone Axe Studies: archaeological, petrological, experimental and ethnographic*, London: Council for British Archaeology Research Report, **23**, 13–23

Smyth, W 1848 'On the Mining District of Cardiganshire and Montgomeryshire', *Memoirs of the Geological Survey*, **2** (2), 655–684

Stanley, H 1850 'Recent discoveries indicative of ancient metallurgical operations in North Wales', *Archaeological Journal*, **7**, 68–6

Strasburger, M 2001 *Early Ochre Mining in the Royal Forest of Dean (Gloucestershire)*, unpublished paper deposited at Clearwell Caves, Forest of Dean

Taylor, J 1994 'The First Golden Age of Europe was in Ireland and Britain', *Ulster Journal of Archaeology*, **57**, (third series), 37–60

Thorburn, J 1990 'Stone Mining Tools and the Field Evidence for Early Mining in Mid-Wales', in P Crew and S Crew (eds), *Early Mining in the British Isles: Proceedings of the Early Mining Workshop at Plas Tan y Bwlch, Snowdonia National Park Study Centre, 17–19 November 1989*, Plas Tan y Bwlch Occasional Paper, **1**, 43–46

Timberlake, S 1987 'An archaeological investigation of early mineworkings on Copa Hill, Cwmystwyth', *Archaeology in Wales*, **27**, 18–20

Timberlake, S 1990 'Excavations at Parys Mountain and Nantyreira', in P Crew and S Crew (eds), *Early Mining in the British Isles: Proceedings of the Early Mining Workshop at Plas Tan y Bwlch, Snowdonia National Park Study Centre, 17–19 November 1989*, Plas Tan y Bwlch Occasional Paper, **1**, 15–21

Timberlake, S 1992a 'Prehistoric Copper Mining in Britain', *Cornish Archaeology*, **31**, 15–34

Timberlake, S 1992b 'Llancynfelin Mine and Nantyrarian Mine', *Archaeology in Wales*, **32**, 90–91

Timberlake, S 1995 'Llancynfelin and Nantyrarian Mines', *Archaeology in Wales*, **37**, 62–65

Timberlake, S 1996 'Tyn y fron Mine, Cwmrheidol', *Archaeology in Wales*, 36, 60–63

Timberlake, S 1998 'Survey of Early Metal Mines within the Welsh Uplands', *Archaeology in Wales*, 38, 79–81

Timberlake, S 2002a 'Mining and prospection for metals in Early Bronze Age Britain – making claims within the archaeological landscape' in J Brück (ed), *Bronze Age Landscapes: Tradition and Transformation*, 179–192.

Timberlake, S 2002b 'Cwmystwyth, Banc Tynddol', *Archaeology in Wales*, 42, 97–98

Timberlake, S 2002c 'Ancient prospection for metals and modern prospection for ancient mines – the evidence for Bronze Age mining within the British Isles', in M Bartelheim, E Pernicka and R Krause, *The Beginnings of Metallurgy in the Old World*, Forschungen zur Archaeometrie und Altertumswissenschaft, **1**, Rahden, Westfalia: Institut fur Archaometrie, Freiberg, Verlag Marie Leidorf Gmbh, 327–358.

Timberlake, S 2003 *Excavations on Copa Hill, Cwmystwyth (1986–1999): An Early Bronze Age copper mine within the uplands of Central Wales*, British Archaeological Reports (British Series), **348**, Oxford: Archaeopress

Timberlake, S 2004a 'Banc Tynddol Beaker Gold Disc', *Archaeology in Wales*, **44**, 137–138

Timberlake, S 2004b 'Comet Lode Opencast, Copa Hill, Cwmystwyth', *Archaeology in Wales*, **44**, 139–141

Timberlake, S 2004c 'Pwll Roman Mine, Tre Taliesin', *Archaeology in Wales*, **44**, 142–143

Timberlake, S 2005 'In search of the first melting pot', *British Archaeology*, **82**, 32–33

Timberlake, S 2006 'Excavations of early mineworkings at Twll y Mwyn (Cwm Darren) and Erglodd, Ceredigion', *Archaeology in Wales*, **46**, 79–86

Timberlake, S 2007 'The use of experimental archaeology/archaeometallurgy for the understanding and reconstruction of Early Bronze Age mining and smelting technology', in S La Niece, D Hook, and P Craddock (eds), *Metals and Mines: Studies in Archaeometallurgy,* London: Archetype Publications/British Museum, 27–36.

Timberlake, S and Mason, J 1997 'Ogof Wyddon (Machynlleth Park Copper Mine)', *Archaeology in Wales*, **37**, 62–65

Timberlake, S and Prag, A 2005 *The Archaeology of Alderley Edge – Survey, Excavation and Experiment in an Ancient Mining Landscape*, British Archaeological Reports (British Series), **396**

Timberlake, S forthcoming 'The origins of metal mining in Britain: The exploration and archaeological excavations of the Early Mines Research Group in Central Wales', *Journal of the Welsh Mines Society*, **1**

Tinsley, H and Grigson, C 1981 'The Bronze Age', in L Simmons and M Tooley, (eds), *The Environment in British Prehistory*, London: Duckworth, 210–250

Tylecote, R 1986 *The Prehistory of Metallurgy in the British Isles*, London: Institute of Metals

Varley, W 1964 *Cheshire before the Romans*, History of Cheshire series, **1**, Chester: Cheshire Community Council and C Tinley and Co

Williams, J 1866 *A Short Account of the British Encampments lying between the Rivers Rheidol and Llyfnant in the County of Cardigan and their connection with the Mines*, Aberystwyth

Williams, J and Davidson, A 1998 'Survey and Excavation at the Graiglwyd Neolithic Axe-Factory, Penmaenmawr', *Archaeology in Wales*, **38**, 3–21

Williams, R 1991 *The Berehaven Copper Mines, Alihies, Co.Cork, SW Ireland*, British Mining, **42**, Northern Mines Research Society Monograph

Wilson, G 1921 *The Lead, Zinc, Copper and Nickel ores of Scotland*, Memoirs of the Geological Survey: Special Report on the Mineral Resources of Great Britain, **17**, Edinburgh: HMSO

8. The demise of the flint tool industry

Chris Butler

Introduction

Of two things we can be fairly certain; that by the end of the Bronze Age the use of flint had declined, and that to a very great extent bronze appears to have taken over as the main material from which tools and weapons were made.

This decline was so complete that by the Iron Age there is virtually no evidence for the continued use of flint for making tools. Although some (Young *et al* 1999) have argued the case, the evidence is slim, and much of the flintwork found could well be residual Bronze Age material. If flint did continue to be used in the Iron Age, it was certainly not produced by any premeditated knapping strategy.

But to say that this decline is as a result of the introduction of metalwork would be to over simplify the causes for the demise of the flint tool industry, which are much more complex than this alone.

To try and understand the reasons for this decline it is necessary to go back and look at how flint knapping strategies changed and developed over previous millennia (Butler 2005). This may then help us to understand why changes in flint working occurred, what prompted those changes and how that is reflected in the archaeological evidence.

The Mesolithic Period

An important influence on the range of tools and equipment needed by a society is the environment in which they live, which ultimately defines their economy, and the organisation and structure of that society. The raw material available will also obviously be a factor, as this will define the types of tool that can be manufactured.

In the Mesolithic period the environment comprised predominantly woodland, and the main food sources were woodland animals, together with plants, which were gathered or collected. The woodland animals needed to be hunted, and this meant weapons were required that were suitable for this task. The throwing spears of the Upper Palaeolithic were useless in a woodland environment, being more suited to an open environment, so instead the bow and arrow were introduced, a trend that may have started in the Final Upper Palaeolithic (Barton 1992).

This new hunting equipment meant that flintworking technology needed to change so that the points and barbs required for the arrows could be produced. Thus the microlith was introduced, and with it a whole new knapping strategy was developed to produce the bladelets required for microlith production (Butler 2005).

But it was not just the microlith that defined the flintworking strategy they used. Their hunter-gatherer society was organised into small mobile groups exploiting territories on a seasonal basis. As they could not carry large quantities of flint around with them, their flintworking strategy had to make the most of the raw material, so that they could take with them all that they needed to make and repair their hunting equipment, *ie* small-sized cores that were carefully curated (Fig 8.1).

Thus the Mesolithic flintworking technology was developed, and is defined by: (a) the selection of good quality flint; (b) cores being well worked-out, and cylindrical or pyramidal in shape. They were curated and discarded only when too small to produce further bladelets; (c) the use of platform preparation, and cores are rejuvenated to get the maximum out of them; and (d) the production of blades and bladelets using a soft hammer, or possibly even a punch to achieve more precision. The bladelets were then used predominantly for microlith production.

A wide range of tools was produced in the Mesolithic (Fig 8.2), including scrapers, burins, microdenticulates, awls and piercers, cutting and chopping tools, together with core tools such as the tranchet adze for woodworking and picks; in total some 18 different basic tool types. These tools tend to be found mostly at longer stay base camps, whereas at hunting camps a smaller range of tools are found including microliths and expedient scrapers.

For the Mesolithic period, we can therefore conclude that the combination of the environment and their economy had defined the range of tools that were required, which in turn drove the flintworking technology needed to produce them. It is also likely that everyone in a hunter-gatherer community was capable of making these tools, and there were no flintworking specialists.

The Early Neolithic Period

In the Early Neolithic a similar thing occurred. The landscape once again changed, the woodland was cleared, and slowly people began

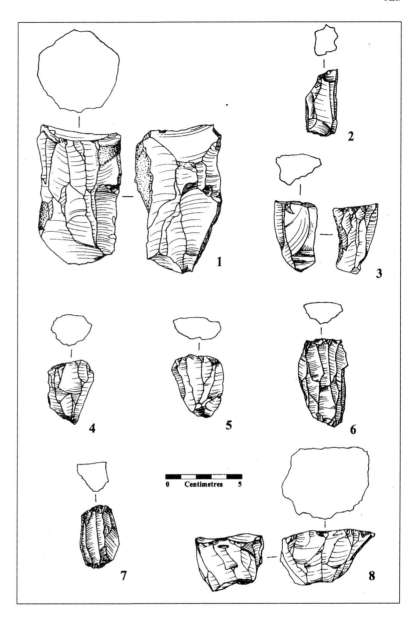

Figure 8.1 (above) Examples of well-worked Mesolithic cores

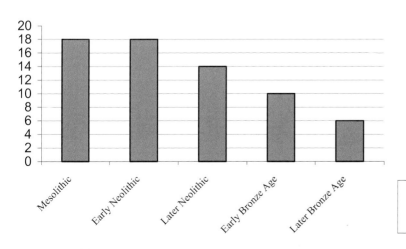

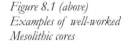

Figure 8.2 (left) Number of stone tool types by period

to settle down and stay in one place, although this was a long process. But this had an effect on the flintworking technology.

The first and most important change was that the microlith disappeared from the hunting toolkit, and with it went the requirement for bladelets and some of the associated manufacturing techniques. The reason for this is simple. The arrow, pointed and barbed with microliths, is a short-range weapon, meant for encounter hunting and not suited for use at longer ranges in the more open landscape that was now emerging. What was needed instead was something more aerodynamic; the result was the leaf-shaped arrowhead (Green 1980). As well as hunting, the suggestion of occasional warfare, for example at Crickley Hill (Dixon 1972), also led to a requirement for longer ranged and more accurate weapons.

Evidence of Early Neolithic settlement is notoriously difficult to locate, and people were still fairly mobile, so a conservative flintknapping technology with an element of curation was still required, and the number of different tool types remained high at 18.

To sum up, in the Early Neolithic people were; (a) still selecting good quality flint; (b) carefully working and rejuvenating cores with prepared platforms; and (c) producing soft hammer blades and long flakes.

But other significant changes were beginning to take place. As people settled down they were able to exploit sources of raw

material more systematically, leading to flint mining on the South Downs (Russell 2000). This development was being mirrored on the continent, for example at Spiennes in Belgium (Butler 2006), and saw the industrial scale production of flint tools, with perhaps the first flintworking specialists making polished flint axes. However, it is likely that most people would still have been capable of making all the remaining types of tool, even the invasively retouched arrowheads and knives.

It is also clear that in the Early Neolithic care was being taken to use specially selected flint for the manufacture of some tools, perhaps those being produced by specialists. At Ringlemere and other sites in Kent the Early Neolithic assemblages have large numbers of tools manufactured on blades and flakes of distinctive Bullhead flint (Butler forthcoming; Fig 8.3). Similar targeting of high quality raw material by flintworking specialists has been suggested on the continent, for example Bartonian flint in the Seine Basin (Barford 2004).

The Later Neolithic Period

By the beginning of the third millennium BC, the population would have been largely sedentary and engaged predominantly in farming. This led to a fundamental change in flintworking technology. As people no longer needed to move around the landscape, they had better, and perhaps continuous, access to raw materials, which could be stored rather carried around with them. Therefore, the careful curation of the flintwork that had previously taken place was no longer required, although where flint was less plentiful this curation appears to have continued even into the Bronze Age.

The range of tools produced appears to have reduced at the same time, now numbering some 14 different types. This reduction was probably driven by the changing requirements of settled farmers. They could make do with a more limited range of tool types, although within some classes of tool types, for example scrapers, there was a marked increase in variation. There were also some new tool types such as single-piece sickles, designed specifically for their new farming economy.

Polished axes continued to be produced in the Later Neolithic, but the South Downs flint

Figure 8.3 Examples of Early Neolithic implements from Ringlemere, manufactured on Bullhead flint

mines ceased production, and Grimes Graves started up, although there is little evidence for the production of axes there (Barber *et al* 1999).

Flintworking technology in the Later Neolithic was defined by; (a) the quality of the raw material was less important; (b) no evidence for platform preparation or core rejuvenation; and (c) the hard hammer production of flakes (any blades are accidental).

Flintworking was probably still a skill practised by most people, but there appears to have been increased specialisation in respect of a limited range of tool types (Durden 1995), especially as we move into the Early Bronze Age.

The Early Bronze Age

The introduction of bronze had very little immediate effect on flintworking technology. The flintworking technology of the Later Neolithic continued into the Early Bronze Age without any apparent change; the debitage from these two periods is inseparable.

What did change however were the tools. Although the number of tool types dropped to 10, there was a significant change in the types of tool being produced. Fancy barbed-and-tanged arrowheads, plano-convex knives, daggers and some other exotics all made an appearance in the Early Bronze Age. These tool types all require a skilled flintknapper, and were probably the result of specialist production. This suggests that although large parts of the population may have still been able to fashion basic flint tools, for anything complex a specialist flint knapper was now required. What is more these exotic tools most frequently occur in ritual situations, such as burials or as votive deposits. However, it is important that we do not take these 'exotics' out of proportion, as they only make up a very small minority of the flintwork that was being produced.

Flint and stone axes disappeared at the end of the Neolithic, and were the first type of flint tool that was completely replaced by its bronze equivalent. However, apart from the axe, all other the early bronze tools and weapons (for example awls and daggers) continue to be produced in flint. So why did the bronze axe replace flint and stone axes?

We should not underestimate the look and effect of a shiny bronze axe over the rather dull, by comparison, flint and stone equivalent – its role as a prestigious item would have been significant. Compare this to the latest must-have gadget in today's society. Given the ritual use of flint axes in the Neolithic, the ritual use of early bronze artefacts should be entirely expected.

Experimentation has also shown that the bronze axe can be more efficient, and is less likely to break than a flint axe, when used to chop down trees. It can take up to 40 hours of labour to produce a large polished flint axe (Harding 1989), although smaller ones may only take some five hours (Olausson 1982). However, a bronze axe takes much less time to make, and if it is damaged or breaks it can easily be melted down and recycled into another axe. It is thought that both polished flint axes and bronze axes were produced by specialists.

There is one function of an axe which has not been fully considered, and that is as a weapon of war. In this case a bronze axe would be significantly superior to any stone axe, and may ultimately have been the reason for the demise of the flint axe, as warfare seems to have become much more important in Bronze Age society.

Finely worked flint daggers (Fig 8.4) are found all over northern Europe, with some particularly fine examples from Denmark. It has been suggested that these were specifically produced as copies of bronze daggers, with

Figure 8.4 Early Bronze Age flint daggers

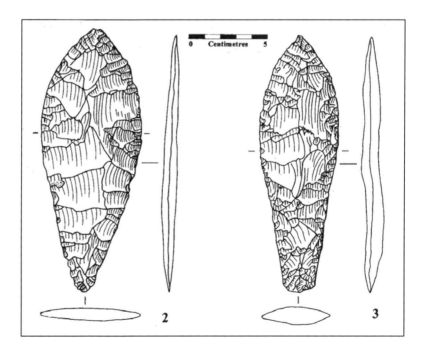

some even replicating the handle, pommel and stitching. As they are often found in ritual deposits (Field 1982), it could be that the flint copies were made to be placed in graves to replace a bronze original that could then be retained in circulation, as the bronze items were too valuable to be 'wasted' as a votive deposit. However, as experimentation has shown that these flint daggers took some 12 hours to produce (Stafford 1998), the reasons may be more complex than this.

Evidence has also been found for copper-tipped pressure flaking tools having been used to produce some of these prestigious flint exotics. So rather than being implicated in the demise of the flint industry in the Early Bronze Age in a ironic way it actually seems

that metal tools were helping to continue the use of flint.

The Later Bronze Age

As we move into the Later Bronze Age there were significant changes in the flintworking technology. Work carried out by Ford *et al* (1984), showed that there was much less variation in flake size and shape on Later Bronze Age sites than at Neolithic sites, whilst a greater proportion of flakes retained cortex.

The Later Bronze Age knapping strategy is simple and straightforward; (a) any flint will do, and is often scavenged (Butler 2001); (b) flakes are removed with a hard hammer until a suitable sized piece is produced. The core is then probably discarded; and (c) the tool is fashioned, utilised and discarded.

The reasons for this change were probably twofold. Firstly, there was a reduction in the range of tool types required by the sedentary farming communities of the Later Bronze Age. Although it is likely that the simple flake continued to be used for cutting alongside bronze tools throughout the Bronze Age, the number of different specific tool types reduced to six, of which only the scraper, piercer, fabricator and notched flakes were common. Fewer tool types would lead to less variation in flake size and shape. A study by Bradley (Ford *et al* 1984) has shown that the mean number of flint implement types per site reduced from seven in the later Neolithic to only three in the Later Bronze Age.

Secondly there is the increasing availability of a much broader range of bronze tools. However, these do not seem to have replaced the flint tools on a one to one basis, and the greatest proportion of bronze pieces found are actually weapons rather than agricultural or domestic tools.

The restricted range of tools might reflect the fact that the remaining flint tools were being used for more specialised tasks for which flint was probably the more efficient raw material. The obvious examples are the scraper (Fig 8.5) and piercer, where the hardness of flint would have outperformed bronze, while sharp fine-bladed flint flakes would also have performed better than bronze bladed tools until the manufacturing techniques of bronze tools improved in the Later Bronze Age.

The use of bronze for weapons is an

Figure 8.5 Later Bronze Age scrapers. The broad variation in form of these scrapers demonstrates the continued importance of some flint tools.

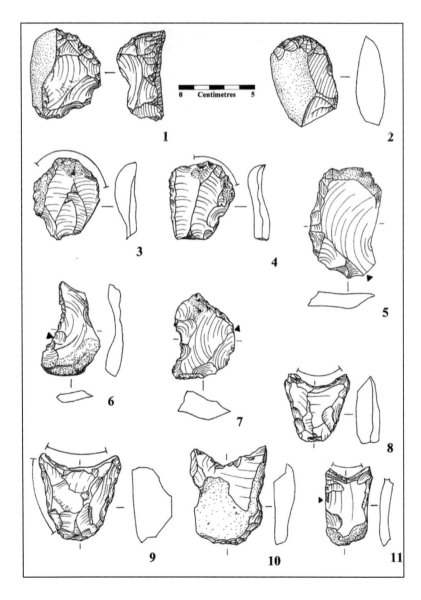

interesting aspect of this new material. Metal axes had already been introduced during the Early Bronze Age, replacing the flint and stone examples. During the Bronze Age swords, daggers and spearheads were introduced, and in most cases were completely new forms of weapon, having no apparent flint predecessor to replace. In the case of arrowheads, flint examples disappear from the archaeological record, but in Britain there are very few bronze examples.

This all suggests that warfare, or at least the status and prestige that goes with the ownership of weapons, was an increasing factor in Later Bronze Age life. It appears that a lot of the initial effort and resources in bronze metalworking was going towards supplying that requirement rather than supplying the domestic and craft needs, which continued to be provided by flint tools.

But nothing is straightforward; we have to accept that we are working with an incomplete database. Whereas flint is almost indestructible, metal is not, and although flint tools could be repaired and adapted quite easily when broken, they were simply discarded when finished with, whereas bronze tools could be recycled when broken. The result is that on the excavation of Bronze Age sites fairly large quantities of flint can be found, but very little in the way of metalwork.

If we look at the example of the Bronze Age site at Black Patch in Sussex, some 2,772 pieces of worked flint were recovered, of which 49 were tools, whilst only five bronze artefacts were found (Drewett 1982). This obviously gives us a problem when trying to interpret the corresponding use of flint and metal on sites.

Ford *et al* (1984) suggested that the extent to which flint was being exploited on a Bronze Age site might be an indirect measure of the metal supply. Little progress on this subject has been made since then, largely due to the problem highlighted above, and other problems of interpretation. Does the absence of a particular flint tool type on a site mean that it had been replaced by a bronze tool, or does it simply mean that the task for which that tool was employed was not undertaken on that site?

Conclusions

As we have seen there was a trend from the Mesolithic period through to the Bronze Age for flintworking technology to change as a result of the new circumstances in which people found themselves. Changes in the environment and economy were driving technological change.

The trend had also been for a general decline in flintworking technology, until skilled specialists were required to produce any exotic items, whilst most of the population appear to have lost their flintknapping skills over this time. Interestingly, this was matched by the specialism seen in metalworking and other emerging industries.

Although in some parts of the country raw material availability and quality did have an effect on flintworking technology, in the south-east, where flint is readily available this has never been an issue; the supply of good quality flint was never a problem throughout prehistory.

The variety of flint tools being produced had reduced significantly by the Early Bronze Age, but was this really due to the introduction of bronze, or was it due simply to changing circumstances. The introduction of bronze was to some extent incidental, having had little impact in the Early Bronze Age apart from the replacement of axes, as flintworking skills and the variety of tools being produced had already begun to decline dramatically at the start of the Later Neolithic, some 500 or so years earlier. However, flint does continue to be used throughout the Bronze Age.

The final demise of the flint tool industry was probably brought about as much by economic and social change as it was by the increase of metal working, although the increasing availability of bronze and then finally iron was probably the final nail in the coffin of an industry that was already in decline.

What we can really be sure about is that by the Iron Age, the use of flint seems to stop abruptly (Saville 1981), so perhaps we should be saying that it was the final replacement of flint by iron and not bronze that led to the final demise of the flint tool industry.

List of references

Barber, M, Field, D, and Topping, P 1999 *The Neolithic Flint Mines of England*, London: English Heritage
Barford, L 2004 'Lithics, culture and ethnic identity', *Lithics*, **25**, 65–77
Barton, R 1992 *Hengistbury Head, Dorset, Volume 2: The Late Upper Palaeolithic and Early Mesolithic Sites*, Oxford

University Committee for Archaeology Monograph, **34**, Oxford

Butler, C 2001 'The Flint' in C Greatorex, 'Evidence of prehistoric ritual traditions', *Sussex Archaeological Collections,* **139**, 27–73

Butler, C 2005 *Prehistoric Flintwork*, Stroud: Tempus Publishing Ltd

Butler, C 2006 'A visit to Spiennes Flint Mines, Belgium', *Lithics*, **26**, 102–10

Dixon, P 1972 'Crickley Hill 1960–1971', *Antiquity*, **46 (181)**, 49–52

Drewett, P 1982 'Later Bronze Age downland economy and excavations at Black Patch, East Sussex', *Proceedings of the Prehistoric Society*, **48**, 321–400

Durden, T 1995 'The production of specialise flintwork in the later Neolithic: a case study from the Yorkshire Wolds', *Proceedings of the Prehistoric Society,* **61**, 409–432

Field, D 1982 'Two flint Daggers from Kingston', *Surrey Archaeological Collections*, **74**, 207–8.

Ford, S, Bradley, R, Hawkes, J and Fisher, P 1984 'Flint-working in the Metal Age', *Oxford Journal of Archaeology*, **3**, 157–173

Green, H 1980 *The Flint Arrowheads of the British Isles*, British Archaeological Reports (British Series), **75**, Oxford

Harding, P 1989 'An experiment to produce a ground flint axe', in G de G Sieveking and M Newcomer (eds), *The Human uses of Flint and Chert*, Cambridge: Cambridge University Press, 37–42

Olausson, D 1982 'Lithic technological analysis of the thin butted axe', *Acta Archaeologica*, **53**, 1–88

Publishing Ltd

Russell, M 2000 *Flint Mines in Neolithic Britain*, Stroud: Tempus

Saville, A 1981 'Iron Age Flintworking – Fact or Fiction?', *Lithics,* **2**, 6–9

Stafford, M 1998 'In search of Hindsgavl: experiments in the production of Neolithic Danish flint daggers', *Antiquity*, **72 (276)**, 338–349

Young, R and Humphrey, J 1999 'Flint use in England after the Bronze Age: Time for a Re-evaluation?', *Proceedings of the Prehistoric Society*, **65**, 231–242

9. Land at the other end of the sea? Metalwork circulation, geographical knowledge and the significance of British/Irish imports in the Bronze Age of the Low Countries

David Fontijn

Dedicated to J.J. Butler

Introduction

Maritime contacts between Great Britain and Ireland and regions on the near continent during the Bronze Age have been a research theme for a long time. Attention specifically focused on the possibility of regular seafaring across the narrow Strait of Dover between Southeast England and Northwest France, and on the marked numbers of metalwork imports and cultural convergences that are believed to result from these overseas contacts. But connections between Britain and Ireland and the near continent are generally thought to have been much more far-reaching than just between the English-French Channel regions; directly or indirectly, contact and exchange networks are thought to have included large parts of the coastal French and Iberian regions that face the Atlantic Ocean, as well as to stretch out towards the regions at the continental side of the North Sea: the Low Countries (Cunliffe 2001). Particularly, research has focused on contacts between Britain – and to a lesser extent Ireland – on the one hand, and Belgium and the Netherlands on the other. Several scholars identified British/ Irish metalwork among finds from the Low Countries (Butler 1963; O'Connor 1980; Verlaeckt 1996), evidencing overseas bronze exchange networks. Similarities between Middle Bronze Age pottery and barrow types from southern England and that of the so-called Dutch/Belgian 'Hilversum culture' have also been interpreted as resulting from mutual cultural influences (Glasbergen 1954). More recent investigations, however, suggest that British/Irish connections might have been less important than traditionally thought. This does not only hold true for similarities in pottery and burial customs (Theunissen 1999), but there are also indications that the flow of metalwork from Britain and Ireland to the Low Countries might have been overrated (Butler 1995/1996, 171). The present study therefore aims to study these British/Irish imports and their significance in the Low Countries once again, dealing with three related topics

1. How numerous are British/Irish imports among metalwork found in the Low Countries?
2. What was the social and ideological relevance of these overseas imports? Did the fact that they originated in far-flung places give them an added significance?

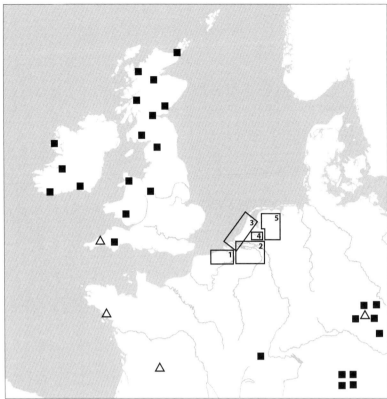

△ tin
■ copper

Figure 9.1 Copper and tin ore sources in north-west Europe and regions discussed (after Fontijn 2002, fig. 1.1). 1 West Belgium, 2 southern Netherlands/ northern Belgium, 3 western Netherlands, 4 central Netherlands, 5 northeastern Netherlands

3. Is there any evidence that Bronze Age people in the Low Countries were aware of the fact that these objects came from regions at the other end of the North Sea? What sort of geographical knowledge could have travelled with the objects?

Bronze Age relations between Britain and Ireland and the Low Countries

The Low Countries are far removed from copper and tin sources (Fig 9.1). However, copper and bronze implements have been used here from at least *c* 2300 BC onwards, and parts of the Low Countries knew a thriving local bronze industry throughout the Bronze Age (Butler and van der Waals 1966; Butler 1995/1996; Butler and Steegstra 1997/1998 and 2002/2003). Copper and tin ores do occur in certain places in Britain and Ireland, and this may partly explain why archaeologists have always assumed that structural – overseas – metal exchange relations must have existed between the Low Countries and Britain and Ireland. Still, this does not entirely explain

why Bronze Age links with the Isles were so prominently discussed in the literature. After all, many continental copper ores were also available and it is widely assumed that much, and probably most, of the copper and bronze in Belgium and the Netherlands ultimately derived from continental sources (Butler and van der Waals 1966). It seems as if – especially – British Bronze Age imports were a subject of more than normal interest. Is this because they imply the existence of prehistoric *seafaring*? Are they regarded as evidence for a prehistoric prelude to the important maritime histories of Britain and the Netherlands in historical times?

Identifying British/Irish imports

All discussions on metalwork exchange between Britain/Ireland and the continent go back to identifications of insular metal or metalwork objects. As the Low Countries lack copper and tin ores, prehistoric bronzes ultimately derive from metalliferous regions, which might be located in southern parts of the continent or in certain areas in Britain and Ireland. The question to be asked is whether insular imports can be distinguished from continental ones. The range of articles and books on cross-Channel exchanges illustrate that it has always been considered possible to recognise insular imports. At the same time, decades of research on insular imports on the near continent involved repeatedly shifting interpretations of the same finds as either British/Irish or continental in origin (compare for example Butler 1963 with Butler 1995/1996 on this topic). Sourcing of metalwork has been done on the basis of formal typology of the object and/or on its metal type. However, a positive identification of typically British or Irish stylistic traits or metal types is anything but undisputed, and particularly, there even appear to be contradictions between formal typology and metal composition. Many of the axes and halberds which were regarded as British and Irish imports on typological grounds, including the contents of the well-known Wageningen hoard, appeared to be made of continental metal (Butler and van der Waals 1966; Harbison 1968). Also, many of the types interpreted as of British or Irish origin can also be regarded as actually lacking distinctive regionally specific traits (like most of the undecorated flat axes conventionally identified as 'Irish' types in West-Belgium) or similar types which appear to have been produced in different European regions (rib and pellet socketed axes, interpreted as of British origin (Sompting type) by some authors; but see Huth 2000). Often, the present state of knowledge simply prevents sourcing of finds; the spectacular ceremonial dirks of Plougrescant-Ommerschans type can both be argued to be of English origin (derived from Kimberley dirks; Needham 1990, 245–248) or of North French origin (related to Tréboul-St Brandan dirks; Butler and Bakker 1961, 203–204). Some finds which figured in earlier discussions should no longer be considered, as closer inspection of museum documents shows that there is no evidence that they were found in the Low Countries (for example, the decorated flanged axe erroneously provenanced 'Nijmegen'; Butler 1995/1996, no. 29).

With this in mind, I went through the published metalwork finds again and made a new inventory of all objects in the Low Countries for which it might be expected that they were produced in Britain or Ireland (Table 9.1). The survey was confined to the area of the Lower Rhine Basin and western Belgium (covering all of the Netherlands, the Belgian provinces of Limburg, Antwerpen, Vlaams-Brabant and west and east Flanders). Unfortunately, there are at present no up-to-date inventories of metalwork finds in the southern and eastern Belgian provinces. The following criteria were used to include objects as 'insular imports' on the list. Given the problems in the identification of British/Irish imports outlined above, I qualified these interpretations with differing degrees of probability.

1. Very likely: there is a match between a characteristic insular form and type of metal (for example, the shield pattern palstaves in the Voorhout hoard which are made of Northover's type M metal)
2. Likely: this is a characteristic insular form, but there is no metal analysis available to support this interpretation (for example, side- and end-looped spearheads, all non-analysed tin items)
3. Possible: the object's form is seen as characteristic for an insular origin by more than one author, but continental products with comparable forms are also known. If a metal analysis is available, it cannot be

unequivocally linked to either insular or continental metalwork circulation zones
4. Disputable: this is an object with a rather indistinctive form for which a British/Irish origin is claimed by some author(s) but disputed by (an)other(s). If a metal analysis is available its interpretation is equally uncertain (examples are undecorated flat axes interpreted as 'Irish' types like Lough Ravel that are ill-defined and are actually quite similar to other flat axes ('Bygholm type') for which metal analyses show that they were most probably produced on the continent (Butler 1995/1996, 166–167).

Using these different categories of probability, the appendix clearly is not a list of British-Irish 'imports' but rather some sort of 'maximum' of objects that potentially can be interpreted as such. It should be realised, however, that the list is mainly confined to interpretations based on typological grounds; systematic programs of metal analyses have not been carried out, apart from material from the Dutch Early Bronze Age, and a small selection of finds from old Belgian collections (Wouters 1990). We are thus blinded to the possibility that insular metal itself might have had a much more prominent role in the continental metalwork than is now suggested by the numbers of (probably) imported objects alone.

Insular metalwork in the Low Countries

The list (Table 9.1) of potential insular imports in the Low Countries is surprisingly low in numbers; it contains only 127 objects (metal and faience; tin nails in the Bargeroosterveld dagger counted as one), of which just 81 are thought very likely to have a British/Irish origin (categories 1 and 2, see above; 38 and 14 of these 81 are from just two finds, Exloo and Voorhout respectively). Taken together, all the items constitute only some 6 per cent of the Bronze Age metalwork in the Netherlands and West-Belgium, a number that is much lower than might be expected from all the attention paid in writing to Bronze Age connections between Britain and Ireland and the Low Countries. Moreover, these are mainly 'British' types, making the evidence for an explicitly 'Irish' link even much less significant (in marked contrast to what was thought in the

1960s and 1970s; Butler 1963; De Laet 1974, 290–291).

As it might be expected that the coastal regions in particular were much better suited for participating in exchange networks across the sea than regions in the interior, I shall discuss imported objects for several regions within the Netherlands and Belgium (Fig 9.1).

West-Belgium

The region west of the river Scheldt, defined here as the present-day provinces of *West-Vlaanderen* and *Oost-Vlaanderen*, is both linked to northwest France via the River Scheldt and its tributaries (like the river *Dender*), but also to the west-Belgian coast which links up with the Channel Region to the south along the coast. It thus seems pre-eminently suited for participating in Northwest-French networks via the river Scheldt or by seafaring along the coast, even though there is not much evidence for inhabitation of the coastal zone (Bourgeois *et al* 2003). Much attention has been paid to identifying metalwork items that attest to cross-Channel connections (De Laet 1974; Warmenbol 1986). Several of the claimed imports are now no longer considered as such (Verlaeckt 1996, 14), and the present list is even more cautious in the identification of insular imports than previous publications. 14 out of 26 in my view qualify as of 'disputable' origin (category 4, see above). These include most of the claimed 'Irish' types. Even if we include all 'disputable' British/Irish imports, only 8 per cent of all Bronze Age metalwork finds published by Verlaeckt (1996) may be evidence of objects travelling across the sea. The recognised imports do contain some interesting finds. Axes are the most numerous. With the exception of a single decorated flat axe, the majority seems to be regular Middle and Late Bronze Age types with traces of a use-life. Many specimens have affinities with types that were probably produced in Northern France rather than at the other side of the Channel and imply the existence of shared conventions among Bronze Age smiths on either side of the Channel. Likely imports also include Middle and Late Bronze Age utilitarian swords and a rare ceremonial dirk of Wandsworth type (Warmenbol 1986, 153– 154). Other conspicuous items are several looped spearheads. These include large

specimens for which it is likely that their main functions were for (ceremonial) display rather than practical use.

The southern Netherlands/North Belgium and the central Netherlands

To the east of West-Belgium is the Dutch-Belgian area roughly bordered by three important European rivers, the Rhine in the north, the Meuse valley in the east, and the Scheldt in the west. The smaller Demer river in the Belgium is usually seen as a southern border (Fontijn 2002, 6–8). The higher grounds to the north, the central Netherlands, are also discussed here. These comprise the *Veluwe*, the Province of Utrecht and the Hilversum area.

Due to the fact that three important major rivers flow through this area, the southern Netherlands/North Belgium are potentially connected to more than one European region. These links are with the German Rhineland, south-western Germany and ultimately Central Europe via the river Rhine, with eastern France and south-eastern Belgium via the Meuse, and with (south)western Belgium and ultimately Northwest France and the Channel zone via the river Scheldt. Inhabitants of the Central River area, where the Rhine and Meuse flow close to each other and are reachable via many of smaller tributaries and streams, were potentially in a pivotal position to have access to downstream river trade routes from different European regions.

This region is traditionally considered as having had a special connection with southern England during the earlier half of the Middle Bronze Age, as the 'home' of the English-affiliated 'Hilversum' culture, particularly because of similarities between Hilversum pottery and types from Wessex. The occurrence of British metalwork in the region is seen as another category of artefacts evidencing regular contacts between Dutch-Belgian and overseas Bronze Age communities. It is then all the more striking that recent reviews of metalwork finds have drastically reduced the number of convincing insular imports in the 'Hilversum culture' region (Butler 1995/1996; Fontijn 2002). A program of metal analyses showed that 'classic' examples of British-Irish imports, like the entire content of the well-known Wageningen hoard or almost all of the 'flanged axes with British-Irish affiliations' all turned out to be of continental origin (Butler and van der Waals 1966; Harbison 1968). The present review even goes further than that. If we even include all objects of which a British/Irish origin is in dispute (category 4), Table 9.1 shows that only 5 per cent of all Bronze Age metalwork in this rich and well-researched region are potentially British/Irish imports. Objects characteristic for north French regions, however, appear to be much better represented among the metalwork (in some periods, like the Middle Bronze Age B, up to 25 per cent; *cf* Butler 1987; Fontijn 2002, table 7.1).

The kind of imported objects known are comparable to those from adjacent West-Belgium. Axes make up the largest part of the imports, and like in West-Belgium, most show traces of use just like regional and other imported axes. Regionally produced axes lack a well-defined style. Rather, they seem to have adapted and even copied stylistic traits of southern, North-French traditions (Fontijn 2002, 123), which in their turn can have similarities to axes produced in Britain (Butler and Steegstra's 'West European types' (1997/1998)). A single exception is once again a visually deviant Early Bronze Age decorated flanged axe from Haren (Fig 9.2), interpreted as one of the very few Irish imports on the basis of both metal composition and typology by Harbison (1968, 182). As in West-Belgium, some regular Middle and Late Bronze Age swords are found which are likely to have been produced in Britain. An insular origin is also possible for the precious and rare dirk-sized ceremonial sword of Plougrescant-Ommerschans type found in Jutphaas.

Western Netherlands

This region is defined by the present-day coastal provinces of Zeeland, Zuid-Holland and Noord-Holland. The Dutch delta had a markedly different outline at this time than it has now (Fig 9.3), and its different geographical situation has important implications for settlement and possibilities for access to other regions. By this time, a rather stable coastline had developed, consisting of closed dune systems and lengthy sand barriers, only interrupted by several estuaries where major rivers discharged into the North Sea; the Scheldt, the Meuse, the Rhine and the smaller Oer-IJ north of it. Sealed off from direct sea influences, major peat bogs developed behind the coast. Bronze Age settlements

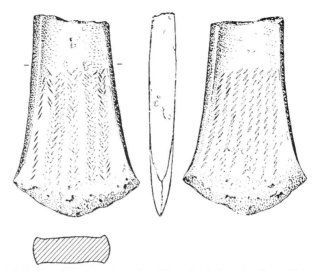

Figure 9.2 Decorated low-flanged axe from Haren (scale 3:4; after Butler 1995/1996, fig 10b: 28). Copyright Groningen Institute of Archaeology (formerly BAI), University of Groningen

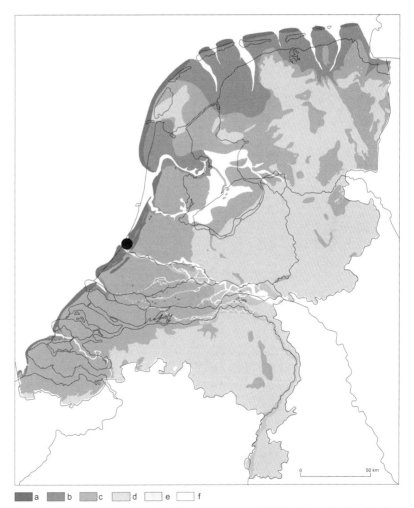

a ▪ b ▪ c ▪ d ▪ e ▪ f

Figure 9.3 Palaeographic map of the Netherlands around 3800 BP based on De Mulder et al 2003: fig. 143; the dot indicates the position of the Voorhout hoard. a) coastal and river dunes; b) peat; c) estuaries and tidal flats; d) floodbasin deposits; e) sand; f) water

Figure 9.4 The Voorhout hoard

were mainly situated in the coastal dune area, and in one area in the interior, on the West-Frisian marshes linked to the Oer-IJ inlet. There is no evidence for inhabitation of the large peat areas that separated the coastal communities from settlements in the southern and central Netherlands. More than those in any other region, the inhabitants of the west Dutch dune area may therefore have been in the best position to get involved in maritime networks. It is unclear whether they maintained regular contacts with communities in the interior via the rivers Meuse or Rhine, or even acted as some sort of 'gateway communities' controlling the flow of exchanged goods from the North Sea to the interior (*cf* Cunliffe 2001, 43; fig 2.18). This would have implied protracted voyages upstream the rivers or lengthy journeys over land. The Bronze Age metalwork found is small in number but differs to a certain extent from that in the adjacent southern Netherlands. There are a number of imports –including an entire warrior outfit (the Velserbroek grave) – that are similar to those of North German, Nordic, traditions (Butler and Steegstra 1997/1998, 175–179). Such objects might have reached the region by seafaring along the coast from the north, although the North Sea coast can be dangerous here as two tidal systems meet just to the north of this region (Thrane 2001, 553). A number of British imports may have reached the region via a southern route along the coast. Only the Acton Park palstaves in the Voorhout hoard (Fig 9.4), two faience beads and the end-looped spearhead from Bodegraven are convincing examples of overseas imports.

The Voorhout hoard was found in the dunes at some distance from the coast near the Rhine estuary (Fig 9.3). It was originally one example

of an entire group of 'merchant's hoards' consisting of identical palstaves, thought to reflect the activities of British merchants on the continent (Butler 1963, 59–62). Later research showed that most of these hoards consisted of continental instead of insular metalwork, except for the one from Voorhout. In this hoard, 13 out of 19 implements appeared to be made of M metal, providing support for Butler's theory that these axes were produced in Northern Wales (Northover cited in Butler 1990, 78)

Altogether, insular imports constitute some 20 per cent of all metalwork, by far the highest percentage of all regions. However, the total number of metalwork finds in the western Netherlands is very low when compared to that of other ones. Also, 16 out of the 19 bronze objects that probably have a British origin are from the Voorhout hoard (faience excluded). If we count the Voorhout hoard as one, the percentage of insular metalwork is some 4 per cent, just as low as that in the other regions.

The north-eastern Netherlands
This region is defined as comprising present-day provinces of Overijssel, Drenthe, Groningen, Friesland and eastern Flevoland. In the Bronze Age, people were inhabiting the gently undulating Pleistocene coversand areas that were on all sides confined by peat bogs (Fig 9.3). There are no important European rivers flowing to the area, and by this time, the salt marshes along the northern coast were not yet populated. Of all the regions discussed so far, this one seems to be in the most isolated position. Nevertheless, it is remarkably rich in metalwork finds, including rare items from far-flung places. Its main links seems to have been with North Germany and Scandinavia, as for example illustrated by the rich Late Bronze Age hoard of Drouwen consisting of a wealth of Nordic imports (Butler 1986). It is unclear whether these reached the northern Netherlands by travelling over land or across the sea, especially since it is known that the North Sea coast can be dangerous for shipping here. Moreover, the north Dutch coast was probably not yet populated and lacked attractive landing sites (Bakker 1976, 68; Thrane 2001). Potentially insular items constitute some 7 per cent of all metalwork known. However, 34 tin and bronze items of the total of 55 possible imports are from the Exloo necklace

(Fig 9.5). Insular imports are far from frequent, but there are some peculiar items. The best example is the composite necklace of Exloo itself, consisting of 4 faience and 4 amber pendants, 9 amber beads, 1 bronze and 25 or 27 tin beads. It has recently been argued that 1 amber bead and 4 pendants might represent a local addition to a necklace that originated in Wessex (Haveman and Sheridan 2005/2006, 125–126). Such a find would have fitted neatly in the sort of links that were originally conceived for the 'Hilversum culture', but it entered the ground in a region that is clearly outside the distribution of the 'Hilversum' pottery. The Early Bronze Age tin nails in the horn hilt of the Bargeroosterveld dagger might have come from English sources, although the metal composition of the copper dagger blade to which the handle is attached is interpreted as of Central European origin (Butler and van der Waals 1966, 87). Axes dominate the possible imports in all regions apart from this one. Only two fragmented palstaves of probably British origin are known (the Bargeroosterveld hoard). Among the few potentially insular imports, there seems to be a marked emphasis on rare ceremonial and display items (the ceremonial weapons from Ommerschans and Tollebeek, the large spearhead from Exloërmond, the Exloo necklace).

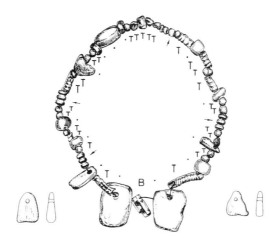

Figure 9.5 The Exloo necklace, after Butler 1990. T = tin, B = bronze, arrows indicate fayence beads. Copyright Groningen Institute of Archaeology (formerly BAI), University of Groningen

The perception of British/Irish imports by Bronze Age communities

This re-assessment of insular objects among Bronze Age metalwork in the Low Countries shows that truly convincing examples of overseas imports are rare. Furthermore, they do not appear to be confined to just one phase or one region. What was the social and ideological significance of such overseas imports? Realising that all the metalwork reached the Low Countries via supra-regional contact and exchange networks, did the fact that this material originated in areas at the far end of the North Sea give them an added significance to communities in the Low Countries?

It is widely assumed that metalwork had a special relevance to the inhabitants of the non-metalliferous regions like the Low Countries and southern Scandinavia (Sørensen 1987; Fontijn 2002). This can be inferred from the fact that metalwork figured in special burial

practices and especially played a prominent – and sometimes almost exclusive – role in depositional practices, where items were deliberately deposited in 'natural' watery places. This remarkable practice of a deliberate 'giving up' of rare materials, which could be entirely re-cycled instead, was a widespread practice in non-metalliferous regions during the Bronze Age (Bradley 1990). Paradoxically, it seems to relate to the special meanings attached to precisely this metalwork; these 'offerings' of objects were not randomly done, but appear to have been a highly structured practice of 'selective deposition' (Needham 1989; Fontijn 2002). The majority of metal was not deposited at all but must have been re-cycled and remains out of view of archaeology altogether. Of the small selection that did end up in such permanent depositions, specific kinds of objects were only placed in specific kinds of places in the landscape, avoiding others (Fontijn 2002). There are also remarkable patterns of association and avoidance between certain categories of objects. In the southern Netherlands and north Belgium, for example, weapons were almost never deposited in burials, but were deposited in major rivers in considerable numbers. Lavish ornaments in the Plainseau tradition of the Late Bronze Age, on the other hand, are also lacking in burials but seem to have been preferably deposited in different contexts (Fontijn 2002, 189–191).

Apparently, there were widely shared ideas on the sort of contexts where specific items could be sacrificed. It also implies that these objects were not just 'things', but meaningful items representing specific cultural values that were to be handled in prescribed ways only. The observation that certain categories of objects were deposited together indicates that the concepts with which they were associated were not considered to be in conflict with each other. Alternatively, the lack of weapons in Bronze Age burials in the southern Netherlands, for example, implies that weapons and references to violence or warfare apparently did not have a place in cultural ideas on the proper imagery and representation of the dead in their graves, whatever these might have been.

Research shows that different treatment of metalwork in deposition relates to the accruement of meaning due to a specific life-path. This includes the function for which an item was originally designed, the social and moral connotations that were attributed to such a function (*eg* the special connotations of items like weapons), the actual life-path of the object; its use and trajectory of circulation. As Kopytoff argues (1986, 66–68), following the life paths of certain items may yield a wealth of cultural information on how they were perceived by the society in question. Tracing patterns in the treatment of foreign items may inform us on what was seen as the culturally desirable 'life-path' or cultural biography of such objects, and therewith, the specific cultural ideas and meanings that go with it. In particular, those biographies which end up in permanent deposition stand a chance of being preserved in the archaeological record. Although the larger part of their previous life-path will remain hidden from us, we might learn something on the way British-Irish imports were interpreted from the role they played in this 'selective deposition'.

The 'otherness' of British/Irish imports

Interpreting objects as 'foreign' is a matter of perception. In the end, all bronze in the Low Countries came from far away places, and the insular imports are not exceptional in this respect. The way in which imported material was understood is a matter of interpretation on the part of local communities on the receiving end of the chain of exchange. This involves a process of 're-contextualisation'; non-local items are consciously and unconsciously compared with norms and material culture classifications as perceived locally. Every society has ideas on what constitutes its 'own' material culture; forms and styles which are known from implements that are used in everyday activities

or which regularly figure in important social events like specific paraphernalia (Sørensen 1987). Perceiving objects as 'close to' or 'alien to' one's own 'style' can be a situational and rarely clear-cut judgement. Nevertheless, such perceived distinctions do exist. Items that are produced in styles and shapes deviant to what is current locally, or of which the production involves crafting skills not available locally, must have been as recognisable to Bronze Age communities as they are to us. Such visual differences alone can be culturally meaningful and may contain the basis for differentiated use and perception (Sørensen 1987, 94). The perception of what is regarded as 'character-istic for' and 'close to' what is considered as a group's 'own' material culture is both created by what is produced by local smiths, as well as by the sort of objects that reach the region via regular exchange networks. It is conceivable that local bronze production and the main supra-regional bronze exchange networks by which bronze reached the local community are closely linked. It may have been important to make local products translatable to objects circulating in the wider bronze exchange system. Making objects look like those from other exchange partners may be one end to achieve this (Fontijn 2002, 251–252). Crafting, then, can be very important in the creation and even manipulation of what is regarded as 'local' and 'current' material culture. Smiths can make local products that are highly distinctive for a particular region, but also work in styles that are highly adaptive and copy elements from styles from other regions (*cf* Sørensen 1987). This is an important point, for thriving native bronze industries based on re-cycling metal are known from at least three regions in the non-metalliferous Low Countries; west Belgium, the southern Netherlands/North Belgium and the north-eastern Netherlands.

In the two southern Dutch and Belgian regions, local production is particularly known from the Middle and Late Bronze Age. In particular, regionally produced axes lack an outspoken regional style. Rather, they seem to lend or even copy elements that are characteristic for both Continental and Atlantic traditions (Fontijn 2002, 165). The mould from Oss-Horzak even shows that distinctive styles thought to be characteristic for mid-German regions like wheel-headed pins, seems to have been rather straightforwardly copied in the southern Netherlands (Fontijn 2002, 138–141). As a whole, regional styles in these regions may be characterised as 'open' rather than 'closed'. Especially regional palstaves can have similarities to products from France (especially with those of the Normand type; Butler and Steegstra 1997/1998, 245).

The north-eastern Netherlands seem to have been more linked with north German and Nordic traditions. Butler's recent study of socketed axes in this region illustrates that these do have distinctive decorations that are typical for the region only (Butler and Steegstra 2003/2004). Also, they show a remarkable variation in form and decoration among themselves. This is in marked contrast to what is found in the southern regions, and especially native crafting traditions from the Late Bronze Age north seem to have been a much more 'closed' tradition than those in the south. Sørensen (1987, 99) has argued that such 'closed' styles prevail in Late Bronze Age-Early Iron Age southern Scandinavia as well.

How 'deviant' were British-Irish imports then from the metalwork that was more current in the Low Countries? The answer to this question depends on which part of the Low Countries is taken into account. In the discussions above of (possible) insular imports in specific regions, it was often hard to make out on typological grounds only whether an object really came from Britain or Ireland. This was especially hard for many axes (palstaves in particular) and swords in West Belgium and the southern Netherlands. Often, a distinction between Atlantic French or British cannot even be made, and authors refer to such types as belonging to one 'West European' tradition (Butler and Steegstra 1997/1998). Such observations, however, may well relate to the 'open' nature of Atlantic crafting traditions, by which objects lack regionally distinctive traits and rather seem to have been made to look like or were translatable to objects from other traditions. Forms that are visually deviant, however, do exist; the Early Bronze Age decorated axes in west Belgium and the southern Netherlands, and the end- and side-looped spearheads. Large numbers of – probably – regionally produced spearheads are known, as well as imported ones. These always have pegged sockets instead of loops. It is interesting to see that particularly the larger examples of such looped spearheads

figure among the finds, which may have had a ceremonial rather than practical role. The rare tin and faience items also must have been deviant from current material culture, though more for their material rather than for their form. In the northern Netherlands, most finds mentioned in Table 9.1, be they genuinely British or not, are very deviant in form from the bulk of metalwork found there. It is also striking that most of the items from the north mentioned in Table 9.1 seem to have been primarily display items (the Exloo necklace) or ceremonial, aggrandised weapons (Tollebeek, Ommerschans, Exloërmond).

How insular imports ended their life

Having discussed the 'otherness' of British/Irish imports among the metalwork current in the Low Countries, we will now seek out whether striking similarities or differences between insular and other metalwork had repercussions for the cultural biographies of British/Irish objects. Large parts of their life-paths will remain hidden from us, like their history of circulation, and not much can be said about their use-life either. This is unfortunate, as ethnographies of exchange repeatedly show that it is precisely in their history of circulation and use that objects can get an added significance. We are informed, though, on the way in which they ended their life-path. Table 9.1 shows that in many cases, these objects were found in watery sites like rivers or peat bogs. In other words, they appear to have figured in depositional practices of the sort described above, like most other Bronze Age metalwork in the Low Countries. Even the Voorhout hoard comes from a depression filled with peat, and can be argued to represent a permanent deposition instead of a cache of temporarily stored trade stock which was never retrieved (Butler and Steegstra 1997/1998; Fontijn 2008). The distribution of British/Irish imports thus mainly represents *depositional* patterns, through filters of post-depositional decay and unbalanced research intensity. It needs not to reflect patterns of circulation. In theory, large quantities of British metal may have circulated in, for example, west Belgium that were never selected for deposition. Distribution of British/Irish metalwork across the Low Countries, therefore, cannot serve as a basis for judging intensities of exchange relations with Britain and Ireland as

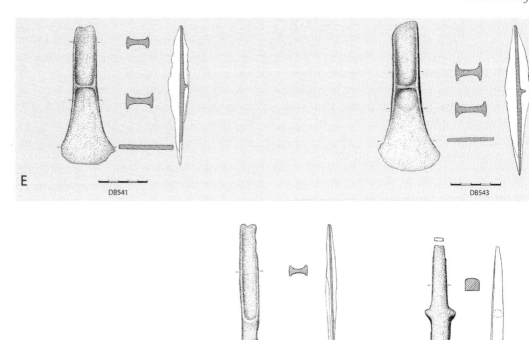

has traditionally been done by archaeologists (*cf* Butler 1963), unless there was a constant relation between numbers of imports in circulation and those in deposition.

In general terms, British/Irish imports were treated in a similar way as other imports from far-flung places in selective deposition. In west Belgium and the southern Netherlands/ northern Belgium, most have been found in 'multiple deposition zones' in major rivers at some distance from settlements (Fontijn 2002, 260– 265, fig 14.2). They rarely figure among depositions in wet places closer to lived-in areas and are practically unknown from farmsteads and their agrarian environment, burials and barrow zones or urnfields. The same applies for those in the north-eastern Netherlands, where they figure in peat bogs away from settled land, which had long histories of use for depositional practices.

In western Belgium and the southern Netherlands/northern Belgium and the cen-

tral Netherlands, there is no evidence that a distinction was made between British/Irish and continental imports; whereas there is evidence that certain central European imports were deposited in a different manner (Fontijn 2002, 93–95; 127–129). Insular imports were placed in the same deposition zones where French imports and regional axes ended up. They also seem to have had a use-life comparable to that of their French counterparts; most axes and swords show traces of use. The side-looped spearhead from 's-Hertogenbosch was even converted into a regular spearhead type with pegged socket. Hoards are rare in the Low Countries, but it is rarely realised that even one of the most convincing examples of British – Welsh – imports in this region, the Voorhout hoard, also consists of a combination of British and 3 or 4 non-British items, probably French types (Fig 9.6; Butler 1990; Fontijn 2008). It thus can no longer be regarded as the classic example of material which travelled 'en bloc' from Britain to the Netherlands. Summing up, there is no evidence that British/Irish imports were treated differently in deposition from other imports. Rather they appear to have been deposited in the same way as – particularly – the more numerous Atlantic French imports with which they often share stylistic traits. The same applies to visually deviant types, like the decorated flanged axes or side- and end-looped spearheads

In the northern Netherlands, but also in the case of the Epe hoard in the central Netherlands, which is rather close to this region, the situation is different. We have already seen that this is true for the selection of items which ended up in deposition; rare ornaments and ceremonial, aggrandised weapons. Axes are rare, and the palstaves from the Bargeroosterveld hoard, the only two convincing examples known, were deposited together with rare continental *Nierenringe*. One axe was damaged, the other broken, which is rather unusual in depositions in the Low Countries. This might suggest that they were seen as metal from an unusual far-away place rather than as implements in their own right. In the Ommerschans and Epe hoards and in the Exloo necklace, on the other hand, special (possible) insular items all seem to have been deliberately linked to local and regional items. In Ommerschans, there is a curious association between a masterpiece of bronze casting (the sword), scrap metal, and presumably locally made flint implements. In Exloo, amber, tin and faience beads in a Wessex tradition of composite necklaces are combined with locally made amber beads (Haveman and Sheridan 2005/2006, 125–126). In Epe, an Oxford type palstave was deposited together with a regional stopridge axe and sickle. All suggest that some sort of 're-contextualisation' or re-appropriation took place. Were 'alien', special items made socially acceptable to the local community by deliberately forging links with regular, local items?

Overseas imports and the concept of land at the other end of the sea

The metalwork from the Low Countries charted so far neatly illustrate its impressive 'cosmopolitan' nature. Bronzes from all directions could end up in hoards, as happened for example in those from Bargeroosterveld and Voorhout. Still, locating the origins of objects in this way is first and foremost an *etic* enterprise, established by modern scholars with modern maps in the back of his or her head. But what would prehistoric people have known on the precise origins of all this material? What sorts of views of the wider world would they have had, and how would they have located the origins of such material? Can we gain any understanding in the indigenous, *emic*, perception of foreign material and its geographical origins? Did inhabitants of the Low Countries know that the objects discussed in this text as 'British/Irish imports' originated on a huge island situated at the far end of the large North Sea? It may be clear that this final question may prove the most difficult one to answer in a satisfactory way. Yet, it is also the one which is rarely or never made explicit, and an affirmative answer to this question is even tacitly assumed in most contributions. It may even be asked whether the entire concept of 'British-Irish' imports is misleading, as such modern geographical denominators may blind us from the possibility that Bronze Age perceptions of origin and geography might have been very different from ours.

Does knowledge on origin and geography travel with objects in long-distance exchange?

It may be assumed that most insular imports reached the Low Countries by some form of exchange, be it ceremonial gift exchange or barter/commodity exchange (*cf* Bloch and Parry 1989). Some members of the local community must have engaged in supra-regional long-distance exchange. Such networks do not only channel the flow of bronze, but also facilitate deviating views on the wider world, as a world that is inhabited by other cultures and other places, by people that may be seen as related to one's own group, but also as deviant, or strange and even as non-human (Helms 1988). Structural exchange of gifts and commodities defines boundaries of ordered society and may include entities that are politically or ethnically separate and distinct yet related through exchange alliances and by acceptance of mutually understood ideologies (*cf* Helms 1993, 95). The social reality of the participants in long-distance exchange may therefore include groups that are hardly or even never met in daily life and areas that are never visited, but who nevertheless must have a place in the view and cosmology of the world as perceived locally.

Anthropological studies of long-distance gift exchanges have provided us with interesting examples how rather exact knowledge on the origin of objects can have travelled with objects in exchanges. Knowledge of an object's path of circulation and former owners can be perceived as crucial information adding up to an object's value. Exchange partners can have some sort of maps in their heads on the circulation of the object so far. The well-documented Melanesian Kula exchange cycle is a case in point (Malinowski 1984; Weiner 1992). Other examples include the extensive desert exchange routes of the Lake Eyre Basin in Australia (McBryde 2000). It links groups half a continent apart and involves the circulation of goods over thousands of kilometres. They rank amongst the world's most extensive networks in a hunter-gatherer society. In spite of the huge distances across which objects travel, McBryde (2000, 244) argues that 'the routes taken by these goods and the nodes they pass through...would all be well known to groups linked to such transactions. Well known also would be the resources of the various countries traversed and the significant places from which these came, *eg* Parachilna red ochre'.

Yet, there are also instances where knowledge of geographical origins of imports is *not* preserved during exchange transactions. Such knowledge may get lost or be considered as irrelevant. Reference to geographical origins may then for example only be in terms of generalisations or simplifications (like 'material coming from the far north' or 'upstream'). Such objects, therefore, simply have no or hardly any histories of long-distance circulation. As Nicolas Thomas (1991) has argued, this must have been the reality in exchange systems which permit alienation and commoditisation of goods. He argues that there is a tendency among anthropologists to project the properties of special, high status gifts on gifts in general (Thomas 1991, 65). In other words, instances as the Kula exchange of which precise knowledge on geographical origins and paths of circulation travel with the exchanged item, are exceptional. A great part of imported material would have reached communities as bulk via other kinds of gift exchanges and – most importantly – via commodity exchange or long-distance trade. It is likely that this also applies to metalwork

exchange during the Bronze Age (Huth 2003; Muckelroy 1981). Such transactions can be rather anonymous ones where objects do not have names, and where there is no knowledge of and no rank increment from the origins and paths of circulation itself (Thomas 1991, 67). This certainly does not preclude the possibility that many of the thus traded objects could take on specialised roles when they were put to use in the local community, and for Bronze Age metalwork it is even very likely that this happened (Bradley 1990, 121–129; Fontijn 2002, 253–254).

There are also ethnographies that show that the place where an object originated was understood in imaginary or mythical terms. The most sacred and precious coppers in the potlatch ceremonies of the Kwakiutl Northwest coast native Americas are a case in point. They consider these coppers as divine objects, given by spirits; objects of an 'enchanted' world (Godelier 1999, 60; Mauss 1993, 45). However, as Godelier recently emphasised (1999, 60–61), these objects were originally made by people. Mauss (1993, 131 note 237) makes some remarks on the place where the raw copper might have been extracted and on the groups that were possibly involved in the manufacture of these precious coppers. In other words, these coppers had a cultural biography in which knowledge on the actual geographical origin and conditions of production became replaced by tales of myth. Similar processes in which specific items become inalienable possessions by links with imaginary origins are well-documented, for example during the creation of Early Christian cult places (Theuws 2003). Another process in which the origin of objects is perceived in mythical terms, or 'cosmologically authenticated' (Weiner 1992, 100–104) is what Helms has termed 'cosmologically driven acquisition' (1993, 95–97). Its aim is not to engage in reciprocal exchange relations and of seeing the mapping the world through networks of contact and exchange, but rather to obtain an exotic special item from an area that is normally beyond the reach of local societies, even by means of their existing long-distance exchange relations. The object thus represents the long reach of a community to places far beyond the world as perceived locally.

What could people possibly have known?

England is visible from the French side of the Channel in good weather circumstances and crossing the Channel is generally considered as possible in the Bronze Age (Clark 2004). The existence of intensive cross-Channel exchanges as documented by many archaeologists is therefore hardly surprising. This is different in the case of contacts between Britain and the Netherlands across the much larger North Sea. Britain is too far to be visible from any place on the Dutch beaches, and whether it was possible or desirable to cross the North Sea from Britain to the Netherlands may be something of an open question given the present lack of evidence (but see van de Noort 2003). It seems viable, however, to use insights in the palaeo-geographical settings of the regions discussed here in combination with the actual insular imports found in them, to outline hypothetical routes of contact.

The southern Netherlands/northern Belgium are at a considerable distance from the coast. The main routes by which metalwork reached these regions must have been by boat, downstream via the major rivers Rhine, Meuse and Scheldt. It is questionable whether the region could easily by reached from the sea, as it would have involved protracted voyages upstream the river by boat or over land, and it is even debatable whether this was done in the Roman Period (Thijs van Maarleveld *pers comm*). Downstream traffic on the major rivers Meuse and Scheldt seems the most logical way by which French metalwork could have arrived here. Realising that British metalwork circulated in Northwest French networks as well, it might be ventured that the small amount of British imports known reached the southern Netherlands together with French metalwork. It is at any rate conspicuous that certain French and British objects not only share stylistic traits, but are also repeatedly found associated in depositions. Does this imply that British/Irish objects were seen as one variety of material which was seen as coming from the far south? A similar situation can be found in the adjacent west Belgian region. Here, downstream traffic from the south via the river Scheldt again seems the most viable route by which metal could reach the region. This region, however, does seem to have had a connection to the coast, even though there is not much evidence for Bronze Age occupation of the coastal zone.

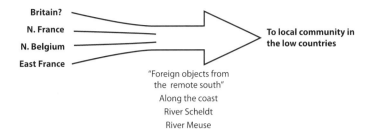

A sea route along the coast from the Channel area might have been travelled with boats of the Dover type. British/Irish metal in that case could have come from the French channel zone by sea, avoiding the much longer and more dangerous crossing of the North Sea from England to the Belgian coast. At any rate, in both scenarios, British material would also reach the area 'from the south' instead of from across the sea, and likewise the origins of 'British/Irish' may also have been located there (Fig 9.7).

The central and north-eastern Netherlands both seem to have a rather isolated position. We have seen that the settled area was at some distance from the coast, which was at that time not yet suitable for inhabitation. The north Dutch coast has also been argued to have been a rather inconvenient and even dangerous coast for seafaring. French imports that are prominent among depositions in the southern Netherlands, are very rare in the north (Butler 1987), and so are British/Irish imports. In the few examples where British imports figure in depositional practices, we are dealing with cases where objects rather figure as 'exotic' material rather than as objects themselves; faience and tin as decorations in the Exloo necklace or in the haft of the Bargeroosterveld dagger, fragments of axes in the Bargeroosterveld hoard. Objects are not associated with other Atlantic imports with which they could have been imported 'en bloc' like elsewhere, but seem to have been linked with regional items (the Epe hoard, possibly Ommerschans, Exloo) or rare items which came from a continental source (Bargeroosterveld hoard). It might therefore be ventured that insular items represent visually deviant, rare imports and that knowledge on their origins was not available (Fig 9.8). Given the emphasis on rare, aggrandised ceremonial items, their origin may even have been conceptualised in mythical or cosmological terms.

Figure 9.7 Possible perception of origins for objects imported from Northwest-France and Britain

*Figure 9.8
Conceptualisation of
known and 'known
about' world via exchange
networks. Rare and/or
'beyond normative' objects
may be conceptualised as
originating in an unknown
world outside the reach of
regular networks. Some
of the British imports
in the northeastern
Netherlands may have been
conceptualised as such.*

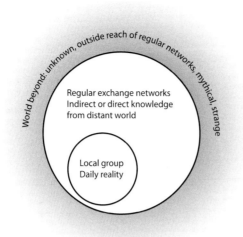

The only convincing candidate for a maritime region is the coastal western Netherlands. Geographically, it is rather isolated from its hinterland, and it is likely that seafaring along the coast, using the tides, might have been a viable route for long-distance contacts. British imports are again rather rare among the metalwork known, but the Voorhout hoard represents one of the best examples we have, with its contents of north Welsh palstaves. It can be considered as a group that was transported 'en bloc', given the worn state of the objects probably as source of metal for re-melting (Fontijn 2008). However, even this convincing set of overseas imports consists of a mix of insular as well as non-British, presumably French Atlantic metalwork (Fig 9.6). Again, it stands for a scenario where British and French metal were shipped together and brought to the Netherlands via a southern route along the French-Belgian coast. Even this genuine British metal is more likely to have been perceived by continental as 'coming from south' rather than as originating on a huge landmass at the other end of the North Sea.

The concept of 'origins' of metal as perceived by Bronze Age communities
How relevant is this concept of origins to metalwork circulation at all? As a material, copper and tin lack visual characteristics from which one can infer where the material was extracted. The Voorhout hoard consisted of material of mixed British-French provenances, but all in worn or even broken conditions, which suggests that they were valued as recyclable material. This collection of scrap was deliberately sacrificed, presumably as some token in order to sanction the conversion of alien metal for local recycling (Fontijn in press). Since the main components of bronze may easily consist of material from different provenances, which was melted down and mixed, even the entire concept of 'unique origins' as current in the case of stone or flint may be upset. It is the smith who can give bronze objects once again a distinctive outlook or 'style', but we have seen that in the case of certain Atlantic items, British and French objects were produced in styles similar to rather than different from each other. This might imply that we should not assume that 'origins' of metalwork were perceived of as locating it to one specific, unique place or area, but rather as 'belonging to a particular circulation zone or exchange network', only defined in broad spatial terms.

Conclusion

This study of metalwork circulation across the sea focused on the much-debated relation between Britain/Ireland and the Low Countries during the Bronze Age. British-Irish imports found in this continental region were central to the discussion. A re-evaluation of objects found in the Netherlands and West-Belgium that were supposed to have been produced in Britain or Ireland nuanced established views that such imports were prominent among the imports in the Low Countries. Even in the southern Netherlands/northern Belgium, traditionally considered as the 'home' of the Wessex-affiliated 'Hilversum culture' no more than 5 per cent of all Bronze Age metalwork might have been imported from Britain or Ireland. Comparably low figures are known for all other regions, including the western Netherlands, the only region with a true maritime setting. Of the (rare) convincing examples of British-Irish imports, practically all represent British rather than Irish objects.

Most insular imports known to us were 'sacrificed' or deposited in watery places. They figured in the more encompassing practices of 'selective deposition' of metalwork, which implied that they were considered as imbued with a special social and/or ideological significance. The fact that they originated on land at the other end of the sea does not seem

Table 9.1 (pp 143–146) An inventory of all objects in the Low Countries for which it might be expected that they were produced in Britain or Ireland

	Type	Date	Context	Remarks	References
North-eastern Netherlands					
Bargeroosterveld '1900 hoard' *(1)*	2 'late' British palstaves 'East English' resp. 'South English' metal	Period IV; Penard/Wilburton-Wallington; LBA	Hoard in barrow? With fragment of bracelet; knife and 2 *Nierenringe*-bracelets	One anciently damaged; other only midsection; anciently broken	Butler/Steegstra 1997/1998, nos 233–234; O'Connor 1980, no 195; metal analysis by P. Northover
Bargeroosterveld *(2)*	Tin nails in horn hilt of copper dagger	EBA	Peat bog	Copper analysis indicates Central European metal	Butler/Van der Waals 1966, 109, no. 54
Bargeroosterveld *(2)*	Basal-looped spearhead (L. 26.5 cm)	MBA–LBA	–	–	Butler 1963, 109, no. 5
Exloo *(1)*	Composite necklace; 4 segmented faience beads, 1 bronze bead, 25 (or 27?) tin beads, 4 amber pendants, 9 amber beads	Haveman/Sheridan 2005/2006; between 19th and 15th century BC	Peat bog	Imported from Wessex, but 1 amber bead and 4 pendants probably locally-made additions	Butler 1990; Haveman/Sheridan 2005/2006
Exloërmond *(2)*	Basal-looped spearhead (L 42 cm)	MBA B	Peat bog	–	Butler1987, 32
Ommerschans *(4)*	Huge ceremonial sword type Plougrescant-Ommerschans; razor, 2 chisels, 1 rod, 2 pins, 4 fragments of metal, spiral; all bronze; flint chisel, flint fragment, stone chisel, flint/stone implement, stone tablet, whetstone	MBA A–B	Peat; all objects on platform of Birchwood stakes	Sword; either French or British origin; other objects unknown, small bronze and flint possibly locally made	Butler 1990, 86–91; Fontijn 2001
Onstwedde *(2)*	Basal-looped spearhead (L 25.5 cm)	MBA B	–	–	Butler 1987, 2
Papenvoort *(2)*	Side-looped spearhead	MBA B	–	–	Butler 1963, 109, no. 12
Tollebeek *(4)*	Ceremonial spearhead w. slits and blade perforations	C14 wooden shaft; 3050 ± 70 BP; but typologically LBA	–	Either French or British origin; wooden shaft present in socket	Butler/Hogestijn 1988; metal analysis by P. Northover
Zwartsluis *(4)*	High-flanged axe type Arreton	MBA A	–	Ground, edge facets	Butler 1995/1996, 59
Western Netherlands					
Bodegraven *(2)*	Basal-looped spearhead type Enfield	MBA B	River?	–	Butler 1987, 32
Den Haag *(2)*	Faience bead, segmented	Uncertain, MBA?	Settlement	–	Haveman/Sheridan 2005/2006, 113
Loosduinen *(4)*	Stopridge axe type Caverton	MBA A–B	Under peat layer	–	Butler 1995/1996, no 152
River Scheldt in Zeeland or Flanders *(4)*	Palstave, looped, trident variant of Type Shelf	LBA (not before Penard phase)	–	Mint condition	Butler/Steegstra 1997/1998, no 221
Vogelenzang *(2)*	Faience bead, ribbed biconical	Settlement remains date MBA A	Settlement	–	Haveman/Sheridan 2005/2006, 112–3
Voorhout *(1)*	14 primary shield palstaves type Acton Park, 2 of which less typical, 5 w. ribbed shield; 2 stopridge axes, 1 high-flanged axe, 1 flanged axe, 1 lugged chisel	MBA A–B	Peat layer	Most worn, some damaged; Acton Park palstaves and chisel; M Metal; N. Welsh imports, 2 stopridge axes type Plaisir; French, high-flanged axe; non-British	Butler 1990, 78–84;Butler/Steegstra 1997/1998; Fontijn in press; metal analysis by P. Northover

	Type	Date	Context	Remarks	References
Southern Netherlands/ North Belgium					
Aijen *(4)*	Stopridge axe type Bannockburn	MBA A	–	Ground, sharpened	Butler 1995/1996, no. 150
Asselt *(4)*	Palstave, type Wantage	MBA–B	River	Blunt, not sharpened	Fontijn 2002, app. 2.5
Cuijk-Maas *(3)*	Dagger, type Keelogue	MBA B	River	Dubious provenance! Find lost	Fontijn 2002, app. 5.2
Eerselen *(4)*	Palstave, type Stibbard	MBA–B	Marsh	–	Butler/Steegstra 1997/`1998, no. 217
Epe *(4)*	High-flanged axe type Arreton	MBA A	–	–	Butler 1995/1996, 60
Epe *(3)*	Palstave type Oxford	MBA A–B	Hoard in hill (barrow?) near valley	Sharpened; in hoard with regional stopridge axe and sickle; objects wrapped in cloth?	Butler/Steegstra 1997/1998, no 218
Groot Haasdal *(4)*	Low-flanged axe 'of British affinities'	EBA	Hill-valley transition	–	Butler 1995/1996, no. 25
Haren *(1)*	Decorated low-flanged axe	EBA	Wet?	–	Butler 1995/1996, no. 28
Heel *(3)*	Dagger, affiliated to Gerloff's (1975) Ridgeway group	MBA A; late Wessex	–	Sharpened	Fontijn 2002, 105 app. 5.1
's-Hertogenbosch *(2)*	British side-looped spearhead	MBA B	–	Converted to pegged spearhead	Butler 1961
Heythuysen-Arenbosch *(3)*	Dagger, type Keelogue?	MBA B	–	–	Butler unpublished document; Fontijn 2002, app.5.2
Jutphaas *(4)*	Ceremonial dirk, type Plougrescant-Ommerschans	MBA	Marsh	Unused; provenance either North France or British	Butler/Sarfatij 1970–71; Fontijn 2001
'Limburg' (unknown) *(4.)*	Short-flanged axe	MBA A–B	–	–	Fontijn 2002, app. 2.4
'Maas' *(2)*	Flange-hilted sword, type Ewart Park	LBA	River	–	Fontijn 2002, app. 5.4
Meers *(2)*	Flange-hilted sword, type Ewart Park	LBA	River	Blade worked	Fontijn 2002, app. 5.4; Roymans 1991, 75, 11
Milsbeek-Maas *(3)*	Sword, type Appleby	MBA B	River	Shortened blade	Fontijn 2002, app. 5.2
Millingen-biesterveld *(2)*	Two flange-hilted swords, both type Ewart Park	LBA (Ha B3)	River	Both sharpened, found on the same site	Fontijn 2002, app. 5.4
Nijmegen *(2)*	Flange-hilted sword type Thames	LBA (Ha B3)	River	–	Roymans 1991, fig 8e
Nijmegen/Arnhem *(2)*	Flange-hilted sword, type Ewart Park	LBA (Ha B3)	River	–	Roymans 1991, fig 8c
Rijsbergen *(4)*	Short-flanged axe	MBA A–B	Stream valley	Expanded cutting edge	Fontijn 2002, app. 2.4
Stevensweert *(3)*	Grooved ogival dagger	MBA A; Wessex 2	River		Fontijn 2002, 105, fig 6.14; app. 5.1
Veldhoven *(2)*	British side-looped spearhead	MBA B	Stream valley	Sharpened	Roymans 1980
Voorst *(2)*	Flange-hilted sword type Ewart Park	LBA (Ha B3)	River	–	Cowen 1967, 449, no. 6
Wessem *(2)*	Flange-hilted sword, type Ewart Park	LBA	River	Sharpened	Fontijn 2002, fig 8.13

	Type	Date	Context	Remarks	References
In Belgium					
Antwerpen *(4)*	Palstave, type Birchington	MBA B	River	–	O'Connor 1980, list 8, 5
Antwerpen *(4)*	Palstave, type Broadward	MBA B	River	–	Verlaeckt 1996, A11
Antwerpen *(4)*	Flanged axe type Arreton	MBA A	–	–	Verlaeckt 1996, no A22
Battel *(2)*	British basal-looped, straight-based spearhead	MBA B	–	–	O'Connor 1980, list 56, 11
Battel *(2)*	Sword, type Cloontia	MBA B	Stream	Rivets torn and repaired (?)	Warmenbol 1986, 155–156
Brussegem *(4)*	Flanged axe of type Arreton	MBA A	–	–	Verlaeckt 1996, no B2
Duffel-Nethe *(2)*	British basal-looped spearhead	MBA B	River	–	O'Connor 1980, list 20, 15
Hunsel *(4)*	Socketed axe type Sompting	LBA–EIA	–	–	Fontijn 2002, app. 2.15
West Belgium					
Aalst *(3)*	Broad-bladed palstave, ribbed shield pattern	–	–	–	Verlaeckt 1996, no 3
Aalter *(4)*	Stopridge axe type Arreton	MBA–A	–	Asymmetrical cutting edge; resharpened	Verlaeckt 1996, no 5
Baasrode *(4)*	Flat axe related to type Ballyvalley	LN–EBA	River	Insular provenance disputable	Verlaeckt 1996, no 16
Deinze *(4)*	Broad-bladed shield-pattern stopridge axe	MBA–A–B	–	–	Verlaeckt 1996, no 27
Ename *(4)*	Socketed axe type Sompting	LBA–EIA	–	–	Verlaeckt 1996, no 43
Gent *(3)*	Trapezoidal narrow-butted sword; *cf* Burgess/Gerloff 1981; group IV with group III affinities	MBA–B	River	2 rivets holes, one torn; damaged edge	Verlaeckt 1996, no 57
Gent (surroundings) *(2)*	Decorated flat axe; very low flanges; 2 frames of 3 and 5 arcs, related to type Killaha and Ballyvalley	LN–EBA	–	–	Verlaeckt 1996, no 284
Gentbrugge *(2)*	Flange-hilted sword type Ewart Park	LBA (Ha B3)	River	–	Verlaeckt 1996, no 66
Gentbrugge *(2)*	Straight-based basal-looped spearhead, 2 rivet holes, type Kergoustance	MBA B–LBA	River		Verlaeckt 1996, no 70
Geraardsbergen *(2)*	Basal-looped spearhead	MBA B	Wet	Damaged blade, part of wooden shaft preserved	Verlaeckt 1996, no 73
Geraardsbergen *(4)*	Flat axe type Lough Ravel/Ballybeg	LN–EBA	–	Insular provenance disputable	Verlaeckt 1996, no 75
Harelbeke (4)	Palstave 'English type'	MBA–B	Dry	–	Verlaeckt 1996, W3
Lochristi *(4)*	Broad-bladed stopridge axe type Arreton	MBA–A	Peat near river	–	Verlaeckt 1996, no 90
Melle *(2)*	Ceremonial sword type Wandsworth	MBA–B (Taunton phase)	River	Not used; no rivet holes; for ceremonial display	Verlaeckt 1996, no 100
Melle *(4)*	Stopridge axe type Arreton	MBA–A	Stream	–	Verlaeckt 1996, no 108
Oudenaarde *(2)*	Straight-based basal-looped spearhead type Enfield, one loop,	MBA B	–	L= 44.6 cm; relatively large specimen	Verlaeckt 1996, no 122
Schellebelle *(2)*	Large basal-looped spearhead, Rowlands 1976 group 2	C14 of wood; 3150 ± 55 BP; MBA–B	Peat near stream	Wooden shaft preserved; L=49 cm; one of the largest on the continent; ceremonial weapon	Verlaeckt 1996, no 134

	Type	Date	Context	Remarks	References
Schellebelle *(3)*	Narrow-bladed palstave, 5 ribs on septum, 3 below	LBA	River; in peat	–	Verlaeckt 1996, no 145; *cf* O'Connor 1980, 132–133
Schellebelle *(4)*	Socketed axe type Sompting	LBA–EIA	River; in peat	–	Verlaeckt 1996, no 147
Schellebelle *(4)*	Socketed axe type Sompting	LBA–EIA	River; in peat	–	Verlaeckt 1996, no 148
Schoonaarde *(3)*	Broad-bladed 5-ribbed shield-pattern palstave	MBA–A–B	River?	–	Verlaeckt 1996, no 170
Tielrode *(4)*	Flanged stopridge axe (related to) type Arreton	MBA–B	Peat	–	Verlaeckt 1996, no 213
Wetteren *(2)*	Basal-looped spearhead with rivet holes, Rowlands 1976 group 3	MBA–B	–	Addition of rivet holes; adaption to continental habits?	Verlaeckt 1996, no 221
Wichelen *(4)*	Socketed axe type Sompting	C14 date of wood; 2465 ± 35 BP	River?	Wood preserved in socket	Verlaeckt 1996, no 248
Wichelen *(4)*	Socketed axe type Sompting	LBA–EIA	River	Wood preserved in shaft	Verlaeckt 1996, no 253
Wichelen *(4)*	Flat-topped axe	LN–EBA	River?	Resharpened; insular provenance disputable	Verlaeckt 1996, no 271

Remarks to the Table 9.1: (1) interpretation of this find as an insular import is 'very likely', (2) 'likely', (3) 'possible' (4) 'disputable'. See the text for further explanation of these qualifications.

LN: Late Neolithic (2900–2000 BC); EBA: Early Bronze Age (2000–1800 BC); MBA A: Middle Bronze Age A (1800–1500 BC); MBA B: Middle Bronze Age B (1500–1100 BC); LBA: Late Bronze Age (1100–800 BC); EIA: Early Iron Age (800–500 BC)

to have influenced their treatment in these depositional practices. In west Belgium, the southern Netherlands/northern Belgium and in the western Netherlands, no distinctions appear to have been made between the much more prominent French (Atlantic) imports and British ones. They were often deposited together, as if they were seen as equivalent or mutually exchangeable. Particularly British palstaves and swords can have striking similarities to types known to have been produced in Atlantic continental workshops. Such affinities may imply that British and French items circulated in the same networks, and may easily be 'mistaken' for each other. The Voorhout hoard, something of an 'archetype' for the significance of British imports on the near continent, is a case in point. It contained both British and French items, all in the same worn state. It is only in the northern Netherlands, where insular imports are extremely rare among deposited items that they seem to have had a different role. There is an emphasis on ceremonial or display items and on materials rather than forms or shapes (tin, faience). There is no expression of links between materials which might have reached

the region together as in the case of French and British material in the southern or western Netherlands.

Although no decisive answer can be given, a reconsideration of plausible routes by which insular material might have reached the Low Countries shows that direct crossings of the North Sea may be less likely than transport by boat from France via the major rivers Meuse and – especially – Scheldt, or by seafaring along the western Belgian-Dutch coast from the French Channel region using the tides. In most regions, British-Irish imports are most likely to have reached the Low Countries indirectly via a French route. This ties in with the frequent association of French and British objects in depositions, and with their mutual visual affinities. Likewise, 'British' material might have been perceived as a variety of material which came 'from the south' (Fig 9.7). This leaves us speculating on the fascinating idea that in the perception of most Bronze Age communities living in the Low Countries, 'Britain' was not a huge landmass at the other end of the North Sea, but was rather located in the far south.

Acknowledgements

Many thanks are due to Peter Clark for the invitation to write this and for his continuous encouragement in the process of finishing it. I am also thankful to Stuart Needham, Alison Sheridan, Harry Fokkens, Thijs van Maarleveld and Roosje de Leeuwe for discussions on metalwork exchange and Bronze Age seafaring, and for Hannie Steegstra (Groningen) for supplying me with quantitative information on metalwork from the north-eastern Netherlands. The Groningen Archaeological Institute was as kind as to allow me to reproduce the object drawings in Figures 9.2, 9.4, 9.5 and 9.6. This contribution is dedicated to Jay Butler, for his pioneering work on the topic of Bronze Age connections across the North Sea.

List of references

Bakker J A 1976 'On the Possibility of Reconstructing Roads from the TRB Period', *Berichten van de Rijksdienst voor Oudheidkundig Bodemonderzoek,* **26**, 63–91

Bloch, M and Parry, J 1989 'Introduction. Money and the morality of exchange', in M Bloch and J Parry (eds), *Money and the morality of exchange*, Cambridge: Cambridge University Press, 1–31

Bourgeois I, Cherretté, B and Bourgeois, J 2003 'Bronze Age and Iron Age settlements in Belgium. An overview', in J Bourgeois, I Bourgeois and B Cherretté (eds), *Exchange and interaction. The role of the Scheldt and Meuse during the Bronze Age and the iron Age*, Wetteren: Universa Press, 175–190

Bradley, R 1990: *The Passage of arms. An archaeological analysis of prehistoric hoards and votive deposits*, Cambridge: Cambridge University Press

Butler, J 1961 'A looped spearhead converted to a pegged spearhead from 's-Hertogenbosch', *Helinium,* **1**, 54–5

Butler, J 1963 'Bronze Age connections across the North Sea. A study in prehistoric trade and industrial relations between the British Isles, The Netherlands, North Germany and Scandinavia, *c* 1700–700 B.C.', *Palaeohistoria*, **9**, 1–286

Butler, J 1986 'Drouwen: End of a 'Nordic' rainbow?', *Palaeohistoria,* **28**, 133–168

Butler, J 1987 'Bronze Age connections: France and the Netherlands', *Palaeohistoria*, **29**, 9–34

Butler, J 1990 'Bronze Age metal and amber in the Netherlands (I)', *Palaeohistoria*, **32**, 47–110

Butler, J 1995/1996 'Bronze Age Metal and Amber in the Netherlands (II: 1). Catalogue of the Flat Axes, Flanged Axes and Stopridge Axes', *Palaeohistoria*, **37/38**, 159–243

Butler, J and Bakker, J A 1961 'A forgotten Middle Bronze Age hoard with a Sicilian razor from Ommerschans (Overijssel)', *Helinium*, **I**, 193–210

Butler, J and Hogestijn, J 1988 'The Tollebeek spearhead', *Palaeohistoria*, **30**, 109–123

Butler, J and Steegstra, H 1997/1998 'Bronze Age Metal and Amber in the Netherlands (II: 2): Catalogue of the Palstaves', *Palaeohistoria*, **39/40**, 163–275

Butler, J and Steegstra, H 2002/2003 'Bronze Age Metal and Amber in the Netherlands. (III: II): Catalogue of the socketed axes. Part A', *Palaeohistoria*, **43/44**, 263–319

Butler, J and Steegstra, H 2003/2004 'Bronze Age Metal and Amber in the Netherlands. (III: II): Catalogue of the socketed axes. Part B', *Palaeohistoria*, **44/45**, 197–300

Butler, J and van der Waals, J 1966 'Bell beakers and early metal-working in the Netherlands', *Palaeohistoria*, **12**, 41–139

Clark, P 2004 'The Dover boat ten years after its discovery', in P Clark (ed), *The Dover Bronze Age Boat in Context. Society and water transport in prehistoric Europe*, Oxford: Oxbow Books, 1–12

Cowen, J D 1967 'The Hallstatt sword of bronze on the continent and in Britain', *Proceedings of the Prehistoric Society*, **33**, 377–454

Cunliffe, B W 2001 *Facing the Ocean, The Atlantic and its peoples 8000 BC–AD 1500*, Oxford: Oxford University Press

De Laet, S 1974 *Prehistorische kulturen in het zuiden der Lage Landen*, Wetteren

De Mulder, F, Geluk, M, Ritsema, I, Westerhoff, W and Wong, T 2003 *De ondergrond van Nederland*, Groningen: Wolters-Noordhoff

Fontijn, D 2001 'Rethinking ceremonial dirks of the Plougrescant-Ommerschans type. Some thoughts on the structure of metalwork exchange', in W Metz, B van Beek and H Steegstra (eds), *Patina. Essays presented to Jay Jordan Butler on the occasion of his 80th birthday*, Groningen/Amsterdam, 263–280

Fontijn, D 2002 'Sacrificial Landscapes. Cultural biographies of persons, objects and 'natural' places in the Bronze Age of the southern Netherlands, *c* 2300–600 BC', *Analecta Praehistorica Leidensia*, **33/34**, 1–392.

Fontijn, D R 2008 '"Traders' hoards": Reviewing the relationship between trade and permanent deposition: the case of the Dutch Voorhout hoard', in C Hamon and B Quilliec (eds), *Hoards from the Neolithic to the Metal Ages: technical and codified practices*, British Archaeological Reports International Series 1758, 5–17

Glasbergen, W 1954 'Barrow excavations in the Eight Beautitudes. The Bronze Age cemetery between Toterfout and Halve Mijl, North Brabant, II: the implications', *Palaeohistoria*, **3**, 1–204

Godelier, M 1999 *The Enigma of the Gift*, Cambridge/Oxford: Polity Press

Harbison, P 1968 'Irish Early Bronze Age exports found on the continent and their derivatives', *Palaeohistoria*, **14**, 173–186

Haveman, E and Sheridan J A 2005/2006 'The Exloo Necklace: new light on an old find', *Palaeohistoria*, **47/48**, 101–139

Helms, M W 1988 *Ulysses' Sail. An ethnographic odyssey of power, knowledge, and geographic distance, Princeton*, New Jersey: Princeton University Press

Helms, M W 1993 *Craft and the kingly ideal: art, trade, and power*, Austin: University of Texas Press

Huth, C 2000 'Metal circulation, communication and traditions of craftsmanship in Late Bronze Age and Early Iron Age Europe', in C Pare (ed), *Metals Make*

The World Go Round. The Supply and Circulation of Metals in Bronze Age Europe. Proceedings of a conference held at the University of Birmingham in June 1997, Oxford: Oxbow Books, 176–193

Huth, C 2003 'Poor Belgium, rich Belgium. Reflections on the nature of metalwork depositions in the Late Bronze Age and Early Iron Age', in J Bourgeois, I Bourgeois and B Cherretté (eds), *Exchange and interaction. The role of the Scheldt and Meuse during the Bronze Age and the iron Age,* Wetteren: Universa Press, 39–60

Kopytoff, I 1986 'The cultural biography of things: commoditisation as process', in A Appadurai (ed), *The Social life of Things,* Cambridge: Cambridge University Press, 64–91

Malinowski, B 1984 (1922) *Argonauts of the Western Pacific,* Illinois: Waveland Press Inc

Mauss, M 1993 (1923/1924) *The Gift. The form and reason for exchange in archaic societies,* London: Routledge

McBryde, I 2000 'Barter…immediately commenced to the satisfaction of both parties: cross-cultural exchange at Port Jackson, 1788–1828', in R Torrence and A Clarke (eds), *The Archaeology of Difference. Negotiating cross-cultural engagements in Oceania,* (One World Archaeology 38), London and New York: Routledge, 238–277

Needham, S 1989 'Selective deposition in the British Early Bronze Age', *World Archaeology,* **20,** 229–248 (also in H Nordström and A Knape (eds), *Bronze Age Studies. Transactions of the British-Scandinavian Colloquium in Stockholm, May 10–11, 1985,* Stockholm, 45–61)

Needham, S 1990 'Middle Bronze Age ceremonial weapons: new finds from Oxborough, Norfolk and Essex/Kent (with a contribution from D Hook)', *The Antiquaries Journal,* **70–II,** 239–252

O'Connor, B 1980 *Cross-Channel relations in the Later Bronze Age. Relations between Britain, North-Eastern France and the Low Countries during the Later Bronze Age and the Early Iron Age, with particular reference to the metalwork,* British Archaeological Reports (International Series), **91,** Oxford: Archaeopress

Roymans N 1980 'A Middle Bronze Age looped spearhead from Veldhoven (North Brabant)', *Helinium,* **20,** 63–67

Roymans, N 1991 'Late urnfield societies in the Northwest European Plain and the expanding networks of Central European Hallstatt groups', in N Roymans and F Theuws (eds), *Images of the past. Studies on ancient societies in North-western Europe,* (Studies in prae- en protohistorie 7), Amsterdam: Amsterdam University Press, 9–89

Sørensen, M L S 1987 'Material order and cultural classification: the role of bronze objects in the transition from Bronze Age to Iron Age in Scandinavia', in I Hodder (ed), *The archaeology of contextual meanings,* (New directions in archaeology), Cambridge: Cambridge University Press, 90–101

Theunissen, E M 1999 *Midden-Bronstijdsamenlevingen in het zuiden van de Lage Landen: een evaluatie van het begrip 'Hilversum-cultuur',* Leiden (Ph.D. thesis University of Leiden)

Theuws, F 2003 'Exchange, religion, identity and central places in the early Middle Ages', *Archaeological Dialogues,* **10,** 121–138

Thomas, N 1991 *Entangled Objects. Exchange, Material Culture and Colonialism in the Pacific,* Cambridge, Massachusetts/London: Harvard University Press

Thrane, H 2001 'Why did the rainbow end at Drouwen – if it did?', in W Metz, B van Beek and H Steegstra (eds), *Patina. Essays presented to Jay Jordan Butler on the occasion of his 80th birthday,* Groningen/Amsterdam, 551–560

Van de Noort 2004 'An ancient seascape: the social context of seafaring in the Early Bronze Age', *World Archaeology,* **35,** 404–415

Verlaeckt, K 1996 *Between river and barrow. A reappraisal of Bronze Age metalwork found in the province of East-Flanders (Belgium),* British Archaeological Reports (International Series), **632**

Warmenbol, E 1986 'British rapiers with trapezoidal butt found in Belgium', *Proceedings of the Prehistoric Society,* **52,** 153–158

Weiner, A 1992 *Inalienable possessions: the paradox of keeping-while-giving,* Berkely/Los Angeles/Oxford: University of California Press

Wouters, H 1990 *Chemical characterization of archaeological copper alloys. Application of X-ray fluorescence and element micro and trace analytical techniques,* (Ph.D. thesis), Antwerpen

10. The master(y) of hard materials: Thoughts on technology, materiality, and ideology occasioned by the Dover boat

Mary W Helms

I assume Claude Lévi-Strauss never saw the Dover boat, but I believe he would like it, for the boat and others similar to it are 'good to think' in the Lévi-Straussian sense of encoding metaphysical perspectives in concert with their material forms and utilitarian functions. A number of modern scholars have found them so (*eg* Kaul 2004; Pryor 2004; Van de Noort 2004), and there is good reason to think that Bronze Age people would have agreed. I would like to ponder several such perspectives as they may have been informed or expressed by project management and constructional technologies evidenced by the Dover boat and other sewn plank Bronze Age vessels from the British Isles.

Various scholars have commented appreciatively on the sophisticated skilled workmanship and the clever technical complexity evidenced in the manufacture of the Dover boat (Clark 2004, 2; Marsden 2004, 17; Clark 2005; *see also* Coates 2004, 28; Cunliffe 2001, 64). They also note that many hands must have contributed to the various processes involved in felling huge oaks, sculpting the timbers, transporting materials to a shipyard, and constructing the vessel, including cutting the holes for stitches and preparing the coppiced yew withies that, twisted through these holes, would hold it together (Gifford and Gifford 2004; Arnold 2004; Clark 2005, 88–91). It

seems reasonable to assume that the basic skills necessary to perform these tasks would have been known to most, perhaps virtually all, adult men since wood was among the most commonly used raw materials (along with clay and sometimes stone) for a wide range of everyday tools and utensils and provided the basic material for ordinary constructional purposes (Coates 2004, 28; Clark 2005, 91; Harding 2000, 188, 242–248; Audouze and Büchsenschütz 1992, 44–45).

While acknowledging the cooperative nature of such an enterprise, it seems equally reasonable nonetheless to assume that a major project, such as the Dover boat, also required the general direction of a project overseer, a master woodwright, personally responsible for particularly tricky sections of joinery, for coordinating the work as a whole, and for its successful completion as a useful and even aesthetic artefact (Clark 2005, 91; *see also* Gell 1992, 52, 54). I begin this discussion by considering more closely the possible roles such a highly skilled artisan might have been expected to play. I start with a digression to briefly examine the meanings associated with the occupation of woodwright several millennia later, during late Antiquity and the early European Middle Ages, where there is relevant linguistic and literary evidence in Old English, Latin, and common Greek. In spite of cultural differences, the general thrust of these interpretations may offer broad guidelines helpful in thinking about the builders and building of the Dover boat.

In Old English the term 'wyrhta' or wright referred in general to an artificer, a craftsman or fabricator and, more particularly, to a craftsman who worked in wood (Toller 1898, 1288–1289; *see also* Lewis 2001, 985–986). Yet working in wood may have carried broader implications. 'Wyrhta' is one of two Old English occupational identifications that could be accorded the Latin occupational term, *faber*. To take one example, on the famous Northumbrian Lindisfarne Gospels, which were copied in Latin about AD 700 and glossed in Old English *c* AD 950, the occupation of Joseph, the earthly father of Jesus, which is *faber* in Latin (Matthew 13.55) is glossed in Old English as 'smiðes ł wyrchta', that is, smith or wright (Hardwick 1858, 113). If both or either Old English terms were regarded as suitable translations for the single Latin word, it would seem that the two Old English terms must have something in common or represent a continuum of related skills. Indeed, it would appear that 'smith' could indicate a worker in either metals or in wood as well as a craftsman who in general fashioned or forged things (Toller 1898, 889; *see also* Lewis 1988, 37–38). In similar fashion, there would seem to be an implication that someone skilled in woodworking might also be somewhat knowledgeable about metalwork and that such an artisan was also recognised more generally as someone of notable ability who could make or control things.

A very similar set of ideas informed the Latin term, *faber*, itself. In basic dictionary definition, *faber* designated someone who showed exceptional skill and ingenuity in working with various hard materials, that is to say, either with wood or stone or metal (ores being initially stone-like; Simpson 1968, 237; *see also* Hahn 1986, 60). It further implies that experts in woodworking, stoneworking, and metallurgy had certain skills in common such that scholars sometimes simply translate *faber* as 'artisan' (*eg* Chorpenning 1997, 277), meaning one who fashions, creates, constructs, puts together or fabricates objects (Eliade 1962, 101; Forbes 1964, 68) as in the title for God in Latin as *Deus faber*, God the Creator (Curtius 1953, 544–546). (More specifically, however,

faber came to refer particularly to metalworking; the medieval *faber* was the smith [*eg* Duby 1968, 20; Forbes 1956, 60; Aelfric 1968, gloss on page 632, line 208; Foster 1987, 441, entry under 'smyth').

Faber was not unique in its meaning, for it is also a translation for the common Greek word, *tekton*, which in the Classical world referred to an artisan skilled in working with hard materials. 'The Greek word (*tekton*), like the Hebrew *charasch*, means a worker in stone, wood, or metal, and the precise reference has to be gathered in each case from the context' (Nineham 1963, 165). To be sure, *tekton* has a more specific application, referring to an artisan who works with wood (Mounce 1993, 446), but even within the context of woodworking the term 'has a wide range of meanings from a shipbuilder to a sculptor, but it generally indicates a craftsman of considerable skill' (Albright and Mann 1971, 172–173 n 55–56). The term is also sometimes translated broadly as 'builder', emphasising construction, whether in wood or in stone (*eg* Morris 1992, 3; Danker 2000, 995; Albright and Mann 1971, 172 n 55–56).

As a master artisan, a *tekton* conveyed the ancient Greek concept of *métis*, the ability to do things or to exhibit special skills by virtue of superb resourcefulness, cleverness, and cunning ('informed prudence') of mind (Meiggs 1982, 112–113; Detienne and Vernant 1978, 11, 235–236, 307–308). Stated somewhat differently, the knowledge commanded by skilled artisans was long thought to evidence wisdom (*sophia*), the organised body of knowledge handed down through the generations within professional groups 'such as those of the blacksmiths and carpenters' (Detienne and Vernant 1978, 315). Wisdom also conveys a sense that divine inspiration informs an artisan's work, imbuing it with elements of the mysterious or the uncanny, at least in the opinion of less informed laymen (*eg* Gell 1992, 51–52), as well as contributing to the old idea that the gods (or God) acted as artisan when creating the cosmos or when instructing humans in skills for living (*eg* Glacken 1967, 14; Proverbs 8). This idea – that skilled craftspersons are replicating the original creativity of the deities and are granted their skills and guided in their work by divine powers or presence – is very widespread among traditional non-industrial societies, past and present (Helms 1993, 13–32).

The significance of the transformational creative work and the unique, even sacralised, role of Classical, late Antique and early medieval 'masters of hard materials' also took into account beliefs concerning the nature of the raw materials, the stone, ore, and wood with which they worked and which also shared certain basic qualities. The fundamental issue is recognition that trees and stone and ore are rooted in and thus derive from the cosmological realm of the living earth. Consequently, these hard materials are themselves alive since they are imbued with the energetics of earth's generative life-force and live and grow (gestate) in association with that chthonic maternity. The potency of trees as living forms is expressed in diverse symbolism, though perhaps most powerfully in the well known concept of the archetypical Tree of Life, an idea common to many cultures (*eg* Eliade 1958, 265–282, 298–300, 309–313; James 1966; Cook 1974). The potency of stone as literally living material (we still speak of the 'living rock') can be evidenced in beliefs (fundamental to alchemy, for example) that ores and minerals are like embryos, slowly maturing and ripening in the earth, from which they receive nourishment (Eliade 1962, 8; *see also* Plumpe 1943).

Since, as living forms, trees, stone, and ores themselves are redolent with supernatural potencies and energies, the harvesting of such materials from the earth and the crafting of objects from them requires awareness and careful management of these intangible forces, just as the end products may be expected to embody some of this extraordinary power, too (*cf* Thomas 1966, 153). Given the ideological context surrounding such enterprises, it is not surprising to find considerable symbolism and ritual associated with these activities (*eg* Eliade 1962; Taçon 1991). This is simply to say, once again, that a master of hard materials must control and manipulate the life forces his resources embody and be involved with supernatural powers. Stated more broadly, a master of hard materials must actively manoeuvre between cosmological realms, between the world of nature or supernature and the world of human living. Consequently, he (or she) in effect becomes a liminal being (not unlike the shaman) who personally embodies extraordinary creative power and, in the role of skilled artisan, assumes a certain sacrality

as well as ritual capabilities and responsibilities (Helms 1993, chap. 4).

Let us now return to the Bronze Age and the world of the Dover boat. The discussion above allows the speculation that the skills, roles, and responsibilities of the master craftsman purportedly in charge of the construction of such a vessel should not be too narrowly defined. I would suggest 1) that such a skilled builder and overseer was a master of hard materials in general, meaning that knowledge of constructional skills not only in wood but also in stone and in some local aspects of metallurgy could be exhibited by the same artisan, though not necessarily utilised in every project; 2) that such a man also would have been expected to negotiate through ritual the cosmological interface between the natural realm that provided wood and stone as ideologically potent raw materials and the human world that controlled these resources and utilised them in the creation of cultural forms; 3) that a master builder who directed (for example) the construction of a sewn plank boat exercised his exceptional skills and knowledge by virtue of close personal association with supernatural powers and would not himself have been an ordinary man but a liminal personage who, at least when acting in his professional capacity, stood somewhat separate from the rest of society.

I offer this description of a skilled master with expertise in various types of crafting, even though I realise that the Bronze Age is recognised as an era when technological techniques and craft specialisation become especially elaborated (*eg* Audouze and Büchsenschütz 1992, 48, 50, 134, 167; Harding 2000, 197, 269; Coles and Harding 1979, 8, 10; Kristiansen and Larsson 2005, 57–58). However, some scholars have also noted more unifying conceptual and technological interrelationships among separate crafts or classes of materials. Thus, pottery decoration styles may mimic the structure of basketry or metal objects may be copied in clay or stone or the same decorative motifs may appear on metal, ceramics, or stone. Likewise, 'the processes for the production of bronzes, pottery, and glass . . . were broadly similar, and the winning of ores, stone and flint also involved comparable techniques . . .' (Coles and Harding 1979, 10). 'In short, starting in the Neolithic and increasing at some speed in the Bronze Age, different classes of objects linked in with each other' (Gosden 2003, 35; Bradley 2005, 101).

Among these interconnections, technologies linking wood with stone or metal – the hard materials interrelated in occupational labels in later millennia – are of particular interest here. In addition to the extensive use of wood in mining ores and the essential role of charcoal as fuel for smelting (Coles and Harding 1979, 63–65), construction techniques could relate wood and stone, too, as evidenced by the well-known use of techniques of joinery common to woodworking on stone uprights and lintels at Stonehenge (Harding 2000, 247; *see also* Audouze and Büchsenschütz 1992, 47). Speaking in an ideological context and with reference to the British Neolithic and early Bronze Ages, Miranda Aldhouse-Green notes that 'within a symbolic context, it may be possible to view wood and stone as belonging to a continuum of being . . .', as in recent archaeological work relating choice of wood and stone for ceremonial monuments to cosmological concepts of life and death (Aldhouse-Green 2004, 98). Indeed, the qualitative relationship between wood and stone is widespread, for Eliade noted the close association between trees and stones as markers for sacred centres at many places throughout the Old World (1958, 269–271).

Returning to a more utilitarian context, given the all-important role of polished stone and then bronze axes in general clearing and woodworking, from tree-felling to all manner of general construction, as well as in social and ideological (ritual) contexts (Harding 2000, 321; Cunliffe 2001, 209, 236), one wonders if the combination of metal (as bronze axes, adzes) and wood (as basic construction material) was regarded as somehow especially meaningful in the construction of the Dover boat. Similarly, to the extent that the Dover boat or others similar to it might have been used to transport bronze ingots or scrap metal or palstaves (Clark 2005, 93, 94), wood and metal again can be said to have formed a conceptually interrelated unit, at least for the duration of the trip. As is well known, various types of wooden vessels and metal are accorded permanent association in the Nordic Bronze Age where images of ships appear on bronze objects – knives, razors, and neckrings, especially in Denmark (Kaul 2004), and boats are famously immortalised in stone on rock carvings in Scandinavia (Gelling and

Davidson 1969, 43–67; Kristiansen 2004, 119; Kaul 2004; Clark 2005, 94; Davidson 1988, 169).

To be sure, any technological and/or qualitative relationships between wood and metal that may have informed the crafting of the Dover boat and/or broadly defined the role of its master builder are evidenced at best only very generally in the boat itself, but there are a few more specific qualities suggested both by the wooden nature of sewn plank vessels and by their basic constructional features that may be considered. With respect to wood, thinking of the ancient belief that trees are imbued with life and remembering Eliade's insight that any ordinary tree of a given species could become a consecrated representative of the archetypical Tree of Life of that species as depicted in lore and ritual (1958, 324), it seems noteworthy that the Dover boat (like the Ferriby boats; Van de Noort 2004, 91) was constructed of oak and of yew. Undoubtedly, in functional constructional terms these species of trees were selected for their material properties of durability, elastic strength, and resistance to rot, but I cannot resist noting that both the oak and the yew were also recognised as cosmologically special trees, even as sacred trees, in ancient lore of Northern Europe and the British Isles.

Sacred groves of yew and of oak were common features of pre-Roman religious life and the several sacred trees mentioned in ancient Celtic (Irish) sources include the ash, the yew (the holy tree of Irish druids) and the oak (Davidson 1988, 170; Anderson 2003, 416; Ross 1967, 33–38; Bevan-Jones 2002, 144, 160–162, 137–139). Similarly, in Nordic Scandinavia and Celtic Germany cosmological trees included not only the ash and the apple but also the oak, associated with the god of the sky, and the yew, related both with death (its leaves, twigs, seeds are toxic to humans and to livestock, though not to game) and with immortality since it is a very long-lived evergreen that frequently resprouts, even after being felled (Davidson 1988, 170, 23; Elliott 1957; Bevan-Jones 2002, 8–12, 23, 44). The yew seems to have been especially important among pre-Christian Celtic peoples, including those in the British Isles, who associated it (along with the oak and the ash) with springs and wells, with royalty, and with ideologically protected places of public assembly (open air meeting sites, churches) where justice could be meted out and who attributed magical powers to it and gave it a special role in saga and folklore and ritual (Elliott 1957, 253–254; 260–261; Bevan-Jones 2002, chap. 5, 92–93, 108, chap. 8, 166).

The qualities of the yew also may have included an association between the red-orange colour of its wood and the red-bronze of its dried foliage and the red-gold colour of bronze (Bevan-Jones 2002, 154–155 regarding a Bronze Age grave in Wiltshire lined with yew wood and with the burial wrapped in abundant yew leaves and interred with a bronze knife). In addition, among other virtues, yew wood with magic inscription could be used as protective amulets, as evidenced (for example) by an inscribed eighth century yew piece from Friesland (the Westeremden B wand) which, in the opinion of some scholars, may have been intended to magically control the waves and protect against drowning (a particularly interesting agency for a sea-faring perspective; *see* Elliott 1957, 256, 260).

As for the oak, in Anglo-Saxon England that mighty tree was recognised as a cosmic axis mundi directly linking people with the gods (Davidson 1988, 24). Such an august association was probably very ancient. For example, Bronze Age northern Europe often utilised the oak as a coffin. Harding comments on the symbolic significance of such an interment, relating the oak tree-trunk coffin to house construction (also predominantly of oak in temperate Europe) and noting the relationship between houses and tombs both in Neolithic and Bronze Age contexts. He mentions, too, the ancient and long-lasting association of yews with graveyards (and churchyards) and the general connection of trees like ash, oak, and yew with longevity or eternal life; burial within a tree carrying the obvious connotation of a return to the source of life (Harding 2000, 108–109; *see also* Bevan-Jones 2002, chap. 3, 76, 91). In like fashion, Aldhouse-Green, in her study of Iron Age and Roman Europe, discusses how long-lived trees, notably oaks and yews, could be readily associated with ancestral origins and serve as linkages with past and future time and with the several realms of the cosmos (2004, 96–97; *see also* Kristiansen and Larsson 2005, 242, 245). In many Irish and English sayings ('lists of ages') the yew in particular is regarded as the oldest living thing in the world and thus leads back

to the beginning of time and to God (Bevan-Jones 2002, 149).

Using various cross-cultural examples, Aldhouse-Green comments on the common belief that the life within trees could be transferred to objects made from them. 'Indeed, the stages of transformation – the tree-felling, preparation of wood, carving and polishing – all may endow the finished product with potent symbolism in which the death of the tree and its rebirth as a boat, house or figurine in the alchemy of transformation may all serve to imbue wooden objects with sanctity and power, with a second life-force' (Aldhouse-Green 2004, 197). In this context the use of yew wood for wall panelling and ornamentation, furniture and utensils in chiefly houses of Bronze and/or Iron Age Ireland perhaps conveyed not only an aesthetic touch but also symbolism relating the qualities of yew to qualities of a good ruler (Bevan-Jones 2002, 140, 141, 186). Similarly, it seems not unreasonable to ask whether, in the eyes of its builders and owners and those who used it, the Dover boat might have been imbued with the energising potency, magical protection, and long life of the oaks and yews of which it was composed and to suggest that one of the constructional responsibilities of the boat's master of hard materials was to ritually direct this 'alchemy of transformation' toward a successful ideological outcome that would mystically protect the lives and safeguard the travel of crew and passengers.

In addition to types of wood, another basic constructional feature evidenced by the Dover boat seems 'good to think'. The building of this boat appears to emphasise themes of boundary and enclosure. Clearly this remark applies as a truism to any vessel whose shape defines and encloses an interior space. However, the constructional techniques used in building sewn plank boats during the Bronze and Iron Ages particularly emphasise the basic integrity of the shell of the boat as a boundary form in and of itself (*see also* later Nordic [Viking] ships; Cunliffe 2001, 74). As Séan McGrail has put it, such boats were designed and constructed 'planking first.' That is to say, 'in prehistoric times, a builder of sewn plank boats thought of his boat in terms of the planking; his planking was hewn to shape and fastened together by lashings of sewing to create the shape of hull he wanted' (2004, 62–63). In contrast, so-called Romano-Celtic vessels of the early AD centuries were built 'frame-first', that is, the builder 'thought of his plank boat in terms of the framing' in that the framing was erected first and planking then attached to that interior skeleton (McGrail 2004, 63).

These contrasting approaches to boat-building are not trivial differences. They seem to imply two fundamentally different perspectives regarding basic principles of construction that may go well beyond boat building per se to express contrasts in fundamental principles relative to the ordering of space and experience, including even landscape organisation and cosmic construction (Barrett 1994, 92, 94–95; Parker Pearson and Richards 1994b, 38). The Romano-Celtic boat seems to signify an 'internal' mode of building in which interior structural forms are primary, while the Bronze Age sewn plank boat gives primacy to creation of a barrier that will separate and distinguish between interior space and exterior space, that which is within from that which is without (Parker Pearson and Richards 1994a, 24).

The barrier or boundary approach evidenced by sewn plank boats is also of interest because the Bronze, as well as the Neolithic and Iron Ages, give evidence of a preference for boundaries and enclosures in a number of other ways that suggest that the concept of enclosures constituted a fundamental ideological construct of the times and its cultures (*eg* Thomas 1996, 184). For example, late Neolithic and especially Bronze Age round houses of the British Isles seem to embody this idea, especially those characterised by a continuous load-bearing wall (such as a ring of posts linked by timbers and/or interlocked branches) supporting a conical roof which sometimes was balanced by a central post but not always (consider also variations on this theme, including enclosures encircling clusters of round houses, that were further developed during the Bronze and Iron Ages; Audouze and Büchsenschütz 1992, 70–74; Parker Pearson and Richards 1994b, 50–51; Harding 2000, 30–36; Clark 2004, 2–4). On a larger scale, southern England's famous henge monuments are defined by ditches and encircling embankments and palisades (Audouze and Büchsenschütz 1992, 85–90; Bradley 2005, 10–12; Cunliffe 2001, 244; Thomas 1996, 183–222). Barrow burials fit this scheme, too, both by virtue of their surrounding ditches and post rings and

when the barrow is viewed as a very thick wall or encompassment separating the world of the living from that of the dead (Harding 2000, 85–89; Pryor 2004, 32; Anderson 2003, 277). In a volume on early Scandinavian and Celtic religions, Davidson notes the prominence of the idea of enclosed sacred space that might encompass images of the gods or sacred objects or 'provide an obvious boundary around holy ground, separating it either temporarily or permanently from the normal world' (1988, 27). Other Scandinavian examples can include the ropes enclosing a court of law, the delineation of an area in which an official duel was fought, or stone settings placed around graves, as well as earthworks or ditches to mark off areas of worship or that contained sacred springs, hearths, pillars, stones, etc. (*ibid*).

It is also instructive to consider the early Germanic approach to space and enclosures in which 'space' is not an abstract concept but a qualitative 'thing' that has relevance as a location or a container for a specific activity (Bauschatz 1982, 130–131). In the same active sense, 'walls' of various sorts, natural and human made, become important as defining the space wherein activity occurs. Walls can be of all sorts: sea-cliffs and headlands that define the edge ('walls') of the sea and enclose the land, mountain ridges that surround a temple; the walls that delineate the hall of the chieftain, the sides of vehicles used in procession. All these structure and define places – spaces – of significant activities and allow important distinctions to be made between the events occurring within the enclosure and those that lie without (Bauschatz 1982, 137–138, 140; *see also* Eliade 1958, 370–371; Thomas 1996, 184).

Returning to the Dover boat, I would suggest that, to the people who made it and those who used it, the 'planking first' vessel constituted a container, an enclosure, for activities situated within it which were considered to be in some sense set apart, even 'sacralised' by virtue of the bounding walls of oak and yew. By its enclosure, the 'space' within the boat was connected with greater cosmological concerns and archetypical conditions of being that the concept and process of enclosing represented. More specifically, the space within the boat would have been preserved, in existential order and safety, from the dangers of the non-sacred or 'disorderly' conditions outside the boat's perimeter.

Francis Pryor, thinking about prehistoric cosmological principles, notes that British Bronze Age people constantly tried to connect human constructions with the 'natural order of things ... they were giving the products of their own hands and minds a wider, deeper meaning and legitimacy that was thought to transcend the normal day-to-day world' (2004, 32). Whether the Dover boat is representative of journeys of some distance and possible danger, such as crossings of the channel, or if it was used only locally to travel the coast or served as a river ferry, all its passages could be embarked upon with a sense of having temporarily stepped out of the mundane into the extraordinary within the protective perimeters of a mystically safe and bounded floating 'place' or centre encircled by the physically strong and mystically potent qualities of oak and yew. As Eliade pointed out (1958, 379, 382, 384–385), even at the very lowest level of immediate religiosity, people tend to draw near to sacred cosmic archetypes and make them present. Thus, not only could any Bronze Age oak be regarded as the Cosmic Tree, but any sewn plank boat could be one expression of the general practice and significance of bounding and enclosing sacred space or place. In practical terms, this role and identification presumably would be achieved by ritual consecration of the boat at some point during its construction. A simple ceremony presided over by the official project overseer, our master of hard materials, perhaps to mark the formal completion of the task, would have been sufficient and appropriate.

Having brought the Dover boat into being by constructional skill and ritual ministration, I wonder if a purported master of hard materials also might have played a ritual role in its demise or at least its 'retirement' from routine active duty as a water transport. Pryor makes an interesting connection between British Bronze Age sewn plank boats as known through archaeological finds and the fact that the Bronze Age overall was an era notably marked by the ritual breaking and deposition of artefacts (2004). He considers the possibility that boats might have been ritually destroyed, perhaps deliberately sunk, and asks whether the Dover boat might have been ritually destroyed and deposed, too, for the boat seems to have been far from worn out, was found

at a cosmologically liminal junction between maritime and inland environments (the edge of a coastal creek), and shows possible signs of ritual destruction in the deliberate removal of side pieces (2004, 34; *see also* Van de Noort 2004).

Although the precise fate of the Dover boat may be debated, in general I view the possible ritual breaking and deposition of boats to be a very understandable action comparable to both votive (and perhaps all) hoards and the rich elite burials for which the Bronze Age is famous and comprehensible within ideological, especially cosmological, contexts of the times. While recognising that the diverse characteristics and possible purposes of hoards and other forms of deposition are multifaceted and have generated much scholarly debate and an extensive literature (for example, Harding 2000, 352–368; Bradley 2005, 145–164), my own position, simply stated, would begin with the assumption that depositional objects, like metals and perhaps boats, derived from raw materials – living wood and living ores (stone) – believed to be redolent with the cosmological life force of the earth that originally generated them. I then posit that Bronze Age people believed, as many traditional cultures have, that if human society takes living, energised materials from the world of nature for human use, then human society has the obligation to return life energy to the earth to replenish the store so that the cosmological cycle of life, the renewal and regeneration of all living things, may continue (Helms 1998, 29–30; *see also* Anderson 2003, 334 regarding Germanic lore).

The form and manner in which this restoration is accomplished, however, takes into account some additional factors. First, the cultural generation of life is always a transformative act of creation that repeats the archetypical acts of creative deities who first brought life energy and living forms into being. People repeat the original cosmological creation of life energy with the conception of every child, with the seeding of every field. Skilled craftsmen become replicators of original creation when they transform raw materials into finished cultural products such as boats, or bronze palstaves, or metal implements and ornaments. Second, since the act of crafting manifests life energy, the crafted product of a creational act becomes, in qualitative terms, a package of rarefied, purified, concentrated life-force. In the process of crafting all extraneous material, all 'impurities' have been removed. All the slag has been drawn off the smelted metal, all unnecessary branches trimmed from the fallen oak that will become a boat. The final product that the craftsman then brings into being will have a definite identity or comprehensibility. Life energy will not be just an abstract idea but will be given a tangible, clearly recognisable shape and form as an object or a matrix-free substance. This 'objectivising' of abstractions, this bestowal of definite shape and form and irreducibility (durability) is what is meant by the very concept of creation, of the bringing into being or actualising of some thing or circumstance.

When the time comes for humans to replenish the energy of the earth, to act as substitutes for the deities and re-create the earth's original potency (regardless of how it has been depleted), one obvious thing to do (though not the only approach) is to place into the earth skilfully crafted packages of pure, rarefied, concentrated, tangible life force, packages with the definitiveness of shape and form and durability that bespeak an act of creativity and the realisation and literal encapsulation of life energy. Such objects – a pile of ingots or of palstaves, a cache of ornaments or weapons, possibly even a boat – vivify and regenerate the earth with the potency that they contain, much as an injection of concentrated medication revives and refreshes the patient (consider Cunliffe 2001, 236, 258–259; also Gelling and Davidson 1969, 50–51, 157 regarding the ship as symbolic of renewed fertility, wellbeing and prosperity). It follows, too, that the longer the effect of the medicine lasts, that is, the more durable the energy-filled material that composes the deposition, the longer the necessary benefit will be obtained, though it is equally plausible that items could be chosen for their ability to decay or be broken or otherwise deliberately manipulated and 'opened' so as to facilitate the release of energy back into the earth (*eg* Pollard 2004). It appears that a good argument can be made that the ritual deposition of crafted goods in the Bronze Age is an outgrowth of, and variation upon, the earlier Neolithic emphasis on the bones of the dead as the preferred medium for expressing a life-enhancing relationship with the supernatural realm (*eg* Jones 2004, 168).

The sheer volume and diversity of crafted goods exhibited by the Bronze Age indicates that skilled crafting in various media, especially those involving hard materials, achieved special prominence during that era and highly skilled artisans were in demand, greatly appreciated, and probably well patronised. By extension, the value of and necessity for a highly nuanced role of general 'master of hard materials' as director and overseer of both technological and ritual aspects and goals of skilled crafting can be especially appreciated. By way of comparison, we may consider the master builders of traditional Irish society, known as Ollamh builders, whose skills included masonry, carpentry, and other talents. Brehan Law tracts indicate that these men were given great rewards, at least equal to those accorded chief poets and teachers (Bevan-Jones 2002, 166). We can also hypothesise that, on an everyday level, the duties of such a Bronze Age master were perhaps not unlike those of the medieval monastery chamberlain (*camerarius*) who, among other responsibilities, was charged with supervising the work of the diverse craftsmen of the monastery workshops – the smiths, leather workers, fullers, woodworkers, etc. who prepared the tools and utensils for the house. The chamberlain, who had his own office and workshop in their midst, conferred with the artisans, assigned workloads, and inspected finished products (Horn and Born 1979a, 335; 1979b, 189, 337, 200; 1979c, 109). The proposed Bronze Age master might also have a parallel in the procedure, still found among some traditional societies, such as the Arawakans of the Upper Xingu area of southern Brazil, in which one way to become a leader, a 'great man', of the group is to become the master of all the arts (Heckenberger 2005, 297–298; *see also* Werner 1981, 365–366). Closer to Bronze Age Britain, we may find the concept personified in the Celtic god, Lugus, whose cult may have been widely distributed throughout the British Isles and also Gaul, who has been described as an all-purpose deity, the multi-skilled god of all sorts of crafts and arts and of commerce who was also appreciated for his intellectual capacities, including magical incantations (closely paralleled by the Germanic Odin, also a magician and patron of the arts and crafts, among other things; Ross 1967, 249, 251–252).

My interpretation of a purported Bronze

Age master of hard materials does not imbue him with such a universal range of abilities, but I do suggest that the construction and intended purpose of a water craft like the Dover boat may well have involved a highly skilled master of diverse crafting and ritual skills who, like the boat that took shape under his direction, essentially was charged with bridging and making connections with realms and regions beyond or outside of local society proper; which is to say, with cosmological realms and cosmographical regions (the boat's destinations) representative of more 'distant' space and time. Through his expertise, living matter, technological skills, and the energising potencies of the cosmos would have coalesced to create a vessel that, in its completed physical form and consecrated social and ideological functions, interrelated and embodied these attributes, too (Thomas 1996, 71–72, 153).

List of references

Aelfric, Abbot of Eynsham 1968 *Homilies of Aelfric, A Supplementary Collection, Volume 2*, J C Pope (ed), Oxford: Oxford University Press

Albright, W and C Mann, trans. 1971 *The Anchor Bible: Matthew*, Garden City: Doubleday and Co

Aldhouse-Green, M 2004 *An Archaeology of Images*, New York: Routledge

Anderson, E 2003 *Folk-taxonomies in Early English*, Madison: Fairleigh Dickinson

Arnold B 2004 'Dover to Bevaix, from the Middle Bronze Age to Gallo-Roman times, from lashing to nailing', in P Clark (ed), *The Dover Bronze Age Boat in Context*, Oxford: Oxbow Books, 82–89

Andouze, F and Büchsenschütz, O 1992 *Towns, Villages, and Countryside of Celtic Europe from the Beginning of the Second Millenium to the End of the First Century BC*, Bloomington, Indiana

Barrett, J 1994 'Defining Domestic Space in the Bronze Age of Southern Britain', in M Parker Pearson and C Richards (eds), *Architecture and Order: Approaches to Social Space*, New York: Routledge, 87–97

Bauschatz, P 1982 *The Well and the Tree*, Amherst: University of Massachusetts

Bevan-Jones R 2002 *The Ancient Yew*, Bollington, Cheshire, UK: Windgather

Bradley, R 2005 *Ritual and Domestic Life in Prehistoric Europe*, New York: Routledge

Chorpenning J 1997 'The Enigma of St Joseph in Poussin's *Holy Family on the Steps*', *Journal of the Warburg and Courtauld Institutes*, **60**, 276–281

Clark, P 2004 'The Dover Boat Ten Years after its Discovery', in P Clark (ed), *The Dover Bronze Age Boat in context: Society and water transport in prehistoric Europe*, Oxford: Oxbow Books, 1–12

Clark, P 2005 'Shipwrights, Sailors and Society in the Middle Bronze Age of NW Europe', *Journal of Wetland Archaeology*, **5**, 87–96

Coates, J 2004 'The legacy of Ted Wright', in P Clark (ed), *The Dover Bronze Age Boat in Context*, Oxford: Oxbow Books, 20–29

Coles, J and Harding, A 1979 *The Bronze Age in Europe*, New York: St. Martin's

Cook, R 1974 *The Tree of Life*, London: Thames and Hudson

Cunliffe, B 2001 *Facing the Ocean*, Oxford: Oxford University Press

Curtius, E 1953 *European Literature and the Latin Middle Ages*, New York: Pantheon

Danker, F 2000 *A Greek-English Lexicon of the New Testament and other Early Christian Literature*, 3rd edition, Chicago: University of Chicago

Davidson, H 1988 *Myths and Symbols in Pagan Europe*, Syracuse: Syracuse University

Detienne, M and Vernant, J-P 1978 *Cunning Intelligence in Greek Culture and Society*, New Jersey: Humanities

Duby, G 1968 *Rural Economy and Country Life in the Medieval West*, Columbia: University of South Carolina

Eliade, M 1958 *Patterns in Comparative Religion*, New York: Sheed and Ward

Eliade, M 1959 *The Sacred and the Profane*, New York: Harcourt, Brace and World

Eliade, M 1962 *The Forge and the Crucible*, New York: Harper and Row

Elliott, R 1957 Runes, Yews, and Magic, *Speculum*, **32**, 250–261

Forbes R 1956 'Metallurgy', in C Singer, E Holmyard and A Hall (eds), *A History of Technology: Volume 2*, Oxford: Clarendon Press, 41–80

Foster, F (ed) 1987 *A Stanzaic Life of Christ*, Oxford: Early English Text Society and Milwood, New York: Kraus Reprints

Gell, A 1992 'The Technology of Enchantment and the Enchantment of Technology', in J Coote and A Shelton (eds), *Anthropology, Art, and Aesthetics*, Oxford: Clarendon Press, 40–63

Gelling, P and Davidson, H 1969 *The Chariot of the Sun*, New York: Frederick A. Praeger

Gifford, E and Gifford, J 2004 'The Use of Half-Scale Model Ships in Archaeological Research with Particular Reference to the Graveney, Sutton Hoo and Ferriby Ships', in P Clark (ed), *The Dover Bronze Age Boat in context: Society and water transport in prehistoric Europe*, Oxford: Oxbow Books, 67–81

Glacken C 1967 *Traces on the Rhodian Shore*, Berkeley: University of California

Gosden, C 2003 'The Expression of Emotion Through People and Objects', in C Gosden *et al* (organizers) *Rethinking Materiality*, Cambridge, Conference papers, McDonald Institute for Archaeological research, March 28–31, 33–36

Hahn, C 1986 "Joseph will Perfect Mary Enlighten and Jesus Save Thee": The Holy Family as Marriage Model in the Mérode Triptych', *The Art Bulletin*, **68**, 54–66

Harding, A 2000 *European Societies in the Bronze Age*, Cambridg: Cambridge University Press

Hardwick, C 1858 *The Gospel According to Saint Matthew in Anglo-Saxon and Northumbrian Versions*, Cambridge: Cambridge University

Heckenberger, M 2005 *The Ecology of Power*, New York: Routledge

Helms, M W 1993 *Craft and the Kingly Ideal*, Austin: University of Texas

Helms, M W 1998 *Access to Origins*, Austin: University of Texas

Horn, W and Born, E 1979a *The Plan of St. Gall: Volume 1,* Berkeley: University of California

Horn, W and Born, E 1979b *The Plan of St. Gall: Volume 2,* Berkeley: University of California

Horn, W and Born, E 1979c *The Plan of St. Gall: Volume 3,* Berkeley: University of California

James, E 1966 *The Tree of Life*, Leiden: E J Brill.

Jones, A 2004 'Matter and Memory', in E DeMarrais *et al* (eds), *Rethinking Materiality*, Cambridge: McDonald Institute for Archaeological Research, 167–178

Kaul, F 2004 'Social and Religious Perceptions of the Ship in Bronze Age Northern Europe' in P Clark (ed), *The The Dover Bronze Age Boat in Context: Society and water transport in prehistoric Europe*, Oxford: Oxbow Books, 122–137

Kristiansen, K 2004 'Sea Faring Voyages and Rock Art Ships', in P Clark (ed), *The Dover Bronze Age Boat in Context: Society and water transport in prehistoric Europe,* Oxford: Oxbow Books, 111–121

Kristiansen, K and Larsson, T 2005 *The Rise of Bronze Age Society,* Cambridge: Cambridge UniversityPress

Lewis, R (ed) 1988 *Middle English Dictionary, Part S.9,* Ann Arbor: University of Michigan

Lewis, R (ed) 2001 *Middle English Dictionary, Part W.8,* Ann Arbor: University of Michigan

Marsden, P 2004 Reconstructing the Dover Boat', in P Clark (ed), *The Dover Bronze age boat in Context: Society and water transport in prehistoric Europe,* Oxford: Oxbow Books, 17–19

McGrail, S 2004 'Northwest European Seagoing Boats Before AD 400', in P Clark (ed), *The Dover Bronze Age Boat in Context: Society and water transport in prehistoric Europe,* Oxford: Oxbow Books, 51–66

Meiggs, R 1982 *Trees and Timber in the Ancient Mediterranean World,* Oxford: Clarendon

Morris, S 1992 *Daidalos and the Origins of Greek Art,* Princeton: Princeton University

Mounce, W 1993 *The Analytical Lexicon to the Greek New Testament,* Grand Rapids: Zondervan

Nineham, D 1963 *The Gospel of St. Mark*, Baltimore: Penguin

Parker Pearson, M and Richards, C 1994a 'Ordering the World', in M Parker Pearson and C Richards (eds), *Architecture and Order: Approaches to Social Space*, New York: Routledge, 1–37

Parker Pearson, M and Richards, C 1994b 'Architecture and Order', in M Parker Pearson and C Richards (eds), *Architecture and Order: Approaches to Social Space*, New York: Routledge, 38–72

Plumpe, J 1943 'Vivum Saxum, Vivi Lapides: The Concept of 'Living Stone' in Classical and Christian Antiquity', *Traditio*, **1**, 1–14

Pollard, J 2004 'The Art of Decay and the Transformation of Substance', in C Renfrew, C Gosden and E DeMarrais (eds), *Substance, Memory, Display: Archaeology and Art*, Cambridge: McDonald Institute for Archaeological Research, 47–62

Pryor, F 2004 'Some Thoughts on Boats as Bronze Age Artefacts', in P Clark (ed), *The Dover Bronze Age Boat in Context: Society and water transport in prehistoric Europe,* Oxford: Oxbow Books, 31–34

Ross, A 1967 *Pagan Celtic Britain*, London: Routledge and Kegan Paul

Simpson, D 1968 *Cassell's Latin Dictionary*, London: Cassell

Taçon, P 1991 'The Power of Stone', *Antiquity*, **65 (247)**, 192–207

Thomas, J 1996 *Time, Culture and Identity*, New York: Routledge

Toller, T (ed) 1898 *An Anglo-Saxon Dictionary Based on the Manuscript Collections of the Late Joseph Bosworth*, London: Oxford

Van de Noort, R 2004 'The Humber, its sewn-plank boats, their contexts and the significance of it all', in P Clark (ed), *The Dover Bronze Age Boat in Context: Society and water transport in prehistoric Europe,* Oxford: Oxbow Books, 90–98

Werner, D 1981 'Are Some People More Equal Than Others?', *Journal of Anthropological Research*, **37**, 360–373

11. Exploring the ritual of travel in prehistoric Europe: the Bronze Age sewn-plank boats in context

Robert Van de Noort

'In many parts of the world and at many periods the practice has prevailed of depositing boats, or models or other representations of them, with the dead, either as a means of facilitating his supposed voyage to another world, or as a symbol of his maritime activities during his lifetime. That the former is generally the correct explanation of the custom there can be no doubt' (Grinsell 1941, 360)

Introduction – why we should be interested in studying travel?

Even before Gustaf Kossina (*eg* 1911) developed his concept of culture and explained cultural change through the process of diffusion, archaeologists have (often polemically and exclusively) advocated particular theoretical models as being the principal mechanisms by which to explain change. These include migration, assimilation, acculturation, (neo-Darwinian) social and cultural evolution, environmental determinism, variants on the Marxist concept of accumulation and internal forces for change, world-system models, peer-polity interaction and many more (*eg* Trigger 1990). However, the archaeological demonstrable activity of travelling has been largely overlooked in this debate, although some important exceptions exist (see below). This is surprising when one considers that in a prehistoric, a-literate society, travelling offers the only opportunity to increase knowledge and understanding once the social memory of one's locale has been exhausted, and it can thus lead to the introduction of new materials and ideas which can in turn result in innovations and cultural change.

The *products* of travel in prehistoric Europe, especially for the later Neolithic and Bronze Age, have been studied extensively and the debate on the acquisition of exotic objects, often referred to as prestige-goods, of the 1980s and '90s is well rehearsed (*eg* Rowlands 1980; Shennan 1982; 1988; Bradley 1984; Barrett 1994; Harding 2000). However, the *processes* by which this acquisition took place have not received the same attention. The significance of these processes, or travel, in archaeology has seen something of a revival since the publication of Mary Helms' *Ulysses' Sail: An Ethnographic Odyssey of Power, Knowledge, and Geographical Distance* in 1988, and several studies have been inspired by her ideas (*eg*

Figure 11.1 The location of the sewn-plank boats and boat-fragments

Beck and Shennan 1991; Broodbank 1993; Needham 2000; Kristiansen 2004; Kristiansen and Thomas 2005). The core of Helms' argument is the association of geographical distance with the value attributed to ideas and goods obtained through travel. This relates to the basic concept that in many societies across the world metaphorical connections exist between geographical distance and time, or horizontal distance, linking great journeys with ancestors, gods or the sphere that acts as the final resting place, as already expressed in Leslie Grinsell's 1940 paper, quoted at the opening of this paper. Thus, exotic or prestige goods are valued because they have been acquired from great distances and can, metaphorically, be associated with this 'other world'. However, the exotic objects themselves may not have been the chief purpose of the journeys, rather they provide a material reflection of the knowledge and understanding, both sacred and profane, that has been gained during the travels. It has been argued that knowledge played a significant role in the social reproduction of the socio-political order and organisations of the later Neolithic and Early Bronze Age, that is in the negotiation, legitimisation and reinforcement of the rights of the newly emerged elite groups over people who did not possess such knowledge.

In several earlier studies, I have endeavoured to incorporate the maritime archaeology of the Bronze Age into the study of prehistoric travel (Van de Noort 2003; 2004a; 2004b; 2006; Van de Noort *et al* 1999). This seemed appropriate as the type of craft that enabled the long-distance journeys to be completed successfully determined the perception of distance; crossing the North Sea today is largely a routine matter because we have the technology to undertake such journeys safely, but the craft that enabled seafaring in the Bronze Age, and the limitations in the knowledge of the sea and what lay beyond the horizon, made crossing the North Sea anything but a routine activity. In this, I have assumed that sewn-plank boats were used for seafaring (*see also* Van de Noort *et al* 1999; McGrail 2001; Clark 2004a). Helms also argues that when undertaking long-distance journeys, the departure from or return to the home territory was frequently marked in early societies by ritual or ritualised activities. Furthermore, specific locales would have been selected as

departure and arrival points, namely those that linked the travellers to the ideological concepts represented in the landscape that gave meaning to long-distance travel. This concept provides a basic archaeological tool. Through the analysis of the landscape context of the sewn-plank boat locations, we can ascertain something of the 'ritual of travel'. For the Bronze Age we may expect to see, for example, a reference to ancestors such as burial places, the presence of 'territorial' markers such as barrows or cairns, or votive/structured depositions, especially of esoteric objects.

At the first Dover Boat conference, I presented an analysis of what can be learnt about the significance of sewn-plank boats from contextualised studies concentrating on the sewn-plank boats from the Humber estuary, notably the boats from North Ferriby and Kilnsea (Van de Noort 2004a). The purpose of this paper is to review the contexts of all known sewn-plank boats, including the Dover boat, and to place this in the context of a broader exploration of rituals associated with travel from prehistoric Europe. It should aid in developing an understanding of the ancient perception of that 'other world' in Leslie Grinsell's quote.

The sewn-plank boats contextualised

The known sewn-plank boat finds (Fig 11.1) include five boats from the Humber estuary and tributaries; F1, F2 and F3 from North Ferriby (Wright and Wright 1939; Wright 1990, Wright *et al* 2001), a single plank discovered on the beach at Kilnsea in East Yorkshire in 1996 (Van de Noort *et al* 1999) and the famous Brigg 'raft' (McGrail 1981). The Severn estuary has provided three craft; a side strake of one boat (Caldicot 1) and up to three additional fragments of another boat (Caldicot 2; McGrail 1997), and two pieces of boat planking from Goldcliff (Bell 1992; 1993). The Dover boat was discovered in 1992 in the River Dour (Clark 2004b). The final fragment, of a single cleat, comes from the River Test at Testwood Lakes excavations, just north of Southampton (Fitzpatrick *et al* 1996; Andrew Fitzpatrick *pers comm*). Table 11.1 provides the most up-to-date calibrated dates for all these craft. The contextualised sewn-plank boats of the second millennium BC are presented below in a broadly chronological order, starting with

Sewn-plank boat	Date	Period (after Needham 1996)	Reference
F3	2030–1780 cal BC	3	(Wright *et al* 2001);
F2	1940–1720 cal BC	3	(Wright *et al* 2001);
F1	1880–1680 cal BC	3	(Wright *et al* 2001);
Caldicot 1	1870–1680 cal BC	3	(McGrail 1997);
Kilnsea	1750–1620 cal BC	3 or 4	(Van de Noort *et al* 1999);
Dover	1575–1520 cal BC	4	(Bayliss *et al* 2004)
Testwood Lakes	c. 1500 cal BC	3 or 4	(Fitzpatrick pers. comm.);
Goldcliff	c. 1170 BC	5	(Bell *et al* 2000);
Caldicot 2	c. 1000 cal BC	6	(McGrail 1997);
Brigg 'raft'	825–760 cal BC	7	(cf. Switsur in McGrail 1981).

Table 11.1 (left) Calibrated dates of sewn-plank boats mentioned in the text

Table 11.2 (below) The contextualisation of the 10 sewn-plank boats from England and Wales

Period	Sewn-plank boat	Immediate context		Landscape setting (2 km radius)	
		Associated ritual deposits?	*Re-use of boat timbers in river crossings?*	*Nearby ancestral monuments?*	*Nearby contemporary monuments?*
Period 3	F3	None	No	None	None
	F2	None	No	None	None
	F1	None	No	None	None
	Caldicot 1	None	No	Neolithic long barrow	Large EBA barrow
Period 3/4	Kilnsea	None	No	Neolithic houses and hengiform monument or circular structure	Several EBA barrows containing beaker pottery
Period 4	Dover	None	No	None known	Possible EBA burials represented by whole a whole Beaker
Period 4/5	Testwood Lakes	Bronze Acton 2 rapier	Bridge	None	None
Period 5	Goldcliff	Human skulls	Trackway	None	None
Period 6	Caldicot 2	Wilburton-type chape, two vessels, an amber bead, wooden objects and a dog skeleton	Trackway or bridge	As Caldicot 1	As Caldicot 1
Period 7	Brigg 'raft'	Bronze axe, spearhead and pin, human and animal bones, pottery	No, but nearby bridge or jetty	None	None

the Humber finds. In the case of Caldicot, however, both craft are discussed under the same header to avoid repetition.

Ferriby 3, 2 and 1 (respectively 2030–1780 cal BC, 1940–1720 cal BC and 1880–1680 cal BC; Fig 11.2)

In previously published research, the boat finds from Ferriby in the Humber estuary have already been placed in their immediate and landscape contexts (*eg* Van de Noort 2003; 2004a; 2006), and the conclusions may be summarised here. The archaeology from the North Ferriby foreshore includes the well-preserved remains of F1 found in an intertidal creek. F2, comprising the two parts of the keel plank joined amidships; and F3, which consists of an outer bottom plank stitched to the remains of one of the lower side strakes, were both found to rest on alder roundwood logs, as if awaiting repair or assemblage (Wright

Figure 11.2 The contexts of the sewn-plank boats from Ferriby, Kilnsea and Brigg

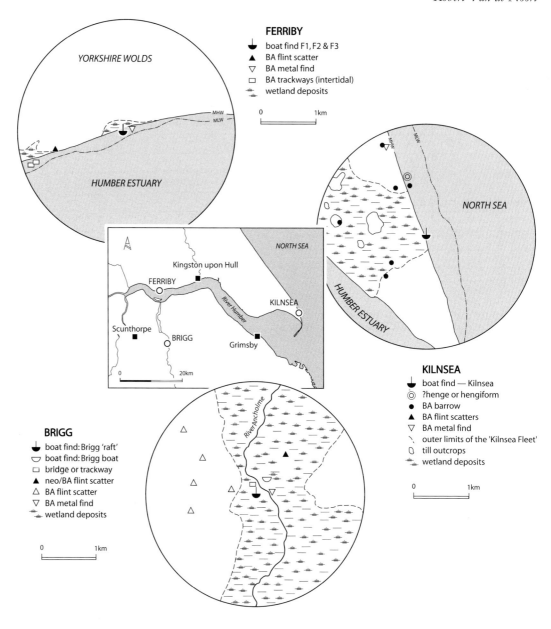

1990). Combined with the oak chips with bronze axe marks and the off-cuts of yew withies that are continued to be retrieved from the foreshore, it was concluded that the North Ferriby site was a prehistoric boatyard. Several other finds from the foreshore reinforce this conclusion, and a number of small finds have been interpreted as shipwright's tools, such as a 'tingle' used for repairing holes and cracks in boats, and the pistol-shaped tool used for stitching the yew withies.

The discovery of at least two paddles and a timber interpreted as the fragment of a capstan are suggestive of the North Ferriby site being used as a landing place for boats, and the North Ferriby foreshore was ideally situated for cross-estuary traffic, connecting it with the area around South Ferriby on the Lincolnshire side of the Humber. Other finds from the foreshore include part of a baked clay sinker, a bronze knife blade and fragments of pottery. Archaeological and palaeoenvironmental evidence is suggestive of pastoral farming on the foreshore. Several hurdle trackways from North Ferriby and other foreshores in the Humber dated to the period *c* 1700–1000 cal BC have now been reinterpreted as crossing places for livestock within intertidal saltmarshes used as grazing land, rather than as trackways used to gain access to the boats (Van de Noort and Fletcher 2001; Van de Noort 2004a). Within the landscape context of the Ferriby boats, pollen analysis indicates that by *c* 1700 cal BC, arboreal pollen was relatively rare suggesting that woodland had been largely cleared (Wright and Churchill 1965). Although this work is now somewhat dated, the palynology implies that during the time of the construction of F1, F2 and F3, the cultural landscape context of North Ferriby was one dominated by agricultural use.

Within the cultural landscape of the Ferriby boats, little exists in terms of monuments. To the west of North Ferriby, the low hill known as Redcliff has been interpreted as a late Iron Age port-of-trade (*eg* Creighton 1990). Flint artefacts and debitage from Redcliff indicate human activity here from the Late Mesolithic onwards, but even though field-based research has been small in scale, this Iron Age port-of-trade remains without a clear Bronze Age predecessor. Evidence for burial monuments, the ritual deposition of artefacts or any other ritualised activities in the landscape around North Ferriby is, however, conspicuous by its absence with the exception of a Late Bronze Age spearhead found to the north of the foreshore, in North Ferriby village. In previous analyses (Van de Noort 2003; 2004a), this landscape was interpreted as one where the construction of sewn-plank boats and their daily use was not imbued with any 'special' meaning. In a recent reappraisal of this analysis, Henry Chapman and Benjamin Gearey (2004) argue that even cross-estuarine travel would have been accompanied by ritualised behaviour. Whilst this may indeed have been the case – and while it is always hard to disentangle the ritual components from everyday activities in the prehistoric period – the fact remains that nothing in the archaeological record of the contexts of the Ferriby boats or their cultural landscape setting indicates that rituals played a significant role here.

Kilnsea (1750–1620 cal BC; Fig 11.2)

The Kilnsea boat plank was found on the beach in the southernmost part of Holderness in 1996 (Van de Noort *et al* 1999). It comprises a single plank, with the bases of two cleats, but with its edge badly eroded. In terms of

the dimensions of the planks and its cleats, it resembles the keel-plank or lower side strake of F1. It is unlikely, if not impossible, for a timber object of Early Bronze Age date to survive either on the beach, or in the sand dunes, or in the glacial tills that form the principle component of the local landscape. Instead, the most likely place where the boat-plank could have survived is in the clays and peats that continue to be exposed during low tides, derived from the so-called Kilnsea Fleet. This was an elongated glacial and glaciofluvial depression cut into the till connected to the Humber estuary. Due to the post-Glacial and Holocene sea-level rise, the Kilnsea Fleet was inundated sometime around 4000 cal BC, and estuarine conditions prevailed here during the Bronze Age, as shown by the numerous fossils of the *Scrobicularia* mollusc in the clays forming the basal deposits within the depression.

Due to the stray character of the find, we have no further knowledge of its deposition context, and it is simply impossible to attest whether or not other boat fragments may have been washed out into sea. The Kilnsea Fleet, however, would have been ideally suited as a landing place for craft crossing the North Sea. It formed the first north-bank tidal inlet within the Humber estuary, and it would have offered a safe landing place for boats, with the tides giving easy access to the chosen landing place.

Much of the original landscape context of the Kilnsea boat has been lost to coastal erosion over the last 4000 years. What remains of the immediate landscape context of the Kilnsea boat is, nevertheless, rich in monuments. The oldest monuments date to the Neolithic, with the remains of two small buildings dated to *c* 3600 cal BC. A pit containing several broken quern stones also belongs to this phase. At some later point, a possible mini-henge or hengiform monument (or other type of circular monument; Harding and Lee 1987) was constructed nearby. The construction of the circular monument has a *terminus ante quem* of *c* 2500 cal BC, given by a cremation burial within its outer ditch. This structure was 30 m in diameter, and had an entrance or interruption in the north-western part, but too much of the site had been destroyed by a marine inundation broadly dated to around 1000 cal BC to ascertain the specific type of this monument. At least two Bronze Age barrows were constructed over the remains of the Neolithic structures. One of the central graves included a jet button, and the skeletal remains of another Beaker-accompanied burial were radiocarbon dated to *c* 2000 cal BC.

When analysing this landscape, it has been commented that the cultural landscape of the Kilnsea site, possibly representing the place of departure to, or arrival from, continental Europe, was embedded with special meaning. The way in which the Early Bronze Age seafarers signified themselves and their world through the landscape includes strong reference to their ancestors and various ritualised activities. At this early date,

the legitimisation of political and religious power without reference to the ancestors is unthinkable, and the space that was passed through during the voyages may have acted as a metaphor for the time span between people and their ancestors (*cf* Van de Noort 2003, 412).

Caldicot 1 and 2 (respectively 1870–1680 cal BC and c 1000 cal BC; Fig 11.3)

The Caldicot boat planks were discovered in 1990 during the excavations of an ornamental lake within the country park around Caldicot

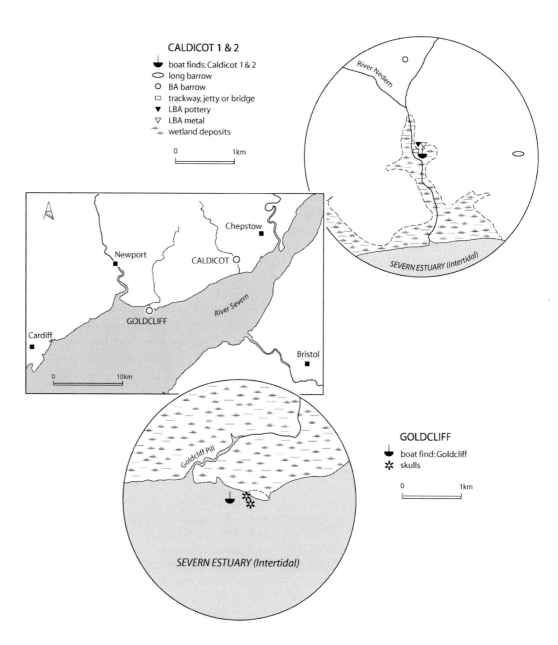

Figure 11.3 The contexts of the sewn-plank boats from Caldicot and Goldcliff

Castle (Nayling and Caseldine 1997). The lake was dug within the floodplain of the River Nedern or Nedern Brook, which offers access to the Severn estuary, about 1100 m due south at Caldicot Pill. Palaeoenvironmental and archaeological deposits within the ornamental lake date from the Mesolithic through to the Iron Age, with the Bronze Age subdivided into six phases. The Caldicot 1 boat fragment belongs to Phase III, Caldicot 2 to Phases VI, VI/VII and VII.

Caldicot 1 was the second or higher side strake of a sewn-plank boat, and includes a number of characteristic features such as the bevelled edge, holes for stitching planks together and the remains of three cleats. The 3.55 m long plank had been broken in antiquity (McGrail 2001, 188). Phase III activity is described as including 'the deposition of a wide variety of wood including scrub clearance, woodworking debris and the boat strake' alongside the deposition of some stone and bones of domesticated animals (Nayling and Caseldine 1997, 261–262) and it seems unlikely that the sewn-plank boat remains are those of a sunken boat. Rather, it and the associated yew ties have been interpreted as 'discarded material, resulting from the repair of a sewn-plank boat' (*ibid* 263). There is no evidence for a structure in the river for this phase.

On the basis of diatom and other biological indicators, it was established that the Nedern Brook at Caldicot was principally a freshwater river during Phase III, although the presence of limited numbers of maritime biota suggests that occasional high tides could have reached as far upstream as the ornamental lake. Further downstream, the Nedern was tidal, providing 'free' transport into this small tributary of the Severn estuary, and the boat could have been landed at, or just above, MHWST at Caldicot.

Caldicot 2 was discovered during the same excavations. Caldicot 2 is used here as a shorthand for three oak fragments, consisting of a possible cleat fragment, a 0.3 m long plank with six holes similar to a bottom plank of the Brigg 'raft' (see below) and another plank with what has been described as a possible cleat ridge, similar to the one known from F2 (McGrail 1997, 215–217). These fragments have not been dated independently through radiocarbon or dendrochronological assay, but are attributed to Phase VI, VI/VII and VII of

the Caldicot site on the basis of stratigraphy.

The context of these fragments is significantly different from that of Caldicot 1. The Nedern Brook, responding to sea-level change and sedimentation of the valley, had become a wider, flat-bottomed channel at the start of Phase VI, *c* 1100–1000 cal BC. Structure 9014, described as a fort, hard or weir, was constructed early in the tenth century BC, and was shortly thereafter followed or replaced by a wooden bridge or jetty and associated trackway (Nayling and Caseldine 1997, 265–268). The River Nedern at Caldicot is believed to have been beyond the tidal limit at the beginning of Phase VI, but by the time the bridge was constructed, the river may have become tidal again at this place. This structure may also have doubled as a fish weir.

From around both structure 9014 and the bridge-and-trackway, numerous cultural deposits have been recovered. 'Systematic dumping' near structure 9014 included 'large quantities of stone, clearance waste, woodworking debris, substantial timbers, bone waste and even wooden artefacts', including the two possible boat-planks (*ibid* 266). From near the bridge came a Wilburton-type chape, fragments of at least two 'finely decorated vessels', decorative bone objects, an amber bead, wooden domestic items and a near-complete dog skeleton (*ibid* 267). The possibility that at least some of these depositions should be interpreted as 'ritual' or votive was raised by the authors of the Caldicot report (*idem*). Recent overviews of the contexts of sewn-plank boats have suggested that Caldicot was associated with ritual depositions (*eg* Champion 2004; Pryor 2004), but these do not differentiate between Caldicot 1 and Caldicot 2 in terms of either date or context.

The environmental component of the landscape context of Caldicot 1 and 2 has been studied in considerable detail (Nayling and Caseldine 1997). During Phase III, that is the phase to which Caldicot 1 is assigned, the floodplain of the Nedern was wet grassland, with ample scope for grazing, and species such as greater plantain and fat hen suggest locally disturbed ground, attributable to human or animal activity. On the dry land either side of the floodplain, the palynology indicates a reduction in woodland density, and increasing pastoral activity with a dominance of sheep over cattle suggested by the animal bone assemblage and some, presumably small-scale, arable landuse (*ibid*). In Phases VI/VII, the meadows on the floodplain are also grazed, and the palynology suggests extensive disturbance of the natural habitat, which is unsurprising in light of the structures that had been built here. The surrounding drylands provide evidence for continued pastoralism and cereal cultivation, alongside signs of woodland management.

The cultural landscape of the Caldicot boats includes several early burial monuments, according to the Glamorgan-Gwent Archaeological Trust SMR/HER. The area within 2 km of the Caldicot boat location includes the Heston Brake chambered long barrow at Portskewett and at least one, and possibly two, round barrows. The chambered tomb is located some 1800 m to the east of Caldicot Castle, northeast of Portskewett village, set on the crest of a spur of land in a narrow valley. Excavations here revealed two internally connected chambers in this 25 m long mound, and the tomb is considered to be of the Glamorgan/Monmouthshire group of Cotswold-Severn type of long barrows, and thus on typological grounds dated to around 4000 cal BC (Lynch *et al* 2000, 66). The location of the Portskewett monument is particularly poignant in that is was located to be visible principally from the water, rather than from the surrounding land, and its entrance faced the Severn. The visual impact of the long barrow on its surrounding landscape is restricted by low ridges several hundred metres to the east and west, and the Nedern Brook is not visible from it. However, an impressive panorama of the Severn estuary can be gained from the top of the remains of the monument and on a clear day the Portskewett long barrow would have been visible from the Severn Estuary as far as modern Cardiff on the horizon. The Portskewett long barrow is not exceptional in this respect (see, for example, Phillips 2004), and this monument could have acted as a clear reference point for later mariners (*cf* McGrail 1997).

To the north of the Caldicot boat site, and overlooking the Nedern Brook valley, lies the Crick Barrow, a large monument measuring 41 m in diameter. Excavations in 1940 revealed an Early Bronze Age funerary deposit within a stone kerb rig with a diameter of *c* 29 m. A nearby low mound of *c* 10 m diameter was thought to be a possible second round

barrow by Crawford in 1921. Within this landscape context, the HER/SMR also records a considerable number of enclosures dated broadly to the prehistoric period, but these remain without obvious function or more precise date. Although the Crick barrow forms part of a small number of Bronze Age burial sites in southern Monmouthshire, the area lies clearly beyond the main concentrations of round barrows in Wales (Lynch *et al* 2000, 82).

Dover (1575–1520 cal BC; Fig 11.4)

The information on the discovery, excavation and analysis of the Dover boat are now available in an outstanding publication (Clark 2004b), of which a brief summary will have to suffice here. A number of features of the discovery are directly relevant to this paper. The Dover boat was found in 1992, and has been dated through radiocarbon assay to 1575–1520 cal BC (Bayliss *et al* 2004). In essence, it consists of four planks, that is two bottom- or keel-planks that were joined together by means of a longitudinal cleat rail, and two ile planks, or transitional strakes (Marsden 2004, 32–33). In design, it shares a number of aspects with all sewn-plank boats, including the use of cleats and transverse timbers to provide the hull with rigidity, and with the Early Bronze Age boats in the use of individual, rather than continuous stitches. Wear and tear, and several repairs to the ile planks where these had split in antiquity, show that the Dover boat had seen considerable service. At the point of deposition, the vessel showed signs of leaking but the structure of the boat was 'quite sound' (*ibid* 44). In its hypothetical reconstruction, this was a 'flat-bottomed boat' which may have been up to 15 m in length (only 9.2 m was excavated) and 2.3 m wide, with a square transom end (based in part on that of the Hasholme logboat; *cf* Millett and McGrail 1987), giving room to a crew of about 20 and generally understood to have been capable of seagoing journeys (Marsden 2004, 94; *see also* alternative reconstructions in Crumlin-Pedersen 2006). Owain Roberts (2004) believes that the Dover boat would have straightforwardly withstood Force 3 winds, and at a speed of 4.5 to 5 knots could cross the Channel in under five hours.

The context of the boat was studied in an equally unparalleled fashion, despite the

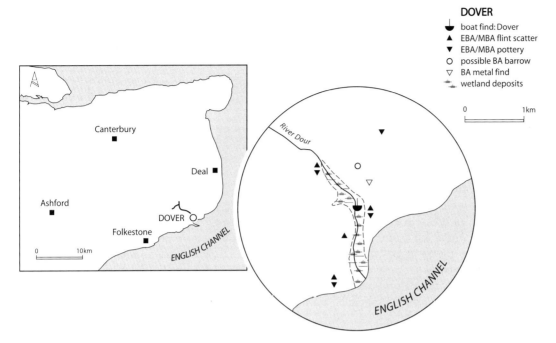

Figure 11.4 The context of the sewn-plank boat from Dover

limitation set by the two cofferdams that determined the extent of excavations. In terms of the palaeoenvironmental setting, the seafaring role of the Dover boat is reinforced by the fragments of marine beach shells in the boat. The boat was found at a depth of −0.04 and −0.75 m OD, and this relates to a contemporary sea-level of between −2.0 and −5.0 m OD (Keeley *et al* 2004, 232–234). With the boat, a considerable amount of flint, debitage pottery and burnt flint was found, alongside animal bones. These have been interpreted as inwash from an upstream but nearby rubbish dump or midden related to Late Neolithic and Bronze Age habitation (Bown *et al* 2004). A small fragment of Kimmeridge shale from Dorset, found in the boat, is seen as a leftover of (one of) the Dover boat's cargoes (*ibid*).

A great deal has been written about how and why the Dover boat was deposited. Unequivocally, the final resting place of the boat was a 'quiet backwater' in the shallow and freshwater stream of the Dour. However, whether the boat was stripped here 'of anything useful' for reuse and then deserted (*eg* Parfitt 2004, 22; Clark in Bown *et al* 2004, 211), or was ritually killed and buried (*eg* Champion 2004; Clark 2004c) remains a topic of debate. During my talk at the Conference, I put forward the suggestion that the Dover boat may have been put in the Dour for storage during the winter months to avoid the timber to crack or warp, but Peter Clark pointed out in subsequent discussions that central rails on the bottom planks had been deliberately cut through to expose the transverse timber 342 (set between bottom cleats 314 and 315), which would have made re-use at a later date very difficult, if not impossible.

Dover's geographical position has made it the principle gateway to Continental Europe from the time that Britain became an island around 6000 cal BC, and the high concentrations of archaeological finds from the Neolithic and Bronze Age reinforces this concept for this period. Obviously, the gateway function of Dover extended beyond the Bronze Age, and this has contributed to the widespread destruction of prehistoric monuments during the Roman, medieval and early modern periods. Consequently, a comparatively large number of antiquarian discoveries are without clear provenance or context. The partial destruction of Dover Museum during the Second Wold War only adds to this problem. For example, the complete Early Bronze Age Beaker from the Maison Dieu fields, discovered in 1883, may well have come from a barrow which had been flattened by the late nineteenth century and the pot itself was reported to be presented to Dover Museum, but neither the

Beaker nor the circumstances of its discovery can be retraced.

Thus, within 2 km of the Dover boat site, the Kent SMR/HER lists no monuments, but includes seven locations containing flint artefacts or debitage of Neolithic and Bronze Age date; three of these sites also include pottery fragments which allow dating of these occupation or activity sites to the Late Neolithic and/or Early Bronze Age. For the period around *c* 1600 cal BC, the landscape incorporates two additional locations where pottery was deposited. One of these locations is within 100 m of the boat site. Although no structural evidence for a Bronze Age settlement has been found as yet, the archaeology of the lower reaches of the Dour valley and the fringing chalk cliffs strongly suggests that people lived here during this period. Notably, the palaeoenvironmental work associated with the Dover Boat found that the Dour valley at this time was a largely treeless landscape with arable fields, and evidence for a nearby settlement comes in the form of a charred hazelnut fragment, cereal grain and animal and fish bones, some with butchering marks, presumably representing the rubbish from nearby habitation (Keeley *et al* 2004). Keith Parfitt and Tim Champion (2004, 266) have suggested that the Western Heights, a chalk headland near the estuary of the Dour, would have been an ideal location for the settlement that produced this rubbish.

Alongside the evidence for settlement, the high number of depositions of high-status artefacts in this small area is most remarkable. These include an Early/Middle Bronze Age hoard of three flanged axes together with a tanged spearhead, a gold armlet found in 1878, a Late Bronze Age gold penannular earring found in 1853, and a group of five Late Bronze Age socketed axes, found in association with a fragment of a sword broken in antiquity, other broken bronze implements and 'lumps of metal'. The context for most of these antiquarian finds is unknown, and two locations are only known by their nearest kilometre grid-square. We cannot therefore determine whether or not the majority of these metal depositions should be treated as 'votive depositions in wet places' (*cf* Bradley 1990), or as hoards. In view of recent discussions, however, this difference may be one based in the preconceptions of archaeologists rather than in the archaeology itself. Martyn Barber (2001, 167), for example, has argued that the return of metal to where it came from was governed by cosmological frameworks, with the precise reason for deposition varying across time and space; this, rather than the difference between ritual and profane deposition may explain the choice of environment.

Peter Clark's recent (2004e) contextualisation of the Dover boat places it firmly in the Middle Bronze Age, and its function has been interpreted within the context of the fragmented society of the bounded landscape that characterises that period (*cf* Brück 2000). However, the sixteenth century cal BC date for the sewn-plank boat dates it to end of Needham's (1996) Period 4, the Early Bronze Age, and the vessel may equally be interpreted as lying within the final stages of the period of the expansive social network. Indeed, in considering the socio-political context of the boat, Keith Parfitt and Tim Champion (2004, 264) consider it principally in the light of Early Bronze Age funerary monuments, rather than the bounded landscape which becomes archaeologically visible in Kent only at the very end of the second millennium cal BC.

Testwood Lakes (*c 1500 cal BC; Fig 11.5*)

The Testwood Lakes boat fragment was discovered in 1996 by staff of Wessex Archaeology, during excavations carried out as part of a watching brief linked to gravel extractions resulting in the creation of the most northerly of the water reservoirs commonly known as Testwood Lakes, namely Meadow Lake (Fitzpatrick *et al* 1996). The reservoir was cut into the floodplain of the River Blackwater, just north of its confluence with the River Test, and *c* 4 km north of the intertidal bay of Southampton Water, which offers direct access to the Solent. The preliminary palaeoenvironmental analysis undertaken to date describes the floodplain around 1500 cal BC as a slow flowing, largely freshwater river, with some brackish but no seawater present. Thus, the Testwood Lakes site was in the Bronze Age at the very top end of the tidal reach, where MHWST may just have had periodical influence. Stands of trees, grasses and reeds would have grown on the riverbank, but further afield, more open grassland

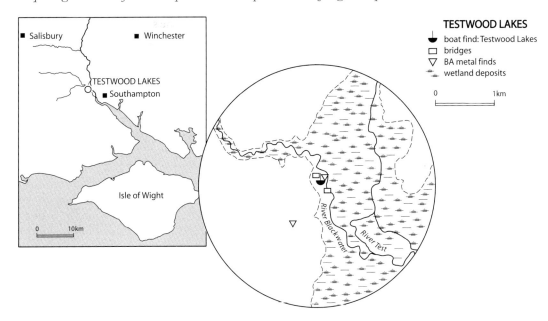

Figure 11.5 The context of the sewn-plank boat from Testwood Lakes

dominated, and the palaeoenvironmental analysis has shown that around 1500 cal BC the floodplain became more intensively exploited for agricultural use.

The Testwood Lakes boat fragment comprises the remains of a single cleat, with dimensions comparable to the cleats of the Brigg 'raft'. The cleat is provisionally dated to *c* 1500 cal BC (Andrew Fitzpatrick *pers comm*; *contra* McGrail 2004). It was found near the remains of three bridges (Testwood 1, 2 and 3) which cross the River Blackwater here, the oldest of which was dated through radiocarbon assay to *c* 1700 cal BC and the youngest to around 1400 cal BC. The oldest and best surviving structure (Testwood 3) comprised two rows of upstanding, mainly oak, timbers extending for *c* 26 m, standing between 1.5 and 2 m apart. Some 15 planks were also found in the former river, presumably forming the superstructure of the bridge, displaying a range of carpentry techniques, including notches, bevels and mortise holes, but no cleats or cleat-like features. The cleat itself had been damaged on one side where it would have been connected to a boat-plank, and the other side was found worn. This may be interpreted as evidence that entire boat-planks had been reused for the bridge decking but that the cleat, being something of a potential obstacle, had been removed from the plank in antiquity and thrown into the river.

As part of the same excavations, a broadly contemporary bronze rapier was uncovered from the riverbed. The Acton 2-type rapier was not broken, but lacked its handle, and pending further analysis should be broadly dated to the middle of the second millennium BC. The possibility that this rapier is a votive deposit in the wetlands of the Rivers Blackwater and Test has not been discounted by the excavators.

Within the landscape context of the Testwood Lakes boat fragment, one other contemporary find has been recorded in the SMR/HER. This is a looped palstave bronze axe, found in 1965 some 700 m southwest of the boat fragment and just beyond the edge of the floodplain of the River Test. No further information on this object is available as it was retained by the finder, but in line with the general dating of looped palstave axes, may be considered as dating to the second half of the second millennium BC.

Goldcliff (c 1170 BC; Fig 11.3)

The Goldcliff boat comprises two planks, both of oak with upstanding cleat ridges through which mortise holes had been cut, similar to the cleat ridge of the Dover boat. Closely spaced 'fastening' holes along the sides, some still containing plant fibre cord, are similar to those of the Brigg 'raft'. The closely-spaced holes suggest that continuous rather than individual stitches had been used to link these planks to other side strakes.

The two planks formed part of a small platform-like structure measuring 1.3 by 1.6 m, together with several other pieces of roundwood. The excavators initially suggested it was a platform used for hunting, fishing or fowling within the intertidal zone of the Severn estuary (Bell 1993, 11) but it is now thought that it was a short trackway crossing a narrow channel within an intertidal context (Bell et al 2000, 82). For one of the two planks, it has been argued that this was not the first time it had been reused. One of the mortised holes would have had no function in the sewn-plank boat, nor did it serve a function in the platform. No other finds have been made from the direct context of these planks.

The Goldcliff site was not close to any dry land, and within the landscape context of this craft, no other indications of Neolithic or Early Bronze Age activity exist (*idem*). However, the discovery of two human skulls of Late Bronze Age date links Goldcliff with the practice of the deposition of human crania, with or without bronze weaponry, which is well documented from wetlands and island contexts in Britain and further afield (*eg* Bradley and Gordon 1988; O'Sullivan 2001; Koch 1998; Pryor 2001; *cf* Bell *et al* 2000, 72).

Brigg (825–760 cal BC; Fig 11.2)

The sewn-plank boat from Brigg in the Ancholme valley in Lincolnshire was discovered in 1888 during clay diggings and it is now conventionally known as the Brigg 'raft', reflecting earlier interpretations and avoiding any confusion with the Brigg (log-)boat. It was initially interpreted as a pontoon bridge, raft, or flat-bottomed boat (Thropp 1887), but after re-excavation in 1907/8 by Rev. Alfred Hunt, who described the craft as a Viking raft or pontoon bridge, and a second full-scale re-excavation in 1973 undertaken by the National Maritime Museum (McGrail 1981), the 'raft' is now accepted as a sewn-plank boat. A series of radiocarbon assays dates it to *c* 825–760 cal BC, and this is therefore the youngest of the sewn-plank boats (*cf* Switsur in McGrail 1981).

At Brigg, the floodplain of the Ancholme narrows to *c* 400 m and this narrowing provided the natural place to cross the river. Around the time of the sinking of the craft, the Ancholme floodplain around Brigg had become inundated with brackish water and, as a

consequence of the sea-level rise, the river had become tidal. The shore vegetation included expanses of reed (*Phragmites communis*), whilst insect analysis indicates that the 'raft' itself was abandoned at or around the high water mark of spring tides. A flat-bottomed 'raft' would have been able to take the ground on a falling tide and would have been especially useful for inland and inshore waters, but was unlikely to function well in open water; however, alternative interpretations exist on the reconstructed hull, suggesting that the Brigg 'raft' may have been a rounded craft in the then long tradition of building seafaring sewn-plank boats (Roberts 1992; 2004b). No other information on the immediate context of the 'raft' was recorded but a number of contemporary artefacts have been found over the years at this natural constriction of the Ancholme valley. These include a Late Bronze Age socketed axe, a leaf-shaped spearhead, a polished stone axehead and a stone battle-axe, pottery, human and animal bones and a bronze pin also of Late Bronze Age date (Davey 1973; May 1976, 112–114; Van de Noort 2004b).

The cultural landscape of the Brigg 'raft' includes ample evidence for activity around 1000 cal BC, but is devoid of any funerary monuments of Neolithic or Bronze Age date. A Late Bronze Age or Early Iron Age trackway was found close to the 'raft', and was dated to 930–350 cal BC (Godwin and Wills 1960). The limited excavations did not establish whether this west–east orientated track offered access to or across the River Ancholme. A very large logboat was discovered in 1886 less than 100 m to the east of the 'raft' and somewhat confusingly known as the Brigg boat. Early radiocarbon dating provides it with a date range of 1260–800 cal BC. These findings have led commentators to conclude that the natural constriction of the Ancholme floodplain at Brigg had functioned from ancient times as a crossing point.

The contextualised sewn-plank boats

The contextualisation of the 10 sewn-plank boats from England and Wales suggest that the boats dated to before *c* 1500 cal BC were perceived rather differently from those dated to after 1500 cal BC. Of the earlier group, comprising F3, F2, F1, Kilnsea, Caldicot 1 and Dover, none is associated with ritual depositions (although alternative views for the Dover boat exist), and the context of several craft suggest that the remains can be linked to boat-building or repairs. Furthermore, for the boat sites from where seagoing journeys may have been undertaken (Kilnsea, Caldicot and Dover), earlier 'ancestral' monuments existed within their immediate landscape setting. Of the later group, comprising the boats from Testwood Lakes, Caldicot 2, Goldcliff and the Brigg 'raft', all were associated with ritual deposition, and all had fragments reused within structures crossing rivers (although the Brigg 'raft' was only found near a trackway). There were no earlier monuments in the landscapes of the Testwood Lakes, Goldcliff or Brigg boats (*see* Table 11.2).

In terms of ritual of travel, this suggests that during the Early Bronze Age seafaring was undertaken with clear reference to the ancestors as exemplified in the ancestral monuments, but that the boats themselves were not considered ritual objects or ritually produced, as indicated by the absence of ritual deposits at North Ferriby and Caldicot 1. Contrastingly, the re-use of boat fragments in the Middle and Late Bronze Age should be understood in the context of the structured deposition and burial of raw materials, waste and human remains, reflecting the idioms of transformation and regeneration which are well established for this period (*cf* Brück 2001).

Other evidence for the ritual of travel in prehistoric Europe

The incorporation of the fragments of sewn-plank boats from Testwood Lakes, Caldicot 2 and Goldcliff into structures that enabled travel across water or wetlands is no surprise, and that this incorporation is understood as the structural deposition/reuse of the craft is no mere speculation. On the contrary, when contextualising this evidence within the greater body of prehistoric water crossings, it is apparent that travel by whatever means may have been accompanied by ritual actions, or that the crossing of water and wetlands may have primarily been understood as ritual components of travel. This is not the place to offer a comprehensive review of the archaeological evidence of the ritual of travel. However, even a quick overview of the evidence from wetlands, where the remains of wooden trackways and bridges have survived and where we have therefore unequivocal evidence of forms of travel, shows that rituals have accompanied journeys from at least the early Neolithic through to the late Iron Age.

For example, in the early Neolithic period, objects were deposited alongside the Sweet Track in the Somerset Levels, dated to 3807/6 BC, including an unhafted and unused polished jadeite axe from central Europe, flint arrowheads and axes, pottery, yew pins, a broken pot filled with hazelnuts, a fragment of a bow, an arrow shaft, a wooden bowl and an object that has been interpreted as a child's toy axe of oak, but which may alternatively be seen as a (votive) token (Coles and Coles 1986). From Bourtanger Moor in the eastern Netherlands, the deposition of artefacts such as the wooden wheels and cart fragments beneath and alongside the Neolithic trackways (most famously the Nieuw Dordrecht trackway, dated to *c* 2900–2450 cal BC), express another aspect of the ritual of travel (*eg* Van der Sanden 2001). For the Bronze Age period, there are votive deposits at Britain's oldest bridge, at Testwood Lake, from where a rapier was found, and on the Crouch estuary in Essex, a Late Bronze Age wooden causeway was associated with two deliberately placed human skulls (Wilkinson and Murphy 1995). At Islandmagrath on the Fergus estuary, a Late Bronze Age wooden trackway was located near the findspot of a gold bracelet (O'Sullivan 2001, 125–128). For the Iron Age, ritually placed deposits have been found at the trackways at Fiskerton in Lincolnshire, and in the Bourtanger Moor, the first century BC Valtherbrug, a 12 km long trackway with adjacent deposits including four bog bodies, all more or less contemporary with the track, at least five querns, and wagons or parts of wagons (Van der Sanden 2001; *see also* Van de Noort and O'Sullivan 2006, 45–55, for an extended discussion on this topic).

There is also a much larger body of objects, especially bronze artefacts, and human skulls from many rivers and wetlands which have been understood as 'votive deposits in wet places' (*eg* Bradley 1990), but many of these may have been linked to crossings, with or without the assistance of wooden bridges and structures that may not have survived.

Indeed, many of the concentrations of such votive deposits were to be found at crossings, including the one across the River Ancholme at Brigg where the 'raft' was found, and one cannot help but wonder whether there is more to the specific locales chosen for the votive depositions than simply presenting gifts to the gods who resided in wet places (Davey 1973). More recent research by Stocker and Everson (2003) in the Witham valley in Lincolnshire, offers an exceptional example of the longevity of the use of specific locales for crossing this river and its floodplain, in this case stretching from the Bronze Age (marking these crossing points with barrow cemeteries), through the Iron Age and Roman period (commemorated with metal deposits, and possibly with fragments of logboats at Fiskerton; Field and Parker Pearson 2003), through to the high medieval period (when important monasteries mark the crossing points).

Alongside the ritual depositions that can be observed alongside trackways and bridges, European prehistory also offers us an extended display of boats and boat-shaped sites and images, as already observed by Grinsell (1940). The first category of archaeological evidence includes the depiction of boats and wagons or carts in the rock art of Scandinavia, and of the ships on bronzes (eg Kaul 1998; 2004). Over 10,000 boat images in the Bohüslan/Vestfold region alone suggests that the journeys undertaken by boats were of great significance and required some sort of commemoration, materially represented in rock carvings (eg Coles 1993; 2000). The second category is the use of (real or specially made) boats in burials, from the Early Bronze Age boat-shaped coffin at Gristhorpe and Loose Howe in Yorkshire to the (Scandinavian Iron Age) boat burials of Slusegaard, Sutton Hoo, Gokstad, Oseberg and other sites (Grinsell 1940; Elgee and Elgee 1949; and contributions by Crumlin-Pedersen, Müller-Wille and Carver in Crumlin-Pedersen and Munch (eds) 1995). Finally, a third category comprises the metaphorical use of boat-shapes in the use of grave settings, such as the 'stone ships' on Gotland and elsewhere in Scandinavia (Capelle 1995). These three categories commemorated in various forms the importance of travel, and by extension expressing something of the significance of geographical distance.

Conclusion: The ritual of travel in prehistoric Europe

Although the previous section offered only a glimpse of ritual aspects of travel, it is evident that suggestion that the sewn-plank boat remains were (re-)used in ritual contexts is not out of the ordinary. Indeed, the link between travel (and especially travel by boat) and its metaphorical significance is a long-standing theme in archaeology, as exemplified by the quote from Leslie Grinsell from 1940 presented at the beginning of this paper. The analysis of the contexts of sewn-plank boat remains have led to a number of assertions about the function of the Bronze Age sewn-plank boats from England and Wales, including the Dover boat (eg Van de Noort 2006). This included the assumptions that sewn-plank boats were used for seafaring, and that this seafaring in the Early Bronze Age enabled the directional acquisition of exotic goods within developing elite networks. The nature of seafaring changed in the Middle and Late Bronze Age and 'down-the-line' exchange of goods became the norm. Sewn-plank boat fragments in this period have been found in secondary contexts, incorporated in bridges, jetties or trackways at Testwood Lake, Caldicot and Goldcliff, and these have been explained as befitting a period where the concepts of transformation and regeneration are represented in many other deposits as well (eg Brück 2001).

This paper has presented the greatest contextual detail on all the known sewn-plank boats to date. It has also placed this evidence in the context of the ritual aspects of travel in prehistoric Europe, showing that objects (and knowledge) obtained from distant parts have been valued within a ritual sense (as evidenced by structured deposits, boat image carvings, boat burials and boat-shaped stone settings) from at least the Early Neolithic onwards. The enduring ritual of travel can, in outline, be explained by returning to Mary Helms' (1988) work on the significance of geographical distance and that for much of the prehistoric period, a metaphorical link existed between geographical/vertical distance and time, or horizontal distance. Thus to travel in prehistory meant in one way or another to reach into the 'other world'.

What the detailed study of the sewn-plank boats implies is that the perception of what this 'other world' was changed during the second millennium BC. During the period up to *c* 1500 cal BC, this 'other world' that could be metaphorically visited on long journeys was primarily the world of the ancestors. This is supported by the ancestral monuments within the landscape contexts of the early Bronze Age boats, especially Kilnsea, Caldicot 1 and Dover, and the deposition of exotic goods such as the jade axe, or artefacts linked directly to travel such as wagon parts and wheels, alongside trackways. In other words, the ritual significance of travel in this period was to connect to the ancestors.

In the period after *c* 1500 cal BC, the perception of this 'other world' seems to have been the earth as a final resting place of the recently deceased, as implied by the inferences made that the incorporation of sewn-plank boat fragments into structures that enabled travel and crossing of wet places links to the concepts of transformation and regeneration. The use of boats and boat-settings in funerary behaviour and deposition of bog-bodies alongside trackways in the later period, seem to reinforce the notion that the perception of the importance of travel and its ritual treatment facilitated the supposed voyage of the dead to the 'other world'.

List of references

Barber, M 2001 'A time and a place for Bronze', in J Brück (ed), *Bronze Age Landscapes: Tradition and Transformation,* Oxford: Oxbow Books, 161–169

Barrett, J 1994 *Fragment of Antiquity: An Archaeology of Social Life in Britain, 2900–1200 BC,* Oxford (UK) and Cambridge (USA): Blackwell

Bayliss, A, Groves, C, McCormac, C, Bronk Ramsey, C, Baillie, M, Brown, D, Cook, G and Switsur, R 2004 'Dating', in P Clark (ed), *The Dover Bronze Age Boat,* London: English Heritage, 250–255

Beck, C and Shennan, S 1991 *Amber in prehistoric Britain,* Oxford: Oxbow Books

Bell, M 1992 'Field survey and excavation at Goldcliff, 1992', in M Bell (ed), *Severn Estuary Levels Research Committee Annual Report,* 15–29

Bell, M 1993 'Intertidal Archaeology at Goldcliff in the Severn Estuary', in J Coles, V Fenwick and G Hutchinson (eds), *A Spirit of Enquiry; Essays for Ted Wright,* Exeter: WARP, The Nautical Archaeology Society and the National Maritime Museum, 9–13

Bell, M, Caseldine, A and Neumann, H 2000 *Prehistoric Intertidal Archaeology in the Welsh Severn Estuary,* York: Council of British Archaeology Research Report, **120**

Bown, P, Bristow, C, Burnett, J, Clark, P, Gibson, A, de Silva, N, Williams, D, Wilson, T and Young, J 2004

'Other artefacts from the site', in P Clark (ed), *The Dover Bronze Age Boat,* London: English Heritage, 211–228

Bradley, R and Gordon, K 1988 'Human skulls from the river Thames, their dating and significance', *Antiquity,* **62 (236)**, 503–509

Bradley, R 1984 *The social foundations of prehistoric Britain,* London

Bradley, R 1990 *The Passage of Arms,* Cambridge: Cambridge University Press

Broodbank, C 1993 'Ulysses without sails: trade, distance, knowledge and power in the early Cyclades', *World Archaeology,* **24**, 315–331

Brück, J 2000 'Settlement, landscape and social identity: the Early–Middle Bronze Age transition in Wessex, Sussex and the Thames Valley', *Oxford Journal of Archaeology,* **19**, 273–300

Brück, J 2001 'Body metaphors and technologies of transformation in the English Middle and Late Bronze Age', in J Brück (ed), *Bronze Age Landscapes: Tradition and Transformation,* Oxford: Oxbow Books, 149–160

Champion, T 2004 'The deposition of the boat', in P Clark (ed), *The Dover Bronze Age Boat,* London: English Heritage, 276–281

Chapman, H and Gearey, B 2004 'The social context of seafaring in the Bronze Age revisited', *World Archaeology,* **36**, 452–458

Clark, P 2004a 'Discussion', in P Clark (ed), *The Dover Bronze Age Boat,* London: English Heritage, 305–322

Clark, P (ed) 2004b *The Dover Bronze Age Boat,* London: English Heritage

Clark, P 2004c 'The Dover Boat ten years after its discovery', in P Clark (ed), *The Dover Bronze Age Boat in Context: Society and Water Transport in Prehistoric Europe,* Oxford: Oxbow Books, 1–12

Coles, B and Coles, J 1986 *Sweet Track to Glastonbury,* London: Thames and Hudson

Coles, J 1993 'Boats on the rocks', in J Coles, V Fenwick and G Hutchinson (eds), *A Spirit of Enquiry; Essays for Ted Wright,* Exeter: WARP, The Nautical Archaeology Society and the National Maritime Museum, 23–31

Coles, J 2000 *Patterns in a Rocky Land: Rock Carvings in South-West Uppland, Sweden,* Uppsala: Department of Archaeology and Ancient History

Creighton, J 1990 'The Humber frontier in the first century AD', in S Ellis and D Crowther (eds), *Humber Perspectives: a Region through the Ages,* Hull: Hull University Press, 182–198

Crumlin-Pedersen, O 2006 'The Dover Boat – a reconstruction case-study', *The International Journal of Nautical Archaeology,* **35**, 58–71

Crumlin-Pedersen, O and Munch, B (eds) 1995 *The ship as symbol: in prehistoric and medieval Scandinavia: papers from an international research seminar at the Danish National Museum, Copenhagen, 5th–7th May 1994,* Copenhagen: National Museum of Denmark, Department of Archaeology and Early History

Davey, P 1973 'Bronze Age metalwork from Lincolnshire', *Archaeologia,* **104**, 51–127

Elgee, F and Elgee, H 1949 'An Early Bronze Age burial in a boat-shaped wooden coffin from north-east Yorkshire', *Proceedings of the Prehistoric Society,* **15**, 87–106

Field, N and Parker Pearson, M 2003 *Fiskerton: An Iron*

Age timber causeway with Iron Age and Roman votive offerings: the 1981 excavations, Oxford: Oxbow Books

Fitzpatrick, A, Ellis, C and Allen, M 1996 'Bronze Age 'jetties' or causeways at Testwood lakes, Hampshire, Great Britain', *NewsWARP*, **20**, 19–22

Godwin, H and Willis, E 1960 Cambridge University natural radiocarbon measurements III, *Radiocarbon*, **3**, 60–76

Grinsell, L 1941 'The boat of the dead in the Bronze Age', *Antiquity*, **14 (60)**, 360–369

Harding, A 2000 *European Societies in the Bronze Age*, Cambridge: Cambridge University Press

Harding, A and Lee, G 1987 *Henge Monuments and Related Sites of Great Britain: air photographic evidence and catalogue*, Oxford: British Archaeological Report (British series), **175**

Helms, M 1988 *Ulysses' Sail: An Ethnographic Odyssey of Power, Knowledge, and Geographical Distance*, Princeton: Princeton University Press

Kaul, F 1998 *Ships on Bronzes: A Study in Bronze Age Religion and Iconography*, Copenhagen: National Museum of Denmark

Kaul, F 2004 'Social and religious perceptions of the ship in Bronze Age Europe', in P Clark (ed), *The Dover Bronze Age Boat in Context: Society and Water Transport in Prehistoric Europe*, Oxford: Oxbow Books, 122–137

Keeley, H, Allison, E, Branch, N, Cameron, N, Dobinson, S, Ellis, I, Ellison, P, Fairbairn, A, Green, C, Hunter, R, Lee, J, Locker, A, Lowe, J, Palmer, A, Robinson, E, Stewart, J and Wilkinson, K 2004 'The environmental evidence', in P Clark (ed), *The Dover Bronze Age Boat*, London: English Heritage, 229–249

Kossina, G 1911 *Die Herkunft der Germanen*, Leibzig: Kabitzsch

Kristiansen, K 2004 'Sea faring voyages and rock art ships', in P Clark (ed), *The Dover Bronze Age Boat in Context: Society and Water Transport in Prehistoric Europe*, Oxford: Oxbow Books, 111–121

Kristiansen and Thomas 2005 *The Rise of Bronze Age Society. Travels, Transmissions and Transformations*, Cambridge: Cambridge University Press

Lynch, F, Aldhouse-Green, S and Davies, J 2000 *Prehistoric Wales*, Stroud: Tempus

Marsden, P 2004 'Description of the boat', in P Clark (ed), *The Dover Bronze Age Boat*, London: English Heritage, 32–95

May, J 1976 *Prehistoric Lincolnshire*, Lincoln: History of Lincolnshire Committee

McGrail, S 1981 *The Brigg 'raft' and her prehistoric environment*, Oxford: British Archaeological Reports (British Series), **89**, and Greenwich: National Maritime Museum Archaeological Series, **6**

McGrail, S 1997 'The boat fragments', in N Nayling and A Caseldine, *Excavations at Caldicot, Gwent: Bronze Age palaeochannels in the Lower Nedern Valley*, Council for British Archaeology Research Report, **108**, York, 210–217

McGrail, S 2000 'The boat planks', in M Bell, A Caseldine and H Neumann (eds), *Prehistoric Intertidal Archaeology in the Welsh Severn Estuary*, 77, Council for British Archaeology Research Report, **120**, York

McGrail, S 2004 'North-west European seagoing boats before AD 400', in P Clark (ed), *The Dover Bronze Age Boat in Context: Society and Water Transport in Prehistoric Europe*, Oxford: Oxbow Books, 51–66

McGrail, S 2001 *Boats of the World*, Oxford: Oxford University Press

Millett, M and McGrail, S 1987 'The archaeology of the Hasholme logboat', *Archaeological Journal*, **144**, 69–155

Nayling, N and Caseldine, A 1997 *Excavations at Caldicot, Gwent: Bronze Age Palaeochannels in the Lower Nedern Valley*, Council for British Archaeology Research Report, **108**, York

Needham, S 1996 'Chronology and periodisation in the British Bronze Age', *Acta Archaeologica*, **67**, 121–140

Needham, S 2000 'Power pulses across a cultural divide: Armorica and Wessex', *Proceedings of the Prehistoric Society*, **66**, 151–194

O'Sullivan, A 2001 *Foragers, Farmers and Fishers in a Coastal Landscape: An Intertidal Archaeological Survey of the Shannon Estuary*, Dublin: Royal Irish Academy, Discovery Programme Monographs, **4**

Parfitt, K and Champion, T 2004 'The boat in its cultural setting', in P Clark (ed), *The Dover Bronze Age Boat*, London: English Heritage, 264–275

Parfitt, K 2004 'Discovery and excavation', in P Clark (ed), *The Dover Bronze Age Boat*, London: English Heritage, 9–22

Pryor, F 2004 'Some thoughts as boats as Bronze Age artefacts', in P Clark (ed), *The Dover Bronze Age Boat in Context: Society and Water Transport in Prehistoric Europe*, Oxford: Oxbow Books, 31–34

Roberts, O 1992 'The Brigg 'raft' reassessed as a round bilge Bronze Age boat', *International Journal of Nautical Archaeology*, **21**, 245–258

Roberts, O 2004a 'Reconstruction and performance', in P Clark (ed), *The Dover Bronze Age Boat*, London: English Heritage, 189–210

Roberts, O 2004b 'Round the headland or over the horizon? An examination of evidence for British prehistoric efforts to construct a seaworthy boat', in P Clark (ed), *The Dover Bronze Age Boat in Context: Society and Water Transport in Prehistoric Europe*, Oxford: Oxbow Books, 35–50

Rowlands, M 1980 'Kinship, alliance and exchange in the European Bronze Age', in J Barrett and R Bradley (eds), *Settlement and Society in the British Later Bronze Age*, Oxford: British Archaeological Reports (British Series), **83**, 15–55

Shennan, S 1982 'Ideology, change and the European Early Bronze Age', in I Hodder (ed), *Symbolic and Structural Archaeology*, Cambridge: Cambridge University Press, 155–161

Shennan, S 1986 'Interaction and change in the third millennium BC western and central Europe', in C Renfrew and J Cherry (eds), *Peer Polity Interaction and Socio-Political Change*, Cambridge: University Press, 137–148

Stocker, D and Everson, P 2003 'The straight and narrow way: Fenland causeways and the conversion of the landscape in the Witham valley, Lincolnshire', in M Carver (ed), *The Cross goes North: processes of conversion in Northern Europe AD 300–1300*, York: Woodbridge Medieval Press, 271–288

Trigger, B 1990 *A History of Archaeological Thought*, *Cambridge*: Cambridge University Press

Thropp, J 1887 'An ancient raft found at Brigg, Lincolnshire', *Association of Architectural Societies Reports and Papers*, **19**, 95–97

Van de Noort, R 2003 'An ancient seascape: the social context of seafaring in the Early Bronze Age', *World Archaeology*, **35**, 404–415

Van de Noort, R 2004a 'The Humber, its sewn-plank boats, their context and the significance of it all', in P Clark (ed), *The Dover Bronze Age Boat in Context: Society and Water Transport in Prehistoric Europe*, Oxford: Oxbow Books, 90–98

Van de Noort, R 2004b *The Humber Wetlands: The Archaeology of a Dynamic Landscape*, London: Windgather Press

Van de Noort, R 2006 'Argonauts of the North Sea: A social maritime archaeology for the 2nd millennium BC', *Proceedings of the Prehistoric Society*, **72**, 267–287

Van de Noort, R and Fletcher, W 2000 'Bronze age human-ecodynamics in the Humber estuary', in G Bailey, R Charles and N Winder (eds), *Human Ecodynamics, Symposia of the Association for Environmental Archaeology No 19*, Oxford: Oxbow Books, 47–54

Van de Noort, R, Middleton, R, Foxon, A and Bayliss, A 1999 'The 'Kilnsea boat', and some implications from the discovery of England's oldest plank boat remains', *Antiquity*, **73 (279)**, 131–135

Van de Noort, R and O'Sullivan, A 2006 *Rethinking Wetland Archaeology*, London: Duckworth

Van der Sanden, W 2001 'From stone pavement to temple – ritual structures from wet contexts in the province of Drenthe, the Netherlands', in B Purdy (ed), *Enduring Records: the environmental and cultural heritage of wetlands*, Oxbow Books, Oxford, 132–147

Wilkinson, T and Murphy, P 1995 *The Archaeology of the Essex Coast: The Hullbridge Survey*, East Anglian Archaeology, **52**, Norwich

Wright, C and Wright, E 1939 'Submerged boat at North Ferriby', *Antiquity*, **13 (51)**, 349–354

Wright, E 1990 *The Ferriby boats: Seacraft of the Bronze Age*, London: Routledge

Wright, E and Churchill, D 1965 'The boats from North Ferriby, Yorkshire', *Proceedings of the Prehistoric Society*, **31**, 1–24

Wright, E, Hedges, R, Bayliss, A and Van de Noort, R 2001 'New AMS dates for the Ferriby boats; a contribution to the origin of seafaring', *Antiquity*, **75 (290)**, 726–234

12. In his hands and in his head: The Amesbury Archer as a metalworker

Andrew Fitzpatrick

Figure 12.1 Selected north-west European sites mentioned in the text

Introduction

Living at the beginning of the Bronze Age in Britain, in what can be called the Copper Age or Chalcolithic, the Amesbury Archer had wide ranging connections. He was one of the first metalworkers in Britain, and he came from far away in continental Europe. These two things help to explain something of why he

was afforded the most well-furnished burial of his age.

The Amesbury Archer

The man

The man we now call the Amesbury Archer lived between about 2,500 and 2,300 years BC (2470–2280 cal BC: OxA-13541; 3895±32 BP). He was buried 5 km south-east of Stonehenge (Fig 12.1) in a small, below ground, timber, chamber that may have been surmounted by a low burial mound. Standing 1.75 m tall, the Archer lived to be 35 to 45 years old, but for much of his life he had been disabled because of a traumatic injury to his left knee.

At his death, his mourners buried him in the way that was typical for the Bell Beaker burial rite which was common across much of Europe. He was placed on his left side in a flexed position, slightly curled up as if he was asleep, with his head to the north-east (Fig 12.2). The offerings placed beside him – the accoutrements of a hunter or warrior and other symbols of status – are also typical of the time. Archery is represented by two stone wristguards and many flint arrowheads that are the equivalent of a quiver of arrows. Other offerings included two gold basket-shaped ornaments, perhaps used as hair tress ornaments, three copper knives, five Bell Beakers, four boars' tusks, many flint tools but also flint flakes or blanks for making new tools, and tools of stone and of antler, including an antler tool for pressure-flaking flint. A black stone, a so-called cushion stone, was a metalworker's tool.

These objects are all typical of their time. What is atypical is the quantity of the grave goods that the Archer was furnished with by his mourners. His burial is also one of the very earliest in the Bell Beaker burial rite, a rite found across much of temperate Europe, yet to have been found in Britain (Fitzpatrick 2003; in preparation).

The 'Companion'

A younger man was buried close to the Archer. Known as the 'Archer's Companion' and dated to 2460–2140 cal BC (OxA-13562; 3892±38 BP), this man had lived to be 20–25 years old. In his grave, which was smaller than the Archer's, were some flint tools, a boar's tusk, and a pair of gold hair tress ornaments similar to those with the Archer. This young man was also apparently of high status.

Although DNA analyses are not currently possible, it has been possible to demonstrate that the two men were related as their feet share an unusual non-metric trait in which bones that are not usually articulated are (the calcanea and naviculars have coalition defects). This trait can only have been transferred genetically.

The radiocarbon dates, though statistically indistinguishable, hint that this second burial is slightly later than the Archer's. Whether the men were brothers, cousins, or father and son is not known. In some way, though, something of the Archer's status had been passed to the younger man but extensive excavations have demonstrated there were no other burials close by.

Copper Age connections

Oxygen isotope analysis of the enamel of one of his molar teeth has demonstrated that as a child the Archer lived in a colder climate than that of Britain today, in central Europe or Scandinavia. The area may be refined by strontium isotope analysis of the tooth enamel. This excludes the northern tracts of the distribution, while archaeological evidence, assuming that the Archer came from a cultural milieu that was using Bell Beaker materials (*cf* Czebreszuk and Kryvaltsevich 2003; Nicolis 2001), points to an origin towards the Alpine region, an area in which metallurgy was long established. In contrast, his 'Companion' could have been raised in southern England. It would, however, be mistaken to think to think that the

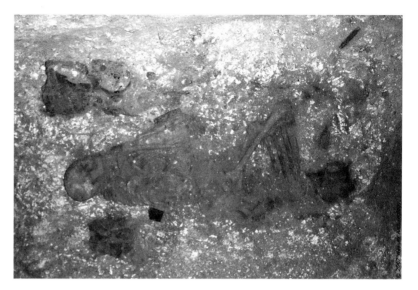

Figure 12.2 The burial of the Amesbury Archer as excavated

Amesbury Archer made his journey alone, or these two burials are those of all the people in this family group.

Relatively small scale mobility or migration within and between Bell Beaker communities has been suggested in Bavaria in central Europe (Price *et al* 1998; 2004; Heyd *et al* 2002–03). Rather longer journeys, either within Britain and Ireland or neighbouring parts of continental Europe, have also been demonstrated in the case of the Boscombe Bowmen whose grave was found less than 1 km from that of the Archer (Evans *et al* 2006), but the Amesbury Archer provides the first example of people travelling great distances at this time. At this time horse riding was apparently a novelty, and, on the basis of the evidence presently available, the Channel would have had to have been crossed in a dug out canoe.

But what is the context of this remarkable story, which might be considered a heroic tale, near the start of the Copper Age in Britain?

The Beaker Folk

As we have seen, the burial rite and the objects buried with the Archer were typical of the time. A similar rite and comparable objects are found in widely separated areas in parts of central, western and Mediterranean Europe. How to explain this similarity in objects, and to a lesser extent mortuary practices in which an idealised representation of a male warrior is often portrayed, has vexed archaeologists for generations (*cf* Harrison 1980). And it continues to do so (*eg* Nicolis 2001; Czebreszuk 2004a;

Guilaine 2007).The principal interpretations may be outlined briefly.

The Three Age system and the importance of the introduction of different metals still underpins the way in which understandings of European prehistory are organised. In particular, the importance of the adoption or acceptance of metallurgy as a factor that caused social change and as a device in increasing social differentiation are still – rightly or wrongly – emphasised in many works. The use of the term Copper Age does little to alter this. It is clear, though, that over much of temperate Europe metallurgy predates the appearance of the 'Beaker Folk' and that even at a later date, metallurgy was not necessarily introduced by groups using the Bell Beaker 'Set' of objects of the types that were placed in the Archer's grave (*eg* Vander Linden 2004, 43; 2006).

Earlier interpretations among Anglophone scholars of the 'Beaker Folk' can be divided into three broad camps. In the first the explanation is sought through ethnicity and immigration. In the second the explanation is sought through status, and in the third it is sought through beliefs (Brodie 1998, 45–48)

In the ethnic hypothesis, Bell Beaker assemblages (sometimes described as 'packages' of material) were taken as symbols of ethnicity and thought to mark the arrival of immigrant 'Beaker People.' Although this interpretation fell out of fashion in some scholarly traditions, it can now be clearly demonstrated that Bell Beaker funerary practices were indeed quite different to what they succeeded and may be regarded as intrusive, leading to a similar conclusion but arrived at by a very different route (*eg* Heyd 2001).

The idea of the travel and migration of individuals and small groups using the Bell Beaker 'Set' of materials has been steadily rehabilitated in more recent works of synthesis (*eg* Brodie 2001; Heyd 2001; Salanova 2001, 96). Now, irrespective of interpretive fashions, isotope analyses studies such as that of the Amesbury Archer and the Boscombe Bowmen, have demonstrated this mobility did take place.

In the second hypothesis, Bell Beaker assemblages were seen as being associated in some way with the appearance across Europe of more individualising status hierarchies or ideologies (Shennan 1976). This idea, popularised by Gordon Childe's conception of the Bronze Age (1930), has been developed in models based either on prestige goods (*eg* Thorpe and Richards 1984) or on symbols of status (*eg* Barrett 1994). What can be termed a 'ranked society,' where societies are led by local chieftains or tribal leaders, is often implied.

The third interpretation, of beliefs, appears in a number of guises and in many ways further develops the status interpretation. Bell Beakers have been seen as representing a cult package in which Bell Beakers symbolise male drinking rituals, participation in which was restricted to certain groups (Sherratt 1987; Rojo-Guerra *et al* 2006). It has also been suggested that the package of bow and arrow, knife, and beaker, is a symbolic hunting set providing for the hunting of big game, its' ritual killing, and the ritual drinking of its blood. This hunt may have been undertaken in either the world of the living or the dead (Case 2004a; 2004b).

Lastly, some have sought to explain these similarities through, or as, a 'phenomenon' and to interpret the material remains as a 'Set'. For example, 'we interpret the Set as the remains of a new knowledge, an ideology' (Strahm 2004a, 122; *cf* Salanova 2000, 15–17). This Bell Beaker network or phenomenon may also have allowed for the use of some form of pidgin language or even a proto-Celtic language (Gallay 2001).

All these hypotheses, which are not mutually exclusive, have some appeal, appearing to explain certain aspects or manifestations in certain times or places, with Bell Beaker-using groups often being considered as the first socially differentiated and male-dominated European people. But none are entirely convincing as pan-European explanations (*eg* Brodie 2001), probably because there is no single explanation. It is clear that there is greater similarity between the evidence from single burials, which enact idealised representations of social identities, than that from settlements. Some scholars therefore identify difference and diversity (Vander Linden 2004a; 2006; 2007) or, put another way, that which is 'similar but different' (Czebreszuk 2004b).

In Britain, the burial of the Amesbury Archer is one of the earliest, if not *the* earliest, Bell Beaker graves yet found and he appears to have had at least some metalworking skills. Even if there is, as yet, little agreement as to the exact meanings of the Bell Beaker phenomenon, it is still important to recognise just how novel these new materials and the burial rite were when compared to those of the Late Neolithic – and perhaps Chalcolithic – societies in Britain. Needham has described this time as one of 'Beaker as [a] circumscribed, exclusive culture, *c* 2500–2350 cal BC' and 'entirely [continental] European in inspiration' (2005, 209), echoing a similar point made about the earliest Bell Beakers in parts of central Europe (Shennan 1976, 233).

The introduction of metalworking

Sources of copper are not evenly distributed across Europe; much of central and north-western Europe has almost none (Strahm 1994, Abb. 27). Many areas to the south and east that had ready access to copper, practised metallurgy from much earlier dates, hundreds or even thousands of years earlier. One of these regions was the possible homeland of the Amesbury Archer; the Alpine region (Strahm 2004b; 2007).

In one of the most elegant attempts to explain this apparent discontinuity, Brodie suggested that for centuries there was a frontier zone, a 'Chalcolithic frontier', between these two areas that either had ready access to copper sources or those areas that did not. He suggested that two important things eventually passed across this frontier. From the south-east came metallurgy, which was adopted in the north-west. From the north-west came the spread of certain Bell Beaker pottery styles into central Europe. Drawing on the evidence of the isotope studies in Bavaria (Price *et al* 1988), the transfer of these skills is suggested to have been enabled by marriage and alliances.

Brodie suggested that the spread of potting styles to the east reflects the marriage of women from communities outside the Chalcolithic frontier into communities inside it (1997; 2001, 492–495). Movement in the opposite direction is symbolised by the introduction of metallurgy, which it is suggested, indicates the movement of skilled metalworkers. These were not the Childean prospectors or itinerant smiths often envisaged in the introduction of metallurgy (Childe 1930, 9), but metalworkers who were invited into a community (Brodie 1997, 306; Brodie 2001, 494). As Brodie put it; 'there was more information embodied in the head and hands of metalworker than embedded in the

substance of a thousand inanimate objects' (2001, 494).

The evidence is slight, and the situation perhaps more nuanced. Metallurgy often appears to have been adopted quite rapidly even if some areas with apparently ready access to copper, for example Bohemia and Moravia, did not choose to adopt do so until the late Corded Ware/early Bell Beaker periods. This may tell us something of the significance of ascribed to metallurgy in the Bell Beaker 'Set' in temperate Europe, and this is not necessarily the same as the introduction of metallurgy.

The emphasis placed by Brodie on the exchange of women as marriage partners might be doubted. Instead, most writers would emphasise the primacy of metallurgy, especially in northern and western Europe (*eg* Needham 2005, 207 208). This was not just a 'practical knowledge' (*pace* Brodie 1997, 306), and the participation in alliances may be reflected in the high status that was, as we will see, afforded to metal workers. Although Brodie doubted whether inter-marriage could account for the introduction of the Bell Beaker 'Set' (or culture) into Britain and Ireland (Brodie 1997, 311), his observation that alliances, and marriages, are flexible institutions that might seek innovation (2001, 494), provided an important insight into the introduction and acceptance of metalworking (*cf* Vander Linden 2007).

As we have seen, this had to involve the movement of people or groups with metalworking knowledge and skills. As the case of the Amesbury Archer, who is entirely European and with wide ranging connections, shows, those journeys could cover long distances in a short time, challenging the idea of a static 'Chalcolithic frontier' or steady and slow diffusion. The journey of the Amesbury Archer is consistent with the discontinuous distribution of groups using the Bell Beaker 'Set' and suggests a series of fluid and rapidly changing scenarios for the adoption of metallurgy.

The origins of metallurgy in Britain and Ireland

The Amesbury Archer stands near the beginning of the metal ages in Britain. In the full Bronze Age in Britain, as elsewhere in Europe, access to and control of ores, ingots

Figure 12.3 The cushion stone buried with the Amesbury Archer. Length 84 mm

and objects is frequently seen as a source of power and status. Metal itself is often thought of as possessing magical properties (*eg* Cowie 1988).

The earliest metals used in Britain and Ireland were gold and copper (Northover 1999). Evidence for the early prospection of gold, presumably in placer deposits in streams, is very difficult to identify. So too is evidence for manufacture, and currently, there is only the evidence of the objects themselves (Eogan 1994, 1–22; Needham 2002). The situation for copper is different, with several mines known, mainly in western Wales (Timberlake 2001; 2003, 51). However, the earliest known is at Ross Island among the Killarney Lakes of County Kerry in the south-west of Ireland, where a mine and associated work camp have been excavated (O'Brien 2004). The earliest mining of the readily accessible and high grade copper dates to between 2500–2200 BC. At the work camp the mineralised rock was reduced through sorting and crushing and subsequently reduced to metal by roasting and smelting. It is thought that the camp was used almost exclusively for this purpose, perhaps on a seasonal basis.

The Ross Island copper has a high arsenic content and it is suggested that the knowledge and skills necessary to produce this metal may have drawn on expertise from continental Europe. In this regard, it can surely be no coincidence that the pottery from the work camp is of Bell Beaker type. O'Brien is clear; 'copper metallurgy first appeared in Ireland at a relatively advanced level, probably through contacts with metal-using groups on the continent' (2001, 561; *cf* O'Brien 2004, 563–565).

Ross Island is a key site in our understanding of the development of metallurgy in Ireland, Britain and beyond. One point may be emphasised here: no metal objects were found, just a single droplet of smelted raw copper. The objects made from the ores, almost certainly copper axe heads, were manufactured elsewhere. However, the evidence for the manufacture of objects at settlements in most Bell Beaker regions in temperate Europe is slight (*eg* Mille and Bouquet 2004; Simpson *et al* 2006, 139–140; Fig 12.1).

The Archer as a metalworker

Metalworkers' graves in Europe

Assuming that the Amesbury Archer himself had used the cushion stone, or metalworking tool, buried with him (Fig 12.3), he is the earliest Bell Beaker metalworker yet found in Britain. This does not, though, mean that metal was not used before this time, or that there were not earlier metallurgists in Britain.

The Archer's grave is one of a group of almost 30 certain or possible Copper Age graves in central and western Europe that contain metalworking tools made from stone and on this basis they have been identified as the burials of smiths or metalworkers (Moucha 1989; Bátora 2002a; 2002b). The great majority are these burials have Bell Beaker associations, but there are also a few Corded Ware examples that appear to be of approximately the same, or slightly earlier, date (Bertemes and Heyd 2002, 217).

Many of the known Bell Beaker-associated metalworker's burials are from Bavaria, Bohemia, and Moravia and they lie relatively early in their local sequences. In several respects, notably the apparent high status afforded to the dead man by his mourners, the burial of the Amesbury Archer has strong similarities with this group, from which it is a marked outlier. The same is true of the cremation burial from Zwenkau (Sachsen Anhalt) in Germany (Campen 2004). However, the burials with metalworking tools found just across the North Sea in the Netherlands (from Lunteren (Gelderland) and Soesterberg (Utrecht)) (Butler and van der Waals 1966), and perhaps also Beers Gassel (Cujik) II (Noord Brabant); Verwers 1990, 30–31, Afb. 16; Van der Beek, 2004, 171–172, fig. 18), are all slightly later in date than the burial of the Amesbury Archer.

First identified as metalworking tools by Jay Butler and Diderik van der Waals on the basis of the examples from the Lunteren and Soesterberg burials, some of the stone tools are often square or rhomboidal stones, which they called cushion stones. The stones were suggested to be multi-purpose tools that could have 'served as small anvils, hammers, polishing stones, or for a variety of these purposes' (Butler and van der Waals 1966, 63). They are accompanied by hammer stones that are often axe head-shaped and some of these may have been manufactured from polished stone axe heads of Neolithic date.

Several metalworkers' graves have two or three stones, which almost always include a cushion stone and an axe head-shaped hammer and some larger groups of stones are also known (*eg* Bertemes *et al* 2000; Campen 2004). In a number of cases boar's tusks have been found, sometimes in direct association with the stones, leading to the suggestion the tusks were also metalworking tools (Bertemes and Heyd 2002, 217), perhaps used as burnishing or planishing (smoothing) tools used on copper and gold, both of which are soft metals.

A number of graves which – as with the Amesbury Archer – contain a single stone have also been interpreted as those of metalworkers. Caution needs to be exercised in the interpretation of these finds, as the stone may simply have been whetstone (*eg* Moucha 1989, 216; Bartelheim 2002, 34). The identification of single axe head-shaped tools as metalworker's tools, particularly if they were, as has been suggested, made from reworked Neolithic stone axe heads (*eg* Moucha 1989; Müller 1987; Turek 2004) is perhaps less certain (*cf* Lynch 2001), even though an axe head-shaped tool associated with a cushion stone in the well-furnished Bell Beaker burial at Turo-vice (Olomouc) in Moravia (Moucha 1989, 216) has yielded traces of metal (Bertemes and Heyd 2002, 216–217). However, in the case of those graves with cushion stones, this identification may be accepted more readily since these stones are a specialist tool with clear metalworking associations.

These burials are invariably of men and are almost universally considered as being among, if not the, most well-furnished graves in their local context (*eg* Moucha 1989, 216;

Bátora 2002a, 43, 46; Bertemes 2004a, 152–153; Delgado Raack and Risch 2006). This interpretation is often based on the presence of metal objects in these graves, which are highly visible in the archaeological record, and reflects the importance traditionally ascribed to the ownership of metals as means of demon-strating and increasing social differentiation. Some of the Bell Beaker graves, particularly in Moravia, are also early in their regional sequences (*eg* Hájek 1966) and the grave from Kirkhaugh, (Northumberland in England), which contained an All Over Corded Bell Beaker and a gold basket shaped ornament, may also include a cushion stone (Maryon 1946).

In view of the isotope evidence for the Amesbury Archer having grown up in western central Europe, it should be emphasised that it is how metalworkers were symbolised in these central and eastern central European burials that is relevant here, not direct geographical and cultural parallels. The discontinuous distribution of groups using the Bell Beaker 'Set' and the variability of their mortuary practices, for example the rarity of burials with Bell Beakers in north-eastern France (Chambon and Salanova 1996; Salanova 2004, 66–69, fig. 4; 2007, 213–217), means that we do not currently know how metalworkers were symbolised in the mortuary practices of the areas between central Europe and Britain, if at all.

Metalworkers: symbol and signifier

The identification of some individuals in Bell Beaker burials as having been craft specialists – from leather workers to potters – was first systematically set out by Clarke (1970, 260–265) and elaborated on by both Brodie (1997, 303–304; 1998; 2001) and Salanova (1998). Metal workers and skilled artisans are often regarded as having a high status (*eg* Bertemes 2004b, 214; Kristiansen and Larsson 2005, 52–57). While the association between the appearance of Bell Beakers and metallurgy has been overstated, the association was nonetheless important and metals appear to have been ascribed an importance by groups using the Bell Beaker 'Set', particularly in temperate Europe. In some areas where metallurgy was already long established, the status ascribed to metal also seems to change after the Bell Beaker 'Set' was adopted (*eg* Kunst

1997; Ambert 2001; Roussot-Larroque 2004). This hints at something of the characteristics of the Bell Beaker phenomenon.

If the Amesbury Archer ultimately came from the Alpine region, he came from an area in which metalworking was well established. This poses the question why this journey was made then – at about the time that Bell Beaker 'Set' was adopted in that region – and not centuries before? The answers may lie in the ways in which the ideas that were shared by what were apparently widely separated groups using the Bell Beaker 'Set' were linked, and the ways in which the adoption of metallurgy was linked to the movement of people (*cf* Vander Linden 2007, 349).

The appearance of the Bell Beaker 'Set' was broadly contemporary in Britain, Ireland and central Europe. How skilled artisans or crafts people were symbolised in central European burials has been discussed by Turek (2004). Turek divided the crafts represented in burials into an archery package, and a metalworking package. The interpretation of the tools associated with working flint arrowheads and other flint tools was seen as unproblematic by Turek. In considering metalworking, Turek asks what scale of craft specialisation might be anticipated at, or shortly after, the introduction of Bell Beaker metallurgy? He suggested that early copper metallurgy was established on a limited scale; with no evidence of either mass production or craft specialisation. Given the rarity of early metal objects in the archaeological record, he suggests that it is unlikely that the men buried with metalworking tools were full time specialists in metal production.

Instead, Turek suggested that the metalworking tools need not indicate that the man they were buried with was necessarily a smith. Instead they symbolised the control of the new technology and the dead men are seen as having had a privileged access to what is regarded as an esoteric knowledge or exclusive technology, one which is widely regarded as having strong ritual and magical associations (*eg* Cowie 1988; Budd and Taylor 1995; Kristiansen and Larsson 2005, 53–57). Turek suggests that this comes from a particular social category and personal status which, he suggests, allowed the control of what is called 'strategic *technologies* and raw-materials' (2004, 151). A related point is made by Kristiansen and Larsson who suggest that

later in the Bronze Age special tools were added to the grave goods of the elite (2005, 57–58).

Defining identities in mortuary rituals is complex (*eg* Thomas 1991; Sofaer Derevenski 2002; Brück 2004; Healy and Harding 2004) but it is perhaps unnecessary to doubt that the men with whom the metalworker's tools were buried could use them; Turek accepts the presence of tools used to produce arrowheads and other pieces of archery equipment as unproblematic. The practical skills needed to work the soft metals of gold and copper are not sophisticated.

Although it could be argued that more metallurgical knowledge and skills were deployed at extraction and production sites such as Ross Island than in the making of small metal objects such as gold hair ornaments or copper knives, it is the ability to make objects that is consistently represented in the burials of Copper Age and Bronze Age metalworkers (Bertemes 2004b, Delgado Raack and Risch 2006; Belgirono 2002; Bartelheim 2007, 206–207). This appears to reflect a separation between the mining of ores and the production of metal on the one hand, and the manufacture of goods on other, which appears to have been accorded a special status (*cf* Bartelheim 2002, 35).

While the tools symbolise metalworking, they also signify access to the new; of knowledge and materials, and also control over the manufacture and distribution of the finished goods. These were almost invariably small items of jewellery and weaponry; objects of adornment used to symbolise status (Turek 2004; Bartelheim 2007).

In many respects The Amesbury Archer could be seen to embody this interpretation. He has a metalworking tool, more if the boar's tusks are also accepted as metalworking tools, but the metal of the copper knives and maybe also the knives themselves come from northern Spain and western France (Fitzpatrick 2003; Needham in preparation). The gold ornaments buried with him are made from a metal that is probably continental European in origin, but they are made in a style that is insular. Perhaps significantly, the only related finds from continental Europe are from lands that face the Atlantic. In Portugal finds are known from the Estremoz (Évora) area, and Ermegeira (Lisboa), while in France there is

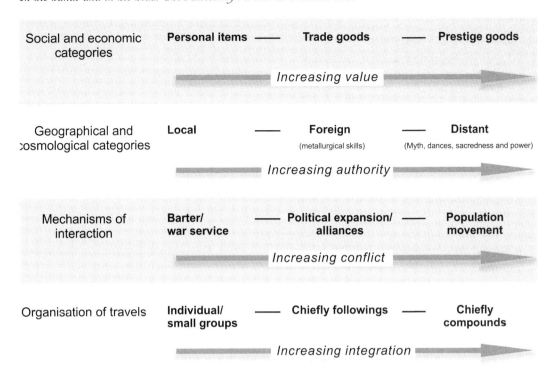

Figure 12.4 Model of processes of interaction and trade (after Kristiansen and Larsson 2005, fig 15)

a find from Armorica at Le Colledic, (Côtes-d'Armor) (O'Connor 2004, 208). The amount of gold required was small and the skills may have been modest, but the *knowledge* of metalworking, access to the metal and control of the distribution of the finished objects within the *chaîne opératoire*, was new, and perhaps priceless.

An Odyssey

At the first Dover Bronze Age Boat conference, Kristian Kristiansen, drawing on the work of Mary Helms (1988; this volume), summarised something of the status that could be accrued by some individuals through travel (Kristiansen 2004). Kristiansen and Larsson have elaborated this in the *The Rise of Bronze Age Society: Travels, transmissions and transformations,* in which they emphasise the magical powers and heroic fame that could be gained in the European full Bronze Age from participating in distant travels and expeditions (Fig 12.4). In doing so, they characterise Ulysses, thought to have lived over a thousand years after the Amesbury Archer, as a Bronze Age archetype (2005, 32–61).

Returning to the journey of the Amesbury Archer, we should note that the Archer can only be shown to have been in continental Europe as a teenager. He may have been raised there, but he need not necessarily have been born there. Nor, if the Archer was indeed born and raised in western central Europe, should it be assumed that he, and perhaps those who may have been with him, made one single journey that ended near Stonehenge. He may have made several separate shorter, but still lengthy, journeys.

Some of the objects buried with the Amesbury Archer, such as the wristguards or the antler pin have similarities with examples from central Europe, but as we have seen, the metal of the copper knives and perhaps the knives themselves come from Atlantic Europe, northern Spain and western France (Fitzpatrick 2003; Needham in preparation). He had travelled far and wide across western Europe and some of these objects may have been acquired on his travels.

This is to emphasise the limitations of our knowledge. It may be speculated that in making his own odyssey, the Amesbury Archer would have crossed many conceptual borders (Kristiansen and Larsen 2005, 43–51), between 'us' and 'other', between land and sea, between the safe – near to home, and the dangerous and distant. As Kristiansen and Larsson argue, the crossing of these borders is likely to have been associated with, and marked by, rituals. They suggest that heroic travels, trade and acquisition integrate in complex ways that can be reduced to neither economy nor myth. Instead, they formed an integrated part of the cosmology of some ancient societies.

Unlike Ulysses or the Bronze Age chief buried at Kivik, Scania, Sweden (Randsborg 2003), used as an exemplar by Kristiansen and Larsson (2005, 186–212), the Archer did not return from his journey to distant lands but settled, close to Stonehenge, which was a place of great religious importance; a place that Kristiansen and Larsson would describe as a distant cosmological centre. The time during which Stonehenge was built is a matter of debate (*eg* Bayliss *et al* 2007; Parker Pearson *et al* 2007), but if, as has been suggested, the Archer made some, or perhaps all, of his travels as a pilgrim seeking healing for his disability (Darvill 2006, 151), these were apparently unsuccessful. Alternatively, if the injury occurred when in Britain, the damage to his knee, whether inflicted accidentally or deliberately – the Greek god smith Haphaestos was disabled – it may have meant that he could not return to the European mainland.

The Amesbury Archer and any fellow travellers arrived into a foreign culture. He came with new and exotic goods – the Bell Beaker 'Set' with its accoutrements of warfare and hunting – and with access to, and some skill in, the secrets and magic of metal. He was a foreigner; he was dressed differently, and he had a name in what was almost certainly a different language. Nonetheless, possessing distance and access, magic and knowledge, he will have carried in his head a map of another world, a *mappa mundi*.

In the foreign land where he died, he was not buried close to sources of copper or gold, but near to Stonehenge, almost as a precursor to the rich Wessex Burials of the Early Bronze Age. Stonehenge was not the only great temple near to where he was buried; the nearby and earlier henge at Durrington Walls is in many ways no less impressive. But the bringing of the great stones to Stonehenge was, and is, unique. It was the greatest temple of the age in Europe. The building of it, the carrying of stones from far away, was a great, and enormously risky, mission. Its organisation would have involved great numbers of people to move the stones, to make the ropes, to prepare food and shelter; and much more besides. It was a phenomenon.

The Archer's journey did not form the origin of the heroic, ranked, warrior society as conceived by Kristiansen and Larsson. However, the successive building and rebuilding of Stonehenge would have been a time of great change in the locality. This may have created a situation where new and different types of status, if not power, could be ascribed or achieved. The nearby burial of the Archer's 'Companion', a descendant who was also afforded a high status in death, shows that something of the Archer's status was transferred to another generation. But, in common with other well-furnished Bell Beaker burials across Europe, the Archer's grave was not to become a focal point for burying the dead of his lineage group.

There were also other journeys to Britain and Ireland; Wessex need not be ascribed a primacy in this. The journeys that the Archer may have made are consistent with the long standing debate over the Atlantic origins of Irish metallurgy (*eg* Sheridan 1983). We have mentioned the people who travelled to Ross Island (O'Brien 2004) and one of the earliest Bell Beaker burials in Britain (and which was cut into Beaker associated settlement material) comes from the Atlantic seaboard, from Sorisdale on the Isle of Coll in the Inner Hebrides (Ritchie and Crawford 1977–78), and there is other related funerary evidence from mainland Scotland (Sheridan 2007; Suddaby and Sheridan 2006, 84).

Unlike the degree of small-scale and routine mobility suggested for contemporary communities within central Europe (Price *et al* 1998; 2004), some of these journeys around Britain and Ireland may have been ones of prospection or associated with the transformation of ores into metal and metal objects.

We should remember that we can also see evidence for exchanges and perhaps other journeys around this time. The recognition of early copper flat axe heads from western France, perhaps from Armorica, in the French Jura close to the western Alps (Klassen *et al* 2007) demonstrates something of the broadly contemporary movements of objects through networks that spanned parts of the journey that the Amesbury Archer, and perhaps others, made. In turn, these journeys echoed earlier exchanges of flint knives and stone axes.

Conclusion

This paper has touched on just a few of the things that can be said about the Amesbury Archer. The high status afforded him is consistent with those of early metalworkers in some other regions in temperate Europe, with their knowledge of and access to the magic that was metal, and their ability to turn it into goods and to control access to them.

But, coming from far away, the Archer would also have brought knowledge of a wider world and this may have added to any aura that surrounded him. Around Britain and Ireland sites such as Ross Island and burials such as the Boscombe Bowmen show that other journeys were being made. But unlike that Bronze Age archetype Ulysses, the Archer did not return from his Copper Age journey. Instead a family was raised. But the place at which he settled would have been known far away as a place of great religious importance.

The temptation to romanticise the story of the Amesbury Archer should be eschewed. And in themselves, magic and myth as abstract concepts do not provide an explanation, but they have a role to play in trying to understand the story of the Amesbury Archer and his Copper Age Connections.

Acknowledgments

Very many colleagues have helped in the course of the work from which this paper is drawn and their kindness can only be briefly acknowledged here, as is the hospitality and help of the Römisch-Germanische Kommission of the Deutsches Archäologisches Institut. The constructive criticism of Alison Sheridan, Andrew Lawson, Ben Roberts and Brendan O'Connor improved an earlier draft of the paper.

List of references

Ambert, P 2001 'La place de la métallurgie campaniforme dans la première métallurgie française', in F Nicolis (ed), *Bell Beakers Today. Pottery, people, culture, symbols in prehistoric Europe*, Proceedings of the International Colloquium Riva del Garda (Trento, Italy), May 1998, Trento, Provincia Autonoma di Trento, Servizio Beni Culturali, Ufficio beni Archeologici, 577–588

Barrett, J 1994 *Fragments from Antiquity: An archaeology of social life in Britain, 2900–1200 BC*, Oxford: Blackwell

Bartelheim, M 2002 'Metallurgie und Gesellschaft in der Frühbronzezeit Mitteleuropas, in J Müller (ed), *Vom Endneolithikum zur Frühbronzezeit: Muster sozialen Wandels?*, Bonn: Universitätsforschungen zur prähistorischen Archäologie, **90**, 29–44

Batora, J 2002a 'Contribution to the problem of 'craftsmen' graves at the end of Aeneolithic and in the Early Bronze Age in central, western and eastern Europe', *Slovenska Archeológia*, **50 (2)**, 179–228

Bátora, J 2002b 'K hrobom metalurgov z obdobia eneolitu v strednej, západnej a východnej Európe', in I Cheben and I Kuzma (eds), *Otázky neolitu a eneolitu našich krajín – 2001. Zborník referátov z 20. pracovného stretnutia bádateóv pre výskum neolitu a eneoliti Čiech, Moravy a Slovenska, Liptovská Sielnica 9.–12.10.2001*, Nitra: Archaeologica Slovaca Monographiae Communicationes, **4**, 35–46

Bayliss, A, McAvoy, F and Whittle, A 2007 'The world recreated: redating Silbury Hill in its monumental landscape', *Antiquity*, **81 (311)**, 26–53

Belgirono, M 2002 'Does tomb no. 21 at Pyrgos (Cyprus) belong to a blacksmith?', in H Procopiu and R Treuil (eds), *Mouldre et Foyer II – Archéologie et Historie*, Paris: Centre National de la Recherche Scientifique, 73–80

Bertemes, F 2004a 'Zur Enstehung von Macht, Herrschaft und Prestige in Mitteleuropa', in H Meller (ed), *Der geschmiedete Himmel. Die weite Welt im Herzen Europas vor 3600 Jahren*, Halle: Landesamt für Denkmalpflege undArchäologie Sachsen-Anhalt – Landesmuseum für Vorgeschichte Halle, 149–153

Bertemes, F 2004b 'Frühe Metallurgen in der Spätkupfer- und Frühbronzezeit', in H Meller (ed), *Der geschmiedete Himmel. Die weite Welt im Herzen Europas vor 3600 Jahren*, Halle: Landesamt für Denkmalpflege undArchäologie Sachsen-Anhalt – Landesmuseum für Vorgeschichte Halle, 144–149

Bertemes, F and Heyd, V 2002 'Der Übergang Kuperzeit/Frühbronzezeit am Nordwestrand des Karpatenbeckens – Kulturgeschichtliche und paläometallurgische Betrachtungen', in M Bartelheim, E Pernicka and R Krause (eds), *Die Anfänge der Metallurgie in der Alten Welt/The Beginnings of Metallurgy in the Old World, Band 1. Forschungen zur Archäometrie und Altertumswissenschaft*, Rahden/Westfalen: Marie Leidorf, 185–228

Bertemes, F, Schmotz, K, and Thiele, W-R 2000 'Das Metallurgengrab 9 des Gräberfeldes der Glochenbecherkultur von Künzing, Lkr. Deggendorf', in M Chytráęek, J Michálek and K Schmotz (eds), *Archäologische Arbeitsgemeinschaft Ostbayern/West- und Südböhmen, 9. Treffen, 23. bis 26 Juni 1999 in Neukirchen b. Hl. Blut*, Rahden/Westfalen: Marie Leidorf, 53–60

Brodie, N 1997 'New perspectives on the Bell-Beaker culture', *Oxford Journal of Archaeology*, **16 (3)**, 297–314

Brodie, N 1998 'British Bell Beakers; twenty five years of theory and practice', in M Benz and S van Willigen (eds), *Some New Approaches to the Bell Beaker 'Phenomenon.' Lost Paradise…? Proceedings of the 2nd Meeting of the 'Association Archéologie et Gobelets, Ffeldberg (Germany), 18th–20th April 1997*, Oxford: British Archaeological Reports (International Series), **690**, 43–56

Brodie, N 2001 'Technological frontiers and the emergence of the Beaker culture', in F Nicolis (ed), *Bell Beakers Today. Pottery, people, culture, symbols in prehistoric Europe*, Proceedings of the International Colloquium Riva del Garda (Trento, Italy, May 1998), Trento, Servizio Beni Culturali, Ufficio beni Archeologici, 487–496

Brück, J 2004 'Material metaphors. The relational construction of identity in early Bronze Age burials in Britain and Ireland', *Journal of Social Archaeology*, **4**, 307–333

Budd, P and Taylor, T 1995 'The faerie smith meets the bronze industry: magic versus science in the interpretation of prehistoric metal-making', *World Archaeology*, **27**, 133–143

Butler, J and van der Waals, J 1966 'Bell Beakers and early metal-working in the Netherlands', *Palaeohistoria*, **12**, 1966 (1967), 41–139

Campen, I 2004 'Unscheinbar, aber bedeutsam. Das älteste Gold Sachsens stammt aus einem Steinzeitgrab bei Zwenkau', *Archaeo*, **1**, 27–29

Case, H 2004a 'Beaker burial in Britain and Ireland: A role for the dead', in M Besse and J Desideri (eds), *Graves and Funerary Rituals during the Late Neolithic and the Early Bronze Age in Europe (2700–2000 BC). Proceedings of the International Conference held at the Cantonal Archaeological Museum, Sion (Switzerland), October 4th–7th 2001*, Oxford: British Archaeological Reports (International Series), **1284**, 195–201

Case, H 2004b 'Beakers and the Beaker Culture', in J Czebreszuk (ed), *Similar but Different. Bell Beakers in Europe*, Poznań: Adam Mickiewicz University, 11–34

Chambon, P and Salanova, L 1996 'Chronologie de sépultures du IIIᵉ millénaire dans le Bassin de la Seine', *Bulletin de la Société préhistorique française*, **93**, 103–118

Childe, V 1930 *The Bronze Age*, Cambridge: Cambridge University Press

Clarke, D 1970 *Beaker Pottery of Britain and Ireland*, Cambridge: Cambridge University Press

Cowie, T 1988 *Magic Metal. Early metalworkers in the north-east*, Aberdeen: Anthropological Museum, University of Aberdeen

Czebreszuk, J 2004a 'Bell Beakers: an outline of present stage of research', in J Czebreszuk (ed), *Similar but Different. Bell Beakers in Europe*, Poznań: Adam Mickiewicz University, 223–224

Czebreszuk, J (ed) 2004b, *Similar but Different. Bell Beakers in Europe*, Poznań: Adam Mickiewicz University

Czebreszuk, J and Kryvaltsevich, M 2003 'The north-eastern border of influence of Bell Beakers idea', in J Czebreszuk, and M Szmyt (eds), *The Northeast Frontier of Bell Beakers. Proceedings of the symposium held at the Adam Mickiewicz University, Poznań (Poland), May 26–29 2002)*, Oxford: British international Reports (International Series), **1155**, 107–116

Darvill, T 2006 *Stonehenge: The biography of a landscape*, Stroud: Tempus

Delgado Raack, S and Risch, R 2006 'La tumba Nº 3 de Los Cipreses y la metalurgia Argárcia', *AlbercA*, **4**, 21–50

Eogan, G 1994 *The Accomplished Art: Gold and Gold-Working in Britain and Ireland during the Bronze Age (c 2350–650 BC)*, Oxford: Oxbow Monograph, **42**

Evans, J, Chenery, C and Fitzpatrick, A 2006 'Bronze Age childhood migration of individuals near Stonehenge, revealed by strontium and oxygen isotope tooth enamel analysis', *Archaeometry*, **48**, 309–322

Fitzpatrick, A 2003 'The Amesbury Archer,' *Current Archaeology*, **16 (4)**, (no. 184), 146–152

Gallay, A 2001 'L'énigme campaniforme', in F Nicolis (ed), *Bell Beakers Today. Pottery, people, culture, symbols*

in prehistoric Europe, Proceedings of the International Colloquium Riva del Garda (Trento, Italy), May 1998, Trento, Provincia Autonoma di Trento, Servizio Beni Culturali, Ufficio beni Archeologici, 41–57

Guilaine, J (ed) 2007 *Le chalcolithique et la construction des inégalités. Tome I. Le continent européen*, Paris: Errance

Hájek, L 1966 'Die älteste Phase der Glochenbecherkultur in Böhmen und Mähren', *Památky Archeologické*, **67**, 210–241

Harrison, R 1980 *The Beaker Folk*, London: Thames and Hudson

Healy, F and Harding, J 2004 'Reading a burial: the legacy of Overton Hill', in A Gibson and A Sheridan (eds), *From Sickles to Circles. Britain and Ireland at the time of Stonehenge*, Stroud: Tempus, 176–193

Helms, M 1988 *Ulysses' Sail*, Princetown: Princetown University Press

Heyd, V 2001 'On the earliest Beakers along the Danube', in F Nicolis (ed), *Bell Beakers Today. Pottery, people, culture, symbols in prehistoric Europe*, Proceedings of the International Colloquium Riva del Garda (Trento, Italy), May 1998, Trento, Provincia Autonoma di Trento, Servizio Beni Culturali, Ufficio beni Archeologici, 387–409

Heyd, V, Winterholler, B, Böhm, K and Pernicka, E 2002–2003 'Mobilität, Strontiumisotopie und Subsistenz in der süddeutschen Glochenbecherkultur', *Berichte der Bayerischen Bodendenkmalpflege* , **43/44**, 2002–2003, (2004), 109–135

Klassen, L, Pétrequin, P and Grut, H 2007 'Hache plates en cuivre dans le Jura Française. Transferts à longue distance de biens socialement valorisés pendant les IVᵉ et IIIᵉ millénaires', *Bulletin de la Société préhistorique française*, **104**, 101–124

Kristiansen, K 2004 'Sea faring voyages and rock art ships', in P Clark (ed), *The Dover Bronze Age Boat in Context: Society and water transport in prehistoric Europe*, Oxford: Oxbow Books, 111–121

Kristiansen, K and Larsson, T 2005 *The Rise of Bronze Age Society. Travels, transmissions and transformations*, Cambridge: Cambridge University Press

Kunst, M 1997 'Waren die 'Schmeide' in der portugiesischen Kuperzeit gleichzeitig auch die Elitem?', in B Fritsch, M Maute, L Matuschik, J Müller and C Wolf (eds), *Tradition and Innovation. Prähistorische Archäologie als historische Wissenschaft. Festschrift für Christian Strahm*, Stuttgart: Internationale Archäeologie, Studia honoraria, **3**, 541–550

Lynch, F 2001 'Axes or skeuomorphic cushion stones; the purpose of certain' blunt' axes', in W Metz, B van Beek and H Steegstra (eds), *Patina: Essays presented to Jay Jordan Butler on the occasion of his 80th Birthday*, Groningen: privately published by the editors, 399–404

Maryon, H 1936 'Excavation of two Bronze Age barrows at Kirkhaugh, Northumberland', *Archaeologia Aeliana*, (4th series), **13**, 207–217.

Mille, B and Bouquet, L 2004 'La métal au 3ᵉ millénaire avant notre ère dans le Centre-Nord de la France', in M Vander Linden and L Salanova (eds), *Le troisième millénaire dans le nord de la France et en Belgique*, Lille: Anthropologica et Præhistorica, **115**/Mémoire de la Société préhistorique française, **35**, 197–215

Moucha, V 1989 'Böhmen am Ausklang des Äneolithikums und am Anfang der Bronzezeit', in M Buchvaldek and

E Pleslová-Štiková (eds), *Das Äneolithikums und die früheste Bronzezeit (C¹⁴ 3000–2000 BC) in Mitteleuropa: kulturelle und chronologische Beziehungen. Actes des XIV Internationalen Symposiums Prag-Liblice 20.–24.10.1986,* Prague: *Praehistorica,* **15,** 213–218

Müller, D 1987 'Gräber von Metallwerkern aus der Glockenbecherkultur des Mittelelbe-Saale-Gebietes', *Ausgrabungen und Funde,* **32,** 175–179

Needham S in preparation 'The Archer's metal equipment', in A Fitzpatrick, in preparation

Needham, S 2002 'Analytical implications for Beaker metallurgy in north-west Europe', in M Bartelheim, E Pernicka, and R Krause (eds), *The Beginnings of Metallurgy in the Old World,* Rahden/Westfalen: Forschungen zur Archäometrie und Altertumswissenschaft, **1,** 98–133

Needham, S 2005 'Transforming Beaker culture in north-west Europe: processes of fusion and fission', *Proceedings of the Prehistoric Society,* **71,** 171–217

Nicolis, F (ed) *Bell Beakers Today. Pottery, people, culture, symbols in prehistoric Europe,* Proceedings of the International Colloquium Riva del Garda (Trento, Italy), May 1998, Trento, Provincia Autonoma di Trento, Servizio Beni Culturali, Ufficio beni Archeologici

Northover, J P 1999 'The earliest metalworking in southern Britain', in A Hauptmann, E Pernicka, T Rehrens and Ü Yalçin (eds), *The Beginnings of Metallurgy. Proceedings of the International Conference, Bochum 1995,* Bochum: Die Anschnitt, Beiheft 9, 211–225

O'Brien, W 2001 'New light on Beaker metallurgy in Ireland', in F Nicolis (ed), *Bell Beakers Today. Pottery, people, culture, symbols in prehistoric Europe,* Proceedings of the International Colloquium Riva del Garda (Trento, Italy), May 1998, Trento, Provincia Autonoma di Trento, Servizio Beni Culturali, Ufficio beni Archeologici, 561–576

O'Brien, W 2004 *Ross Island: Mining, Metal and Society in Early Ireland,* Galway: National University of Ireland, Bronze Age Studies, **6**

O'Connor, B 2004 'The earliest Scottish metalwork since Coles', in I Shepherd and G Barclay (eds), *Scotland in Ancient Europe: the Neolithic and Early Bronze Age of Scotland in their European Context,* Edinburgh: Society of Antiquaries of Scotland, 205–216

Parker Pearson, M, Cleal, R, Marshall, P, Needham, S, Pollard, J, Richards, C, Ruggles, C, Sheridan, A, Thomas, J, Tilley, C, Welham, K, Chamberlain, A, Chenery, C, Evans, J, Knüsel, C, Linford, N, Martin, L, Montgomery, J, Payne, A and Richards, M 2007 'The Age of Stonehenge', *Antiquity,* **81 (313),** 617–639

Price, T, Grupe, G and Schröter, P 1998 'Migration in the Bell Beaker period of central Europe', *Antiquity,* **72 (276),** 405–411

Price, T, Knipper, G, Grupe, G. and Smrcka, V, 2004, 'Strontium isotopes and prehistoric migration: the Bell Beaker period in central Europe', *European Journal of Prehistory,* 7, 9–40.

Randsborg, K 1993 *Kivik: Archaeology and iconography,* Copenhagen: Acta Archaeologica, **64 (1)**

Ritchie, J and Crawford, J 1977–78 'Recent work on Coll and Skye: (i) Excavations at Sorisdale and Killunaig, Coll', *Proceedings of the Society of Antiquaries of Scotland,* **109,** (1978), 75–84

Rojo-Guerra, M, Garrido-Pena, R, Garciá-Martínez-de-Lagrán, Í, Juan-Tresseras, J and Matamala, J 2006 'Beer and Bell Beakers: drinking rituals in Copper Age inner Iberia', *Proceedings of the Prehistoric Society,* **72,** 243–265

Roussot-Larroque, J 2004 'Première métallurgie du sud-ouest atlantique de la France', in P Ambert and J Vaquer (eds), *La première métallurgie en France et dans les pays limitrophes. Actes du colloque international de Carcassonne 28–30 septembre 2002,* Paris: Mémoire de la *Société préhistorique française,* **37,** 159–174

Salanova, L 1998 'Le statut des assemblages, campaniformes en contexte funéraire: la notion de "bien de prestige"', *Bulletin de la Société préhistorique française,* **95,** 315–326

Salanova, L 2000 *La question du Campaniforme en France et dans les Iles anglo-normandes: productions, chronologie et rôles d'un standard céramique,* Paris: Société préhistorique française and Comité des Travaux Historiques et Scientifiques

Salanova, L 2001 'Technological, ideological or economic European union? The variability of Bell Beaker decoration', in F Nicolis (ed), *Bell Beakers Today. Pottery, people, culture, symbols in prehistoric Europe,* Proceedings of the International Colloquium Riva del Garda (Trento, Italy), May 1998, Trento, Provincia Autonoma di Trento, Servizio Beni Culturali, Ufficio beni Archeologici, 91–102

Salanova, L 2004 'The frontiers inside the western Bell Beaker block', in J Czebreszuk (ed), *Similar but Different. Bell Beakers in Europe,* Poznań: Adam Mickiewicz University, 63–76

Salanova, L 2007 'Les sépulture campaniformes: lectures sociale', in J Guilaine (ed), *Le chalcolithique et la construction des inégalités. Tome I. Le continent européen,* Paris: Errance, 213–228

Shennan, S 1976 'Bell Beakers and their context in central Europe', in J Lanting and J van der Waals (eds), *Glockenbeckersymposion, Oberried 1974,* Bussum/Haarlem: Fibula-van Dishoeck, 231–240

Sheridan, A 1983 'A reconsideration of the origins of Irish mettalurgy', *Irish Journal of Archaeology* 1, 11–19

Sheridan, A 2007 'Scottish Beaker dates: the good, the bad, and the ugly', in M Larsson and M Parker Pearson (eds), *From Stonehenge to the Baltic: living with cultural diversity in the third millennium BC,* Oxford: British Archaeological Reports (International Series), **1692,** 91–123

Sherratt, A 1987 'Cups that cheered', in W Waldren and R Kennard (eds), *Bell Beakers of the Western Mediterranean,* Oxford: British Archaeological Reports (International Series), **331,** 81–114

Simpson, D, Murphy, E and Gregory, R 2006 *Excavations at Northton, Isle of Harris,* Oxford: British Archaeological Reports (British Series), **408**

Sofaer Derevenski, J 2002 'Engendering context: Context as gendered practice in the Early Bronze Age of the Upper Thames Valley, UK', *European Journal of Archaeology,* **5,** 191–211

Strahm, C 1994 Die Änfange der Metallurgie in Mitteleuropa', *Helvetia Archaeologia,* **25,** 2–39

Strahm, C 2004a 'Das Glochenbecher-Phänomen aus der Sicht der Komplementär-Keramik', in J Czebreszuk (ed), *Similar but Different. Bell Beakers in Europe,* Poznań: Adam Mickiewicz University, 101–126

Strahm, C 2004b 'L'introduction et la diffusion de la

métallurgie en France', in P Ambert and J Vaquer (eds), *La première métallurgie en France et dans les pays limitrophes. Actes du colloque international de Carcassonne 28–30 septembre 2002*, Mémoire de la *Société préhistorique française*, **37**, 27–36

Strahm, C 2007 'L'introduction de la métallurgie en Europe', in J Guilaine (ed), *Le chalcolithique et la construction des inégalités. Tome I. Le continent européen*, Paris: Errance, 47–71

Suddaby, I and Sheridan, A 2006 'A pit containing an undecorated Beaker and associated artefacts from Beechwood Park, Raigmore, Inverness', *Proceedings of the Society of Antiquaries of Scotland*, **136**, 77–88

Thomas, J 1991 'Reading the body: Beaker funerary practice in Britain', in P Garwood, D Jennings, R Skeates and J Toms (eds), *Sacred and Profane. Proceedings of a conference on archaeology, ritual and religion, Oxford, 1989*, Oxford: Oxford University Committee for Archaeology Monograph, **32**, 33–42

Thorpe, I and Richards, C 1984 'The decline of ritual authority and the introduction of Beakers into Britain', in R Bradley and J Gardiner (eds), *Neolithic Studies: A review of some recent research*, Oxford: British Archaeological Reports (British Series), **133**, 67–84

Timberlake, S 2001 'Mining and prospection for metals in early Bronze Age Britain – making claims within the archaeological landscape', in J Brück (ed), *Bronze Age Landscapes. Tradition and transformation*, Oxford: Oxbow Books, 179–192

Timberlake, S 2003 *Excavations on Copa Hill, Cwmystwyth (1986–1999). An Early Bronze Age copper mine within the uplands of central Wales*, Oxford: British Archaeological Reports (British Series), **348**

Turek, J 2004 'Craft symbolism in Bell beaker burial customs. Resources, production and social structure at the end of [the] Eneolithic period', in M Besse and J Desideri (eds), *Graves and Funerary Rituals during the Late Neolithic and the Early Bronze Age in Europe (2700–2000 BC). Proceedings of the International Conference held at the Cantonal Archaeological Museum, Sion (Switzerland), October 4th–7th 2001*, Oxford: British Archaeological Reports (International Series), **1284**, 147–156

Van der Beek, Z 2004 'An ancestral way of burial. Late Neolithic graves in the Netherlands', in M Besse and J Desideri (eds), *Graves and Funerary Rituals during the Late Neolithic and the Early Bronze Age in Europe (2700–2000 BC). Proceedings of the International Conference held at the Cantonal Archaeological Museum, Sion (Switzerland), October 4th–7th 2001*, Oxford: British Archaeological Reports (International Series), **1284**, 157–194

Vander Linden, M 2004 'Polythetic networks, coherent people: a new historical hypothesis for the Bell Beaker phenomenon', in J Czebreszuk (ed), *Similar but Different. Bell Beakers in Europe*, Poznań: Adam Mickiewicz University, 35–62

Vander Linden, M 2006 *'Le phénoméne campaniforme dans l'Europe du 3e millénaire avant notre ère. Synthèse et nouvelles perspectives*, Oxford: British Archaeological Reports (International Series), **1470**

Vander Linden, M 2007 'What linked the Bell Beakers in third millennium BC Europe?', *Antiquity*, **81 (312)**, 343–352

Verwers, W (ed) 1990 *'Archeolgische Kroniek van Noord Brabant 1985–1987*, Waalre: Stichting Brabants Heem, 30–31